C0-CCO-069

The Burma Road to Poverty

The Burma Road to Poverty

Mya Maung

Foreword by
Everett E. Hagen

PRAEGER

New York
Westport, Connecticut
London

0694573

~~129098~~

Library of Congress Cataloging-in-Publication Data

Maung, Mya.
The Burma road to poverty / Mya Maung; foreword by Everett E. Hagen.
p. cm.
Includes bibliographical references and index.
ISBN 0-275-93613-9 (alk. paper)
1. Burma—Social conditions. 2. Burma—Economic conditions—1948–
3. Socialism—Burma. 4. Burma—Politics and government—1948–
I. Title.
HN670.7.A8M38 1991
306′.09591—dc20 90–27555

British Library Cataloguing in Publication Data is available.

Copyright © 1991 by Mya Maung

All rights reserved. No portion of this book may be reproduced, by any process or technique, without the express written consent of the publisher.

Library of Congress Catalog Card Number: 90–27555
ISBN: 0–275–93613–9

First published in 1991

Praeger Publishers, One Madison Avenue, New York, NY 10010
An imprint of Greenwood Publishing Group, Inc.

Printed in the United States of America

The paper used in this book complies with the Permanent Paper Standard issued by the National Information Standards Organization (Z39.48-1984).

10 9 8 7 6 5 4 3 2 1

To my children,
Christopher, Michael, and Melanie Maung,

and the students and freedom fighters of Burma

Contents

0694573 ~~129098~~

Foreword

When the Chinese military killed students calling for democracy in Tiananmen Square in June 1989, the World, or at least the West, reacted in shock, but the West had paid little note to the massacre of a greater absolute number of students (and others) and greater violence in Myanmar (then Burma) during five months of the previous year. Yet a student of political structure may take special interest in the modern history of Burma. Mya Maung traces the most recent two decades of that history—not only the facts and the results of the military takeover, but the way in which the military leaders seemed to believe that the economy as well as the people ought to behave as they wished. Though Mya Maung's graduate study and then professional work have been in economics and finance, the present volume is distinguished not so much by analysis in those fields as by analysis of why the military leaders thought it would be effective to behave as they did. They did not behave as all dictators do. This is a study of "why Burmese leaders behave like Burmese" (my phrases, not his). It is this discussion which in my view is more intriguing and penetrating than that in any of the several other studies of recent Burma. A student of political structure may well ponder this question, and try to apply the answer at which he arrives to other countries that puzzle him.

Everett E. Hagen
Massachusetts Institute of Technology

Preface

The Burma Road to Poverty began with the illegal seizure of political power by General Ne Win in 1962 from the constitutionally elected civilian government of U Nu. The main objective of this study is to explain how and why this road was established historically in terms of the interrelationships between the socio-political and economic factors. It will attempt to travel this road by treating the economic stagnation of Burma as a phase of total socio-cultural development in light of the backward and forward linkages of Burmese society, polity, and economy. The main purpose of this study is to come to an understanding of how and why a country relatively rich in natural resources attained the status of one of the least developed nations in the world by the end of 1987. This cannot be accomplished without an understanding of the non-economic parameters of economic development. This is really nothing new in the history of the economics of development, which received a great deal of attention and research during the years immediately following the Second World War when development fever spread throughout the less developed world of newly independent nations. It is the contention of this study that the process of economic change is an integral phase of total socio-cultural change.

With the above views in mind, I will undertake the venture of traveling the Burma Road to Poverty on both a personal and societal level. The sad saga of Burma's impoverishment will be given in terms of case studies and an overall appraisal of societal change and conflict among personalities and social groups that came to shape the destiny of Burma in the aftermath of its independence in 1948. The data I have gathered is primarily personal and derived from interviews with a number of individuals and families outside Burma as well as from accounts written by those who have experienced the effects of various policies and programs of the civilian and military governments of Burma during the past forty years.

In view of the isolation and oppression of Burma during the twenty-eight years of military rule, the only course of inquiry into the poverty of a reclusive nation has to be the traditional approach of what the Burmese termed *pazat thamine*, oral history which was practiced by Buddhist monks with respect to Buddha's preachings. This tradition of recording and learning the history of a particular society is a common heritage of all ancient cultures prior to the development of systematic writing. Some of the accounts of Burmese history I use in this study were taught to me orally by my parents, elders, and teachers. This method of intergenerational transmission of knowledge is expressed in a Burmese saying "the younger heard the words of the older"—*thetkyee zagar thetngel kyar*. I also employed the opposite method of "the older heard the words of the younger"—*thetngel zagar thetkyee kyar* by talking and listening to many young men and women from my native land whose stories and experience of the Burmese Way to Socialism were most illuminating and invaluable for my research.

The method adopted in my endeavor was taught to me in my youth while learning the traditional Burmese folktales. It was the method used by a folk hero named Maung Pauk Kyine, a commoner with no capacity for higher education. After many disappointing years of studying at an institution of higher education, he was forced to give up. His teacher, his *sayah*, taught him to remember only three basic maxims to succeed in life: ask many times as it begets words or answers, travel many times as it begets distance, and stay awake as it begets longevity of live—*may-bar myar zagar-ya, thwar-bah myar kha-yee yauk* and *ma-ate ma-nai athet-shai*.[1] By employing the three methods on his homeward journey, he ultimately became a king known as Maung Pauk Kyine, *naganaing minyahzah*, the conquering king of the dragon. I relied heavily on the first of the three maxims for my research, asking many times and cross-checking the words or the answers from all sources. I practiced this method with extreme diligence by traveling back psychologically in my thoughts to my native land during the course of interviews and conversations with many Burmese. Hundreds of hours of interviews were conducted on the phone and in person to learn about the events and experiences of those who have lived through the twenty-eight year military rule over Burma.

Having left the country more than two and a half decades ago, my venture seemed as troublesome as the Burma Road to Poverty. Yet, after more than three years of attempting to invoke a link back to the culture I was brought up with, I began to have a better and clearer understanding of the relationship between economic and noneconomic factors in modernization. My youthful years which I spent as "a student in a Buddhist monastery," *hpongyi kyawnthar*, a high-school student at Myoma National High School, a Rangoon University student, and a classical Burmese musician, all greatly helped me to understand the basic Buddhist cultural determinants of Burmese behavior and thought in the traditional society of Burma.

In order not to be misleading, my interest and effort in understanding the relationship between cultural values and economic change began during my graduate studies in the United States where I was sent in 1954 by the civilian government of U Nu to obtain the degree of Ph.D. in economics under the State Scholarship Program. My own experiences from 1961–1962 as a field researcher on the Cooperative Movement of Burma were of immense value in understanding the peasantry of Burma. As the Head of the Economics Department of the Defense Services Academy at Maymyo from 1962–63, I came into contact with several military personalities and obtained an understanding of their views, outlooks, and behavior. Since that time, I have looked deep into the theories as well as empirical research findings of social change and economic growth in Burma. I was fortunate to be able to leave Burma for the United States as my views were in direct conflict with the illegal seizure of political power by the military elite and the philosophy of the Burmese Way to Socialism.

Soon after the military coup of 1962, I advanced hypotheses relating to the economic future of Burma in several journals and a book, most of which have been confirmed.[2] This by no means suggests that the chronicle of developments covering the last twenty-eight years of military rule in this book is either conclusive or definitive regarding its validity. Some of the analyses are going to be hypotheses which I hope will be tested and confirmed in future studies of Burma. This is due to the fact that, like the rest of the outside world, scholars and researchers, with the exception of a handful, have been shut off throughout the military rule from conducting empirical studies of social change and economic development inside Burma. The paucity of materials and reliable statistical data is as painful as the grinding poverty of Burma itself. Yet, there is enough evidence for the Burma Road to Poverty for the purpose of scholarly analysis and historical record.

In a way, the road to poverty of Burma parallels my own personal experience of acculturation to western value-systems, thoughts, and codes of conduct loaded with failures, traumas, and maladjustments similar to those of developmental endeavors of both the civilian and military governments of Burma. At least in my own case, the quest for success and happiness with life and work in my adopted country of the United States seems to have reached a point of relative calm, although the same has not been true for my native land and in its failure to develop and adjust to the modern world of the twentieth century. Instead, it seems to have traveled backward in time to the dark ages of the Burmese kings and the British colonial subjugation with respect to freedom and democracy. This is not to claim that I am totally adjusted to Western thoughts and values and I sincerely do not believe that I can ever accomplish this during the rest of my life. There is a Burmese saying that "only streams and ditches fade away but not your racial or more correctly cultural roots," *chawn-yoe myawn-yoe thah tein-gaw mel, lu-yoe myo-yoe ma tein-gaw bu*. My own reflections on the ways the Burmese are trained and nurtured as children concur deeply with some of the analyses and evaluations made by Professor Everett E. Hagen with respect to authoritarian personality formation and the reasons for lack of economic growth in a traditional society on a global scale.[3]

Following the traditional Burmese custom of paying homage to the teachers, *sayahs*, I would like to acknowledge the encouragement, knowledge, and inspiration given to me by various teachers and professors of my native land. The first person to whom I wish to pay respect and acknowledgment is the most reverend Venerable U Wimala. The same accord is due to Professors Kenneth E. Boulding, who taught me at the University of Michigan, and the late Max F. Millikan, who taught and helped me while I was at M.I.T. I would especially like to thank Professor Everett E. Hagen for his lifelong interest in Burma and me and the encouragement he has given me throughout my academic career. Professor Hagen read and raised various questions on the first draft of this manuscript which are of immense value for the substance of this book. I am also grateful to Professors Robert Meagher of the Fletcher School of Law and Diplomacy and Joseph Silverstein of Rutgers University for urging me to write once again about Burma.

I would also like to thank many Burmese friends, families, and intellectuals, including Buddhist monks, students, civil servants, politicians, businessmen, dealers in the border trade, and retired army officers, for providing me with scarce materials and information. Among them are my lifelong friend U Than Tin of New York, U Kyaw Than of Germany, U Kyin Oo, U Oung Myint Tun of the British Broadcasting Corporation, London, Daw Mi Khin Khin Soe, and Chao Tzang Yawnghwe (Eugene Thaike), and Harn Yawnghwe of Canada, two sons of the late President of the Union of Burma, Thamadagyi Saw Shwe Thaike, who was jailed by Ne Win in 1962. Of all the Burmese who helped me in writing this book, U Thaung (Aung Ba La) of Florida, provided me with invaluable references, information, and penetrating discussions on the history of Burmese politics based upon his own personal experiences and knowledge. He is a former journalist and owner of the Burmese newspaper, *The Mirror*, who was arrested and jailed by the Ne Win regime in 1964. Special thanks are due to Sayah U Than Tun for his penetrating advice and correction, and for reteaching me the historical facts about ancient Burma.

Although I wish to mention the names of many talented Burmese scholars, reporters, researchers, and ordinary folks at home and abroad who have helped me, most of them wish to remain anonymous for fear of repercussions, reflecting the state of political conditions in Burma today. This study also would not have been completed without the moral and financial support of Dean John Neuhauser and Dr. Hassen Tehranian, Chairman of the Finance Department, of the School of Management of Boston College. Last but not least, I am deeply indebted to my friend and colleague, Dr. George Aragon for his careful reading and comments, and to Professors Robert Taggart, Nikolaos Travlos, reading and comments, and to Professors Robert Taggart, Nikolaos Travlos, and the rest of the Faculty of the Finance Department for reading and commenting on some technical chapters of the book. I am most grateful to Miss Maggie Galvin, the Secretary of the Finance Department, for her meticulous reading, editing, and corrections of the first draft of the manuscript.

NOTES

1. In most cases, my own spellings of the Burmese words, followed by Pali words or conventional English spellings in parentheses, will be used.
2. See Mya Maung, "Socialism and Economic Development of Burma," *Asian Survey* (Berkeley: University of California, December 1964); "The Burmese Way to Socialism Beyond the Welfare State," *Asian Survey* (Berkeley: University of California, June 1970); and *Burma and Pakistan: A Comparative Study of Development* (New York: Praeger Publishers, Inc., 1971).
3. See E. E. Hagen, *The Theory of Social Change: How Economic Growth Begins* (Homewood: The Dorsey Press, 1962).

Introduction

For many generations dating back to the times of the Burmese kings, the Burmese society, its culture, language, and the character of its people have always confused and confounded Western observers, travelers, and scholars alike. The very name of the country now called Myanmar has been confusing to many. I would like to stress that for many generations the English writings and spellings of Burmese names, towns, and the country itself have been inconsistent. One of the main reasons for this is the very nature of the Burmese language. It is a monosyllabic tonal language whose sounds are difficult for a Westerner to hear correctly. For example, the word *ma* has three basic tonal variations: a sharp and abrupt sound of *ma* as opposed to the soft and elongated *mah*, which is pronounced in English as if one were addressing one's mother, and the last sound of *mar* which is pronounced as in the Bostonian accent or in referring to the planet of Mars. All three have different meanings in Burmese.

As the Burmese pronounce the name of the majority ethnic group of Burma, it should be spelled or spoken correctly as *Myanmah* (in writing) and *Bamah* (in speaking) with the soft and elongated "h" ending. Hence, even today both the Burmese English and Western newspapers and journals wrongly spell the name of the country as *Myanma* (the adjective of *Myanmah*) or *Myanmar* (no meaning at all in Burmese) interchangeably with "a" and "r" endings. The obvious reason for this is that to a Western ear the three sound the same. In order to be fair, a few nineteenth-century British writers, the most distinguished among them being Sir George J. Scott or Shwe Yoe, seemed to notice the tonal variations and used the correct spellings of Burmese words. For example, the word *Burmah* (correctly spoken name for the majority ethnic group of Burmese) instead of "Burma" was used by Mr. Holt Hallett, F.R.G.S., in his article on "Burmah, Present and Future: in *London Times Weekly* on December 25, 1885.

One should also notice that the term "Myanmar," which is the illegitimate new name given to Burma by the Saw Maung government, does not mean "country" at all in Burmese. It should be *Myanmah Pyi* or *Myanmah Nainggan*, which signifies the country, *pyi* or *nainggan*, of the majority ethnic group called *Myanmah*. Throughout this book I will use Burma instead of Myanmar and my own spellings which I consider correct tonal variations of the Burmese words as the Burmese write or speak; they are often completely different from the traditional or conventional English spellings. For example, for some unknown reason, the British called the capital of Burma Rangoon, whereas the Burmese always call it *Yangon* or *Dagon*.

One other confusing aspect of Burmese customs relates to Burmese names, which have no bearing on family relationships. The most common names assumed by Burmese such as the "Maungs" and the "Oos" (phonetically correct spelling) or "Us" (conventional spelling) exemplify confusions engulfing the entire spectrum of Burmese society and its unique customs. For example, my own name of Mya Maung has no relationship to the present Head of the State, General Saw Maung, even though to Westerners we have the same last name. Not only names but also the Burmese society itself have confused many outside observers. As Sterling Seagrave, the son of the famous Burma surgeon, Dr. Gordon Seagrave, remarked: "Burma is a Cheshire cat country, look the other way for an instant and it vanishes, leaving only a vague and slightly perverse smile, the smile of Buddha. Look again and it is inside out, upside down, confusion."[1]

It has been called the "land of contradictions" by many scholars throughout the entire history of Burma with respect to its politics, social character, and personality. One of the contradictory portrayals of Burmese society relates to the relaxed, pacific, and happy-go-lucky character versus the tense, violent, and stressed to the point of being paranoid nature of the Burmese. This seemingly split personality of the Burmese has led many observers and analysts to draw two opposing inferences with respect to the propensity of Burmese society to develop into a modern nation.

At one end of the spectrum of assessments is the view of immense potential for development and at the other end is the view of total societal impotence for modernization. The latter view is to be found in the writings of a group of western observers who came into contact with old Burma before the British colonial annexation in the eighteenth and nineteenth centuries. Most of them belonged to a group of Portuguese and American missionaries whose predilections and religious biases tended to describe the Burmese social character as depraved, cunning, cruel, barbarous, and vile. As Ann Judson wrote, the Burmese were sunk in "gross idolatry . . . . and susceptible to the wicked inclinations of their depraved hearts" and "cannot live without telling lies (*mutha*)."[2] Even among the missionaries, the exception to this generalized model of Burmese social character was often acknowledged by recognizing other good qualities. As Father Sangermano wrote, "indeed there are some persons whose affability, courtesy, benevolence, gratitude, and other virtues contrast strongly with the vices of their countrymen."[3]

The misconception of Burmese Buddhism as a religion propagating the worship of idols was clarified by those western observers who came to know Burma and its people well. Among them, F. Tennyson Jesse, the grandniece of Alfred Lord Tennyson, was the most astute and objective observer of Burmese social character and culture. Thus, she wrote: "No one worshipped them (idols of Buddha), such a thing was expressly forbidden by the Buddhist religion. No one even worshipped the Buddha. The "idols" were only to help the devout mind to concentrate on the idea of the Buddha, the just man made perfect."[4]

It must be pointed out here that though her remark is largely correct in terms of what the pure teachings of Buddhism suggest with respect to the worshipping of Buddha as an idol, the fact that the Burmese kings and the Buddhist masses constructed thousands of pagodas and statues of Buddha as deeds of merit reflects a deviation from what Buddhism prescribes. Indeed, not only the idols of Buddha but also images of good and bad spirits, *byamahs* or *thagyars* and *nats*, abound in the daily religious rituals in the life of a Buddhist Burmese reflecting the persistence of supernaturalism and the worship of spirits. However, a gap between what religion sanctions and how people actually behave is common to all societies. As Jesse asked, "the Burmese were intensely superstitious, but was there really much difference between believing in the Holy Coat of Treves or in the Footprint of Buddha?"[5]

George Orwell's *Burmese Days* is a classic case in point of a Westerner siding with the native view of the undesirable impact of colonial rule. In speaking of the British rule, he said "the Indian Empire is a despotism—benevolent, no doubt but still a despotism with theft as its final object."[6] Apart from Orwell, there were a host of Western scholars whose analyses and evaluations of traditional versus colonial Burmese society tended to favor the positive and stable characteristics of Burmese culture. The most outstanding among them were Captain C.J.F.S. Forbes and Sir James G. Scott whose works on the native manners, customs, religion, and social character exemplified the value-neutral analyses and positive evaluations of Burmese culture in contrast to the highly negative and value-loaded observations of G. E. Harvey and Michael Symes.

At this point, it is worthwhile to show how Western scholars themselves could have held two diametrically opposed views and evaluations of Burmese cultural patterns. The classic example of this can be discerned in the remarks of Captain Forbes in his comments on Symes's observation of Burmans as "destitute both of delicacy and humanity, considering women as little superior to brute stock of their farms." Forbes replied "in Burma women enjoy a freer and higher position than elsewhere in the East; indeed, in some matters they have attained rights that their sisters in England are still seeking to obtain, or have lately gained."[7] He went on further to say that "from the easy, indolent disposition of men, and their own energy and natural *savoir faire*, the women rule the roost in Burma."[8] He also corrected the common faulty observation made by a typical westerner on the thoughtlessness of the Burmese with respect to family and its future.[9]

The basic reason for the persistence of the dichotomous appraisals by outside observers of a particular society must be the projection of one's own preconceived ideas and notions of what a society is and ought to be and the personality and background of the observer himself when assessing an alien culture. As Forbes correctly warned, in describing a society or social system which bears no resemblance to your own such as Burma or Thailand or for that matter any unfamiliar culture, "all familiar ideas of social organization must be abandoned."[10]

The positive aspects of the traditional Burmese society that are commonly noticed include egalitarianism, absence of rigid class barriers, elastic social system, freedom of women, individualism, and affability of its people. As Professor Hagen noted: "Egalitarianism extended to virtually all social and political relationships in the society. Strong social sanction prevented even the king from encroaching on the rights and privileges granted by custom to the individual."[11]

Of course, he was referring to the positive aspect of Burmese society under the reign of the benevolent Burmese kings, not the terrible and unjust ones. The latter certainly outnumbered the former by thousands in the *Glass Palace Chronicle of the Kings of Burma*.[12] Indeed, there were no castes or hereditary landed aristocracy and even the royal succession to the throne had no strict rule of primogeniture—a fact with tragic consequences of disorder.[13] After noting the generous and ascetic conduct of the Burmese, Hagen concluded that "the typical Burman was—and is—remarkably tolerant of the behavior of others.... Every visitor to Burma who became acquainted with the people commented on the absence of anxiety."[14] However, by the time he wrote *The Theory of Social Change*, he had come to recognize some of the negative aspects of the authoritarian personality of the Burmese in explaining the failures of the civilian government's attempt at economic development.[15]

The most negative assessment is exemplified in the works of Lucien W. Pye. His was a variant of the missionary view re-dressed in neo-Freudian terms, emphasizing the psychopathology and collective neurosis of the Burmese society and its polity based upon narrow studies of Westernized personalities.[16] He explained the negative economic performance of Burma after the liquidation of British colonial rule in terms of Burmese childhood rearing patterns and paranoid tendencies of the Burmese polity. The result, of course, was a misinterpretation of traditional cultural values and overgeneralization of total societal impotence for modernization.[17] The opposite viewpoint is exemplified in the works of H. F. Hall, J. S. Furnivall, B. O. Binns, and a host of native writers who stressed the damaging impact of British colonial rule on the socio-political and economic systems. For example, B. O. Binns and Furnivall assessed the net impact of British colonial rule as negative in terms of "unrestrained individualism"[18] and creation of a "plural society."[19]

The latest contradiction between what is ideal and what is real or the gap between the normative behavior sanctioned by religion and the deviant behavior that shocks various observers was the violent massacre of demonstrators by their own army during the political upheaval of 1988. The Weberian thesis of pacifism and sanctity of life sanctioned and mandated by Buddhism seems to have been totally invalidated by the atrocious violations of human rights on the part of the ruling military elites and the violent responses of the masses across Burma. For those who were brought up in the ethos of traditional Burmese culture, these outbursts of violence and killings can be explained by the ancient Burmese traditions of absolute authoritarianism and despotic social order, which were deliberately revived by the military autarchy. The twin aspects of ruthless violence and gentleness coexist in every culture inasmuch as they are part of every human being. In its propensity to be simultaneously violent and peaceful Burma is like all other societies.

From this perspective, the process of social change and development may be thought of as conflicts and conflict-resolutions between what is new and what is old or what is alien and what is native. Identification of the traditional barriers to social change is a prerequisite to the understanding of modernization or the lack of it in a particular society. Instead of identifying them in esoteric theories and terms, traditional myths, legends, and folklore of the Burmese will be used as allegories to explain the Burma Road to Poverty. They seem to have served as models for the ruling elite, civilian and military, since 1948, when Burma attained its independence from the British. It may be suggested that the Burma Road to Poverty stemmed from its leaders' attempts to travel back to the ancient times envisaged in their idealization of an omnipotent and prosperous state with different symbols of glory and power.

With the dawning of military rule over Burma, the trend of economic performance has shown a monotonically declining pattern reaching its abyss in December 1987 with Burma as one of the least developed countries in the world. The fact that it took two and a half decades to transform itself from the position of *Rice Bowl* to *Rice Hole* of the world and Asia is indicative of the enormous natural wealth Burma has for potential development, a fact commonly recognized and emphasized by various analysts and observers. The answer to the riddle of what went wrong in such a rich country obviously lies in the human factors of mismanagement and ineffective strategies and policies of development adopted by the military managers. This view has been held by only a limited number of Burma scholars, myself, Joseph Silverstein, and the late Dr. Maung Maung Gyi.

There were a number of writers who viewed the Burmese army as the benevolent and effective modernizing agent of Burma. These sycophantic studies of military rule over Burma exemplify a variant on the positive assessment of traditional Burmese culture in which the modernizing role of the Burmese military elites is glorified. This view is represented in the works of Professors Anderson and Taylor and of Aung Thwin.[20] Neither of these views is correct due to their neglect of "common sense as a cultural system."[21] The idea of the modernizing role of the Burmese army was first advanced by Lucien Pye in 1962.[22] Prior to 1987, and even after Burma applied for and was granted the status of one of the least developed countries in the world, the two scholars who championed the benevolent and modernizing impact of the military rule over Burma in their studies have been Taylor and Aung Thwin. As Robert Taylor eulogized, "Ne Win has achieved the status of a founding father of modern Burma, equal only to the assassinated Aung San."[23]

Differing from his view, Ne Win may be thought of as a "founding father of traditional and decadent Burma," equal in status to Marcos, Sukarno, Pinochet, Castro, Noriega, and many other totalitarian dictators around the globe. This is not to imply that there have not been any changes within Burma, but to assert that the changes that have been made by military rule over Burma have resulted in the intensification of traditional barriers to social change and economic growth. The common denominator of military regimes around the world is the modernization of the army and intelligence arsenal in order to oppress the freedom and security of the people in the name of "law and order" and their supposedly benevolent ideologies.

Just as Taylor exalted Ne Win and his military regime as modernizers of Burma, Michael Aung Thwin assessed the civilian government era from 1948 to 1962 as the mythical period of independence. He contended that true independence for Burma was achieved under the benevolent and unifying rule of military benefactors. He wrote:

> In terms of general economic principles, the post-1962 and current economic system are, in my view, modern versions of the pre-1886 indigenous form, rather than of the colonial and post-1948 form. Today's Burmese way to socialism might be considered a modern version of Karl Polayani's model of economic redistribution, including the presence of more-or-less free markets within the larger, administered, system.[24]

This incredible depiction of the post-1962 economic system of Burma in terms of the precolonial model of economy is wrong in reflecting not only his limited knowledge of the economic history of Burma but also of the comparative economic systems of the modern world. It also reflects what the Burmese term *hpaw hlan-hpar*, eulogizing to gain favor from the ruling military elite. This type of historical writing glorifying the rules of Burma is not without precedent. For example, the *Mahah Yahzawin*, the Great History of Kings, written by U Kala was a prototype for Aung Thwin's eulogy of the Ne Win regime. To equate or even compare the military command economy with the economy of the type put forth by Karl Polayani in his *Great Transformation*, is as mythical as his assessment of the myth of independence from 1948 to 1962.

The model of economy designed by the philosophers and economic thinkers of the Burmese Way to Socialism was anything but indigenous or Burmese and *ipso facto* a duplicate of the Sino-Soviet model. Be that as it may, Michael Aung Thwin's view typified the outlook of the Burma Socialist Programme Party (BSPP), which envisaged an ideal socialist economy of "planned proportional development" on the basis of "the participation of all for the general well-being of all, sharing the benefits therefrom."[25] This obviously classic Marxian prescription for the establishment of a classless communist society of "from each according to his ability and to each according to his needs" apparently escaped Aung Thwin's perception. He is, however, correct in asserting that "the principles that underlay the economic, the political, and the social institutions of traditional Burma were subtly re-established,"[26] returning Burma to the dark ages of the absolute despotism of the Burmese kingdoms by the military rulers annihilating whatever democratic institutions had been left by the colonial and civilian governments.

In fact, George Orwell's description of British Burma seems to fit the real socio-political and economic life of Burma under military rule for the last twenty-eight years more than the ideal depiction of Aung Thwin. In the words of Orwell: "It is a stifling, stifling world in which to live. It is a world in which every word and thought is censored .... Free speech is unthinkable. All other kinds of freedom are permitted. You are free to be a drunkard, an idler, a coward, a backbiter, a fornicator; but you are not free to think for yourself." [27]

Thus, it seems that the military rulers of Burma simultaneously resurrected precolonial and colonial Burma in the name of "the Burmese Way to Socialism." The present political conditions in the newly named country of Myanmar do not seem to deviate much from those described by Orwell.

The political saga of Burma under the military rule of Ne Win and his successors cannot be comprehended without an understanding of the persistent traditional symbols, customs, and myths of state that form inner necessities for the central power-holders to emulate. This is in line with Geertz's view that "thrones may be out of fashion, and pageantry too; but political authority still requires a cultural frame in which to define itself and advance its claim, and so does opposition to it."[28] The cultural frame in which the military as well as the civilian political leadership of Burma have defined and claimed legitimacy has been the traditional culture with its age-old symbolic images of the "sacred center," *nagaya*, and "kings," *yahzahs*, whose authority over the "periphery," *daitha*, or the subjects is defined in the polity of absolute despotism, *padaithayit*.[29]

NOTES

1. Sterling Seagrave, "Burma on Edge," *Geo: A New View of Our World* (New York: Grunner & Jahr USA Inc., 1979), p. 50.

2. Cited by Helen G. Trager, *Burma Through Alien Eyes: Missionary Views of the Burmese in the Nineteenth Century* (New York: F.A. Praeger, Publishers, 1966), p. 143.

3. Ibid., p. 146.

4. F. Tennyson Jesse, *The Lacquer Lady* (New York: The Dial Press, 1979), pp. 365–366.

5. Ibid., p. 365.

6. George Orwell, *Burmese Days* (New York: Time Incorporated, 1962), p. 60.

7. Captain C.J.F.S. Forbes, *British Burma and Its People: Native Manners, Customs, and Religion* (London: Spottswood & Co., 1878), p. 55.

8. Ibid., p. 56.

9. Ibid., p. 59.

10. Ibid., p. 46.

11. E. E. Hagen, *The Economic Development of Burma* (Washington, D.C.: National Planning Association, July 1956), pp. 7–12.

12. See Pe Maung Tin and G. H. Luce, *The Glass Palace Chronicle of the Kings of Burma* (Rangoon: Rangoon University Press, 1960).

13. Hagen, *Economic Development*, pp. 7–12.

14. Ibid., p. 9.

15. Hagen, *The Theory of Social Change*, Chap. 18.

16. See Lucien Pye, *Politics, Personality, and Nation-Building: Burma's Search for Identity* (New Haven: Yale University Press, 1962), p. 86.

17. See Mya Maung, "The Burma Road to a Modern Nation," Joseph Fischer ed., *Foreign Values and Southeast Asian Scholarship* (Berkeley: University of California Press, 1973).

18. See B. O. Binns, *Agricultural Economy of Burma* (Rangoon: Government Printing and Stationery, 1948), p. 2.

19. See J. S. Furnivall, *Colonial Policy and Practice* (New York: New York University Press, 1956), p. 307.

20. The classic case of sycophantic glorification of Ne Win's military dictatorship by Professors Anderson and Taylor can be observed in their personal attacks on Ian Bruma. See Ian Bruma, "The Road to Mandalay," in *New York Book Review* (New York: New York Times, October 23, 1986). As for Michael Aung Thwin's works, the classic sycophantic study was presented in his "1948 and Burma's Myth of Independence," Joseph Silverstein ed., *Independent Burma at Forty Years: Six Assessments* (Ithaca: Cornell Southeast Asia Program, 1989).

21. See Clifford Geertz, *Local Knowldege: Further Essays in Interpretive Anthropology*, (New York: Basic Books Inc., 1983), pp. 73-75.

22. See Lucien W. Pye, "Armies in the Process of Modernization," John J. Johnson, ed. *The Role of the Military in Underdeveloped Countries*, (Princeton: Princeton University Press, 1962.) See also the comments made by Joseph Sil-

verstein on Pye's views in his unpublished article given at the Symposium on Southeast Asian Politics at the University of Michigan, 1987.

23. Robert Taylor, *The State of Burma* (Honolulu: University Hawaii Press, 1987), p. 366.

24. Aung Thwin, p. 27.

25. *The Philosophy of the Burma Socialist Programme Party: The System of Correlation of Man to His Environment* (Rangoon: The Ministry of Information, 1963), p. 45. For a critical account of this, see Mya Maung, "Socialism and Economic Development."

26. Aung Thwin, p. 26.

27. Orwell, pp. 60–61.

28. Geertz, p. 143.

29. Clifford Geertz, *Negara: The Theatre State in Nineteenth-Century Bali* (Princeton: Princeton University Press, 1980). This corresponds directly to the classical polity of Geertz's "*negara*" versus "*desa*," or "town" (state, capital, realm, etc.) versus "villages" in nineteenth century Bali.

The Burma Road to Poverty

1

Traditional Dual Society and Polity of Burma

Burma is a traditional society in which "ways of behavior continue with little change from generation to generation."[1] Other characteristics of such a society include authoritarianism, ascriptiveness, personalism, fractionalism, a "somewhat loosely structured social system,"[2] and low economic productivity. The persistence of these characteristics may be thought of as the result of a process of resistance to social change and economic growth by both "elites" and "simple folks" alike. This is not to suggest that there have not been any changes in the historical evolution of Burmese society, but to assert that the changes have not been substantively sustained enough to alter the ways of behavior towards modernization. In the case of Burma, a host of factors have kept the society from the required transformations of the traditional social system, among which the personality, policy, and value-orientation of the tradition-bound nationalist political leadership are most conspicuous.

Historically, the Burmese society has been held by powerful elites who impose their will on simple folks thus sustaining traditional ways of behavior with great stability. Despite the continual strife and disorder among the power-seekers and various social groups, the most oustanding aspect of the traditional Burmese social system has been the continuation of authoritarianism for millennia on personal, family, and societal levels. This continuum may be attributed to the acceptance of authoritarian rule by the simple folks.[3] In order not to overstate this view, it should be further added that, in both traditional and modern times, the rule of force has also been deployed by central power-holders to sustain their authoritarian reigns.

THE TRADITIONAL DUAL SOCIETY

From a structural-functional perspective, the traditional society of Burma is primarily dual with the powerful elite occupying the "center" made up of one or two cities and the subservient simple folks inhabiting the "periphery" made up of villages.[4] This duality of center, *nagaya*, and periphery, *daitha*, corresponds directly to the classic polity of Geertz's "*negara*" and "*desa*" in nineteenth century Bali. This correspondence is, of course, not accidental since both the Bali and Burmese kingship system was born out of the Indic heritage. This model of traditional society is described by Hagen: "Every traditional society of any importance is a dual society. It consists on the one hand of villages and on the other hand of some larger towns plus one or more central cities. The cities are the king's court, the center of government, regional strong points, or commercial centers."[5]

The powerful elite occupying the center of a traditional society manages the social organization empowered with opportunities and privileges drastically different from and relatively more abundant than those of simple folks whose interests are relegated to those of the central power-holders. Traditional Burmese society under the despotism, *padaithayit*, of various kings was like all traditional societies, prior to the emergence of deviant social groups who eventually destroyed this dual social structure. This third group of traders-financiers or the middle class in Burma was very small in number by virtue of the rigid socio-cultural and political sanctions against their behavior.

THE SOURCES OF BURMESE TRADITIONS

The basic sources of Burmese traditions are to be found in the Indo-Chinese cultural configuration of ancient Burma, with later proliferations and modifications during the reign of various Burmese kings and the British colonial rule. The twin influence of Indian and Chinese cultures on Burmese customs is immediately apparent in the formal attire of a Burmese male made up of a sarong, *longyi*, and a jacket, *tikepon aingyi*. The two represent the Indian and Chinese patterns of dress, respectively. The sarong is common apparel for the Thais, Cambodians, Indonesians, south Indians, and Ceylonese and indicates the impact of Indic culture. The jacket is the apparel of the Chinese. The Shans, Kayins, Kachins, and other hill tribes of the eastern regions of Burma bordering China, however, wear jackets and pants similar to those of the Chinese, and show an affinity to and the greater influence of Chinese customs. The Burmese language itself is a by-product of Indo-Chinese languages. The script and alphabet in Burmese writing are directly linked to the South Indian culture, while the tonal nature of spoken Burmese is primarily Chinese.

PRE-BUDDHIST ANIMISTIC MYTHS AND SPIRITS

The patterns of culture and ways of behavior that the Burmese followed for many centuries prior to the British colonization of Burma in the nineteenth century are derived from two types of belief systems, the pre-Buddhist and the Buddhist. The animism and worship of spirits, *nats*, dated back to many centuries before the arrival of Buddhism in the eleventh century of the Pagan Dynasty. Like most primitive and ancient cultures, the worship of supernatural powers in the form of gods, demigods, mythical beasts, demons, and spirits is a part and parcel of Burmese culture not drastically different from the classical mythology that can be discerned in ancient Greece, Rome, Britain, and all traditional societies prior to the Age of Reason and Science. The reliance on the role of the medicine men or shamans, astrologers, *baidin sayahs*, fakirs or wonder-makers with supernatural power, and savior kings, and their power to solve personal and social problems reflect traditional Burmese man's incapacity to cope with the harsh and demanding physical world around him.

A myriad of mythical animals and spirits pervaded the entire belief system, among which the dragon, the ogre, the demon, the spirit, *nat*, the tiger, the witches and warlocks, the ghost, and a host of others served as symbols of harmful power or evil in the life of a Burmese. The *nagar* and *balue* are also the names of two major tribes which inhabited the northwestern hills and southeastern region of ancient Burma. The hill tribe of *nagar* still exists in Burma today, while the account of *yetkhas* and *balues* conquered by the Mons was given in the stone inscriptions of the Mon kingdom.[6]

The evidence of the persistence of animistic mythology can be directly found in the customary Burmese practice of naming their children according to the day the child was born. Each day of the week is symbolized by a mythical animal such as the Vishnu warrior-bird, *galon*, for Sunday, the dragon, *nagar*, for Saturday, the tiger, *kyar*, for Monday, the lion, *chin-thaik*, for Tuesday, the elephant, *sin*, for Wednesday and so on. Thus, a person born on Wednesday like myself is named with the Burmese alphabet *ma* for Mya Maung symbolizing the elephant for wisdom, while the persons born on Saturday such as U Nu and Ne Win are named with the alphabet *na* symbolizing the dragon for bravery and courage. It must be noted here that the appropriate Burmese alphabet is used in the first part of the name, the Burmese names having no first, middle, or last name as such. Thus, U Nu has only one name: "Nu" is designated for the son born on Saturday, while "U" is a title similar to "Sir." It should also be mentioned that Ne Win's original Chinese name, Shu Maung, indicates that he was born on Thursday rather than on Saturday according to the above custom. The parallel customs in Western and Chinese cultures are the use of astrological Zodiac signs for assigning certain qualities or personality traits to persons born in certain months or years. In Burma, the statues of animals assigned to each day of the week can be found at various parts of a pagoda where the Burmese pay homage to them and perform rituals for good fortune and power in life.

ASTROLOGY AND NUMEROLOGY

Derived from the source of Hindu cosmology and planetary system, various superstitious rituals are performed by the Burmese to counter unforeseeable but prognosticated signs of misfortunes. From the role of Hindu-Brahmanic astologers, *ponnars*, employed as regular advisers by the Burmese kings, to a host of palmists, medicine men, and astrologers, *baidin sayahs*, a Burmese relies heavily upon their allegedly supernatural power to help and guide his life's ventures. Even the washing and cutting of one's hair are to be done on the specified days of the week. This is essentially not too different from the recent scandal caused when the astrologer, Mrs. Quigly, was consulted by Mrs. Ronald Reagan prior to the launching of important government projects or ventures by President Reagan in the United States.

One of the most common practices for sustaining one's success, power, and fortune is known as *yadayah chai* according to specific rituals to be performed as stipulated by astrologers. In the performance of these rituals, the number "9" played a vital role as a numerological cure for misfortunes. The Burmese called it *koenawin chai*. This powerful number of fame and fortune for a Burmese is primarily based upon the Hindu-Brahmanic planetary system in which there are many divinatory planets. Among them are "9" major planets of the Sun, the Moon and others, which the Burmese called *gyoes*. Each *gyo* has a life of certain numbers and is assigned to a specific day of the week. The astrological week has 9 days represented by the nine planets (Wednesday having two *gyos* and another independent *gyo* named *kike*). For example, Sunday *gyo* is assigned the value of 6, Monday *gyo* 15, Tuesday *gyo* 8, Wednesday *gyo* 17, Thursday *gyo* 19, and so on. The total value of the numbers of the lives of the 9 *gyoes* of the week adds up to 108 whose cumulative value is "9" $(1+0+8=9)$.

The significance and the use of the number "9" cut across both the Oriental and Occidental Numerology associated with major religious myths, mainly with the myth of the Mother Goddess of Earth. The Book of Genesis gave the time period from Adam to Noah or from creation to the year of the flood as 1,656 years whose cumulative value is "9." In the Hindu sacred epics and puranas, the present cycle of time is given as 432,000 and the great cycle, *mahahyuga*, as 432,000,000, both of whose cumulative values are "9." Joseph Campbell found the affinity of these mythical numbers between the Hindu and the Western mythology in association with the war between gods and anti-gods. He observed: "But then reading in the Icelandic Eddas, I discovered that in Orthin's (Wotan's) warrior hall, there were 540 doors, through each of which, on the "Day of the Wolf" (that is at the end of the present cycle of time), there would pass 800 divine warriors to engage the anti-gods in a battle of mutual annihilation."[7]

He noticed that 540 times 800 gives 432,000 years. The Indian numerological connection of "9" with this myth can be found in the Hindu festival called Navaratri. The name of this festival literally means "9 Nights" when Goddess Parvati, consort of Lord Shiva, fought and won the victory over the Demons on the "9th" night. In Roman Catholic Europe, the Virgin's conception of the Savior is celebrated by the Angelus tolling "9" times. The death of the Pope is followed by "9" days of mourning for absolution in Rome. The

Baha'i religion, which originated in Persia or Iran, also uses "9" by assigning numerical values to each of the Arabic alphabet in the name of its Prophet, Baha: "b" having a value of 2, "a" of 1, and "h" of 5 whereby the total cumulative sum of the values of the name Baha equals "9." The commonness of the belief in the mystical power of "9" was shown in the ancient Mesopotamian, Babylonian, and Indian mythology.[8] Indeed, "9" is the only number whose multiples by any other integer number produce the cumulative value of "9" ($9 \times 1 = 9$, $9 \times 2 = 18$ whose sum $1 + 8 = 9$, $9 \times 3 = 27$ whose sum $2 + 7 = 9$, etc.).

The modern psychological explanations for the persistence of traditional values and beliefs may be made in neo-Freudian terms in the formation of authoritarian personality. As Hagen put it, "One gains an understanding of most of the facets of authoritarian personality if one assumes that as a child the authoritarian individual acquired no perception of the phenomena around him as elements in systems whose operation is amenable to analysis and responsive to his judicious initiative."[9]

He went on further to assert that the reason for this attitude stems from the two basic perceptions of the world acquired by such an individual, namely, the arbitrariness of the world and the need to submit to greater willful powers than his.[10] As to how such perceptions are acquired, the answers can be found in early childhood experiences to explain the negative aspects of authoritarian personality. It may be suggested that Hagen's assumption is largely correct, although it is by no means exhaustive in explaining how these perceptions are sustained as barriers to social change and economic growth, or how and what causes the personality and thought transformation on the societal level to bring about modernization.

THE ORIGIN OF THE BURMESE

One of the confusions with controversial interpretations throughout the history of writings on Burma relates to the origin of the majority ethnic group, Myanmah. The history of the racial origin of the ethnic groups in Burma is shrouded in mysteries, myths, and legends. The basic reason for this is a lack of reliable records in writings and empirical findings. According to legends, the racial origin of the people of Burma, the Burmese in particular, has been believed to be twofold. A common theory learned by Burmese students asserts that the two waves of migration into ancient Burma were the Tibeto-Burman and the Mon-Khamer. The Myanmahs or Bamahs, as they are called (in writing and speaking) in Burmese, were supposedly a strain of Tibeto-Burman race, whereas the Mons or the Talines, as they are called by the Burmese, were considered to be a subfamily of Khmer racial stock. Later theories and research proved that the two major waves of migration were the Tibeto-Burman and the southern Indian linguistic group of the Austric Family with its two subfamilies of Austroasiatic and Austronesian.[11]

THE WESTERN VERSUS THE EASTERN ORIGIN

Similar to the dichotomy of views regarding the Burmese social character, there are two opposing versions of the racial origin of the Burmese, the Western and the Eastern. In effect, these two versions somewhat reflect the Indo-Chinese cultural configuration of traditional Burmese society. The Western view stressed that the early Tibeto-Burman migration into and settlement in the Upper Irrawaddy region came from the Ganges' Valley linking it to the non-Aryan race of the Turanian families. Their migratory path was traced to the western mountain range of Yakhine or Arakan Yoema inhabited by some savage hill tribes along the seaboard. These tribes were described as ***balues*** or ***beloos*** in the Burmese legends. It may be suggested that the characterization of a person or people as ***balue*** by the Burmese is basically associated with some savage tribes with ominous physical features which they encountered in ancient Burma. In fact, the mythical giantlike beast of ***balue*** in Burmese legends and the drama of Yahma (Ramayana) represents such a creature with fierce and savage looks. It may be allegorically inferred that the initial inhabitants of Negroid racial stock in ancient Burma might appear to the Tibeto-Burman settlers as ***balues*** to explain the root of this mythical creature.

THE LEGEND OF TAGAUNG ABIYAHZAH

According to the most well-known legend of how and when the Burmese kingdom began, the Burmese racial heritage was traced to the Indian King Abiyahzah, the founder of the Tagaung Dynasty in Upper Burma, of the Satkyah (Sakya) caste of Northern India long before the birth of prince Thaitdahta (Siddhartha), the prince Buddha.[12] According to the legendary tale told and taught to young Burmese, King Abiyahzah had two sons named Kanyahzah-gyi and Kanyahzah-ngel (literally meaning "Older King of Kan" and "Younger King of Kan"). The King either by intent or neglect did not designate the next heir to his throne, ***ainshait min***, during his reign. Upon his death, a power struggle broke out between the two sons; a wise minister intervened, asking them to settle their dispute in a contest. The contest was to build a large religious pavilion or almshall, ***mundut***; whoever accomplished the task first would be the successor to the throne. They agreed and the younger brother outwitted and beat his brother by cheating and using simpler construction materials to become the next ruler of the Tagaung Dynasty. The older brother was supposed to have left the Kingdom, traveling down the Irrawaddy river, and founded his own kingdom in the Arakan state at Dannyawadi after installing his son as the King of Phyus.

This legend is an example of the power of myths and symbols in shaping the belief system of a particular culture. In the absence of concrete scientific evidence presented in written records, such myths and legends became the main force for establishing national identity. The Burmese came to believe and assert that Bamahs or Myanmahs are the direct descendants of this kingly race which the Burmese called Tagaung Abiyahzah Thahgiwin Minmyo. The most famous and powerful song of the nationalist political organization known as the We Burmese, the forerunner of the Thakin political organization, and its followers invoked this racial heritage of the Burmese being born of royal blood, *thahgiwin minmyo*, dating back to the Tagaung Dynasty.

Although this belief is unfounded in terms of empirical evidence and archaeological discovery, it remains an unshakable symbol for asserting racial and political pride of the consecutive rulers of Burma. As Captain Forbes correctly noted, "Burmans [Burmese] assert that the progenitors of their nation came into their present seats from the West, from the Upper Valley of the Ganges, and claim a Rajpoot origin of the people; while royal family pretend to trace their descent from the Sacred Solar and Lunar dynasties of Hindustan."[13]

It is apparent either from this legendary tale or from the actual discovery of the ruins of cities in Upper Burma that the cultural if not racial origin of the Burmese is deeply rooted in Indic civilization and its rulers, a fact of ambivalence among the Burmese. Culturally, the influence of India on Burmese traditions can be found in the beliefs, myths, legends, music, art, and architecture of ancient Burma under the Burmese kings. That the very language of Burmese is imbued with the ancient Indian languages of Sanskrit and Pali, in particular, confirms the immense Indian influence on the cultural configuration of the Burmese society. This fact is never psychologically acknowledged by the Burmese whose anti-Indian sentiments seem to be much stronger than their anti-Chinese sentiments. The Chinese, for example, are often called Pauk-hpaws, a congenial term signifying blood brother and born-together, in contrast to another term, Tayoke, which is sometimes used in a derogatory way.

THE EASTERN ORIGIN

Contrary to the above view, the opposing view traced the racial and cultural roots of the ethnic groups of Burma to various migratory waves of settlement from northeastern Tibet and the northwestern regions of ancient China rather than from the Himalayan or northwestern regions of India.[14] The racial origin of the major minority ethnic groups of Shans and Kayins or Karens were directly traced to the Yunan province of China and Thailand. The T'ai racial stock of Tibeto-Burman grouping to which the Shans and Karens belonged is considered to be related to the Chinese. The Burmese together with the Shans were also supposed to have inhabited the western part of China for almost two thousand years prior to their settlement inside Burma. The Mons, whose civilization and kingdoms occupied Lower Burma at Thaton, are considered as a separate and distinct race from the Tibeto-Burman, belonging to the Austronesian race, the southern or oceanic Austric race.[15] This ethnic minority group which the Burmese called the Mon, and sometimes Taline, began the earliest civilization and later Buddhist cultural configuration in Lower Burma dating back to 250 B.C.[16] The existence of the ancient Mon kingdom known as the Thuwanabhumi (Suvannabhummi) was mentioned in the 550 stories of Indian *Jatakas* and the map of Ptolemy.

The classic dichotomy of the Western or Indic versus the Eastern or Chinese connections of the Burmese racial and cultural origin may never be solved in scientific terms since the real written records in the Burmese language date only to about the twelfth century A.D. Although the *Mahah Yahzawin,* the Great Chronicle of the Burmese Kings, a collection of stories and legends of Burmese kings, attributed to the sycophantic work of U Kala in the early eighteenth century, contained the chronicles of legendary dynasties dating back many centuries before Christ, it is not what modern historians consider to be a true archive of systematically written and recorded history.

A somewhat more objective and truer depiction of the Burmese monarchy was given by a group of researchers and scholars in their classic book, the *Mhan-nun Mahah Yahzawin Tawgyi*, the *Great Glass Palace Chronicle of the Kings of Burma*, completed towards the end of the eighteenth century. As a matter of fact, the stone inscriptions of the Pagan Dynasty in the eleventh century were mostly written in the Mon language. Thus, the development of language, customs, and writing occurred first among the Mons, the Phyu (a defunct race often considered as the vanguard of the Burmese), and the Yakhine (Arakan), many centuries before the Burmese developed their own. The mentors of the Burmese, then, were these ethnic groups through whose agency the cultural foundation and configuration of the Burmese were established some nine hundred years ago. The earliest usage of the name of the majority ethnic race Myanmah was traced to A.D. 1190, while the name of the country called Myanmah Pyi (the Country of the Burmese) appeared in A.D. 1235 recorded in the stone inscriptions of the Pagan Dynasty.[17]

THE MYSTERY OF BURMESE RACIAL ORIGIN

The question of the racial origin and cultural identity of the Myanmahs is a mysterious and often confusing matter subject to heated debates and violent quarrels. There is a Burmese saying that the history of the Burmese kings of Pagan cannot be discussed without carrying sticks for fighting on the shoulder—*Pagan Yahzawin doat-hturn*. As a matter of fact, even the skin color and physical features of a typical Burmese are not definitively established and known to the people of Burma themselves. For example, there is a saying in Burmese which construes the skin color of a true Burmese to be brown and bluish in tone signifying the royal blood—"white skin does not make a true human being (meaning Burmese), since the brown-bluish skin reflects the birth on royal throne"—*athar-yel phyu lu-bai-moe-lar, athar-daw nyopyah-nyet-kel nundaw-htet hpwar*.

It is further alleged that the first Burmese Dynasty of Pagan was founded by the Phyus migrating from the Lower to Upper Burma after their kingdom was destroyed. They were supposedly absorbed into the majority ethnic group of Myanmah. From these speculations another legend was born which contends that the beginning of the Burmese race occurred at Kyauksel, a city whose ruins were excavated to reveal the settlement of Phyus—*Myanmah-asa Kyauksel-gha*.[18] Based upon these legends, it may be suggested that the existence of so-called pure Myanmahs or Bamahs in Myanmar today is a myth and that they are a mixed ethnic group similar to the *mestizos* of Latin America.

The Burmese sensitivity with respect to skin color as an aspect of racism can be discerned in the usage of the term *kalar*. This term initially was used to connote all foreigners in the nineteenth century Kingdom of Thibaw, the last Burmese king before the British colonial annexation of Burma.[19] During and after the British rule, the term *kalar* came to specify Indians. This word in Hindustani means "black" indicating the racial element in its usage by both Indians and Burmese. In order not to exaggerate this, most Burmese have no knowledge of this meaning, although many derogatory remarks are made about the *kalars*.

The British colonial policy and practice of employing Indians in the administration of colonial Burma reinforced the deeply-rooted psychological wound of mistrust and resentment against foreigners in general. Thus, the terms *myet-nah phyu*, white or pale face, *sahphyu*, white letter or Christians, were commonly used to designate Western Europeans. Also in the Delta region of Lower Burma, the Kayins who were converted into Christians are called *sahphyu* Kayins as opposed to the Buddhist Kayins, *taline* Kayins. The English were also called Thakins or Boes meaning Masters or Chiefs. In the independent period, the title of Bo designated army officers who seemed to have symbolically replaced the colonial masters in the governance of Burma.

RACIAL IDENTITY CRISIS

It may be further suggested that the mystery of the racial identity of the Burmese, reinforced by the highly disorganized custom of naming persons according to astrological signs with no backward and forward genealogical linkages, has produced a deep psychological wound infested with ethno-linguistic group conflicts and fragmentations. The traumatic effect of this identity crisis tends to be most pronounced in the psyche of individuals with mixed blood, particularly the ones with alien blood such as the Anglo-Sino and Indo-Burmese. Certainly, the intermingling of various ethnic groups has taken place for many centuries, creating this traumatic identity crisis. The evidence of this historical intermingling between the majority Myanmahs and other minority ethnic groups can be discerned most clearly in the Delta regions of Irrawaddy and Salween where the majority of Karens and Mons were absorbed by the former in terms of language and writing. This may also be taken as one of the basic reasons for the intense Burmese chauvinism and the xenophobia of the people of Burma in general.

Indeed, the early settlement of Burma by migrating bands warring continuously for suzerainty may be thought of as the historical conditioning factor for the problem of national unity and identity throughout the history of Burma.[20] For example, the demise of the Phyu Dynasty was attributed to the onslaught of Kayins (Karens), while the southward migration of the original Tibeto-Burmans, the vanguard of the Burmese, into Upper Burma from the northwestern areas of China was due to the Chinese aggression of the Nancho Dynasty.[21] The history of the races of Burma with all their conflicts and conquests over each other from the very beginning of their migrations laid the foundation for a tension-and-war-ridden society with intense ethnic differentiation and fragmentation. Either from the west or the east or from the north or the south, the intruding migrating bands with their chieftains and rulers had subjugated the initial primitive tribes or each other at the very outset of various settlements and after the founding of various kingdoms in Burma. Foreign invasions of ancient Burma by Chinese, Indians, and Mongols further fortified this heritage.

THE EGALITARIAN SOCIETY

The traditional Burmese society based and structured upon the solid foundation of Buddhism and its clerical order tends to promote and preserve authoritarianism and nonegalitarian ranks in real social relationships, if not in theory. In theory, Buddhism from its very inception in Brahmanic India emphasized equality among all its followers and historically represented a revolutionary departure from the social structure of castes, classes, and tribes. The same was true of Christianity when it began in Judea. In Burma, higher power, authority, and status were historically bestowed upon or rather claimed by kings, royal family members, ministers, and priests together with parents, teachers, elders, and lately military commanders.

The conflict between State and Church, the controversies over the divine rights of kings and the investiture contests in the development of Western European civilizations are cases in point of the power struggle between the sacred and the secular. Although such a struggle was not as vigorous and violent in the traditional Buddhist society of Burma, the sacredness and the divine rights were granted to or rather claimed by Burmese kings in light of the secular origin of the Buddha to-be prince, *Hpayarlawn*. It should be pointed out here that the issue of the divine rights of Buddhist kings was never a serious one in Burmese Buddhism, since it does not recognize the existence of a Supreme Being or monotheism. Gautama Buddha was neither the Son of God nor the Messiah of the Supreme Being, making the Theravada Buddhism primarily atheistic as opposed to Hinduism, Judaism, Christianity, and Islam.[22]

The sacred Trinity of Buddha, Hpayar, his Preaching, Tayar (Dhamma), and Disciples (Thangahs), known as the Three Venerable Jewels, Yadanah Thoanpars, were transformed into an authoritarian framework of total deference and obedience by adding the two other secular personalities of parents and teachers. In fact, these five authorities are considered to be five omnipotent and supreme objects of veneration equal in status and rank, although it is not certain that Buddha himself had mandated this ranking. They are called and revered as Anandaw Ananda Ngarpar, Five Deservers of Immeasurable Deference and Gratitude, by Buddhist Burmans. It is not asserted here that giving such reverence and rank to them is wrong or bad as such, but it is shown that the impact of this in the hands of those who came to possess power can be a potent source for developing authoritarianism. The evidence of this was observed by Bishop Bigandet in 1858: "Buddha means wise, intelligent. Phra [Hpayar in Burmese] is an expression conveying the highest sense of respect, which was applied originally only to the author of Buddhism, but now, through a servile adulation, it is applied to the king, his ministers, all great personages, and often by inferiors to the lowest menials of Government."[23]

He went on to further observe that "the word Phra [Hpayar], coupled with that of Thaking [Thakin in Burmese], which means Lord, is used by Christians in Burmah to express the idea of God, the supreme being."[24] Indeed, the two terms were often jointly used as Thakin Hpayar in both ancient and colonial Burma when addressing the king or the British administrator. It must be pointed out here that the term *hpayar* is not indiscriminately used by the Burmese in addressing the Buddha, clergymen, and kings. They are addressed with prefixes such as Myartswah Hpayar, Ashin Hpayar and Hpayarshin, respectively. The prefix of Myartswah is reserved only for Buddha to signify the most Reverend Supreme Being, although not in the Christian sense of God as such. Yet, the fact that the word *hpayar* appears in all three addresses seem to indicate almost equal ranking among them to confirm the Bishop's appraisal. It will be argued then that this cultural norm or value-orientation has been used and abused by the central power-holders to their advantage throughout the history of Burma. In short, the gap between what is preached and what is practiced has widened by negating the sacred in favor of the secular or "desacralization"[25] during the course of the socio-cultural configuration of Burmese society.

TRADITIONAL DUAL POLITY AND ITS LEGACIES

The traditional dual society of Burma with respect to its structure and function found its duplicate in the polity of the Burmese kingdoms in which political power was centralized in the person of the king, *min yahzah* (raja), who was extolled as the Great Arbiter of Existence and Ruler of the Universe (Satkyahwaday Mintayargyi), the Great Owner of Life, Head, and Hair of his subjects (Thetoo Sanpine Mintayargyi), and the Descendant of the Boddisattava, Buddha-to-be (Boddithartta Hpayarlawn). The traditional polity of Burma was similar to all other traditional polities in being primarily dual with powerful monarchs and their families and bureaucracy occupying and controlling the "center," while the "periphery" functioned according to traditional customs and arbitrary laws created and enforced by the former.

The central political power was personalized in the ruling monarch whose numinous qualities were derived from the myths of legendary Buddhist kings of ancient India. It may be best described as the archetypal creation of a sacred state in the psyche of both ruling elites and simple folks. Symbolically, the insignias of a peacock and a hare on the flags and seals of the Koanbaung Kings of Burma reflect the evidence of the belief that the Burmese kings were the direct descendants of the Solar (Peacock) and Lunar (Hare) rulers dating back to the beginning of the Unvierse in Hindu mythology. This myth of the sacred Burmese state was later personalized in the legendary and actual rulers of Burma.

Structurally, the political power and administration were centralized in the person of a king of the central city assisted by his bureaucracy which nominally functioned as the body of legislature, judicial organ, and political administration. This body was called Hlutdaw or Hluttaw comprised of ministers, *wungyis*, which literally means those who bear the burden, in this case the burden of administering the wishes of the king. Formally, there was a Prime Minister as the top administrator out of the Four Major Ministers who formed the inner-circle of political control. The Hlutdaw contained a number of other officials called *mingyis, wundauks,* and *amarts*. The authority of the Hlutdaw was nominally greater than the wish and will of the king and his royal family, but in reality all the officers of that body were either appointed directly or with the approval of the king. This real structuring of political authority and administration was best summed up by Scott:

> The Government of Upper Burma under the native Kings was purely despotic. The King's power was absolute; his only restraints were his voluntary respect for Buddhist rules and precepts, generally for all believers, or particular to the Kingly estate . . . . Official position was the only sign of rank and all officials were appointed or dismissed at the King's will. Dismissal usually meant absolute ruin, a step from the Court to the gaol.[26]

The security and strength of political power depend on the character of the king himself in such a despotic system of governance. Even the strongest and most powerful king, however, faced a threat to his throne, which historically was fought for by multiple royal and nonroyal contenders. This forced a king to be highly cautious and insecure in guarding against his potential demise. The choice of an inner-power group loyal to him became then an absolute necessity and the frequency of the turnover of the members of this group was a way of life in the politics of royalty.

This numinous ruler was further bestowed with the absolute ownership of water and sea, *yaymyay pineshin*, along with white elephants, *sinbyu pineshin*, the white umbrella, *hteebyu pineshin*, and precious gems, *yadanah pineshin*. In addressing a Burmese king, his subject called himself Kyaydaw Myo or Kyundaw Myo, a person in pecuniary bondage or a slave of the king. In fact, the most polite form of the subjective pronoun, used in Burmese conversation when addressing an older person or superior, is *kyundaw*. There are historical records in the stone inscriptions of the Pagan Dynasty that the kings of Burma often declared an entire village to be pagoda slaves, *hpayarkyuns*, to indicate their absolute ownership of their subjects. The pagoda slaves are social outcasts in Burma even up to the present day.

This ownership by Burmese kings of almost everything in the material world is signified by the prosaic Burmese words *pine* (to own) and *pineshin* (owner). The situation was amazingly similar to that of other Southeast Asian kings of Indic cultural origin. Geertz poignantly assessed the ownership of the king of Bali:

> The general relationship between the king and the material world was summed up in a deceptively prosaic word whose apparent ease of translation has been the chief bar to scholarly understanding of it: druwe. Druwe (madruwe, padruwen) means "owned" ("to own," to "possess;" "property," "wealth"). That is not the problem. The problem is that, used in connection with the king, it was applied to virtually everything: not just to his private lands and personal possessions, but to the country as a whole, all the land and water in it, and all the people.[27]

As was pointed out before, even though the word Payar (correctly spelled and pronounced Hpayar)[28] was primarily reserved for the Lord Buddha and his disciples, *yahans*, who were addressed by the devotees as Myartswah Hpayar and Ashin Hpayar, the kings of Burma ostentatiously put themselves in the same sacred rank with Buddha and the *yahans*. The Burmese king was addressed sycophantically by his ministers and subjects as Ashin Min Hpayargyi, the Great Reverend Lord King, to reflect the sacred status ostensibly claimed by a Burmese monarch.

Although neither Buddhism nor actual norms of Burmese culture ranked kings among the sacred objects of veneration such as the Three Venerable Jewels, Yadanah Thoanpar, and the Five Deservers of Immeasurable Deference and Gratitude, Anandaw Ananda Ngarpar, the sacred position was historically bestowed upon the royalty and his family. This process of sacralizing the secular is deeply rooted in the kingship of ancient India and the legendary proclamation of Buddhist kings in India and Burma as the direct descendants from the Sun Dynasty. Lord Gawdama Buddha himself was claimed to be a direct descendant of the Sun Dynasty. This mythical claim was honored and endorsed by the subservient masses throughout the history of Burmese kings.

However, the Burmese also considered a king to be one of the Five Major Enemies of life—water, fire, king, thief, and hater (*yay, mee, min, khothu*, and *machit mahnit thetthu*). This ranking of kings among the ominous enemies of life indicates the immense danger and awesome power the Burmese king historically wielded over those who served him and simple folks in general. In fact, the status or fortune of a man in the service of a king was analogously compared to that of a tree on the precarious bank of a river—*minkha yaukkyar karnnar thitpin*. These two seemingly opposing views of a Burmese king must not be taken as totally contradictory. The two are consistent with each other if one understands the nature of an authoritarian personality with its simultaneous needs to dominate and submit or more correctly the aggression-submission need. The net effect of this combined need is usually extreme "deference."

These two combined views of kings in the Burmese belief system can be taken as a reflection of the symbolic power and sacredness of the "center," on the one hand, and the historically subdued status of the "periphery" in the power structure of the traditional Burmese polity, on the other. It also reflects the rule of will enforced by the ruler and ascribed to him by his subservient subjects. The framework within which the Burmese monarchy claimed its political legitimacy is the traditional Buddhist culture in which the legends of Burmese Buddhist Kings were made as the Ruler of the Earth or the Southern Continent Island, Zabudipah (Jambu Dipa) Letyah Taungkyune. The root of this claim is to be found in the legends of pre-Gawdama-Buddha and post-Gawdama-Buddha rulers of the Sun Dynasty dating back to the beginning of the universe. This is exemplified in the most famous Buddhist King of India, Asoka, who was proclaimed to be the ruler of the entire Universe, Jambudvipa.[29]

THE DUAL MYTHS OF THE BURMESE STATE

The dual myths of the Burmese state, personified in the king as a sacred and a mighty ruler, were derived from two sources of myths: the pre-Gawdama rulers of mythical kingdoms of India and the myth and legend of the life of Gawdama Buddha. They symbolized the two basic priestly and soldierly qualities of an ideal ruler or king, lucidly juxtaposed by Sir George Fraser in his *Golden Bough*.[30] The personalities of Burmese kings and political leadership throughout the entire history of Burma may be presented in terms of the symbol of power, based upon the two myths of god-man and hero. The chronicles of the Burmese kings pivoted around these two myths which seem to have persisted in the contemporary politics of Burma.

THE MYTH OF THE GODLY KING

The Burmese king as the Ruler of the Universe was born out of the pre-Gawdama-Buddha mythical kingship and dynasties of India and later magnified in the hands of the legendary and actual Buddhist kings of Burma. The clearest evidence of this belief can be discerned in the very beginning of the *Glass Palace Chronicle of the Kings of Burma* which opened with the prayer to "Lord Supreme Sakyan King" (*Thartbyi-nyue Satkyah-wateet Yahzah Min)* who conquered over all enemies and ruler of the three world systems or the universe, with the sacred preaching."[31] The Burmese variation of the term "Sakya," the name of the Indian caste which also means "mighty," as Satkyah or Satkyah-wadday used as one of the many titles of a Burmese king, came to signify the concept of "the Universal Ruler" or Chakkavatti.

This ideal concept of a mighty ruler of the universe was supposed to have been what prince Buddha's father wished his son to become. The first king at the beginning of the world was named Mahah Thamada Min (Mahasamata King), a direct descendant of the solar kings, *nayminnwel*, who ruled the universe by copying, recording, and obeying the sacred moral laws and avoiding the four sins. The Southern Continent Islanders (Jabudipans) gave gifts and homage to that king who ruled the earth by observing the "ten moral codes of conduct" prescribed to a king, *minkyint-tayar selpar*. His twenty-eight children, grandchildren, and great-grandchildren succeeded him to rule the cosmic worlds forming the Dynasty of Myitsima Daitha, the Dynasty of the Middle Country in the mythical world of ancient India.[32] The most important king among them was Mahnda Min, who ruled the Four Cardinal Islands of Four Great Oceans surrounded by two thousand small islands with Myint-motaung (Mt. Meru) at the center. He was appropriately called Satkyahwaday Mahnda Min who lived and ruled for hundreds of thousands of years of blissful luxury, glory, and longevity similar to those of the thirty-six angels, *thagyars*.[33]

Certainly, tracing the lineage of the Burmese kings to the Sun Dynasty and the metaphoric glorification of their power and rule as the illuminating sunlight dispelling the darkness are the representation of the mythical symbol of the godly man. This myth was shown to be common to all ancient cultures expressed in the form of what Freud called "archaic remnants" or Jung termed "archetypes." The belief of the Pueblo Indians that they are the children of the Father Sun, the Egyptian myth of Osiris-Horus and the Sun Disk above the throne of pharoah Tutakhamen, the Sun Disk circumscribed behind the heads of Christ and Buddha, and the Shintoist divine Sun may be thought of as the common archetypal symbol of the man-god as the deliverer and the redeemer of life in general.

THE MYTH OF THE HERO

The above religious symbol of the just and benevolent Buddhist king is also closely associated with the hero myth common to all primordial belief systems. As Carl Jung wrote, "The universal hero myth, for example, always refers to a powerful man or god-man who vanquishes evils in the form of dragons, serpents, monsters, demons and so on, and who liberates his people from destruction and death."[34]

The political legitimacy of a Burmese king derived its *raison d'etre* from the very legend of Gawdama Buddha's background. It must be pointed out once again that the very racial identity and background of the prince Buddha, Thaitda-hta Minthar, seemed to be shrouded in mysteries and different interpretations. A lack of an early biography of him as well as his teachings has left a legacy of dichotomous views and conflicting interpretations similar to the entire spectrum of writings on Burmese society, its culture, and peoples. Some said that Buddha belonged to an Aryan race and the warrior caste of Kshatriya, while others contended that the Sakyas, Gautama's own people, were Mongolians like the modern inhabitants of the Tarai of Nepal. The name of Buddha's father, Thudawdana (Suddhodana), is supposed to mean "Pure Rice" suggesting that they were an agricultural people.[35]

The twin mystic qualities of a Burmese king, as a just and benevolent ruler with Buddha-like personality belonging to the nonviolent agricultural caste and a conqueror of all enemies belonging to the Shatriyan caste of warriors, found their profound expressions in the chronicles of the Burmese Kingdoms. What is significant here is to note that the history of the Burmese kings pivoted around these two attributes of a king as the defender of Buddhism and the conqueror of various city states, the kingdoms of ethnic minority groups, in particular, and foreign kingdoms.

THE LEGENDARY GODLY BURMESE KINGS

The legendary Kingdom of Tagaung, also called Thingathaya-hta (Sangassaratta), was supposedly ruled by an unbroken line of kings numbering thirty-three in all with order and tranquility befitting the ideal Buddhist state. It should be recalled that the very first Kingdom of Burma at Tagaung was supposedly founded by King Abiyahzah who left the legacy of competition between his two sons for succession to the throne after his death. The younger brother Kan Yazah-ngel won the throne and the elder brother left Tagaung and eventually founded his own Kingdom in the Arakan state. The Arakanese Chronicle acknowledged the reign of this king to establish the fact that the Burmese and Arakanese Kings were blood brothers. This was not acknowledged in the Burmese Chronicles of Kings. Nevertheless, there were two consecutive kingdoms at Tagaung, namely the pre-Gawdama-Buddha Dynasty of King Abiyahzah and the post-Gawdama-Buddha Dynasty founded by the second migration of another Indian Kshatriyan King by the name of Daza Yahzah. The fall of the first Dynasty was attributed to the onslaught of invaders from the land of Tsin or Sin, which corresponded with Yunan. Thus, the very first Kingdom of Burma was presumed to fall under the attack of the Chinese, Tayoke, the same fate suffered by the Kingdom of Pagan many centuries later. The defeated descendants of the First Kingdom of Tagaung split into three different groups and established different kingdoms, one near Pagan and another in the Shan state.[36]

THE LEGENDARY PAGAN KINGS

At the very outset, it must be warned that the following chronicle of kings of Pagan is primarily based upon legendary tales written in various Burmese chronicles rather than actual records of stone inscriptions. For example, even the names of these kings are not the same as those inscribed in various stone inscriptions of Pagan.[37] These legendary tales are, however, useful for allegorical accounts of the nature and functioning of the polity of ancient Burma. Mythically, the sacredness of the "center" or "throne" became absolute in the person of a Burmese king. Moreover, the dialectic or rupture between the sacred and the profane, as it occurred in the Western political cultures of Christianity and the growth of modern states, never was a serious issue in the traditional polity of Burma. A polity of absolute despotism, *padaithayit*, was established by Burmese kings by exalting themselves to a sacred status equal in rank to those of Buddha, his preachings, and his assembly. This was made possible by the somewhat complete detachment of the Buddhist clerical order, Thangah, from the profane world, *lawki*, mandated by Buddhism itself.

The Burmese monarchs, like all other rulers of traditional societies, were archaic men whose views and behavior were best described by Eliade: "Just as modern man proclaims himself a historical being, constituted by the whole history of humanity, so the man of archaic societies considers himself the end product of a mythical history, that is of a series of events that took place *in illo tempore*, at the beginning of Time."[38]

He further elucidated the meaning of life or living to a man of archaic or traditional society as "for archaic man, there is nothing truly real except the archetype" and that he "must refuse history, the contingent events of actual time, must set himself in opposition to a series of events that are irreversible, unforeseeable, possessed of autonomous value."[39] This amazingly fits the authoritarian personality's view of the world, as described by Hagen and previously cited.

The mighty warrior symbol of an ideal king began to emerge and supersede the symbol of a priestly ruler in the legendary tales of Paukkan or Pugan or the Pagan kings before the most famous founder of the Pagan Dynasty, King Anorya-htah. One of the salient aspects of these kings and their kingdoms was the absence of order or primogeniture in the succession to the royal throne—a seed planted in the very first legendary kingdom of Burma at Tagaung by King Abiyahzah. This departure from the legacy of an unbroken succession of pre-Gawdama-Buddhist kings of ancient India in Burma may be thought of as a consequence of the process of warfare, power struggles, and personal crises developed during the socio-political configuration of ancient Burma. It is directly linked to the mystery of racial origin and the mythical identity of the Burmese rulers compounded by the customs of neglecting genealogical linkages, polygamy of kings, and intermarriages among various ethnic groups.

This legacy was most prominent in the legendary stories of the kings of Pagan which were filled with either a commoner or a banished prince engaged in the professions of a stable boy, a gardener, a Buddhist monk, or a king's serviceman rising to the kingship either by the accidental or deliberate killing of a reigning king. For example, Salai Ngakway Min, the first king of the legendary Fourth Kingdom of Pagan, was supposedly a banished prince working as a stable boy for the reigning king. After he got involved with the consort of the king who visited the stable regularly, he assassinated the king and captured the royal throne.

In the same kingdom, a common gardener, *taungthu*, became king after accidentally killing the reigning king who wandered into a cucumber field on his hunting trip and ate a cucumber without the permission of the angry gardener. He was appropriately named the Taungthugyi Min (the Gardener King). This legacy of killing the reigning king persisted throughout the entire chronicles of the Burmese kings which contain brutal tales of hunting down potential successors to the royal throne, *minlawns*, patricide, fraticide, and mass slaughters of princes and princesses. There were also stories of various bloody intrigues and plots to install a successor to the throne involving ministers, princes, and queens in the political saga of that kingdom.[40]

THE LEGENDARY TALE OF SACRED ANORYA-HTAH

The most legendary Burmese king of the authentically recorded Pagan Dynasty, symbolizing the image of the great Buddhist King of India, Athawka (Asoka), was King Anorya-htah (his real title being Aniruta) whose reign lasted from A.D. 1044 to 1077. He introduced Buddhism throughout the land by importing it from the Mon Kingdom which he conquered. He was also supposed to have eradicated the animistic religion of the worship of dragons, *nagars*, under the influence of Hindu hermits called *ayeegyis* in his kingdom. Splendid pagodas, temples, and shrines dedicated to Buddhism were constructed in his reign as deeds of merit—a legacy left for all the successive Burmese kings and their dynasties. In him the two requisite qualities of an ideal ruler, the sacred priestly person and the mighty warrior, were fused together to form a role model for his successors.

The priestly function of a benevolent king was stipulated in the ten ethical conducts which mandated that he give alms, *ahlu*, observe five and ten commandments, *Thila*, contribute to various charities, control anger, as well as show honesty, patience, tenderness, kindness, and justice and not oppose the peoples.[41] The most famous story of the giving of alms, *ahlu*, by an ideal king named King Waithandayah was told in the Jatakas. This highly religious king performed the greatest *ahlu* by giving away his queen, white elephant, and even his daughter and son, Ganah and Zali, to Brahmanic priests called *Ponnars*—

the astrologers of the Burmese kings.[42] Of course, such an act of religious and moral excellence was never performed by Burmese kings nor did they fully abide by the ten moral conducts sanctioned for a Buddhist king. However, the majority of them constructed bridges, lakes, pagodas, and gave alms to the Buddhist monks. Even at that, these deeds of merit were often performed by a Burmese king to atone for sins he had committed during his reign.

That the above ideal image of a benevolent Buddhist king can be ostensibly associated with King Anorya-htah of Burma should not be carried too far so that he is regarded as the most benevolent Buddhist Burmese monarch. Such an association was implicitly made by Michael Aung Thwin in his incorrect assessment of the fall of the Pagan and other dynasties of ancient Burma as a result of the transfer of wealth—in the forms of giving alms, pagoda slaves, *pay-akyuns*, and land resources—by Burmese kings to the realm of the Buddhist clerical order. Neither reliable statistical facts nor written records of such a transfer can confirm this erroneous and conjectural assessment. The very title of his book *Pagan: The Origins of Modern Burma* misrepresents a true and factual account of ancient Burmese kingdoms similar to U Kalar's *Mahah Yahza-win* with new twists.[43] Contrary to this assessment, it will be suggested that the process of "desacralization" of the sacred by the despotic Burmese monarchs in general underlies the fragility and downfall of the Burmese kingdoms. For even the supposedly most benevolent King Anorya-htah, like many other bad Burmese kings, was ruthless and insecure when it came to the monopoly and safety of his throne and other resources.

His story seems to have left the legacy of purging and destroying many potential challengers to the throne or "the next king-to-be," *minlawns*, under the advice of Brahmin astrologers, *ponnars*, and soothsayers—a practice revived and most vehemently followed by the military dictatorship of Ne Win during the last thirty years. Neither did King Anorya-htah completely abandon the worship of Hindu celestial beings, *nat daiwahs*, and local spirits, *nats*. The evidence of this can be seen in the various pagodas and temples congested with mythical spirits of Byamahs and Thagyars at Pagan. Further evidence of this can be found in the halls of the most famous pagoda built by him, called Shwe-zeegon Zaidi, where various statues of spirits, *nats*, were housed for worship. Among "the next kings-to be," *minlawns*, who were hunted down was the legendary mighty warrior king Kyansitthar, whose story deserves a brief account.

THE LEGENDARY TALE OF HEROIC KYANSITTHAR

The heritage of the tumultuous and fragmented polity of traditional Burma, characterized by violent power struggles of succession to the throne, wrathful killings of rivals, hunting down of potential *minlawns*, and savage warfare among city states, can be traced to the very beginning of the Pagan Dynasty. King Anorya-htah himself came to the throne by killing his own brother after a violent confrontation and battle on horseback. The story of the third king of the Pagan Dynasty, Kyansitthar or Htee-hlaing Min (A.D. 1084-1113), his real title recorded in the stone inscription, may be thought of as a classic case in point of an insecure monarch seeking to destroy a potential contender to his royal power. In fact, his name Kyansitthar used by Burmese historians literally means "a Left-over Soldier" which will become clear in the following unfolding of the romantic story of his life.

Although he was supposed to have been one of the sons of King Anorya-htah according to the contradictory legendary stories given in the *Glass Palace Chronicle*, it was not really verified on the basis of authentic written records or stone inscriptions.[44] All that is certain is that he was in the service of the King and that his life story testifies to the chaotic and disorderly process of royal succession inherent in the socio-political culture and customs of traditional Burma. The stories of the commoner kings discussed earlier exemplify this aspect of the traditional Burmese polity, which must have plagued the psyche of any reigning monarch whose throne and power were in a continuous state of jeopardy.

According to the legendary account of Kyansitthar, he was the son of King Anorya-htah, conceived by a princess from the Middle Country of Waithahli who was sent to the king. The king's emissary in charge of bringing the princess to the kingdom fell in love with her on the homeward journey. The princess was banished on the basis of not being a true princess, a lie told to the king by the treacherous emissary for fear of being discovered. The conception of Kyansitthar by the exiled princess and King Anorya-htah (not from the union between the princess and the emissary) was attended by earthquakes, thunder, and other signs. These events were read by the king's astrologers as a signal of the emergence of a *minlawn*, which terrified the insecure reigning king. Thus, following the advice of astrologers covering many years of the child's growth, the apprehensive king ordered that thousands of pregnant women, nursing babies, and boys who took care of cows, cow-herds (*nwar-kyawnthars*), be hunted down and slaughtered as the years passed.

The young Kyansitthar miraculously escaped each of these mass killings under the protection of the dragon king, *nagar min*, indicating the persistence of the animistic worship of *nagars* in that kingdom. When the hunted one entered the Buddhist clerical order, the astologers once again conveyed their knowledge of it to the king. Not daring to violate the cultural sanction against killing the sacred monks, the king invited them to eat at his palace. Thus, the king was able to detect and discover the identity of the *minlawn*, whose mouth radiated brilliant lights when eating. Upon this discovery, the king asked his astrologers whether or not this monk would take over his throne immediately. The ironical answer given was that the *minlawn* was only second in line to succeed him after his death.

The king, remorseful and guilt-ridden over all his useless killings, began to perform many deeds of merit including the construction of pagodas for the atonement of his sins. He also made Kyansitthar one of his commanders, whose exploits as a courageous and loyal soldier became classic legends in the history of Pagan. The sequel to this story was told when Kyansitthar was assigned the task of saving the Mon Kingdom of Pegu, Oatthah Pellgu, from the attack of another city state, at the request of the king of that kingdom. After the successful completion of the task, the grateful king of Pegu sent gifts among which was his beautiful daughter, Princess Maneet Sandah or Khin Oo. Like King Anorya-hta's emissary who became involved with his mother, Kyansitthar fell in love with the princess on the journey back to Pagan. The infuriated king hunted him down and the rest of his life was spent in hiding from the long arm of the king until the king's death.[45]

At any rate, Kyansitthar symbolized a mighty warrior king with exceptional sacred qualities the Burmese termed *kan* and *hpoan*. His long title of "the Most Great and Glorious Majesty, King of Sunnaparan, Zapudipah, Lord of Many White Elephants, Lord of Gold, Silver, Rubies and Amber, Lord of the Sea and Land, Lord of the Rising Sun, Arbiter of Existence, etc." was to become the ritualistic usage of all Burmese kings in their ceremonies and official communiqués. Kyansitthar also completed the construction of the Shwezeegon Pagoda which was left unfinished by King Anorya-htah. He also built another famed Buddhist temple of immense architectural achievements at Pagan, the Temple of Anandah.[46] The image of Kyansitthar as a savior king born outside the royal family or a *minlawn* with unusual power and ability, *hpoan*, was cast in the various personalities of the Burmese kings and contemporary political rulers of Burma.

Similar archetypes of political cultural patterns can be discerned in ancient Egypt, Greece, Rome, and European nations in the Middle Ages with respect to the problems of royal succession involving killings, exiles, and disputes over divine right. For "archaic man believes himself—in his deepest being—to be a product of mythical history, thus he makes himself by shaping his life in accordance with a series of archetypal models believed to have been established at the beginning of Time by the gods or by his ancestors."[47]

The names of saintly kings of benevolence given in various sacred books and chronicles of Burmese kings were King Waithandayah of Jatakas, King Athawka of Buddhist India, Kings Anorya-htah, Alawnsithu, and Nayapatisithu, of the Pagan Dynasty, King Bayintnaung with alternate titles of Sinbyushin Mintayargyi or Hanthahwaddy Mintayargyi of the Tounggu-Hanthahwaddy Dynasty, and King Min Doan of the Koanbaung Dynasty. As for kings symbolizing the hero myth of a mighty warrior king, Anorya-htah and Kyansitthar of the Pagan Dynasty, Tabinshwehtee and Bayintnaung or Sinbyushin Mintayargyi of the Tounggu-Hanthahwaddy Dynasty and Alawn Hpayar of the Koanbaung Dynasty, stood out most prominently in Burmese history. Their conquests included various city states and kingdoms of minority ethnic rulers inside Burma, along with conquests of Assam and other foreign kingdoms, particularly the conquest of Thailand and the destruction of its capital, Ayuhtiya.

0694573

THE LEGACY OF THE KOANBAUNG DYNASTY

The legacy of the last kingdom of Burma, the Koanbaung Dynasty, contained all the basic weaknesses of the Burmese kingship system: violent and chaotic accessions to the throne, warfare among city states governed by Burmese and other minorities, and wars with foreign kingdoms. The vulnerability of the Burmese kingdoms to foreign attacks dated back to the Pagan Dynasty. In fact, when the founder of the Koanbaung Dynasty, Alawn Hpayar, came to the throne in 1752, the preceding Burmese Kingdom in Lower Burma was vanquished and Upper Burma was overrun by the Mons or Talines from Lower Burma with the help of the French. The Thai King also invaded Lower Burma in revenge for Burmese raids made by previous kings. Alawn Hpayar's successful revolt against and conquest of the Mons, by amassing forces from forty-six or so villages around his village of Moatsobo, became a legend in the chronicle of Burmese kings. His further feats of conquest included the subjugation of the Arakanese, Shan, Manipuri, and Thai kingdoms. The two myths of a heroic and a priestly king were revived and glorified in the two major personalities of Alawn Hpayar and Min Doan in the chronicle of the Koanbaung Dynasty.

THE HERO MYTH: ALAWN HPAYAR (1752-1760)

It must be pointed out that the Great Chronicle of Burmese kings, *Mahah Yahzawin*, reported that Alawn Hpayar was ostensibly born of royal blood and was a descendant of the king of the Pagan Dynasty, Nayapatisuthu. The Arakanese Chronicle also claimed that he was of pure royal Arakanese blood, born from an exiled chief queen of a deposed Arakanese king named Sanda Thuriya of the Dhannyawadi Dynasty. She was supposed to have fled to Upper Burma and settled in Shwebo under the care of its headman.[48] These claims cannot be proven one way or the other due to the reasons given before. Both of these claims seem rather far-fetched in view of the fact that the Pagan Dynasty fell some 400 years before and given the unreliable genealogical records of the chronicles of Burmese kings.

However, it is certain that he was the headman of the village of Moatsobo which later became the capital of Shwebo and the seat of his reign. He was nicknamed Moatsobo U Aung Zaiya, referring to that village. Likewise, his conquest over the Talines was mythically glorified as due to his unusual power, *hpoan*, in beating the enemies of great military might with a simple "bamboo stick." The supernatural signs and omens associated with his unusual power were "when he slept his arms shone like fire; vultures perched on the house of his enemies; gorgeous butterflies and gay-plumaged birds and strange animals entering his dwelling; he dug up an ancient image of the Buddha not far from his doorsteps . . . . He possessed a sword that flew through the air and cut off heads etc."[49]

Real accounts of his rise to the throne and victory over the Mons attributed his success to a unified armed force of many villages and a well-entrenched fortress around his village plus the overconfidence of the invading Mon army. His march and subjugation of the Mons in the Delta region of Lower Burma were also conditioned and caused by the Anglo-French conflict as well as by the procurement of arms and support from the British. His soldierly conquest and ruthless treatment of the rebellious Mons in 1755 testified to the immense psychological scars left by the majority Burmese rulers on successive generations of minorities whom they had raided continuously. With respect to this, *History of Kings* reported:

> His Majesty Aungzeya [Alaungpaya] was of a very fierce and cruel disposition, and made no account at all of life. He put to death many monks, and their iron alm bowls and silk robes were taken away, and the homespun robes were made into footmats. Of some they made pillows, of some they made belts, and of some they made sails. The monks' robes were scattered all over land and water. It is said that when he took Pegu he found more than three thousand monks in the place, and that he had them put to death.[50]

It should be pointed out that he also massacred the English residents on the island of Negrais, a British possession, off the western shore of Bassein. This legacy of ruthless massacres of enemies irrespective of age, sex, or sacred persons may be contrasted with the hero myth of a benevolent Burmese king glorified by the royal historians of Mahah Yahzawin. The violation by Burmese rulers of the Buddhist mandate of the sanctity of human life seemed to be not the exception but the rule.

BODAW HPAYAR (1782-1819)

Like his grandfather, Bodaw Hpayar was a fierce and ruthless ruler whose reign was marred by countless massacres of those who were either actually or suspected of being involved in the conspiracy against him. Among his victims was the famous general Mahah Thihathura, the father-in-law of Sintku Min and the prominent general of the army of Alawn Hpayar, executed for suspicion of conspiracy. Another conspirator, Myatpun, as well as hundreds of men, women, and even monks suspected of conspiracy, were burnt alive and their villages razed to the ground. According to Father Germano "his very countenance is the index of a mind ferocious and inhuman in the highest degree."[51]

Like his predecessors, he would later build pagodas and perform deeds of merit for the atonement of his sins. The most famous pagoda he built, constructed by thousands in forced labor, was the Minkun Zaiditaw along with a gigantic bell which stands today as testimony to that tradition. Following the tradition of moving the capital for fear of being haunted by the ghostly spirits of his victims and to escape uninhabitable ground of the palace infested with limbs and corpses, he moved his royal capital from Ava to another site at Amarapura. He also embarked upon various public work projects such as the famous irrigated lakes of Aungpinlel, Nandah, and Mate-htilah and established his divine rights *in toto* over the Buddhist clerical order.

From these accounts of the Koanbaung kings, it is obvious that Burma under the successive Koanbaung monarchs was a tumultuous polity and a war-ridden country internally and externally. The historical heritage of internal warfare between the Burmese and other minority ethnic groups of Burma was further intensified by Western interest in the natural resources of Burma since the seventeenth century. It increased at a rapid rate in the eighteenth century with growing competition among colonial venturers for trade, market, and wealth. Thus, the fall of the Koanbaung Dynasty was imminent both endogenously and exogenously. From the very beginning of the dynasty, the chief minority ethnic groups of Arakanese, Mons, Shans, and Karens welcomed any foreign power in preference to the ruthless imperial rule of the Burmese kings. This factor can be clearly discerned in the accounts of their cooperation with and seeking help from the British as well as the French and the Portuguese in the history of Burmese foreign relations. With the exception of those of King Min Doan, the foreign policies and relations of the Koanbaung Kingdom were characterized by direct conflict and confrontation with the British colonial power.

THE MYTH OF THE GODLY KING: KING MIN DOAN (1852-1878)

The personality of King Min Doan exemplified a benevolent and priestly monarch along the lines of the first Buddhist rulers of mythical India and Asoka of historical India. From the holding of the Fifth Buddhist Synod to the study of Buddhist scripture, King Min Doan or "Mindon" (common spelling) since childhood was more engrossed in the purification of the Buddhist faith, the aggrandizement of an ideal Buddhist state, and benevolent kingship than in meeting the impending danger of British annexation. King Min Doan's religious zeal and preoccupation with performing deeds of merit rather than facing the mighty military strength of the British further weakened the inherently vulnerable state of Burma.

He undertook many benevolent acts of religious reform, public-work projects, and construction of pagodas, including the erection of a new umbrella, *htee*, studded with precious stones for the famous Shwe Dagon Pagoda of Rangoon, for his political legitimacy in the tradition of just Buddhist kings. The putting up of an umbrella or a spire at the pinnacle of a pagoda is the last act in the construction of a new pagoda and sometimes it may be replaced by a new one as a deed of merit. In fact, he extolled the divine rights of his kingship over the Buddhist order in terms of laws for purification and penalties for misconduct committed by Buddhist clergymen. He, like other Burmese kings, sacralized the Burmese kingship.

His religious reform measures did not receive favorable responses from various Buddhist clerical orders of Lower and Upper Burma. The tradition of Dhama Yahzah, King Over Sacred Preachings, as the purifier of Buddhism and clerical order was a legacy left by King Asoka of India. The right to invade the ecclesiastical or sacred domain of Sangha when its members did not abide by its code, Winaya, was fully exercised by King Min Doan and left a political legacy for the rulers of independent Burma. In fact, he issued the drastic and controversial Dhamma Winaya Act on February 15, 1856, which included prohibitions against wearing footwear, smoking and chewing bettle, causing protests from the major heads of the clerical order, Sayahdaws, throughout his kingdom.

He also followed the royal legacy of polygamy to the extreme by having more wives than any other Burmese king before him. The list of his queens and wives was reported by the London *Times Weekly* on December 25, 1885:

> The late King Min-Don-Min [Min Doan], who was a religious monarch and who especially prided himself on the title of "Holder of the Fifth Ecclesiastical Synod," a title not borne by his successor [Thibaw] had 53 recognized Queens, besides a few scores of inferior wives. Thirty-seven of his recognized Queens survived him. By his Queens he had 110 children, of whom 72 were alive at his death.[52]

Twenty-two of his sons or princes were potential successors to the throne at the time. Indeed, the problem of naming the next successor to his throne plagued him continuously after his sons murdered his brother, Kanaung Min, whom he had originally named as the next successor to the throne. Like the first Burmese king of the Tagaung Dynasty, King Abiyahzah, he left the question of royal succession in a state of suspense primarily due to fear for the life of the ordained successor to the throne and violent power struggles among his forty-eight sons, none of whom were sons of his four major queens.

His own personal life was beset with the problem of rebellion by dissatisfied sons and nephews, as well as feuds among queens, ministers, and leaders of the Buddhist clerical orders, *thahthanah-paings*. He continued the tradition of recruiting loyal officials in building a strong bureaucracy to guard his hold on political power. In other words, despite the benevolent image of a priestly Buddhist king, King Min Doan suffered from the same defects of the traditional Burmese kingship system which made Burma a fairly easy target for colonization by a modern power.

Under the bombardment of internal and external problems of political chaos, King Min Doan, like all of his predecessors, relied upon the power of the occult, astrology, and the supernatural to solve his personal and national problems. As Myo Myint wrote:

> Men of prowess tend to be fascinated by severe ascetics. In Mindon's [Min Doan's] court there were some people who wielded influ-

> ence not because of official position but because of their "spiritual power." Those ascetics included Hlutkhaung Sayadaw and the Shwegin Sayadaw, holy men, the nun Mai Kin, and a Manipuri Brahman. Interested in the occult, astrology, and alchemy, King Mindon supported all these ascetics.[53]

This legacy of Burmese kings relying upon men of allegedly supernatural knowledge and power is an aspect of traditional Burmese culture dating back to the mythical kingdoms of ancient India. The Brahmanic astrologers, *ponnars*, enjoyed special privileges not accorded to any other official in the Burmese royal court. Relying upon them to make predictions and to prescribe actions to counter potential threats and political misfortunes was an integral part of the behavior of the Burmese kings.

The basic aspect of the dual polity of traditional Burma relates to the way in which the powerful elite of the "center" and the simple folks of "the periphery" lived by different sets of rules and enjoyed different privileges. The Burmese King claimed himself as "the Lord of Life and Death" over his subjects, Bawashin Mintayargyi, a title given and repeatedly used by Burmese historians in their chronicles. The absolute ownership of everything by a Burmese king is a legacy of statism left for contemporary rulers of Burma to emulate. The rule of will rather than the rule of law then is the primary feature and functioning of the Burmese monarchy. In such a polity, Hume's "general will" or "volonté générale" has no meaning for either the ruler or the ruled. For the one who is ruled looks upon the groups above him (the humanistic intellectual, the religious functionary, and the powerful elite in ascending order) as belonging to "a world far beyond his ken" and considers "their status as higher or lower, but also as not merely appropriate but proper."[54]

The most unique aspect of the traditional Burmese polity was a lack of systematic primogeniture. The turnover of Burmese kings during the various dynasties after the founding of the Pagan Dynasty was relatively more frequent, with duration of a king's reign averaging less than ten years. For example, there were thirty-six kings of the bloodline of Tabinshwehtee and the duration of his Toungoo Dynasty was given as sixty-seven years from A.D. 1530 to 1597 giving a turnover rate of a little over two years. The last Kingdom of Koanbaung with eleven kings of the bloodline of Alawn Hpayar lasted for 133 years from A.D. 1752 to 1885 giving a turnover rate of a little over twelve years. Thus, from A.D. 1530 to 1885 the average frequency of the changing of kings on the Burmese throne was once every seven years. The Anorya-htah Pagan Dynasty's turnover rate was close to twenty-five years with thirteen kings over a period of 324 years from A.D. 1044 to 1368.[55] This relative increment in the frequency of the changing of kings may be directly attributed, on the one hand, to the polygamous expansion of the kings of various dynasties and, on the other, to a greater number of wars fought among various city states governed by a Burmese king's kin and other ethnic minority rulers.

129098

NOTES

1. Hagen, *The Theory of Social Change*, p. 55.

2. This characteristic of "somewhat loosely structured social units" may be contrasted with Embree's model of "a loosely structured social system" in that it means a lack of corporatist organizational structure in various social units of traditional Burmese society rather than the total social structure as such. Cf. Embree, "Thailand—A Loosely Structured Social System," Hans-Deiter ed., *Loosely Structured Social Systems: Thailand in Comparative Perspective* (New Haven: Yale University Southeast Asia Studies, 1969).

3. Cf. Hagen, *The Theory of Social Change,* p. 71.

4. See Ibid., pp. 58–59.

5. Ibid., pp. 58–59.

6. See U Than Tun, *Ancient Burmese History: Studies in Burmese History No. 1* (In Burmese) (Rangoon: Mahah Dagon Press, 1964), pp. 11–12.

7. Joseph Campbell, *The Inner Reaches of the Outer Space: Metaphor as Myth and as Religion* (New York: Harper & Row, 1986), p. 35.

8. Ibid., pp. 35–37.

9. Hagen, *The Theory of Social Change*, p. 97.

10. Ibid.

11. Than Tun, pp. 20–21.

12. See U Hpo Kyar, *A Brief Modern History of Burma* (In Burmese) (Rangoon: Myanma Gonyai Press, 1937), pp. 8–9. See also Forbes, p. 36. Notice also that the words in parentheses are Pali terms as opposed to the Burmese words using my own spellings.

13. Forbes, p. 36.

14. See Lieutenant-General Sir Arthur P. Phayre, *History of Burma* (London: Trubner & Co., 1883), pp. 1–5.

15. U Than Tun, pp. 22–24.

16. Taline is the later name given to the Mon by the Burmese who were supposed to have intermarried with Indians from the province of Tilingana. This may be a legend, although actual historical accounts of Indian travelers to the Kingdom of Mons, Thayaykhittayah, are commonly recorded by historians. For a detailed account of Mon civilization, see U Than Tun, pp. 81–97.

17. Ibid., pp. 185–186.

18. Cf. Sir James G. Scott (Shwe Yoe), *Burma: From the Earliest Times to the Present Day* (London: T. Fisher Unwin, Ltd., 1924), pp. 20–23. See also, Central Committee of the Burma Socialist Programme Party, *Fundamental Political History of Burma, Part I* (In Burmese) (Rangoon: Sahpay Beikmhan Press, 1962), pp. 204–207. The settlement of the original Myanmahs at Kyauksel was the view of Professor Luce confirmed by various stone inscriptions.

19. See Tennyson Jesse, pp. 193-194.

20. This point was suggested to me by Professor Hagen when I asked him why there seems to be so much fragmentation in the present political conditions of Myanmar.

21. U Than Tun, pp. 109-110.

22. P. Bigandet, *The Life or Legend of Guadama: The Buddha of the Burmese*, (London: Trubner & Co., 1880), Vol. II, p. 261.

23. Ibid., Vol. I, p. 2.

24. Ibid.

25. Cf. J. J. Altizer, *Mircea Eliade and the Dialectic of the Sacred* (Westport: Greenwood Press, 1975), pp. 1–10.

26. Sir James G. Scott, *Gazetteer of Upper Burma and the Shan State*, (Rangoon: Government Printing Office, 1900), Part I, Vol. II, p. 469.

27. Geertz, *Negara*, p. 127.

28. Other writers used the spellings of either Phara or Paya which are not phonetically correct in terms of Burmese. The way Burmese used and pronounced this term is Hpayar; the word "hpa" is a sound somewhere between "pa" and "ba" in tone.

29. E. Sarkisyanz, *Buddhist Backgrounds of the Burmese Revolution* (Hague: Martinus Nijhoff, 1965), p. 31.

30. See Sir James George Frazer, *The Golden Bough* (New York: The Macmillan Company, 1963), Chap. XVII.

31. U Tin Shaing ed., *The Glass Palace Chronicle* (In Burmese) (Rangoon: Pyigyi Munnaing Pitaka Press, 1963), Vol. 1, p. 1.

32. Ibid., pp. 17–18.

33. Ibid., pp. 19–20.

34. Carl G. Jung, *Man and His Symbols* (Garden City: Doubleday & Company, 1964), p. 79.

35. See K. J. Saunders, *Gotama Buddha: A Biography* (New Delhi: Light and Life Publishers, 1978), p. 11.

36. See Phayre, pp. 9–10.

37. Cf. Tin and Luce, p. 14.

38. Cited by Altizer, p. 45.

39. Ibid.

40. See U Hpo Kyar, pp. 18–106.

41. U Tin Shaing ed., p. 68.

42. See for details, Dagon U Tun Myint, *Ten Great Stories* (In Burmese) (Rangoon: Baho Press, 1989), pp. 280-340.

43. See Michael Aung Thwin, "The Role of *Sasana* Reform in Burmese History: Economic Dimensions of a Religious Purification," *Journal of Asian Studies*, August, 1979. See also his, *Pagan: The Origins of Modern Burma* (Honolulu: University of Hawaii Press, 1985), pp. 186-195. See also Victor B. Lieberman, "The Political Significance of Religious Wealth in Burmese History: Some Further Thoughts," *Journal of Asian Studies*, August, 1980. Both of them seem to suggest and agree on the possible demise of the Pagan Dynasty due to the transfer of wealth from the secular to the sacred order of Thangah. I suggest that both of them are wrong and cannot statistically prove such a tenuous hypothesis one way or the other, since it dates back to the twelfth cen-

tury, in addition to the fact that the Burmese were highly disorganized in keeping records of kings, let alone of statistics. This point was suggested to me by Dr. Than Tun.

44. See Thwin, *Pagan*, pp. 199-211.

45. See U Than Tun, pp. 120-124.

46. See Phayre, pp. 38-39.

47. Altizer, p. 44.

48. See Maung Shwe Lu, *Burma: Nationalism and Ideology* (Dhaka: The University Press, 1989), p. 14.

49. J. G. Scott (Shwe Yoe), *The Burman: His Life and Notions* (New York: W. W. Norton & Co., 1963), p. 447.

50. Quoted by B. R. Pern, *A History of Rangoon* (Rangoon: American Baptist Mission Press, 1939), p. 41.

51. Quoted by Phayre, p. 231.

52. Correspondent at Rangoon, "King Thebaw," *The Times Weekly Edition*, London, December 25, 1885, p. 6.

53. Myo Myint, *The Politics of Survival in Burma: Diplomacy and Statecraft in the Reign of King Mindon* (Ithaca: Ph.D. Dissertation submitted to Cornell University, May, 1987), p. 124.

54. Hagen, *The Theory of Social Change*, p. 97.

55. See for details of U Hpo Kyar, pp. 70–73.

2

The Colonial Triple Society and Its Polity

Toward the end of King Min Doan's reign, the weakening economy was further undermined by the loss of human resources to the more prosperous British or Lower Burma. King Thibaw inherited all the problems of the dying Burmese Kingdom with all its weaknesses. The internal strife, power struggles, and weakening economy in the hands of a weak king, Thibaw, ignited the inevitable Third Anglo-Burmese War and the Changing of Crowns in the Golden Land. The transition from the traditional monarchy of Burma to the British colonial rule has been analyzed and evaluated in a dichotomous vein like everything else about Burma.

KING THIBAW (1878–1885) AND THE FALL OF BURMA

The British interest in and contact with Burma began long before the last Koanbaung King Thibaw came to the throne. It took three separate wars to totally capture Burma. These three wars between England and Burma covered a span of sixty-one years from A.D. 1824 to 1885. These wars were fought during the reigns of three Koanbaung kings: Bagyidaw Min (1819–1837), Pagan Min (1846–1852) and Thibaw Min (1878–1885). None of these kings symbolized the hero myth of a mighty soldier presented earlier. The basic insecurity of the Burmese kings remained unchanged in each and every dynasty and violent measures to safeguard the central power were the rule not the exception of royal politics.

The most publicized and historically-noticed atrocities committed by a Burmese king have been those of the last King of Burma, King Thibaw. His very ancestry or lineage seemed to suggest that he was traumatized and born insecure among the many more pure-blooded royal princes in contention for the throne.[1] His name was taken from a town in the Shan states and "his mother, Meebayah, the Loungshay Queen, was a half-breed woman of the wild Shan tribes. She ranked seventh among the recognized Queens of Min-Done-Min [Min Doan], the late King of Burmah."[2] It is a drama woven with plots, counterplots, romance, tragedy, murders, and brutality in the execution of ministers, queens, princes, and princesses. The atrocities committed shocked not only foreign observers and writers but also the Burmese themselves. In fact, the sad tale of the slaughtered members of the royal family was told, written, and performed in many Burmese dramas, *pwes*, bringing tears to the eyes of audiences when their bodies were put in velvet sacks and floated down the river.

This incident of mass killing in the royal courtyard of Thibaw was most vividly described by the author of the *Lacquer Lady* through the eyes of the main character, Fanny:

> Distracted with terror, she turned and saw the whole earth dug up into a huge pit that had been hastily refilled. As she stared at it she saw the ground heave as though with a monstrous and unnatural life of its own. . . . The figure of a girl came rushing out from the woman's gaol on the further side of the pit, and Fanny recognized the younger sister of the Thahghaya Prince. . . . The next moment two big naked men had seized her and forced her downward. . . . They killed her after the Burmese fashion, with blows from a club across her smooth young neck.[3]

According to the Burmese custom, not a drop of royal blood must spill to earth because it may bring misfortune to the king and the country as a whole—the reason for using a club and velvet sacks to float the bodies down the river or burying the victims alive.

These unspeakable acts committed by a bad monarch (some accounts blamed the chief queen of Thibaw, Supayalat, and her mother) should not be used to negate either the Burmese kings or the Burmese social character as a whole. From ancient biblical times to the present, central power-holders have slaughtered their rivals, dissenters, and innocent subjects with the same kind of brutality on small and large scales. Not too long ago, the holocaust on a grand scale occurred in fascist Germany followed by more than half-a-century of brutal suppressions and killings behind the Iron and Bamboo Curtains and elsewhere in various continents; and more recently, by the Cambodian genocide and the Sino-Burmese massacres. It reminds us of power-holders' inhumanity and their fall from their sacred ideologies and utopian ideals.

COLONIAL SOCIETY

At the outset, the basic structure of Burmese society under British colonial rule did not change in being dual with respect to the coexistence of a few central cities and large numbers of peripheral villages. Although there was a definite increase of urban communities, the central core of power, administration, and commerce was confined to a handful of cities, particularly Rangoon, Moulmein, and Mandalay. What is different about the structure of the British colonial society of Burma was the influx of foreigners, especially foreign Orientals (Indians and Chinese) who came to dominate the economy as well as the polity of Burma. In fact, the population of Rangoon during the colonial period was more foreign than native in numbers. For example, the Indian population alone accounted for 60 percent of the population of Rangoon in 1921 and 53 percent in 1931.[4] The decline in 1931 was primarily due to the spread of Indians to other cities. As of 1931, it was recorded that over 40 percent of the total urban population of Burma was alien, 70 percent of whom were Indians.[5]

This is not really unique to Burma, since many countries colonized by European powers had a similar outcome of alien domination of the urban centers or cities. For example, in 1860 Mexico City experienced the same situation with respect to its population, which contained a larger number of Spanish, French, German, English, Italian, Swiss, and others outnumbering and dominating the native Mexicans during the Spanish colonial era.[6] What is unique about the Burmese case, however, is not only the complete domination of the top and middle layers of society by aliens but also the massive importation of foreign labor, alienating the entire urban or modern sector of the society. This is essentially what Furnivall called the classic "plural society" of British tropical dependencies or colonies and what Hagen termed the "doubly colonial society" of Burma.

THE TRIPLE COLONIAL SOCIETY

The term "the triple colonial society of Burma" will be used from a structural-functional perspective by modifying and incorporating both the models of Furnivall and Hagen. It is a triple society in the sense that there were three distinct social layers with respect to socio-political and economic power where the two top layers were the realm of the aliens, making it racially "plural" and politically "doubly colonial." Relative to the dual society of precolonial Burma, the group of what Hagen called traders-financiers was much larger and dominated by the foreign Orientals, Indians, and Chinese. The new dimension of the center or the central cities was the preponderance of the alien population, overpowering the native population in administration, trade, commerce, finance, and labor. The core of the center with respect to the control of political power and administration was simply moved from the ancient capital of the

Burmese king, Mandalay, to Yangon (Rangoon),[7] the seat of the Governor of British Burma. Lower Burma, where Rangoon is located, also became relatively more developed in terms of modernization.

The periphery or rural communities continued to function as before, subservient to the wishes and the will of the powerful elites who occupied the center or urban communities. The simple substitution of native central rulers by alien ones was further aggravated by the domination of the modern economic sector by foreign traders, businessmen, and financiers. The net result of this double replacement of natives by aliens was the magnification of the social pluralism and fragmentation of traditional Burmese society. This feature of the British colonial society of Burma was best described by Furnivall in his exposition of a plural society: "A plural society is a form of social organization in which several distinct races or classes live side by side but separately with no common interest except in making money."[8]

He attributed the primary force in creating such a form of social organization to the unleashing of unrestricted colonial capitalism in Burma. Although his assessment of the colonial economic impact on social organization was largely correct, it does not sufficiently explain the process of socio-cultural transformation on the societal level.

A PLURALISTIC AND FRAGMENTED SOCIETY

The Burmese king, like the colonial ruler, held the diverse ethnic social units or groups together by force of will and laws established to fulfill the needs of the central power-holders. In both societies, the formation of a unified social system on the basis of social will and common good did not and could not transpire to engender a homogeneous social order. In fact, the added layers of alien social groups created a temporary state of subdued ethnic group conflicts among the natives and at the same time added new dimensions to the base of group differentiation. The relative success of missionaries in converting members of certain minority ethnic groups and hill tribes and a few Burmese in the urban centers to the Christian faith added an extra dimension of religion to the traditional group differentiation. At the same time, it provided a unifying force for the Buddhist masses to put aside their ethno-linguistic differences and resist the alien cultural invasion. Repulsing foreign religious intrusions into the firmly established Buddhist culture of Burma was to become the main driving force for the nationalist movement against British colonial rule in the 1930s and 1940s.

The highly simplified triple social structure presented above must be modified to show that the strict alien-native differentiation between the two top layers and the bottom layer was not complete. In fact, alien populations, particularly the Indians, could be found in all three layers. The greatest barriers to native entry into all three layers were to be found in the urban centers where even the bottom layer of laborers was heavily occupied by the cheap Indian laborers.

A few natives began to emerge in the top and middle layers in the latter part of the British colonial rule. Even though the upward mobility of the indigenous population to the top and middle layers was extremely difficult due to competition and insurmountable barriers erected as a result of British colonial policy and practice, there emerged a deviant native social group made up of individuals with different degrees of acculturation to Western thoughts, values, and ways of life. They were ethnically and culturally mixed in terms of blood, religion, and social background. The Anglo-, Indo-, and Sino-Burmese, the converted Christians, the displaced royal civil servants of the Burmese kingdom, and the wealthy were among those representing what sociologists term "cultural brokers."

THE COLONIAL SOCIAL ELITE

The elite which emerged from the traditional sector of the colonial society of Burma was by no means homogeneous with respect to the degree of acculturation to Western European culture, English culture in particular. There were basically two subgroups within this elite group: the foreign-educated and the domestically-educated in terms of English and, to a lesser degree, European education. Not all but a majority of the former were highly anglicized and assumed titles such as "Dr." (both medical and Ph.D.), I.C.S. (Indian Civil Service), "Sir", and "Justice." The most well-known names among the Anglophile group were Dr. Ba Maw, Dr. Ba U, Dr. Ba Han, Sir A.J. Maung Gyi, Sir Paw Tun, etc. They were educated and trained in various European countries such as England, France, and Germany. The majority of them, of course, were trained and educated in Britain. They included individuals with attitudes and behavior apathetic to traditional customs and values. Their children were given English first names (Michael Aung Thwin, for example) and sent to local missionary schools and abroad for further education.

The second group was made up mostly of domestic English-educated individuals with less exposure to modernized European cultures and ways of life. It also represented nationalists who were ambivalent or indignant about the alienation of traditional Burmese culture. Among them were U Shway Thwin, U Kyaw Yan, U Ba Pe, U Saw, Thakin Ba Thaung, Thakin Tin, Thakin Nu, Thakin Ba San, Thakin Aung San, and other prominent student leaders of Rangoon University.

There were two basic types of modern schools in colonial Burma, public and private. The public schools, known as the National Schools or Anglo-Vernacular Schools, were made up of both fully subsidized and partially subsidized schools. The latter were semiprivate schools with native principals and teachers from which the native intelligentsia and political leaders emerged, while the former were run by the British school administrators. The private schools were of two types in the urban centers, semiprivate national schools with native teachers and missionary schools with foreign teachers. The latter were introduced before and during the colonial annexation of Burma by various Western European missionaries, while the former were introduced during the latter part of the British colonial period. Some of the famous missionary high schools in Rangoon, also in other major cities, were the St. John, St. Paul, St. Peter, St. Philomena Convent, Good Shepherd Convent, St. Joseph Convent, Diocesan, American Baptist Missionary, and English Methodist Schools. As for the former, the Myoma National High School in Rangoon graduated a number of prominent political leaders of independent Burma, Premier U Nu, for example.

National schools with a Vernacular and Anglo-Vernacular subdivision were introduced all over the country, from which many nationalist political leaders emerged in colonial Burma. The dual school system of private missionary versus semipublic or partially-subsidized national schools was instituted in major central cities of Burma such as Bassein, Prome, Mandalay, and Moulmein. In the beginning, a great majority of the prominent political figures and civil servants, as well as their offspring, received their education from the missionary schools. In the latter part of British colonial rule, however, the national school system produced many tradition-bound political leaders who came to challenge the anglicized political elite of the missionary schools. After independence, even the children of these staunch nationalist political leaders attended and graduated from various missionary schools.

This dual rival system within the non-Buddhist schools of the urban communities was paralleled by a nationwide dual educational system of monastic versus lay schools. The decline of the traditional monastic educational system run by Buddhist monks relative to the lay school system was reflected in the supercilious attitudes of the urban educated class. For example, the monastic pupils were abusively labeled by the pupils of urban lay schools as beggars—*hpongyi kyawnthar tadawnsar*. The economic aspect of this bigotry and discrimination on the part of the city dwellers was reflected in their looking down on the villagers as *tawthars*, meaning literally the jungle-born. On the other hand, Rangoon was thought of by country folks as Lawki Nateban, a Nirvana of the mundane world with luxurious life styles. Another example of regional bias can be discerned in that those from the relatively more developed Delta region of Lower Burma characterized the Upper Burmans as stupid, *ar-ny-ahthar ar-tata*. This is one of the legacies of British colonial rule which seems to have persisted in the mentality of the urban population in the independent era.

MARGINAL CULTURAL BROKERS

From these two groups another important group made up of their offspring and others with mixed blood emerged as cultural brokers whose aversion to trade, commerce, finance, and technical professions was less strong than that of their parents. Among the most prominent cultural brokers were the Anglo-, Sino-, and Indo-Burmans who took the lead in these professions. In the universities as in various walks of life, the outstanding students and professionals tended to come from this group. Their rise to elite status and conflict with the tradition-bound political leaders set the stage for the development of the dual society of independent Burma with new twists and dimensions of social fragmentation.

THE COLONIAL POLITY AND CHANGING OF CROWNS

Structurally, the British colonial rule over Burma did not substantively change the polity of Burma with respect to its duality. The Burmese monarch was simply replaced by a foreign monarch or his governor at the "center," while the simple folks of the "periphery" continued to serve and function according to the wishes and will of the central power-holders. The main objective of British colonization was primarily economic; their goal was to exploit the rich natural resources of Burma, not to create a democratic state. This view may be modified by the fact that the Burmese did experience a representative form of government in which the Westernized political elite participated during the last two decades or so of the British colonial rule. Yet, as far as real political change for democratization is concerned, the transition from the rule of a Burmese monarch to the British colonial rule represented simply the "Changing of Crowns."

THE COLONIAL IMPACT: POSITIVE OR NEGATIVE

At this juncture, a dichotomy of views regarding the impact of the British colonial policy and practice is appropriate for our purpose. The two opposing views of positive versus negative changes brought about by the British rule over Burma were best described in Orwell's *Burmese Days* in the polemical conversation between the main character, Flory, and an Indian medical doctor named Veraswami, who spoke of the Burmese incapacity to modernize: "Could the Burmese trade for themselves? Can they make machinery, ships, railways, roads? They are helpless without you. What would happen to the Burmese forests if the English were not here? They would be sold immediately to the Japanese, who would gut them and ruin them. Instead of which, in your hands, actually they are improved."

Flory's reply to this typifies the nationalist Burmese response to the intent and impact of British colonial rule: "We've never taught a single useful trade to the Indians [Burmese]. We daren't; frightened of the competition in industry. . . . The only Eastern races that have developed at all quickly are the independent ones. I won't instance Japan, but take the case of Siam—."[9]

These two extreme views on the impact of British colonial rule over Burma, or any colonial rule over any other country, are politically and emotionally charged. Yet they represent the psychological conflicts and traumas left by the colonial legacy for the nationalist political leaders of former colonial countries.

The primary British objective in colonizing Burma was purely economic; to think otherwise would be to deny the historical truth about the colonial expansion of all the western European powers. The report on "Burmah, Present and Future" by Mr. Holt Hallet, F.R.G.S., presented before the Society of Arts on December 25, 1885 in London directly affirmed this:

> Upper Burmah and the Shan States lying to the east of it, which were until lately under its control, should be of greatest interest to us as a trading nation, for they are interposed between the two most populous empires in the world, India and China. In these days with foreign competition getting keener every day, and hostile tariffs not only shutting the European markets against us but in a lesser degree American and English colonies also, with the race for fresh colonies and new markets among European powers, it is of importance that we should avail ourselves of our present opportunity for an inland connexion and commercial alliance with Indo-China and China, and thus acquire new markets of transcendent promise. Burmah and the Burmese Shan States are highly favored by their geographic position.[10]

The statistical data on the profitability and the revenue of British Burma was further given by him as "in the ten years ending 1883, the State outlay in British Burmah was £11,228,282, or an average of £1,122,828 per annum. During this period the revenue rose from £1,565,186 to £2,702,086, or an improvement of £1,136,000 [correct figure should be £1,136,900] between the first and last years of the decade."[11] Under the competitive pressure of French colonial ambition, the fate of Upper Burma to become a British colony was sealed from the very beginning of Anglo-Burmese relations.

THE RULE OF LAW

Another equally fascinating and controversial issue of the impact of British colonial rule over Burma relates to the "rule of law" introduced by the benevolent British rulers in lieu of the "rule of will" of the Burmese monarchs. The opposing views of Dr. Veraswami and Flory further demonstrate this. Flory replies to the former's glorification of "the unswerving British Justice and the Pax Britannica"[12] that it was "Pox Britannica" designed to benefit "the money lender and the lawyer" to promote "more banks and more prisons."[13] Further negative views on the concept of the "rule of law" of the British colonial policy and practice can be found in the writings of Furnivall and another famous colonial administrator, Maurice Collis. The latter spoke of the British Penal Code of Sedition, Section 124A:

> Tradition says it was drafted by Macaulay. 'Whoever by words, either spoken or written, or by signs, or by visible representation, or otherwise brings or attempts to bring into hatred or contempt, or excites or attempts to excite disaffection towards His Majesty or the Government established by law in British India, shall be punished,' etc. The penalty could extend to a long term imprisonment with hard labour, a sentence from two to five years being quite usual.[14]

This law does not seem to differ in substance from the Burmese king's law called *yahzathart* which prohibits all of the above types of behavior and more, including a simple lifting of the head to look at the king without permission. Collis further enunciated that "by a wink which attempted to bring the Government into contempt with those who saw the wink you might be committing sedition. If at the mention of His Majesty you shrugged your shoulder, your intention being to excite your companions to disaffection towards him, you could be convicted."[15] In order to be fair, however, the enforcement of this law by the colonial rulers was less universal, ruthless, and instantaneous than by the Burmese kings who usually called for beheading. At least, some semblances of the rule of law in the forms of *habeas corpus, habeas martinus* and others were introduced in the latter part of the colonial rule to appease the nationalist movements.

A somewhat less derogatory assessment of the British rule over Burma was made by another imperial civil servant of colonial Burma, Leslie Glass. His appraisal of the personal background of Orwell as being a loner and hater of Europeans in general, contrasted with his evaluation of his own background, seems to confirm my earlier explanation of why the colonizers themselves could have two entirely divergent views of Burmese society as a whole.[16] Notwithstanding that there were many fair, friendly, and objective administrators in colonial Burma, the fact remains that colonization means subjugation of one nation by another. In the end, like Orwell and many other friends of Burma, Glass also concluded:

> Instinctively we believed in the superiority of the Western way of life, and that we were bringing the Burmese higher standards of efficiency, honesty, hygiene, communication, democracy, rule of law, and so on. We had the same feeling of superiority about our cultural heritage. . . . The educational system we devised for Burma was a Western one, teaching Western cultural values. Perhaps the first crack in our self-satisfaction came from the realization that Buddhism could hold its own moral grounds with Christianity.[17]

He went on further to observe that the British administrators began to cast doubt about the applicability of British institutions to Burmese society and that the final awakening and pressure for freedom from colonial rule came from below, from the Burmese themselves.[18] It should be added that this awakening came about through the very Western education that the British imparted to the nationalist Burmese reinforced by the changing political thoughts and international circumstances in the latter part of the British colonial rule. On the whole, from a political perspective, the British rule over Burma represented to the Burmese political leaders and masses a process of "the Changing of Kings"—the appropriate title of Glass's book.

THE COLONIAL LEGACIES AND TRAUMAS

One of the most important aspects of the colonial legacy inherited by the Burmese has been the forceful implementation of the so-called "rule of law" in the name of preserving peace, law, and order. The efficiency with which the British enforced these laws in subduing the insurrections and protests against its rule in both colonial India and Burma cannot be given here except to point out that it left a permanent heritage in both countries. This is not to assert that the British violated all the fundamental human rights of the peoples of Burma throughout its administration, but rather to point out the historical continuum of prohibiting sedition against the state in the colonial polity of Burma. Apart from Section 124A, there were over a thousand more Sections, including the infamous Sections 109 and 110, which allowed local administrative officials to detain anyone found vagrant or unemployed for twenty-four hours. Although there was some freedom of the press, freedom of private property and enterprise, the suppression of "freedom of expression and assembly" under the above Law of Sedition may be thought of as a legacy of the rule of force which became an integral part of the polity of independent Burma.

Despite the undeniable fact that there were many important structural changes in the legal system and jurisprudence which were to become the colonial heritage to be emulated by the civilian government of independent Burma, the concretization of truly democratic political institutions did not and could not occur in colonial times because they were introduced only nominally by employing alien civil servants, mostly Indians. Very few natives acquired administrative skills in the enforcement of laws and the running of the modern machinery of government. For example, all the law-enforcement agencies were primarily made up of Indians, Anglo-Burmans, and other minorities prior to 1937 when Burma was separated from British India. This fact is most poignantly noticed by Furnivall who stated: "English visitors were sometimes puzzled because institutions with English names and forms did not function in the same way as in England. This was unreasonable. Institutions could not operate in the same way as in England because they had different functions to perform."[19]

The difficulty of establishing and running a constitutional government in independent Burma was further assessed by him as being due to a lack of correlation between form and function, on the one hand, and the inability to make proper changes involving laws and practices, on the other.[20]

The legacy of the British colonial administrators as "Thakins" or "Masters" was *de facto* a traditional legacy of considering the king's employees as superiors, even though there were virtually no class barriers or distinctions in the traditional Burmese society. Yet, when it came to political authority and power, positions of high rank became *de facto* a nobility or aristocracy in both ancient and colonial Burma. Thus, the titles of *wungyi, wundauk, myoesar, ywahsar,* and *ahmudan*, which referred to a king's employees, were simply transformed into the titles of Minister, Commissioner, District Commissioner (D.C.), Sub-Divisional Officer (S.D.O.), Township Officer (T.O.), Assistant T.O., Officers, and others in both colonial and independent Burma. Their elitist status and behavior recreated to a great extent the sacred positions of the kings, of the members of the royal family, and of the royal bureaucracy. This reflects the psychological necessity of the authoritarian personality of the elites to differentiate themselves from the simple folks as superiors.[21] The ritualistic aping of the colonial masters became a common pattern of the political elite's behavior in the newly independent states around the world. The simple folks themselves also seemed to sanction the elite's claim of its superiority over them for many generations.

ANTICAPITALISTIC AND XENOPHOBIC TRAUMAS

More than anything else the impact of British colonial rule over Burma magnified and traumatized the inherent xenophobia of traditional Burma. Some aspects of this were already discussed in the emergence of "the triple colonial society" or "doubly colonial society" of Burma as a result of the massive importation of foreign Orientals by the British colonization process. A few statistics which will be given in the next chapter will help to highlight the nature and functioning of such a society and to increase understanding of the immense psychological wounds of the consecutive Burmese nationalist leadership of independent Burma. The cause of this anticapitalist and xenophobic trauma was best explained by Furnivall: "Because capitalism had worked to their disadvantage they mistrusted capital. And because capital is derived from profit, they mistrusted capital as an incentive to industry. And they associated capitalism with foreign rule."[22]

Another factor in this mistrust was the cultural sanction against the pursuit of material wealth and pleasures by Buddhism itself, which caused traumatic and violent indictments against the foreign capitalists as cutthroat moneymongers who had come to dominate the colonial economy of Burma. The Burmese themselves are not totally ascetic and do not completely abide by the religious sanctions against worldly goods and pleasures. Yet the negation of capitalism and its evils is a socio-political necessity for the Burmese nationalist leadership in order to claim its legitimacy culturally on the basis of traumas suffered during the British colonial rule.

THE NATIONALIST MOVEMENT

The nationalist movement against British rule derived its main strength and momentum from Buddhism and the Buddhist clerical order at the very outset and was directly linked to the anticapitalist xenophobic traumas presented above. This cultural parameter of nationalism was first invoked by forming lay Buddhist political organizations and later magnified in the hands of Western-educated political leaders who were basically split into the two groups of the foreign-educated versus the domestic-educated in the colonial plural society of Burma. The traditional hero myth of the Burmese kings was also revived and employed by a few nationalist Burmese rebels in their uprising against the British colonial rulers.

THE INVOCATION OF THE HERO MYTH AND THE THAKIN MOVEMENT

These nationalist rebels took a more militant stance by reviving the hero myth and invoking the legacy of the soldierly kings of ancient Burma. The mythical kingly race of Burma was vigorously invoked in their political slogans to promote nationalism among the masses. Their first leader, Thakin Ba Thaung, as a defiant move took on the title of "Thakin" or "Master" which was reserved for the British administrator. He started the political organization of Doe Bamah (We Burmese), a forerunner of that most powerful political organization, the Thakin Party, which was responsible for gaining independence from the British. The most famous song of the We Burmese Party invoked the racial heritage of the Burmese kings by asserting that "the Burmese were the descendants of the ruling race of the first Burmese king Abiyahzah of the Tagaung Dynasty—*Tagaung Abiyahzah Doe Bamah Thahgiwin Minmyo*. This song, written by Thakin Tin, would become the official song of the Thakin Party and was sung throughout Burma in various political rallies.

The invocation of the sacred and hero myths of the kings of ancient Burma was the essence of the entire Thakin political movement during its formative years. It must be noticed also that the changing political thought in Western Europe, the upsurge of liberalism in England, and the nationalist movements in British India themselves helped to ignite and perpetuate the Burmese nationalist student movements in the 1920s. The Thakin political organization, made up mostly of young nationalist Burmese students, was by no means totally united with respect to its leadership and ideologies. It was characterized by splits and struggles for leadership reflecting the traditional Burmese heritage and character of fragmentation during the history of its development. The original formation and functioning of the party was relatively strong and somewhat united, but in the early 1930s the struggle for leadership between Thakin Ba Thaung and other founders of the Thakin Party was in full bloom.

The depression years of the early 1930s saw eruptions of violent political protests against British rule: the Indo-Burmese riot of May 26, 1930, the famous Sayah San Peasant Revolt of December 22, 1930, and the Rangoon jail break in 1931, along with an earthquake at Pegu and Rangoon and a fire at the Shwe Dagon Pagoda. The Peasant Revolt of December 22, 1930 headed by the famous Sayah San began at the grass-roots level in the Village of Yetaik in the Thahyahwady District of Lower Burma while Sir Maung Gyi was the acting Governor of British Burma. It occurred over a question of unfair taxation. This rebellion had mythical overtones similar to the rise of the heroic Burmese kings who were not of royal blood but came from the common people. Sayah San, a former Buddhist monk, was a local Burmese medicine man of astrological knowledge whose right arm supposedly shone like fire when he slept as an omen for greatness similar to that in the story of Alawn Hpayar. The use of this kind of mythical hoax to arouse local interest and followers occurred many times in colonial Burma.[23] Yet they are powerful instruments for conventional politics in amassing followers.

In fact, Sayah San proclaimed himself King Thupannaka Galuna Yahzah on October 28, 1930, using the symbol or the name of the mythical "Vishnu peacock-king," *galon yahzah*. Likewise, his followers also called themselves *galons*, symbolizing conquerors over the *nagars* or dragons representing the evil British rulers and foreigners in general. This revolt was quite successful in drawing rural support due to the invocation of both the traditional hero myth and the anticapitalist xenophobic traumas suffered by the Burmese peasantry. This was reinforced and magnified further by the economic impact of the 1930s' depression. The main assaults were made on the Indians and Chinese in Lower Burma. In 1931 Sayah San was arrested while the peasant unrest continued for another year. In the end, their leader along with 128 followers was hung and more than nine thousand were arrested between 1930 and 1932. From the very outset this rebellion had no chance of succeeding pitted as it was against the superior force and modern arms of the British. Yet, this revolt for patriotism and the hero myth left a legacy for successive generations of nationalist leaders to invoke.

In the late 1930s and 1940s, the anti-Western political elite emerged triumphant over the Westernized political elites who had unsuccessfully managed British Burma after Burma was separated from British India in 1937. During the same year Dr. Ba Maw was elected Premier and formed a Coalition Government for British Burma; he could not, however, succeed in forming a majority Ministry from among the representatives due to the fact that the strongest party with more representative seats was the Party of U Ba Pe of the United G.C.B.A. He did succeed later by amassing the support of minority representatives. In 1939, U Pu became Premier and succeeded in forming a majority ministry. An important personality named U Saw entered the political scene with his pocket army called Galon Sittart. He was elected to the House of Representatives of the U Pu Government and served as the Minister of Forestry. He served as the Premier of British Burma from 1940 to 1941.

The Second Student Strike or the Rangoon University Boycott of 1936 marked the emergence of a new political elite with staunch nationalism whose target of attack became not only the British but also all previous pro-Western native administrators of British Burma. The center of protest was the Rangoon University Student Union which left a permanent legacy of protest for the polity of independent Burma. Thakin Nu and Thakin Aung San came into the political limelight during that strike. However, there were many fragmented political organizations with various names at that time. As of 1936, there were several political parties: Sin yellthar (Poor) of Dr. Ba Maw, a coalition of five parties; Ngarpwint Saing (Five United Flowers or Parties) or the United G.C.B.A. of U Ba Pe; Myochit (Patriot) of U Saw; Twenty-One G.C.B.A. of U Chit Haling; Golden Valley G.C.B.A. of Sir Maung Gyi; Thatpan G.C.B.A.; Fabian Party; and Koemin Koechin Party (the Doe Bamah or the Thakin Party).[24]

The two important personalities emerging out of this chaotic leadership struggle were Dr. Ba Maw and U Saw, the two consecutive Premiers of Burma after its separation from British India. The former played a vital role throughout the era of Dyarchy Rule and came to fame as President of Burma under the Japanese by assuming the titles of Ahnahshin (Owner of Power) or Adipadi (Head Ruler). The latter was a self-educated petition lawyer who came to fame during the Peasant Revolt by representing the peasant rebels. He came from the same district of Thahyahwady from which the leader of that Revolt, Sayah San, came. Both of these personalities used the Burmese myths of kings in their bid for political leadership. Dr. Ba Maw was a Eurasian with Armenian blood;[25] he was originally a Christian and later converted to Buddhism to woo the Burmese Buddhists for political support. In fact, he would name his children Ganah and Zali after the names of the famous pre-Guatama Buddhist king, Waithandayah, as reported in the Jatakas.

Dr. Htin Aung contended that Dr. Ba Maw's wish "to be a king was obviously a malicious rumor."[26] However, he went on to admit that unofficially Dr. Ba Maw used the royal title of Ashin Mingyi as the Burmese kings did.[27] It seems obvious that all the successive political leaders of British and independent Burma somehow emulated the ancient Burmese royalty in their conscious or unconscious acts. On the other hand, U Saw, following the example of Sayah San, called himself Galon to symbolize the mythical peacock bird. This mythical bird symbolized the sun and the Sun Dynasty of the Burmese kings and a mighty conqueror of evil dragons. He succeeded in ousting Dr. Ba Maw and became Premier of British Burma in 1940. In 1941, he led a mission to England to demand a dominion status for Burma from Churchill.

This relentless scrambling for political leadership among individuals of different backgrounds is a Burmese cultural heritage which dates back to the times of the ancient Burmese kings and persists up to the present. In British Burma, however, the struggle for leadership occurred primarily between the old political elites and the newly emerged student political leaders, the Thakins, in the closing years of British rule. It continued throughout the 1940s until the latter succeeded in discrediting and dislodging the Europeanized political elites of the British colonial era by the end of that decade.

Indeed, the momentum of the Thakin political movement accelerated at a rapid rate after the Student Strike of 1936 when a student leader named Bo Aung Kyaw died at the hands of the British police force. The Thakins were also successful in igniting workers' strikes among which the most famous was the 1940 Oilfield Workers' Strike ignited and organized by Thakin Aung San. He rose to national leadership by ousting another prominent Thakin leader, Thakin Ba Sein. Although all the communist revolutionary symbols and terms employed by the Thakins seemed to indicate that they originally drew their political inspiration from the rising tide of communist revolutionary movements in the Western world, a split between the socialist-minded and the communist-minded Thakins occurred in the late 1940s.

By 1945, the extreme leftist Thakins led by Thakin Than Tun, Thakin Soe, and Thakin Thein Pe, the founders of the Burma Communist Parties, came into direct conflict with moderate Thakins led by Aung San and U Nu within the Thakin Party itself. This conflict increased greatly at the very eve of and after Burma gained independence. Numerous splits among political leaders of different socio-economic backgrounds, outlooks, and ideologies within each of these two groups proliferated in the 1950s to confirm the persistence of the tumultuous and fragmented traditional polity of Burma. It should be added further that the philosophies of democratic thinkers were also studied and learned by the student leaders of Rangoon University, including U Nu, U Aung San, U Kyaw Nyein, U Ba Swe, U Tun Pe, U Ba Sein, and many other prominent political leaders.

THE IMPACT OF JAPANESE OCCUPATION

The political impact of the Japanese occupation of Burma during the Second World War may be presented in terms of the revival of the two myths of the traditional Burmese polity, on the one hand, and the laying of the foundation for the revival of the tumultuous and fragmented power struggles among the contenders to the central political power, on the other. The hero myth dominated that era in which a group of military elite emerged out of the Thakins to spearhead and lead the armed resistance movements against both the British and later the fascist Japanese rulers. With the help of the Japanese, the Burmese army in the tradition of the heroic Burmese kings came into existence for the first time since the fall of the last Burmese kingdom in 1886. The name of General Aung San, formerly Thakin Aung San, would become a legend as the founding father of independent Burma. At the same time, Colonel Ne Win, changing from his original name of Shu Maung, began to appear alongside General Aung San in the annals of the Burma Independence Army.

THE HEROIC THIRTY COMRADES OR YELLBAW THONEGYATE

The Thirty Comrades or Yellbaw Thonegyate, as they were gloriously called by the Burmese, symbolized the hero myth of saviors or *sakyah mins* whose courage and power captured the imagination of the Burmese masses during the Japanese occupation. They were supposedly bonded together as blood brothers by performing the sacred ceremony of drinking blood from each other's arms. Their secret mission to Japan for military training, the formation of the Burma Independence Army (B.I.A.), the operations of the Japanese military intelligence, and its occupation of Burma cannot be given in detail here.[28] What is important and relevant for this study is the fact that a solid foundation was laid down during that period for the Burmese governments to build a modern intelligence service and a Burmese army in the governance of independent Burma. Not only Japanese but also British military intelligence and technology would play a vital role in the rise of this military group to the position of central political power-holders during the independent period.

GENERAL AUNG SAN (1916–1947)

In essence, the rise of the military elite by assuming the title of Bo in contrast to their initial title of Thakin was in line with the twin personality of the warrior-king versus the priestly-king image of political leadership. Both of these titles were used in reference to the British administrators: Bo means "Boss" or "Army Officer" and Thakin means "Master" or "Owner of Slaves." The charisma of General Aung San and his rise to the status of the liberator from foreign rule were in keeping with the symbolic image of a warrior king. As a Western-educated intellectual, his thoughts and behavior in politics were somewhat tempered by the modern concepts of the rule of law and democratic ideals. His own background was linked to the Burmese royalty since his grandfather was supposedly in the service of King Thibaw in resisting the British annexation. His evaluation of the traditional polity of the Burmese kings directly revealed the influence of modern political thought that he had absorbed as a student at Rangoon University. He spoke of the political system of ancient Burma thus: "Before the advent of British imperialism the system that prevailed in Burma was feudalism tinged with some patriarchal remains. The King who was the liegelord was the absolute monarch possessing land, water and even lives of his subjects."[29]

Although he had an equal admiration for the Soviet Union and the United States with respect to their antifascism and preservation of democracy, his view on capitalism and the economic role of state definitely favored socialist controls. He asserted that: "If the people of Britain desire to build a new and prosperous Britain with plenty for all, the only way for them to do is to apply Socialist programme to all problems, domestic, colonial and international. At home, the state must take the primary responsibility for economic welfare of the people and should not leave it to the whims of private capital."[30]

In many of the speeches he delivered at various political meetings, the communist terms of "Comrades," "Petit Bourgeois," and "Proletariat" were frequently used. He would also assert that he was not a communist, although he admired a communist "planned economy." This obsession with socialism and optimistic view of it as a cure for socio-economic ills typified the philosophy of most political leaders of various colonies at the end of World War II. With the rising tide of nationalism, demanding freedom and embracing socialist ideologies seemed to go hand in hand at that juncture in the history of world politics.

THAKINS VERSUS BOES

General Aung San simultaneously became the President of the Anti-Fascist People's Freedom League (A.F.P.F.L.) and the President of the People's Volunteer Organization (P.V.O.). The former represented a continuation of his role as one of the leaders of the Freedom Bloc, President of the Rangoon University Students' Union, one of the founders and presidents of the All-Burma Students' Union, and the General Secretary of the Thakin Political Party. The latter represented the continuation of his military leadership and the creation of a military political group since most of its members were drawn from former servicemen of the War and the anti-Japanese resistance movement. More importantly, General Aung San created a new political elite called Boes out of the Thakins, military officers of the B.I.A., and others who were important in the resistance movements against both the British and the Japanese.

To the Burmese masses and the majority of ethnic minorities, this charismatic leader represented a modern hero with high personal integrity, honesty, and unusual power as well as the traditional hero myth of a mighty soldier of Burma. This image was not necessarily endorsed by other displaced political leaders of the colonial era, particularly the politicians and administrators of British Burma. Among them, the most dissatisfied political personality was Galon U Saw, the last Premier of British Burma. The traditional legacy of power struggles between the Thakins and the old politicians of the colonial era continued throughout Burma's struggle for independence during the years following the War. This legacy greatly intensified after General Aung San and most of his cabinet members were assassinated by U Saw and his followers in 1947. Unfortunately for U Saw, despite the traditional legacy of killing the reigning king for the royal throne, he was not installed as the next political leader of Burma.

The A.F.P.F.L. Party of the Thakins peacefully installed Thakin Nu or U Nu as the immediate successor of leadership, marking the end for U Saw (who was sentenced to death) and for most of the Westernized political elite of the colonial era.[31] Beneath this peaceful transfer of political leadership was the emergence of the military elite group under the command of Colonel Ne Win whose prominence was hardly noticed in the political arena at that time. Yet his secret but powerful role as the commander of the Sabotage Group trained thoroughly by the Minami Kikan, the Japanese army intelligence service, and later as the Commander-in-Chief made him occupy a key position in "the center" of the transitional Burmese polity. His early achievement and popularity as a professional soldier were hailed by the British Commissioner for his role in the resistance movement against the Japanese and for disarming the Red Flag Communist Party's rebels.[32] His involvement in the assassination of General Aung San and his cabinet members in 1947 and of U Tin Tut (one of the framers of the Constitution of the Union of Burma) in 1948 has been a well-kept secret. It was only recently revealed by one of the student rebels.[33] This will be discussed in a later chapter dealing with the origin of the military dictatorship of Ne Win.

The impact of the War and the Japanese occupation produced two important social changes: a larger role for the tradition-bound Burmese in the functioning of the polity and an opening for the traditional actors to enter the modern sector, through such channels as politics and military service. The socio-political and economic mobility created during that period was, therefore, highly significant in reviving the two most important traditional heritages, political autonomy and military power, which were embodied in the Thakins and the Boes. The interchange of the top political statuses and roles between the Western-trained elite and the Thakins in the administrative machinery of the Japanese interregnum widened the socio-political horizons of nationalist tradition-bound leaders. They successfully invoked nationwide sentiments and myths of the glorious past. For example, many popular songs about the glory of the head of state, Ba Maw as Adipadi, and the courage of the Thirty Comrades under the leadership of Ko Aung San in the gaining of Burma's independence (a song still being broadcasted by the Burmese Section of the B.B.C. of London on various commemorative occasions) were sung throughout Burma. In short, the path to a return to the glorious days of the Burmese kings was firmly laid down by the Japanese occupation.

NOTES

1. See for detail, Rangoon Correspondent, "King Thebaw," *The Times Weekly*, London, December 25, 1885, p. 6.
2. Ibid.
3. Jesse, p. 180.

4. J. J. Bennison, *Census of India* (Rangoon: Government Printing & Stationery, 1933), p. 224.

5. Ibid., pp. 44–45.

6. See F. Lopez Camara, *La Structura Economia y Social de Mexico en la Epoca de la Reforma* (Mexico: Siglo Veintiuno Editorios, 1967), pp. 19–20.

7. Notice that the Burmese names for these towns are sometimes completely different from the names given to these cities by the British which are in parenthesis.

8. J. S. Furnivall, *The Economy of Burma* (Rangoon: Privately Published Paper, January 28, 1952), p. 3.

9. Orwell, pp. 32–34.

10. Holt Hallet, "Burmah: Present and Future," *Times Weekly*, London, December 25, 1885.

11. Ibid.

12. Orwell, p. 35.

13. Ibid.

14. Maurice Collis, *Trials in Burma* (London: Faber & Faber, 1938), pp. 85–86.

15. Ibid., p. 87.

16. Leslie Glass, *The Changing of Kings: Memories of Burma 1934–1949* (London: Peter Owen, 1985), p. 36.

17. Ibid., p. 38.

18. Ibid.

19. J. S. Furnivall, *The Governance of Modern Burma* (New York: Institute of Pacific Relations, 1958), p. iii.

20. Ibid., p. 1.

21. Cf. Hagen, *The Theory of Social Change*, p. 177.

22. Furnivall, *The Economy of Burma*, p. 9.

23. Cf. Scott (Shway Yoe), *The Burman*, pp. 447–448.

24. Maung Maung Pye, *Burma in the Crucible* (Madras: The Diocesan Press, 1951), pp. 6–7.

25. See Hugh Tinker, *The Union of Burma* (London: Oxford University Press, 1961), pp. 389–390.

26. Maung Htin Aung, *The Stricken Peacock: Anglo-Burmese Relations* (Hague: Martinus Nijhoff, 1965), p. 114.

27. Ibid.

28. See for detail, Won Z. Yoon, *Japan's Scheme for the Liberation of Burma: The Role of the Minami Kikan and the 'Thirty Comrades"* (Athens: Ohio University Center for International Studies, 1973).

29. Aung San, *Burma's Challenge 1946* (Rangoon: The New Light of Burma Press, 1946), p. 9.

30. Ibid., pp. 63–64.

31. For details see, Maung Maung Pye, *A Trial in Burma: The Assassination of Aung San* (Hague: Martinus Nijhoff, 1962).

32. Cf. Hugh Tinker, *Burma Struggle for Independence 1944–48* (London: Her Majesty's Stationery Office, 1984), p. 455.

33. See Maung Htoo (R.A.S.U.), "The Last Journey to Democracy," *Burma Review* (New York: Privately Published Journal, Feb. 1990).

3

The Colonial Double Dual or Triple Economy

The most important impact of British colonial rule over Burma was its economic transformation of the semibarter traditional economy into a quasi-modern economy with its unique feature of what Furnivall termed "dual economy."[1] The duality of the colonial economy of Burma also reflected the dual or triple structure of the colonial society and its polity. The concept of a dual economy refers primarily to the coexistence of a small modern sector with a large traditional sector and the unique functioning of the economy on the basis of both modern and traditional technology. The segregation between these two sectors was almost complete with respect to the modernization of the "central cities" in contrast with the "peripheral villages."

THE DOUBLE DUAL OR TRIPLE ECONOMY OF COLONIAL BURMA

In terms of modernization, the colonial economy duplicated the dual structure of traditional and colonial polities. The main feature of the dual economy of colonial Burma was the coexistence of a small modern sector and a large traditional sector with two separate and different production functions. In this sense, it may be conceived of as a "double dual economy." Modern technology and methods of production were confined to a few urban centers necessitated by the nature and goals of colonial economic enterprises to capture profit in the world market. Traditional modes of production were employed at the originating phases of producing export products dominated by cost considerations, thus generating a typical dual colonial economy. In the case of Burma, upon this duality of the economy was superimposed another duality of alien dominance in terms of numbers and control of economic power at the center as well as the periphery, generating a "doubly dual economy."

In terms of functional economic groups, the structure of the double colonial dual economy of Burma may be thought of as triple. It was made up of three separate layers of socio-economic classes: the Europeans, foreign Orientals, and the natives. The former dominated the top and middle layers with respect to economic power, wealth, and entrepreneurial function, while the natives belonged primarily to the bottom layer. Even in the bottom layer, there was a preponderance of Indian manual laborers competing directly with the native labor force. The dearth of laborers due to the sparseness of native population was the dominant factor for the massive importation of alien laborers, mainly Indians, by the British in their effort to expand agricultural and commercial enterprises.

The basic transformation of the precolonial barter economy into a monetary colonial economy was made by deploying the alien labor force and attracting the migration of the Upper Burman population to the relatively more prosperous and rapidly expanding economy of British or Lower Burma.

THE PRODUCTION FUNCTION

In agriculture and major extractive industries, labor- and animal-intensive methods of production were employed to develop the colonial economy into an export-oriented agrarian economy based primarily upon cost considerations of the colonial ruler. The importation of modern technology was made horizontally at the final stages of production and distribution of raw materials rather than vertically for industrialization of the economy as a whole. In rice as in timber and mineral extraction, the traditional technology of production was heavily relied upon by using man and animal labor power. The methods of planting and harvesting paddy remained essentially primitive throughout the colonial period. Mechanization occurred only in the milling and polishing of rice at certain urban centers in the Delta Region, while timber extraction was primarily done with elephants and men.

Indeed, mechanization of production functions would have been more costly or rather inefficient in most of the basic industries of colonial Burma where rainfall exceeded more than 200 inches in some parts of Lower Burma. For example, the efficiency of using the traditional method of cutting down and hauling heavy teak logs in the rain forests of Burma was noted by a British observer: "No mechanical contrivances have yet been developed as economical as the elephant for timber work under the conditions prevailing in the teak forests of Burma."[2]

Either on the rocky, precipitous and heavily wooded terrain or in muddy water, the skill and efficiency of a tame elephant were unexcelled by man or machine. A good baggage elephant could carry a maximum load of up to twelve hundred pounds and drag on the average two hundred tons of logs per season of timber extraction.[3]

An astonishing feature of the colonial agrarian economy was that major export industries underwent little or no change with respect to the techniques of production. It was an aspect of the colonial dual economy of Burma in which the coexistence of primitive production functions with modern industries was made possible by the perpetual force of the alien monopoly of industry and commerce. Adaptation to the modern exchange system or market economy was primarily made at the final stages of the production process and in the urban centers. Modern methods of processing and marketing agricultural products were partially adopted in milling, packaging, transporting, and storing products near the points of final export, a handful of cities. Most of the cultivation of land and growing of paddy remained untouched by modernity as did the majority of Burmans in the rural communities. Plowing, planting, and harvesting of rice fields proceeded according to the traditional labor-intensive methods (man and animal). Even in the transportation of paddy to the urban mills, natural waterways and native boats manned by men, not by machines, were used.[4]

Milling and marketing of agricultural products were quite modern, since most of this was done by alien entrepreneurs. The rapidity with which the economy of the Delta Region of colonial Burma was developed by the British was truly impressive and was helped by the fortunate natural factor-endowment of Burma itself. The required factors of production apart from rich land resources were extracted mainly from alien sources with the net effect of alienation of the economy in terms of wealth and technology. In 1940–1941, the monocultural specialization in rice was reflected in the fact that two-thirds of the total arable land of colonial Burma was planted to paddy, 12.5 million out of 18.18 million acres. Four-fifths or 80 percent of the paddy acreage, 10 million acres, was located in the Delta region of Lower Burma.[5] In agriculture and extractive industry, men and animals were the primary inputs for production. In the 1940s, it was estimated that there was a bovine population of about 5 million, with 2.6 million working oxen and .5 million working buffaloes. The majority of the working buffaloes was employed in the timber industry, which also employed about 23,000 tame elephants.[6]

ALIEN ECONOMIC DOMINANCE

The total alien dominance of the modern sector economy was reflected in the financing or capital formation in agriculture and industry. In terms of the alien dominance of the modern sector, the colonial dual economy of Burma may also be defined as a "triple dual economy" in referring to the emergence of the third socio-economic group of trader-financiers in the economy. Europeans and Indian money lenders, Chettyars, together financed the entire industrial sector and large-scale businesses with their numerous firms, while the

Figure 1

General Percentage Distribution of Occupations within Each Racial Group

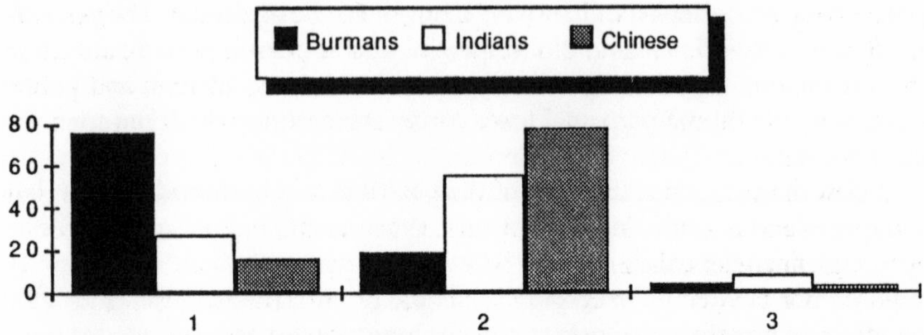

1=Agricultural and Raw Materials Production, 2=Industry and Commerce, 3=Public Services

Source: *Census of India, 1931, Vol. XI, Burma, Part I*, p. 134.

latter and Chinese pawnshops provided the capital for small-scale businesses throughout colonial Burma. For example, it was reported that more than 80 percent of the financing of agriculture was made by Chettyars. They also dominated in financing one-half of the small-scale business enterprises.[7] The exorbitant rates of interest charged by both the Indian and Chinese money lenders to finance the needs of native rural and urban families produced the dramatic loss of 70 percent of the land holdings of the Burmese peasants in the 1930s. This was also caused by the cultural habit of not saving and the Buddhist Burmese inability to adapt to the modern capitalism introduced by the British. Despite some authors' contention that there were enough native entrepreneurs, creditors, and businesses to indicate a positive colonial impact on the economic incentives of the Burmese,[8] neither the statistical facts nor various economic reports on colonial Burma bear this out.

A glance at Figure 1 reveals that in terms of occupational specialization, the Burmans were primarily engaged in agriculture compared with foreign Orientals.

According to the 1931 census, the percentage distribution of occupations within each selected racial group (all workers and working dependents) showed a disproportionate pattern between the Burmans and the foreign Orientals. In agriculture and raw materials production (including forestry, stock raising, fishing, and hunting), the percentages for the Burmans, Indians, and Chinese were given as 75.3, 27.3, and 16, while in industry and commerce the reverse patterns of figures were given as 19.3, 55.7, and 77.2, respectively. It is obvious from these data that the foreign Orientals' domination of the industry and commerce of the colonial economy was almost complete. The causes of this dominance were both economic and social in character. The economic factor was related to colonial economic policy and practice, while the social factor was linked to traditional cultural values supplemented by apathy towards foreigners and foreign rule. This is directly reflected in the fact that, in public services, a much less uneven percentage distribution of occupations within each racial group of Burmans, Indians, and Chinese can be discerned. The percentage figures were 4.1, 7.3, and 2.6, respectively.[9] The pursuit of more attractive and prestigious traditional professions such as teachers, lawyers, and public servants by the Burmans was discussed earlier and this statistical data confirms this information.

In view of the fact that the entire export industry was in the hands of foreign enterprises and that the financing of agriculture, trade, and industry was done by foreign financiers, the growth of native entrepreneurial function was neither required nor favored in an economic climate of unrestrained capitalism. The net effect, as was discussed before, was the anticapitalist and xenophobic traumas of the Burmese in general. The entrepreneurial impotence of the natives should not be exaggerated since some marginal cultural brokers with mixed blood, between alien and natives as well as between Burmese and other ethnic minorities, began to emerge in the latter part of the British rule. Despite the inequity in the distribution of wealth and economic power between the aliens and the natives, the efficiency with which the dual economy of colonial Burma performed was undeniably one of the highest in Asia. It is attested to by the cliché of labeling Burma as the "Rice Bowl of Asia".

ECONOMIC PERFORMANCE

The performance of the Burmese economy from the days of British rule to the present has been one of monotonic regression rather than progression. Using prewar data on the production and export of the major industries of Burma as standards, the economic performance under the management of its native rulers has been rather depressing. Some writers might argue that the use of prewar economic performance as a standard is unfair or inappropriate for the purpose of evaluation, since it neglects the "equity" of income distribution or the welfare aspect of economic fruits reaped by the natives rather than foreigners. Others, Burmese nationalists in particular, might argue that freedom from alien rule is worth more than economic loss or inefficiency.

A point of clarification is needed in discussing the economic performance of colonial Burma. The conventional sectoral division of the economy into agricultural and industrial sectors needs to be modified in assessing the efficiency of production and export. If one follows the standard definition of a modern economy by relative contribution of agricultural products and industrial or manufactured goods to real output, the colonial economy of Burma was primarily agrarian in that more than 70 percent of its output was rice, timber, and other extractive raw materials. If one considered them as major export goods commercialized and developed with modern techniques of production at the final stages of production and marketing, then they may be thought of as ex-

Table 1
Average Annual Values of External Trade (Private Merchandise)*
(Rs. in Millions)

	(1915-1920)		(1920-1925)		(1925-1930)		(1932-1937)	
	Export	Import	Export	Import	Export	Import	Export	Import
	425	253	642	398	735	392	537	224
Surplus	172		244		343		313	

*Source: *Annual Statements of the Seaborne Trade and Navigation of Burma* (1920–1937).

port industries. The development of the colonial economy of Burma was synonymous with the development of the export industries to capture the rapidly expanding world market for primary products and raw materials. As Forbes correctly observed, "there seems to be every sign that as fast as Burma, with its limited population, can increase the outturn, it will be absorbed by commerce."[10]

EXTERNAL TRADE

The balance of trade of colonial Burma did not experience a single year of deficit from 1886 to 1940. Even the Depression years did not produce trade imbalances, attesting to the relative strength of the foreign sector of the colonial economy to withstand deteriorating world market conditions. In fact, there were some signs of slump in rice exports in the late 1920s under the competing pressure of other exporting Southeast Asian countries. Yet the continual trade surplus of rice and other export products throughout that period reflected the natural strength and relative richness of the Burmese economy. The data in Table 1 testify to the continual surplus position in the trade balance of colonial Burma.

Figure 2 shows that the share of rice exports in the total value of exports for the three periods of 1915–20, 1920–25, and 1932–37 averaged close to 50 percent annually, indicating the monocultural export-orientation of the colonial economy of Burma to rice.

The percentages of rice exports for each of the above periods were 50, 56, and 40, respectively. Using 1937–1941 as the standard period for comparative evaluation of precolonial versus postcolonial Burma's economic performance in foreign trade, the average annual value of the external trade totaled Rs.642.1 million, with exports accounting for Rs.493.9 million and imports for Rs.248.2 million. Thus, the average annual export surplus was more than Rs.245 million or $51 million, accounting for about 70 percent of the total value of external trade. It should be pointed out that nearly 50 percent of co-

Figure 2

The Share of Rice Exports in the Average Annual Value of Total Exports

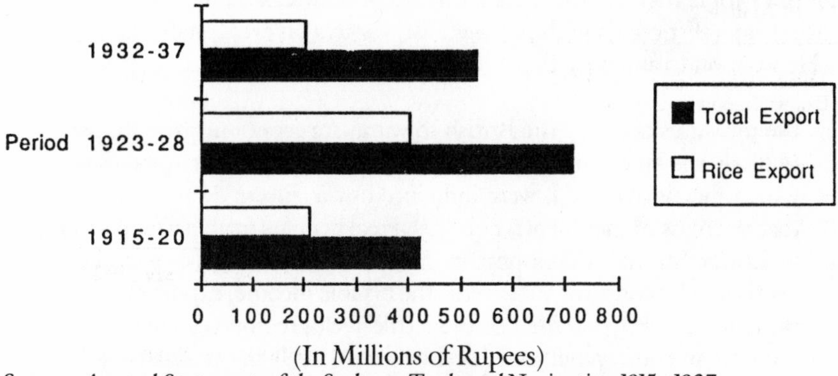

Source: *Annual Statements of the Seaborne Trade and Navigation 1915–1937.*

lonial Burma's exports was accounted for by India alone. Agricultural products also accounted for 60 percent of the total value of exports, with rice alone accounting for 50 percent.

COLONIAL ECONOMIC IMPACT: POSITIVE OR NEGATIVE

The above macroeconomic indicators on the performance of the colonial economy of Burma seem to suggest nominally that it was a healthy economy and outperformed the precolonial economy under the Burmese kings in all aspects. However, the crucial question to be raised in conjunction with positive or negative economic impact relates to "equity" in income or wealth distribution rather than absolute growth rates of production and external trade. Even using the macroeconomic indicators, the colonial economy was by no means a developed industrial economy in that more than 70 percent of its working population earned their livelihood from agriculture and raw materials production. The peasantry of the "periphery" of colonial Burma continued to function economically with preindustrial modes of production, although it was exposed to the modern form of market economy and the use of cash. Their adaptation to the capitalism or market economy of the colonial ruler was made without choice. In other words, the patterns of economic life were imposed from outside rather than internalized in the economic culture of Burma.

The classic pro-British or positive assessment of the colonial economic impact on Burma was made by a host of writers among which the views of Michael Adas seemed to coincide with those of the Indian Dr. Varaswami, a character in Orwell's novel cited earlier. He indicted Geertz's view of the central motive of colonial enterprises as wrong: "The case of Lower Burma clearly contradicts the persistent notion that 'the central desire of *all* imperialist enterprises [was] the wish to bring a people's product into the world economy but not the people themselves; to have one's economic cake and eat it too by producing capitalist goods with precapitalist workers on precapitalist land.' "[11]

He went on to assert that:

> the measures taken by the British to stimulate economic growth, particularly the land tenure system oriented to the "peasant" proprietor which they introduced, were influenced by a sincere desire to insure that the mass of the Burmese obtained real benefits from participation in Lower Burma's development. The fact that the British were also motivated by concerns to increase the taxable income, export production, and market potential of the fertile Delta region complemented rather than contravened their desire to raise the living standard of the area's inhabitants.[12]

Offering neither concrete quantitative living standards of the peasants nor statistical distribution of land holdings between the aliens and the natives, he went on to state verbally that "throughout 1852–1941 period, Burmese not only made up most of the labor force in agricultural production, but Burmese small landholders and large landlords also controlled most of the land on which surplus paddy was produced."[13]

ALIENATION OF LAND AND THE FINANCIAL SECTOR

The most glaring aspect of the double dual economy of colonial Burma was the alien ownership of the land and its monopoly of the financial sector. For example, in Lower Burma more than 40 percent of the occupied land was let to tenants and about 25 percent in Upper Burma between 1920 and 1930. In 1939, the figures climbed to 59 percent and 32 percent, respectively. For the total occupied area of colonial Burma about 49 percent was operated on the system of tenancy at fixed rent. The rentier class was made up primarily of nonresident nonagriculturalists, Chettyars, middlemen or village traders (mostly foreign Orientals), and a very few native landowners.

According to the 1931 census, less than 35 percent of the Burmese peasants were cultivating landowners, while 24 percent were cultivating tenants and 41 percent were cultivating laborers. The same was true of Indians but more than 80 percent of the Chinese were cultivating landowners.[14] The tenants were the sole bearers of the burdens of rent, repair, protection, and cultivation of the land. The leases were made from year to year and the rents varied from 15 to 55 percent of the total output. The rents were often paid in kind and native tenants were constantly changing land with a hope of increased yields to cover their costs of cultivation. The statistical data on the Burmese losing more than one-half of the land in Lower Burma to nonresident alien landowners in the 1930s seemed to have completely escaped the analysis and evaluations of Adas.

The alien dominance of the financial sector of the colonial economy was complete. The financial activities of the Chettyars in the agricultural sector, the most important sector of the economy, began as early as 1880 and reached their peak by the 1930s when the native cultivators were caught in a storm of depression and indebtedness unparalleled in any other colony of the world. During the 1930s, it was estimated that about 940 firms out of a total of 1,100 district firms of Chettyars controlled the entire source of capital in the thirteen rice-growing districts of Lower Burma. By 1939, the total number of Chettyars' firms climbed to 1,900.[15] Their local knowledge and historical financing of the rural agricultural economy surpassed any other alien banking firm. Michael Adas' allegation of the existence of able native creditors and financiers in the development of the Delta region of colonial Burma was not only unsubstantiated but also contrary to the observations of many well-known authorities and government reports on the functioning of the colonial dual economy of Burma.[16]

The testimony and observations of Leslie Glass, a British administrator, based upon his experiences during that period negate the so-called benevolent economic impact of British rule. He wrote: "On the whole in the mud of the delta I understood better why Eric Blair [Orwell] had disliked Burma. Here in its most acute form was the worse problem which flowed from the British occupation of Burma. Two-thirds of rice-lands were held by non-resident land owners (mostly Indian money-lenders)."[17]

He went on to observe "more sinister were the Kabulis [Afghan money lenders]—huge, baggy-trousered North Indian Figures—armed with long staves, to be met with in many parts of Burma. They asked for no receipt for their loans, they merely announced the interest rate and due date of repayment and noted them in their registers."[18] He further testified that if the debtor could not pay, he got whacked by the great staves and should he die the Kabulis would visit the grave and give it symbolic whacks of chili powders.[19] Indeed, there were many stories of the plight of native cultivators in debt who not only lost land but also their teen-aged daughters—debt repayment in kind to the alien money lenders.

In fact, by 1940 the Chettyars came to own over one-half of the land in the hands of the nonagriculturalists in the thirteen principal rice-growing districts of Lower Burma. The estimated volume of total indebtedness of the native cultivators was between Rs.500 million and Rs.600 million or an average of about $115.5 million. It was estimated that about 60 percent of the cultivators were in debt and on the verge of losing their land. They did and by 1940 two-thirds of the land of Lower Burma fell into the hands of nonagriculturalists, most of whom were aliens. The average per capita indebtedness of the three major districts was reported to be Rs.341 or $71, a figure more than the estimated per capita output of Burma in 1941 which was given as Rs.300 or $63.[20] The fact that the British government of Burma allowed Chettyars to charge exorbitant rates of interest in the rural economy and Chinese pawnshop owners to do the same in the urban communities alone testified to the neglect of social welfare. For example, on crop-loans involving payments in paddy, *sabar pay*, the rate of interest per month reached a maximum of 15 percent or 180 percent a year. The annual cash rates of interest on secured and unsecured loans reached up to 24 percent and 30 percent in the latter part of the colonial period. Likewise, the cash rates of interest charged by Chinese pawnshops in urban communities rose to an annual rate of 42 percent.[21]

For example, there was not a single private bank of any significance owned and operated by Burmese in any of the cities of colonial Burma apart from the European banks and other alien firms. Walinsky reported, however, that in 1941 there were three banks "native to the country" compared with eighteen foreign banks in Rangoon.[22] The term banks "native to the country" does not mean banks owned and operated by the Burmese. It seems likely that this reference was made to quasi-governmental co-operative banks. Contrary to Walinsky's assertion, J. L. Christian observed for the same period that "there is not in Rangoon a single banking, insurance, shipping, manufacturing or import firm of any size that is owned and managed by Burmese."[23] In any event, in 1941 there were altogether thirty-eight banks, twenty-one of which were located in Rangoon. The rest of them were mostly located in the cities of relatively more developed Lower Burma.

This fact alone is sufficient to indicate that the colonial agrarian economy of Burma functioned primarily on a cash basis throughout the colonial period. Financial institutions, native or otherwise, never developed in the rural economy for acculturation to modern ways of economic life. In fact, most of the native population never acquired either the knowledge or habit of using checks, savings accounts, and financial instruments other than cash during the colonial period and still have not up to the present. In other words, the modern financial system was never institutionalized in the colonial economy of Burma.

INCOME DISTRIBUTION

An indirect assessment of the alien dominance and inequality in the share of income or wealth was made by Thompson based upon Baxter's report which provided the native share relative to the Indians in the industrial sector of the colonial dual economy. Furnivall made his assessment in terms of the native versus the foreign origin of foreign trade. The basic statistical data used by Thompson was that 67.5 percent of the total workers in Burma's industries were Indians relative to 30.7 percent for the Burmans, which remained constant in the 1930s.[24] The increased pressure of the colonial Dyarchy Government on foreign firms to employ more natives in industries, after the separation of Burma from India in 1937, caused a slight shift in these percentages, although most improvements took place in the government services sector.

Furnivall, however, contended that the alien dominance of the economy intensified by using trade data on the basis of native versus foreign origins of exports and imports for consumption versus production. He showed that the native origin of exports declined, while import for consumption by natives increased during the 1930s. Based upon these data, he concluded that the control of industry and trade by British firms, Indians, and Chinese was greatly increased during the decade prior to the Second World War.[25]

The direct evidence of inequity in income distribution cannot be given since there were no quantitative data on economic exploitation of the masses gathered by the central economic power-holders of precolonial and postcolonial periods. From the indirect evidence of the Burmese king's ownership of everything, it may be inferred that there were some improvements in the economic lot of the masses after colonization, for there was no forced conscription of labor or state monopolies of trade and commerce. Yet, the system of unrestrained free enterprise and the functioning of the colonial economy were such that it generated a different form of inequity for the native population. It erected insurmountable socio-economic barriers which kept the natives from sharing the fruits of economic growth. This would become the basis for the successive nationalist political leadership of postcolonial Burma to reject capitalism as a system of unjust exploitation or to adopt socialism as a just economic system.

The alien dominance of the economy was the most traumatic psychological wound left by the colonial legacy for the Burmese who came to conceive capitalism as synonymous with economic immiserization and foreign rule. The Burmese inability to adapt to the unrestrained capitalism and market economy introduced by the British was most prominent in the field of finance which was conditioned and caused by both cultural and economic factors. Culturally, professions connected with finance, trade, and commerce are contrary to both traditional and Buddhist sanctions, while economically natural affluence in basic necessities and an abundance of land tend to promote a low propensity to save, invest, and innovate. For example, it is not accidental that the entire agricultural sector of the colonial dual economy of Burma at the grass-roots level functioned more or less on a cash and barter basis. In fact, the payments of wages, interest, and the discharge of debts were mostly made in kind and personalized in the rural economy of colonial Burma. This indicates that very little had changed between the precolonial and colonial economic systems with respect to the persistence of traditional economic culture.

What had changed, however, was the landlords who were now alien moneylenders and British tax collectors. This change was to ignite major racial riots and nationalist political movements in the 1930s under the impact of the Depression and the political awakening of the native educated class. The major Indo-Burmese riot of 1938 with all its violence and racial overtones was preceded by the Sayah San Revolt of 1930 which targeted not only the British as scapegoats, but also the Indians and Chinese. This explosion of anti-Indian sentiments, and to a lesser degree anti-Chinese sentiments, coincided with the stagnated state of the colonial economy of Burma. Under the impact of the Depression, previously affluent Burmese peasants were thrown into a vicious circle of agricultural indebtedness and economic insecurity, igniting various race riots. Thus, the racial and political riots of the 1930s were directly linked to the structure and functions of the colonial double dual economy. Their experiences of socio-political degradation and the economic inequity of perverted colonial capitalism under the British rule magnified their general innate mistrust of aliens.

Against the foil of both the ancient and the colonial economic history of Burma, the lag or lack of economic acquisitiveness on the part of the Burmese comes into focus as a consequence of the traumatic experiences suffered by both nationalist elites and simple folks. In the days of the Burmese kings, arbitrary seizure of property, wealth, and income along with forced conscription of labor made the Burmese lethargic towards accumulation of wealth. The introduction of an unrestrained market economy by the British and the creation of a double dual economy compounded the innate repugnance against acquisitive capitalist ventures which the Burmese came to associate with foreign rule and foreigners. Although there was complete freedom of enterprise and no forced usurpation of property or wealth under the colonial rule, the functioning of the colonial economy was such that the natives lost control of their economic life and power at the hands of more capable alien entrepreneurs and aggressive laborers. This anticapitalist xenophobic trauma came to shape the main thrust of the economic policy of successive Burmese governments.

NOTES

1. Cf. Furnivall, *Colonial Policy*, p. 304.

2. F. T. Morehead, *The Forests of Burma: Burma Pamphlet No. 5* (Bombay: Orient Longmans, 1956), p. 10.

3. Ibid., pp. 10–15.

4. See for detail, *Burma Rice: Burma Pamphlet No. 4* (Bombay: Orient Longmans, 1956), pp. 5–11. Also, Furnivall, *Colonial Policy*, Chapter 5.

5. From the source of *Season and Crop Report* (Rangoon: Government Printing & Stationery, 1941), pp. 22–23.

6. *Burma Facts and Figures: Burma Pamphlet No. 9* (London: Longmans, Green & Co., 1946), pp. 13–15.

7. See *Report of the Burma Provincial Banking Enquiry Committee* (Rangoon: Government Printing & Stationery, 1931), pp. 253–264.

8. See Michael Adas, *The Burma Delta: Economic Development and Social Change on an Asian Rice Frontier, 1852–1941* (Madison: University of Wisconsin Press, 1974), pp. 209–210.

9. From *Census of India 1931: Vol. XI, Burma, Part I* (Rangoon: Government Printing & Stationery, 1933), pp. 154–155.

10. Forbes, p. 5.
11. Adas, p. 209.
12. Ibid., pp. 209–210.
13. Ibid.
14. *Census of India*, p. 154.
15. See Tun Wai, *Burma's Currency and Credit* (Bombay: Orient Longmans, Ltd., 1953), p. 51. Also, *Report of the Banking Enquiry Committee*, p. 204.
16. See Tun Wai, *Economic Development of Burma from 1800 to 1940* (Rangoon: University of Rangoon, 1961), pp. 63–98. Also, the works of Christian, Furnivall, Andrus, Andrew, and *Report of the Banking Enquiry Committee*.
17. Glass, p. 206.
18. Ibid.
19. Ibid.
20. Louis J. Walinsky, *Economic Development in Burma 1951–60* (New York: The Twentieth Century Fund, 1962), p. 31. Notice also that before July 1, 1952, Rupee (Rs.) 1 = Kyat (K.) 1. Kyat is used as the legal tender after independence.
21. For details see J. R. Andres, *Burmese Economic Life* (Stanford: Stanford University Press, 1947), p. 67. Also, see *Report of the Ganking Enquiry Committee*, p. 204.
22. Walinsky, p. 52.
23. J. L. Christian, *Burma* (London: Collins, 1945), p. 128.
24. Tun Wai, *Economic Development of Burma*, pp. 89–94.
25. J. S. Furnivall, *Progress and Welfare in Southeast Asia* (Shanghai: The Willow Pattern Press, 1941), pp. 77–78. Cited by Tun Wai, *Economic Development of Burma*, p. 129.

4

From British Burma to the Union of Burma

The political history of Burma after the liquidation of British colonial rule may be divided into the two major eras of Pyidawthah under the civilian government and Pyidawchah under the military rule. The two Burmese terms connote "a country of peace and prosperity" as opposed to "a country in a state of lamentable depression." These are not literal translations of the terms. A literal translation of the term Pyidawthah, made wrongly by Michael Aung Thwin, conveys the meaning of "a Pleasant Honorable Country."[1] It also indicates his lack of understanding of the classical Burmese language and political implications associated with Burmese jargon. The first part of the word Pyidaw means "a Great or Glorious Country" rather than "an Honorable Country" and the adjective ending, *thah*, connotes "prosperous or pleasant." By a play on words, the adjective ending *chah* in the word Pyidawchah signifies rotten or degenerate.

The Burmese are historically fond of coining satiric political terms to express their evaluations of political actions and events. For example, the term Pyidawchah was used to criticize the failures of the civilian government of U Nu, particularly the famous "Pyidawtha Plan" launched in 1952. At any rate, the historical demarcation of the two eras made here by these two Burmese terms refers not to the failures of the civilian government but rather to the relative periods of prosperity and freedom in Burma under the governance of civilian politicians as opposed to poverty and lack of freedom under the military regimes. In general terms, the time periods for these two eras were from 1952 to 1962 and from 1962 to the present. It will be shown that since 1962, after the illegal seizure of political power by General Ne Win, Burma became a Pyidawchah or a country of political repression and economic depression.

THE ROAD TO INDEPENDENCE: THE CHAOTIC TRANSFER OF POLITICAL POWER (1945–1948)

The dissolution of the colonial polity was immediately followed by disorder and power struggles among the leading contenders for the political throne reminiscent of the royal politics of ancient Burma. The major struggles were between the old political elites of the colonial era and the Thakins, on the one hand, and among the Thakins themselves, on the other. The result of the former which culminated in the assassination of General Aung San and his seven cabinet members in 1947 by U Saw has already been discussed briefly. The loss of these leaders set into motion a series of splits among various Thakins, even though U Nu came out triumphant as the new leader of the Anti-Fascist People's Freedom League (A.F.P.F.L.), the major political party responsible for gaining independence from the British in 1948.

During the three years prior to 1948, there were already signs of fragmentation and struggle for political leadership among the Thakins with different ideological inclinations and political views concerning the future of Burma. Even though General Aung San wielded an immense power and influence over the Burmese populace with his charismatic personality befitting the myth of the heroic king of ancient Burma, there were other Thakin leaders of prominence who did not agree with his views and policies. Although on the surface the nationalist independence movements against the British and Japanese, stretching from the 1930s to the 1940s, seemed to be unified, factionalism cut across the entire spectrum of Burmese political leadership. The splits within the Thakin political organization have already been discussed.

Apart from the rightist politicians of the colonial era, Dr. Ba Maw and U Saw, there were anticommunist leaders such as Thakin Ba Sein, Thakin Tun Oke, U Ba Pe, and U Ba Cho representing the traditional and older generation of nationalist politicians who did not subscribe to the Marxist ideology over and above Buddhism. As was pointed out before, the younger Thakins were all leftist in their political thought, subscribing to Marxist ideologies and slogans. Even during the Japanese occupation of Burma itself, conservative and radical groups among the primarily leftist Thakins seemed to have already appeared in the forms of socialists and communists. The communist Thakins led by Than Tun, Soe, and Thein Pe formed the anti-Fascist League, while the noncommunist but socialist Thakins led by Aung San and U Nu formed the People's Freedom League. The two were united and merged into the Anti-Fascist People's Freedom League (A.F.P.F.L.) with the common cause of getting rid of the Japanese rule.[2]

Immediately after Burma was liberated by the British in 1945, the communist faction of the A.F.P.F.L. came into direct conflict with Aung San's faction with respect to the policies and strategies of negotiating with the British government for independence and the future form of government. By 1946, major rifts occurred not only between these two factions but also among the communists themselves under two separate leaders, Thakin Than Tun and Thakin Soe, with two parties known as the Burma Communist Party (also called the White Flag Party) and the Red Flag Party, respectively. In late 1946 both of them were expelled from the A.F.P.F.L. Meanwhile, the rightist politicians of the colonial era vied for political leadership unsuccessfully against the heroic leader, General Aung San, without being able to form a united opposition force with the communists. They temporarily joined with the triumphant A.F.P.F.L. and were members of an Executive Council formed by Sir Hubert Rance, the newly appointed governor of Burma. Thakin Ba Sein, U Saw, U Tin Tut, U Kyaw Nyein, and U Ba Swe accompanied General Aung San's mission to London for negotiations on independence. Thakin Ba Sein and U Saw refused, with considerable ostentation, to sign the Aung San–Attlee Agreement of January 27, 1947. Their refusal was mostly motivated by their personal loss of political leadership to General Aung San.

THE RESURGENCE OF ETHNIC CONFLICT AND THE PINLON OR PANGLONG AGREEMENT

The challenge to the leadership of General Aung San, his mission to London and the Agreement he signed with the British government by the rightists, the communists and minorities, primarily the Karens, did not sway public opinions against the leftist but not communist and socialist-dominated A.F.P.F.L. The minorities' deep-seated mistrust of the majority Burmese was clearly noticed by General Aung San who twice attempted to persuade the main minority leaders of the Shans and Kachins to support his demand for independence. The news of thirty-three Shan *sawbwars*, who cabled a message of dissatisfaction with his mission and demanded a separate invitation to England, was the cause of the first informal conference between the majority and the minority leaders, particularly the Shan royal rulers, *sawbwars*, as the Burmese called the *chaofas* (Shan terminology).

U Nu along with U Pe Kin of the A.F.P.F.L. travelled to the Shan state to meet with them and persuade them to show unity in demanding independence. This campaign was warmly received by Nyangshwe Sawbwar Gyi and the issue of the union or separation of the minority Frontier States was temporarily put aside to focus on the immediate task of gaining independence. Mass rallies of Shans were held under the auspices of the A.F.P.F.L. at Taunggyi and two telegrams, containing the message of the support of the majority of the Shan populace, were sent to General Aung San during his mission to London.[3]

The proliferation of fragmentation among the rightists, leftists, communists, and older politicians ensued in 1947 and the age-old feud between the majority Burmese and the minorities began to surface once again. The restive Karen and Shan leaders who were not involved or invited to participate in the aforesaid Agreement lodged protests against the Agreement. The key minority group challenging General Aung San and the majority Burmese leaders was the Karenni of the Salween frontier region in southeastern Burma. Some Karen leaders resigned from the Executive Council and formed the Karen National Union (K.N.U.) which became the major Karen insurgent organization fighting against the majority Burmese government since that time. It should also be noted that the Karen leaders themselves were not totally united and another organization called the Karen Youth Organization or the Union Karen League was formed under the leadership of Mahn Ba Khaing, who was a member of the Executive Council of General Aung San.[4]

THE PINLON ACCORD

The resurgence of the traditional fragmentation of Burmese society and the surfacing of the age-old conflict between the majority Burmese and the minorities were temporarily submerged under the charismatic personality and leadership of General Aung San. Important Shan *sawbwars* and Karen leaders of central Burma sided with and participated in the independence movements. The promise of making one of the famous Shan *Sawbwars*, Thainnee Sawbwar, the first President of independent Burma seemed to have temporarily subdued the problem of the Shans. The momentum of nationalism that swept across various ethnic groups during this transitional period of independence temporarily superseded the age-old conflict at the Pinlon or Panglong Conference of February 12, 1947, attended by General Aung San, other leaders of the A.F.P.F.L., U Saw and various minority leaders of the Sans, Kachins, Chins, and others under the supervision of the Frontier Areas Committee of the British government. Some nominal agreements as to autonomy of administration and the union of the minorities with the Burmese and the right to secede were made. The Karens of Salween District, however, demanded "a separate administration from Burma proper and under the direct control of the British Government as far as possible."[5] It should be noted, however, that the Karenni delegation to that conference did not participate until the last day of the conference.

The traditional ethnic conflicts and warring kingdoms of Burma have left a deep psychological wound on Burmans in general. It is not strictly racism *per se* as it is understood and practiced in the West, for at times ethnic intermingling of blood and peaceful cohabitation have existed since the days of the Burmese kings. It involves a mutual phobia based on mistrust and fear historically generated by the warring kingdoms of ancient Burma. Neither the commonness of the Buddhist religion nor the cultural and racial affinity of being Mongolian in origin supersedes the traumatic experiences of age-old wars between the majority Burmese and the minorities. It has been shown before that the

British colonial interlude postponed this innate mutual fear and feud for a period of time. Once the colonial protection of minority rights was removed this phobia precipitated once more in the political arena.

The Pinlon Accord of 1947, under the able leadership of General Aung San in cooperation with the imminent Yawnghwe Sawbwargyi (most popularly known in Burmese as Nyaunshwe Sawbwargyi Saw Shwe Thaike) and Minepuen Sawbwargyi, was a historic agreement to overcome the age-old problem of ethnophobia and wars. The first President of the Union of Burma was Thamadagyi Saw Shwe Thaike from 1948 to 1952. The third President was also elected from the minority group, Mahn Win Maung of the Karen minority (1956–1960). Although this appeasement seemed to have stalled the traditional ethnic feuds, it was not totally endorsed by all the minorities, particularly the Kareni and Karens of Salween region. Yet, most of the main minority leaders, Shan, Kachin, and Chin in particular, seemed to have accepted the Accord, since it contained some formal recognition of the minority rights to freedom and autonomy in the newly independent state of Burma. The nine points of the Accord dealt with the issues of appointing a Counsellor in charge of the Frontier Areas, his duties and responsibilities in representing the Hill Peoples, the question of the establishment of a separate Kachin state to be decided by the Constituent Assembly, full autonomy of administration for the Frontier Areas, and equal sharing of revenues by Kachin and Chin Hills as in the case of the Federated Shan States.

The basic success of the Pinlon Accord was due not to the establishment of the letter of the law concerning the Frontier Areas but to the personalities and pragmatism of both General Aung San and the minority leaders, the imminent Shan *sawbwars* in particular. Thus, the son of the first President of the Union of Burma, Chao Tzang Yawnghwe (Eugene Thaike) wrote:

> Given a correct perception and grasp of political and historical realities and politics by Burmese leaders, there seems little reason why national unity cannot be achieved without resort to war and bloodshed. That this is possible had once been proved by no other than Aung San. It would serve present Burmese leaders as well as future ones to examine why leaders of the Frontier Areas agreed to sign the Pinglong Agreement with him. . . . More than anything, it was because the leaders of the Frontier Areas, lacking education and political sophistication were nonetheless very practical men, Aung San, in his own way, was one of them.[6]

Despite the seething dissents, splits and chaotic transfer of political power from the colonial ruler to the Burmese, there was a general endorsement of Aung San's leadership and the A.F.P.F.L. as evident in the successful outcome of the April 1947 elections for the Constituent Assembly. The opposition forces, Ba Sein, Dr. Ba Maw, U Saw, Thakin Soe's Red Communist Party, and the Karen National Union, boycotted the election, but failed to discredit the leadership and the popularity of the A.F.P.F.L. The newly elected Assembly was made up of imminent political leaders of both majority and minority ethnic groups and the transition to independence seemed smooth and successful. This process was sadly halted when the ancient problem of killing the potential successor to the throne, *minlawn*, was set into motion by a rival contender for the political throne.

The most degraded and angered politician was U Saw, a former Premier of colonial Burma, whose militant and authoritarian personality symbolized by his nickname Galon (Mighty Vishnu Bird) U Saw, led him to resort to violence. His imprisonment by the British during the war in Uganda, his fading political status under the shadow of General Aung San, and a narrow escape from an assassination attempt on his life in 1946 were the main determinants of his violent path. Failing legally and peacefully to dislodge General Aung San from his imminent position in the political arena, he staged a rightist coup with his gunmen, murdering seven experienced politicians and members of the Council on July 19, 1947. U Nu, the speaker of the Council, was miraculously spared to take over the leadership. The result of this tragedy was correctly appraised by Adloff and Thompson:

> Although U Saw failed in his objective and was eventually hanged for his instigation of the crime, the elimination of so many of Burma's few qualified leaders has since proved disastrous for the country's stability and rehabilitation. It has also had the important consequence of so completely discrediting the prewar politicians—even those not directly implicated in the plot, such as Ba Sein, Ba Maw and Tun Oke—that the forces of the Right have been leaderless and their opposition to the AFPFL unorganized and ineffective.[7]

Thus, the political leadership was passed onto the parties of the Left which in turn were engulfed with a number of splits among the moderates, extreme radicals, and conservatives. The only unified and organized force seemed to be the Army under the control and command of Ne Win.

THE ROLE OF THE ARMY AND NE WIN IN TRANSITIONAL POLITICS

The role played by the Burma Independence Party and its commanders other than General Aung San during that period's political events might seem rather unimportant. Yet Ne Win, who was made the Commander-in-Chief of Dr. Ba Maw's government during the Japanese occupation, and his commanders, were very much tied into the political drama with the only organized, disciplined, and armed organization. As General Aung San became a full-time political leader, Ne Win seemed to have inherited the task of leading the defense forces of the not yet independent Burma. In fact, an earlier attempt on U Saw's life has been attributed to the work of Ne Win by a student from Rangoon University.[8]

Although the authenticity of this indictment cannot be confirmed since there was no detailed probe into the assassination of the legendary hero of Burma it is a commonly acknowledged story in Burmese circles. The person who supposedly made an attempt to search for the answer to the assassination of Aung San and his council members was also killed in 1948. This was a highly visible, prominent, and foreign-educated person by the title of I.C.S. (Indian Civil Servant) U Tin Tut, a high-ranking government official of the colonial era (Secretary of Finance in 1939) who accompanied U Saw when the latter visited London and met with Churchill in 1942, one of the framers of the Constitution of the Union of Burma and a trusted adviser of Aung San. He also figured prominently as an able negotiator at the Panglong Conference. He was the Minister of Foreign Affairs in 1948 and later assumed the new position of the Inspector General of the Auxiliary Forces with the rank of Brigadier. He was assigned to reform the defense forces at that time and was killed by a mysterious bomb planted in his car in the same year. His death was attributed to his knowledge and possible uncovering of the true perpetrators of Aung San's murder.[9]

Behind the tumultuous scenes of power struggles among the civilian political leaders, the rise of a unified political force in the hands of Bo Ne Win and his associates was in the making. He was by no means apolitical even though his name was overshadowed by General Aung San and other Thakins of the major political organization of the transitional period, the A.F.P.F.L. In fact, his political affiliation was not with General Aung San but with his mentors, Thakin Ba Sein and Thakin Tun Oak, who were replaced by General Aung San within the Thakin Party. His role as the keeper of law and order and subduer of various dissident political groups, communists, minorities, and disgruntled veterans, was firmly established during that period.[10]

All of the names mentioned above would become prominent in the independent politics of the Union of Burma. The most important political base that Ne Win established during that period was the veterans of the dispersed Burma Patriotic Forces, Burma National Army, and Burma Independence Army whose economic life and future were in disarray after the resistance movement and liberation of Burma in 1945. The major organization of these war veterans was called the People's Volunteer Organization (P.V.O.) formed in 1945 under the leadership of General Aung San whose premature death led to the emergence of another dispossessed political group. The loyalty Ne Win received from both inside the so-called reformed Burmese Army and from these veteran groups would play the most vital role in his challenge to the political legitimacy of the fragmented civilian political rule.

The pragmatic choice of occupation he made, during the transitional heyday of independent politics when Thakins and communists were reaping a rich harvest, was correctly assessed by Maung Maung.[11] Ne Win supposedly remained in the army upon the advice of General Aung San.[12] If he had stood beside General Aung San in the political arena, he would have been a second fiddle in view of the fact that his name was never a household word in the resistance movements despite Maung Maung's ostentatious contention to the contrary. However, his choice to stay in the Army behind the limelight of civilian party politics was in line with the Machiavellian politics of the survival of the fittest. Indeed, he would amass not only political loyalty but also military and economic strength for his future entry into the politics of Burma.

From these accounts of Ne Win's role, it is fairly obvious that he had established a loyalty base and a strategic political force among the military personnel at the very outset. Both the internal and external political circumstances favored his eventual rise to power in the transitional politics of Burma's independence movements during and after the War. He was the Commander-in-Chief of both wartime and postwar Burmese governments. He was also the Minister of Defense and Home Affairs from 1949 to 1950 and became Prime Minister in 1958. These important positions and the military intelligence technology which he gathered from both the Japanese and the British became the most important weapons for his success in overthrowing the civilian government of U Nu.

THE RESURGENCE OF A TUMULTUOUS POLITY

With the death of General Aung San, the myth of hero was replaced by the myth of a god-man in the person of U Nu. The invocation of the myth of a benevolent godly king also provoked power struggles and splintering of various contenders to the political throne. The softness and inability of U Nu to deal with the resurgence of a tumultuous polity of Pyidawthah led to the revival of the hero myth by Ne Win and his military commanders. The name "Nu" itself means in Burmese "soft", "gentle," or "youthful." After 1947 the politics of Burma were beset by the emergence of tens of political parties and rebellions by the communists, minority insurgents, and disgruntled veterans with their own factional groups. Fragmentation cut across the entire spectrum of various political organizations, including the minority insurgent groups. Some cases in point were the splits of the Communist Party into the White and the Red Flag Parties, the People's Volunteers Organization into White and Yellow Factions, and the Socialist Party into Communist and anti-Communist Factions, the K.N.U. into the Karen Youth Organization and the Karen National Defense Organization, etc. By 1948, there were several dissatisfied rebel groups who went underground to fight against the U Nu government.

From 1948 to 1952, the newly independent Union of Burma saw political turmoil and disorder reminiscent of the royal ascension to the political throne in the days of the Burmese kings. The three basic challenges to political leadership and power came from the communists, the Red Faction in particular, the Yellow P.V.O., and the K.N.U. Confronted with the communist insurgency, U Nu sponsored a unified Leftist or Marxist League with the 15-Point Communist-oriented Leftist Unity Program. The support he sought was the P.V.O. which had very close ties with the Burmese army. He failed to appease the P.V.O. which demanded not only a greater role in the government but also the inclusion of the insurgent communists in the political leadership.

The most dangerous and violent assault was made by the Karen National Defense Organization (K.N.D.O.) whose army units nearly captured Rangoon itself in early 1949. They were successful also in inciting the Mons into armed rebellion. Their wish and demand were for a separate Karen-Mon state or to secede from the Union of Burma. The dangerous possibility that the Burmese majority might be subjugated by these ancient minority enemies from Lower Burma led to a unified Burmese resistance force under the command of the Burmese Army. The K.N.D.O. also failed to extract support from other minorities, Kachins, Chins, Shans, and Arakanese, to overthrow the majority Burmese government. This fragmentation among the majority and minority political groups reflects the basic nature of the traditional polity of Burma which remains vulnerable to the rule of force by an organized military political organization.

Having been able to stop the Karen minority insurgency by a temporary unification of divided Burmese political groups, U Nu emerged as a national figure. He accomplished this by invoking not the communist-oriented image of a socialist state but the image of the ideal Buddhist state of ancient Burma endorsed overwhelmingly by the Buddhist clerical order and the Buddhist masses. This departure from the extreme left to a moderate posture in building a polity of democratic socialism seemed to establish his political legitimacy not only inside Burma but also in the Western world. In 1951 he and his party were elected by an overwhelming majority of Burmans to usher in an era of experiment with a parliamentary democracy. The sacredness of the center was reaffirmed with the traditional myths of the Burmese state and the image of an ideal Buddhist state of peace and prosperity, Pyidawthah, became the political motto and legitimacy of his leadership in 1952.

U Nu came out by accident as the leader whose personality fitted the image of a priestly ruler capable of building a modern welfare state designed in the symbolic image of the ideal Buddhist state similar to those of Kings Asoka, Abiyahzah, and Min Doan. Indeed, the term Pyidawthah was coined by him reflecting his ideals of peace, prosperity, and morality based upon Buddhism and the traditional Buddhist state of the Burmese kings. Despite all the failures of his socio-political and economic programs, this immensely pious political leader has wielded popular support and power over the tradition-bound Burmese Buddhist masses even up to the present. Associated with him was the myth of god-man or the priestly and benevolent ruler that has been the traditional political heritage of Burma.

THE PYIDAWTHAH ERA OF U NU (1952–1962)

Generally, the transition of Burma from colonial to independent polities may be thought of as a journey back to the traditional polity of the Burmese kings in terms of ideals and goals. The nationalist political leadership of independent Burma, civilian and military, shared the traditional heritages of authoritarianism and the historical anticapitalist xenophobic traumas suffered under the British rule. The political legitimacy claimed by them could only be based upon the outright denunciation of the politico-economic system of the colonial era and the revival of the myths of the Burmese state presented previously. This process whereby the two dominant political figures, U Nu and General Ne Win, resurrected the ancient Burmese Kingdoms may be symbolically thought of as the revival of the myth of the priestly ruler and the myth of the mighty hero which were the dual myths of the legendary kings of Burma.

This is not to imply that this backward linkage of the independent polities of Burma in the hands of the civilian and military rulers of postcolonial Burma is totally traditional and identical in their emulation of the ancient despotic system of government. The British colonial legacy also exerted influences on the administrative systems of government as well as on the thoughts and behavior of both civilian and military power-holders. The only period in which the Burmese masses experienced "freedom" and "parliamentary democracy" was the period of Pyidawthah under the civilian government, no matter how short and defective it may have been. The concept of "the rule of law," as it is understood in Western democratic political systems, was introduced and the appropriate institutions of free press, free election, and constitutional government were incorporated into the polity of the Union of Burma. The name of the Union of Burma was constitutionally adopted by the duly elected civilian government of U Nu in 1948 when Burma was granted its independence by the British.

This view certainly was not shared by a few scholars in the West, although some of them have recently changed their views regarding the military dictatorship that has held power for the last twenty-nine years in Burma. The most illustrative case of negating the civilian government's rule was made by Michael Aung Thwin whose views were discussed previously.[13] His amazing allegation that the civilian government era from 1948 to 1962, with an eighteen-month interlude of military Caretaker Government (1958–60), was "a myth of independence" was made on the basis of his predilection for military regimes more than anything else. The basic flaw of his thesis lies in his lack of comprehension of the nature and functioning of the political systems of Burma since the days of the Burmese kings. Apart from him, there were a few scholars who failed to conceive and assess the real changes in the structure and operations of the military rule over Burma under the banner of "the Burmese Way to Socialism" relative to those of "the Pyidawthah." Their views and writings will be dealt with later at length.

THE REVIVAL OF THE MYTH OF THE BUDDHIST STATE AND THE PYIDAWTHAH POLITY

The political legitimacy sought and claimed by U Nu after his inheritance of leadership was based upon the traditional myth of an ideal Buddhist state, invoking the symbolic image of a benevolent priestly king of Burma. Although the leftist or rather socialist dominance of the political ideology of the A.F.P.F.L. was unquestionable, the role of the traditional myth of the god-man overshadowed all the Marxist ideologies and beliefs when U Nu assumed its leadership. The latter were used to invoke the anticapitalist xenophobic traumas, while the former was invoked to obtain popular support. The invocation of the traditional myth of the Burmese state and the resurrection of the legendary kingdoms of ancient Burma can be discerned in the broadcast of U Nu upon the declaration of Burma's independence. He stated that "thousands of years have passed since a Prince of the Sakyan race founded the Burmese Kingdom at Tagaung in the Upper Irrawaddy, the great river which is so intermingled with our history."[14]

From the August 1945 Naythuyein Conference until the 1947 Rehabilitation Conference of Sorrento Villa in Rangoon, the central vision and emphasis of independent Burma were a socialist state with large-scale power and measures of the state to correct, combat, and control the economic ills of the capitalist colonial state. The very Constitution of the Union of Burma, drawn up in 1948, proclaimed that "the state is the ultimate owner of all lands,"[15] and mandated the socialization or state ownership of all the major industries and natural resources.[16] The Constitution of the Union of Burma placed more emphasis on the omnipotent power and rights of the state to run the socio-political and economic life of Burma than on the rights of the people.

Paradoxically, however, the lingering impact of the colonial political legacy with respect to freedom, democracy, and the rule of law made the polity of Pyidawthah simulate more the welfare state of Western democratic socialism rather than the monolithic socialist polity of the communist world. Although the nationalist leadership of the Union of Burma expressed rigorous and outright denunciations of capitalism, colonialism, and the exploitation of private enterprises, neither the communist approach nor its philosophy were accepted superseding Buddhist philosophy to build a communist state in the Union of Burma. The ousting of various communist leaders and their parties from the political arena seemed to confirm that Western political ideals and philosophies still played a role in the political thought of primary tradition-bound Burmese leaders.

THE MYTH OF GOD-MAN

In order to understand the basic meaning and ideal of Pyidawthah as a political state, one must examine the background and personality of its author, *U*

Nu, Saturday's Son (the title of his autobiography). His boyhood and adolescent years which he narrated himself were deeply molded in the Buddhist Burmese traditions loaded with not only pure Buddhist values but also with pre-Buddhist beliefs and customs. His very name was chosen for him by his father on the basis of astrological advice and omens. Educationally, he was a product of primary and secondary education received from the Anglo-Vernacular National Schools and not from the private missionary schools. His college life at Rangoon University was filled with the typical process of acquiring modern Western education and socialization during the colonial period.[17]

Like most Burmese children, religious education and knowledge of the Buddhist views of life and cosmic order were directly conferred upon him by his father, elders, and customary practices. After taking the Buddhist vow as a novice in the monastery during his college years, the personality and religious zeal of U Nu flowered when he began to make "an inquiry into Buddhism." The following account of his aspiration to become a *hpayar*, Buddha, and of his religious training indirectly show the origin of his attempt to resurrect the ideal Buddhist state in terms of the myth of god-man.

> Leading Maung Nu before the family altar, his father made him sit in a respectful manner before the images of Buddha. He got him to worship the Three Noble Gems [Yadanah Thonepar] with humility. Finally with fingers joined in adoration, Maung Nu vowed, through application of mind and body to their fullest extent, that he would dedicate himself to acquiring ten parami [the prerequisites to Buddhahood] in their thirty layers and prayed that he might one day become true Buddha.[18]

In the same manner by which the Kings of the Koanbaung Dynasty, Alawn Hpayar, Bodaw Hpayar, and Min Doan, for example, aspired to and proclaimed themselves as Buddha to-be, the entire adult life of U Nu and his political career since his premiership have been overwhelmed by this religious goal more than by mundane politics.

In the 1951 election of the Union of Burma, U Nu attained political legitimacy and mass support via the symbolic image of a priestly ruler of benevolence and defender of the Buddhist faith—a prerequisite of Burmese kingship. The launching of the Pyidawthah Plan in 1952 marked a short-lived peaceful period up until 1958 during which the very unifying political impact of Buddhism in the nationalist movements against the British became a target of attack by both modernized civilian political elites, communists, and minorities, religious minorities in particular. The ideal of a modern welfare state was consistently advanced in terms of Buddhist values and philosophy of life more so than the Marxian dialectical materialism.[19] U Nu further speculated on the political state of nature as "once upon a time, all commodities were common property and everybody had the right to use them for his or her benefit."[20] He went on to denounce profit and profit-motivation as the cause of creating the "haves" and "the have-nots" in a Marxian vein of thought and concluded that they were the roots of all sufferings, *dokkhas*, or evils.[21]

This curious but unsuccessful blending of the ascetic Buddhist philosophy of life with the Marxian theory of class struggles and exploitation, attempted by both U Nu and later leaders of the Burmese Way to Socialism, has had very little impact on the actual outlook and behavior of the Buddhist masses. Contrary to what this tradition-bound political leader urged and professed as their ideals and goals, neither socialism nor communism has been able to penetrate the deeply-rooted cultural values of the Burmese. Corruption and struggles for political power and economic privileges became rampant among the framers and implementors of the Pyidawthah Plan, despite the fact that U Nu has been consistently recognized as a truly honest and moral person by many observers.[22]

THE SIXTH BUDDHIST SYNOD AND THE PROMOTION OF BUDDHISM

The clearest evidence of U Nu's attempt at the creation of an ideal Buddhist state via the revival of the myth of god-man was to be found in his holding of the Sixth Buddhist Synod [the legacy of King Mingdoan who held the fifth Synod], the construction of his Peace Pagoda, and the creation of the Buddha Sasana Council. Various legislative acts, such as the Ecclesiastical Courts Act, the Pali University and Dhammacariya Act, etc., were passed to promote a nation wide campaign of revitalizing Buddhism. These actions were, of course, in the tradition of a benevolent Burmese king whose two basic religious functions for political legitimacy were the promotion and protection or rather regulation of Buddhism. As Smith correctly observed "the monarch's religious functions as the promoter and the protector (and regulator) of Buddhism were universally acknowledged as valid by monks and laymen alike, and there was an unbroken continuity in their performance by the kings regardless of dynasty or ethnic identity.[23]

THE FALL OF PYIDAWTHAH AND THE END OF CIVILIAN RULE

On the surface, the Road to Pyidawthah from 1952 to 1958 seemed promising and calm with the revival of traditional values and culture in a political framework of parliamentary democracy in the hands of U Nu and his A.F.P.F.L. Party. The Union of Burma was a relatively open society and a polity of neutrality dealing with both the Western and Eastern Bloc. Underneath the seeming political stability, the country was beset with the age-old problem of fragmentation among the majority Burmese political parties and between the majority and the minorities who had openly taken arms against the central

Burmese government. The challenge to the majority party and U Nu's leadership came from both within his party and from a host of dissatisfied political groups and minorities.

The fall of Pyidawthah began in 1958 when the challenge to U Nu's political legitimacy based upon Buddhism came from within his own party. The two personalities associated with this challenge were his ministers U Kyaw Nyein and U Ba Swe who formed a coalition to discredit U Nu's philosophy and policies. They were both high ranking ministers of U Nu's Cabinet before the rift in the A.F.P.F.L. in 1958. Their political ambition and power struggle to oust U Nu were reminiscent of royal politics. The central ideological rift between the Premier and these two was the issue of the superiority of Marxism over Buddhism as well as the compatibility of the two. As was shown before, most Thakins of the nationalist movements absorbed and used Marxism in their slogans against British colonial capitalism and rule. As early as 1948, the question of the relationship between Marxism and Buddhism caused various splits among the Thakins. To U Nu, Marx and Marxism represented "less than one-tenth of a particle of dust that lies at the feet of our great Lord Buddha.[24] This led to the defection of forty-three left-wing Socialists in 1950 from the Socialist Party within the A.F.P.F.L. to form their own Burma Workers and Peasants Party (B.W.P.P.) which remained aboveground, unlike the militant communists.

By 1954, adherence to the concept of an ideal Buddhist state was at its peak after the construction of the great Cave and the holding of the Sixth Buddhist Synod or World Buddhist Council at the cost of over $2 million. Unfortunately, not only the construction of pagodas, the most famous being the Kabah Aye or Peace Pagoda of U Nu, but also animistic folk religion was revived. It included rituals of sacrificial offerings to celestial and local spirits. The power and strength of the Buddhist clerical order also increased at a rapid rate and so did its political role in the Pyidawthah of U Nu. By 1956, it was quite apparent that modern socialism based upon Marxism was secondary to Buddhism in the construction of the Pyidawthah polity of U Nu. He resigned from premiership in 1957 to reorganize his party, whose victory in the election of 1956 was less than impressive. U Ba Swe became a temporary Premier and U Nu resumed his premiership in 1958. At the 1958 A.F.P.F.L. Conference, he emphatically rejected Marxism as inferior to Buddhism and emphatically asserted that the two were not compatible. The issue of making Buddhism the state religion of the Union of Burma was also hinted at during that Conference.[25]

This philosophical stance was taken not only on religious but also on political grounds in order to repel the open confrontation of the Ba Swe–Kyaw Nyein faction. The latter were two staunch socialists who viewed Marxism and Buddhism as completely compatible and attacked U Nu's use of religion for political fame. The power struggle between U Nu and the Ba Swe–Kyaw Nyein faction broke out into the open and the country was in turmoil with communist and minority insurgency on top of numerous political splits. The resignation of U Ba Swe and U Kyaw Nyein from the Cabinet and the political chaos led to the transfer of political power to General Ne Win in 1958, initially for six months, but then for an additional twelve months, thus ushering in a military rule over the Union of Burma which would eventually sound the death knell of the civilian rule in 1962. This taste of political power by the military elite in a climate of political fragmentation among the civilian political leaders and their parties marked the beginning of the fall of Pyidawthah.

The eighteen-month Caretaker Government of General Ne Win backed the Ba Swe–Kyaw Nyein faction of the A.F.P.F.L. called the Stable Faction, while U Nu in alliance with the communist-dominated National United Front (N.U.F.) supported by a large majority of the Buddhist masses regained political power in the election of 1961. The issue of making Buddhism the state religion and the myth of god-man in the person of U Nu together were responsible for the landslide victory of U Nu and his Clean A.F.P.F.L. (later renamed the Pyidaungsu Party) in that election. During this period of power struggles and elections, it became increasingly apparent that the rule of force involving intimidation and arrest would become a political ritual. U Nu himself was not reluctant to endorse the use of forceful methods to impose his will and wish to make Buddhism the state religion. The political fragmentation of this traditional polity now had a major problem of religious minorities to contend with resulting in a few riots between the Buddhists and the Muslims and violent demonstrations by minorities. On March 2, 1962, General Ne Win and his rising military elite seized the political throne in the name of "saving the country" by deposing and arresting U Nu along with major political figures to end the idealistic Buddhist state Pyidawthah and parliamentary government in the Union of Burma.

BASIC WEAKNESSES OF U NU AND THE PYIDAWTHAH POLITY

There are two basic explanations or evaluations of the failed democratic socialism of the civilian government of the Union of Burma. One attributes the causes of the failure to the personality or psychological neurosis of the civilian politicians as Lucien Pye has done based upon the cultural patterns of Burmese childhood training. The other is a variant of this view with an historical twist of the perpetuation of the colonial political legacy and institutions by the civilian politicians as the cause of political chaos and disorder during the period of civilian rule. According to the latter view, consequently, a truly independent or genuine modern Burmese state was created by the military political elite. Both of these views were originally those of Pye[26] endorsed by a host of later writers, particularly Messers Aung Thwin–Taylor–Anderson discussed earlier. These two views are closely intertwined and were advanced after the newly independent nations underwent a chaotic process of searching for national identity and unity without too much success in either emulating Western democracy or Eastern socialism.

Both of these views are wrong in their neglect of the process of reviving the traditional cultural heritages in all of these nations and the historical conditioning of the polity by both endogenous and exogenous forces. From the accounts of the nature and functioning of the traditional and colonial polities of Burma given earlier, it is fairly obvious that the prerequisites of a free and democratic government were absent in the socio-cultural framework of traditional Burma. Neither the ancient nor the colonial political institutions as they were practiced contained the modern concepts of democracy in terms of "social will," "freedom," "equality," and "the rule of law."

The errors made by the civilian regime of U Nu did not lie in the aspirations for a sacred and benevolent Buddhist state or the use of religion in politics *per se*, but in the revival of other defective values and modes of behavior inimical to the process of modernization. They included animistic beliefs, superstitions, corruption, and actions contrary to what the modern world terms rational and scientific. Yet the basic political necessity of a clear division between what is secular and what is sacred, which modern states had resolved centuries ago to establish a cohesive political order, did not occur in the Union of Burma. The separation of Church and State totally escaped the political vision of U Nu, who aspired to be a Buddha. In fact, despite being a married layman, U Nu took a vow of celibacy in 1948 following in the steps of a Buddhist monk. He donned the yellow robe six times after he became prime minister, mostly in times of political crises.[27]

The pattern of U Nu's behavior with respect to seeking a monastic life in times of personal and national crises is an aspect of the traditional authoritarian personality which can be discerned among many other Burmese political leaders. Apart from such behavior, other rituals include reliance on astrologers, ritualistic actions against bad omens, *yadayah chai*, sacrificial offerings to and building shrines for the spirits, *nats*, feeding monks, and construction of pagodas.[28] In fact, to "avert pending dangers and to achieve complete peace and tranquility in the Union," U Nu called for the construction of 60,000 symbolic sand pagodas in 1961.[29] Not only U Nu but also many politicians and military rulers, including Ne Win, followed more or less the same methods, indicating that contemporary Burmese politics is based more upon traditional than modern cultural practices. These methods fit amazingly well the description of a typical authoritarian personality given by Hagen:

> He comes to believe in the rightness of authoritarian behavior, in the spiritual forces, and in the wrongness of transgressing on their authority with a belief that transcends reason and makes reason unnecessary. Thereafter, like the elders before him, he appeals to the unseen spirits [*nats* in the Burmese case] only with the proper ritual (magic or its equivalent) and with the aid of a religious practitioner [astrol-

> oger, *baydin sayah*, in the Burmese case]. In the technology of production his efforts become concentrated not on technical explorations which the modern world would term rational but on methods of appeasing the spirits and assuring their favor.[30]

Indeed, when it came to claiming power and maintaining political stability, the ancient means of subduing political foes by force rather than by legal means or popular choice became the preferred option of the contenders for the political throne. Even Aung San and U Nu employed some rule of force, although not massacres, and enacted various laws according to their personal wishes and will. For example, Furnivall noted that between 1945 and 1947 more than two hundred Acts were passed, while between 1948 and 1956 about five hundred different Acts were passed dealing with all aspects of governance of the Union of Burma.[31] One of the most infamous laws was known as Poatma Ngar, Law No. 5 which allowed the police or other law enforcement officers to arrest political dissidents.

The neglect of the military power and force needed to maintain political power and stability and inattention to the danger of a rising military leader spelled the demise of the civilian government of U Nu. In the words of Cady, "Thakin Nu could not qualify as a new king [although he laboriously and faithfully followed the royal legacy in words and deeds of merit befitting a king], for he lacked authentic hereditary claims, a fortified palace, and strong dependable army."[32] It was not only that the civilian political leadership failed to notice the growing politico-economic strength of the Burmese army, but also some of them sided with the ambitious military elites in destroying the political legitimacy and power of U Nu. U Nu himself trusted the loyalty of his Chief-of-Staff, General Ne Win, to take care of the political reins in 1958–an irreversible political blunder or perhaps an action taken without having a choice on his part.[33]

Although during the political campaign of 1960 the Caretaker Government of General Ne Win intimidated and arrested many followers of U Nu and his Party, the handing over of the political power back to the triumphant Premier Nu seemed to give some hope of the survival of freedom and democracy. It may be stated that there were "freedom" and "democracy," no matter how defectively they may have been institutionalized, in the Pyidawthah era. In reality, however, the growing political strength and economic power of the enforcer of law and order, Ne Win, and his loyal military commanders during that period, were the main reason for the illegal seizure of political power from a highly respected leader who wished to be a Buddha rather than a prince.

NOTES

1. See his, "1948 and Burma's Myth," p. 27.

2. See for details, Richard Adloff and Virginia Thompson, *The Left Wing in Southeast Asia* (New York: William Sloane Associates, 1950), pp. 86–88.

3. See U Pe Kin, "The Seeds of Pinlon Accord" (In Burmese), *Collected Articles of the Working People's Daily, Vol. 4* (Rangoon: Ministry of Information, March 1989), pp. 362–372.

4. See J. F. Cady, *A History of Modern Burma* (Ithaca: Cornell University Press, 1958), p. 553.

5. Tinker, *The Union of Burma*, p. 25.

6. Chao Tzang Yawnghwe (Eugene Thaike), *The Shan of Burma: Memoirs of a Shan Exile* (Singapore: Institute of Southeast Asian Studies, 1987), p. 53. For details of the conference and terms of agreement see U Pe Kin's articles.

7. Adloff and Thompson, p. 90.

8. See Maung Htoo, p. 8.

9. Ibid.

10. See Maung Maung, *Burma and General Ne Win* (New York: Asia Publishing House, 1969), pp. 166–167.

11. Ibid., p. 165.

12. Ibid.

13. See Chap. 1.

14. Maung Maung Pye, pp. 210–211.

15. *Constitution of the Union of Burma* (Rangoon: Government Printing & Stationery, 1948), Section 30, p. 7.

16. Ibid., Section 31 and Chap. IV.

17. See U Nu, *U Nu, Saturday's Son* (New Haven: Yale University Press, 1975), Prologue and Chap. 1.

18. Ibid., p. 48.

19. See U Nu, *Forward with the People* (Rangoon: Ministry of Information, 1955), p. 28.

20. Ibid., p. 29.

21. Ibid.

22. Cady, Tinker, Hagen, Smith, and many Western writers made this observation.

23. Donald E. Smith, *Religion and Politics in Burma* (Princeton: Princeton University Press, 1965), p. 36.

24. U Nu, *From Peace to Stability* (Rangoon: Ministry of Information, 1951), pp. 106–109.

25. See Smith, p. 127.

26. See Lucien Pye, "The Army in Burmese Politics," John J. Johnson ed., *The Role of the Military in Underdeveloped Countries* (Princeton: Princeton University Press, 1962).

27. Smith, p. 317.

28. Ibid.

29. Ibid., p. 171.

30. Hagen, *The Theory of Social Change*, pp. 151–152.

31. Furnivall, *The Governance of Modern Burma* (New York: Institute of Pacific Relations, 1958), p. 2.
32. J. F. Cady, pp. 584–585.
33. See Walinsky, pp. 246–248.

5

From the Union to the Socialist Republic of Burma

The year 1962 in which Ne Win illegally seized political power marked the beginning of the Burma Road to Poverty both politically and economically. This is by no means to suggest that the political and economic performances of the Pyidawthah era accomplished the task of modernizing the traditional society of Burma or that the civilian managers of the Burmese society were technically more efficient than the military commanders. It means that the socio-political and economic life of Burma during the Pyidawthah era was relatively far more peaceful and prosperous than that of the repressive era of the military dictatorship. Indeed, the type of traditional polity that was and has been revived in Burma by the military rulers is a political rule based upon the legacy of violence and the rule of force which characterized the ominous and inhumane kings of Burma. Under the charade of the "Socialist State" of Burma, the ancient system of despotism, *padaithayit*, was reintroduced by the military rulers with modern twists and arsenals of repression.

NE WIN AND THE MYTH OF THE HERO

While U Nu invoked the myth of god-man in the construction of the Pyidawthah polity, Ne Win revived the myth of the hero for the political legitimacy of his socialist state. These two myths of state of the traditional Burmese kingship, presented in detail earlier, are symbolized in the legendary Burmese kings. The symbolic images of benevolent kings such as King Asoka of ancient Buddhist India and Min Doan of the Koanbaung Dynasty were emulated in the thoughts and behavior of U Nu; the symbolic images of soldierly kings such as Kyansitthar of the Pagan Dynasty and Alaung Hpayar of the Koanbaung Dynasty characterized the thoughts and behavior of General Ne Win. In terms of the basic psychological needs of an authoritarian personality, the myth of god-man relatively requires more deference than aggression and the converse is true of the myth of the hero. It could also be suggested that the ideal of democratic socialism fulfilled the need for deference of godly U Nu, while the ideal of monolithic socialism gratified the aggressive need of soldierly Ne Win.

In order not to carry the contrasting psychological profile of these two dominant political figures of independent Burma too far, it should be noticed that they both came from the same generation of Thakins of Rangoon University and shared traditional values, nationalism, and anticapitalist xenophobia of the colonial past. They both rose to political prominence under favorable states of political events such as the death of General Aung San and political disorders in the late 1950s. Antipathy towards the West and Western cultures can also be discerned in the thoughts and behavior of both personalities, although Ne Win took more aggressive measures of rejecting them by suppressing Western writings, music, and education on a national level. The ambivalence towards Western patterns of culture can also be detected in that both of them sent their children to the missionary English Methodist School in Rangoon.

Biographical accounts of Ne Win relating to his ethnic background and youthful life are not publicly available in detail as much as in the case of U Nu. His supposed Chinese ancestry is a highly sensitive and closely guarded secret which may eventually be authenticated. However, most Burmese conclude that he is a Sino-Burmese by virtue of his original Chinese name, Shu Maung, which was changed to Ne Win when he was one of the Thirty Comrades during the Japanese occupation of Burma. Ne Win himself repeatedly denied this Chinese heritage and his faithful biographer, Dr. Maung Maung, implied that the name Shu Maung is Burmese which means "apple of one's eyes."[1] It should be noted here that the name Ne Win means "Bright Sun" in Burmese. Perhaps, it is not accidental that Ne Win adopted this symbolic name of "Sun" to link his heritage to the Sun Dynasty or "Sun Kings," Ne Min Yahzahs, of the legendary Burmese kings. It is also a fact well-known among the Burmese that Ne Win thought of himself as the descendant of the Kings of the Koanbaung Dynasty.

According to Maung Maung, the lifelong admirer and supporter of the General, Ne Win was born in the town of Paungdale in Prome or Pyi District of Lower Burma. His account of the birthplace of Ne Win itself was contradictory in stating that "he was born on May 24, 1911 (some writers said 1910), at Paungdale, in Prome District."[2] However, after describing how his father brought the bride to his first "home where Shu Maung arrived," Maung Maung went on to say that "the family later moved to Paungdale.[3] According to more authentic sources, he was born in the small town or rather the village of Pauk Hkawn, some twenty-four miles northeast of Prome, in the same district. It was a village with a population of about 3,200 according to the 1953 census. It seems that the genealogy, name, and place of birth of Ne Win are not really recorded and known. This mystery in itself reflects that, unlike General Aung San and U Nu, Ne Win was secretive and maintained a low profile throughout his political life. He was a *min lawn* from a relatively unknown and common background.

Unlike U Nu, neither religious training nor interest in religion seemed to have played a dominant role in his youth and college life. According to Maung Maung, his mother, Daw Mi Lay, was a dominant figure in shaping his frugality, diligence, and work habits, traits which are usually not associated with the typical Burmese social character. In any event, one can confirm from the accounts of his later adult life that he was not born of gentry like Aung San or trained deep in the Buddhist traditions of civility and deference like U Nu. Thus Maung Maung wrote: "The father tended to spoil the child. Daw Mi Lay gave him all her young mother's love and a good upbringing too. She was thrifty, she taught the boy to be so. She worked hard, she taught the boy to acquire a steady work habit. When the boy was a little older, and a young sister was born, he washed the dishes and the diapers."[4]

This pattern of childhood upbringing is totally contrary to typical Burmese patterns. For example, washing dishes and diapers is never a part of the duties assigned to a male child in most Burmese Buddhist households. Be that as it may, the adult behavior of Ne Win with all his violence, vulgarity, and personal abuse of kin and subordinates seemed to contradict Maung Maung's biographical accounts of the General.

Maung Maung contradictorily eulogized the aggressive behavior and foul language of Ne Win: "Bo Ne Win used the strong and salty language of the soldier—his school mates say that he had the language even before his army days—and the young men felt good with him even if he cursed them sometimes in his pithiest prose. To him they unburdened their thoughts and brought their literature."[5]

What the biographer missed in his zealous defense of the General's obscenity is the traditional Buddhist taboo against what the Burmese call *hparoat-tha wahsah*—a deed of demerit or sin committed by the utterance of foul words. Not only by words but also in deeds, the General has continually violated the Buddhist sanctions against the ten deeds of demerit known as *a-kutho*.[6] From a modern political perspective, the above behavior and other related violent abuses of the people around him or enemies reflect the aggressive needs and conduct of Orwell's authoritarian Big Brother in a totalitarian state.

With respect to Ne Win's violent behavior, another astute native writer correctly explained it as a ritualistic aping of the behavioral patterns of a bad Burmese monarch. As Maung Maung Gyi aptly put it: "Ne Win is well known for lapsing into rabid foul language when he is displeased. While a Burmese King of yore would chase a minister with a spear when he was easily annoyed, Ne

Win would lambaste his ministers with shafts of filthy abuse. Promotion, demotion, exile, deportation, abrupt transfer, sudden recruitment, sudden dismissal, and incarceration of military officers or civilian officials, whether high or low, are done at his bidding."[7]

From these observations, it may be inferred that the myth of the hero invoked by Ne Win fell far short of the ideal one that was associated with General Aung San who came from the family background of "well-to-do gentry and a distinguished line of patriotic ancestors."[8] His civility, integrity, and charisma contrasted with the vulgarity, violence, and womanizing of Ne Win.

Ne Win's adult life further revealed other aspects of a typical authoritarian personality: chauvinism, rage, multiple marriages, degradation of kin, friends, and foes alike, and falling back on the tradition of reliance upon superstitious rituals to atone for his sins in the same manner as a bad Burmese king had done in the past. He was supposedly married seven times, including his first unknown affair with a Burmese girl while he was at college and working as a postal clerk, leaving behind illegitimate children, and twice marrying the same woman of Anglicized background, Katy Ba Than. Despite his overt denunciation of Western culture and lifestyles, he regularly entertained many foreign diplomats and Europeanized Burmese guests and held parties with Western music and dances in his Ady Road palace while he was married to Katy Ba Than prior to 1962. Some of the infamous violent attacks he committed included punching a man caught flirting with his wife at a party, chasing and beating with a golf club a man he suspected of intimacy with his wife, breaking drums and kicking musicians for playing loud music at a party across from his residence, and booting a Western diplomat.

His children, including the most famous or rather infamous Sanda Win born of Katy Ba Than, numbered more than ten (nine legitimate ones and others), reminiscent of the polygamy of a Burmese king. His ritualistic performances for the atonement of his sins following the traditional behavior of the Burmese kings will be dealt with later. For now, it is sufficient to say that Ne Win's background, personality, and life seemed to fit the image of a ruthless Burmese king more than that of a benevolent one. In order not to overstate this, it must be pointed out that he was by no means unintelligent or weak. Like most successful dictatorial rulers, his practical intellect and dexterity in Machiavellian politics must be acknowledged. This is evident since he held the political throne in Burma for nearly three decades; his dictatorship was the longest among the Southeast Asian countries.

Beginning in the late 1960s and throughout his tenure as dictator, he began to portray himself as a true Burmese devoid of undesirable Western cultural influences by prohibiting horse racing, gambling, Western music, dances, and parties as well as English as a medium of instruction in various schools. He also performed religious acts and deeds of merit to woo the tradition-bound Burmese Buddhists. At the same time, however, he opened up a number of golf courses all over Burma and made regular trips to England and Western Europe without too much publicity. He was primarily a tradition-bound authoritarian ruler whose effective utilization of modern means of suppression seems to suggest the false image of a rational or modern leader of Burma to some writers. For example, Robert Taylor thought of Ne Win as "a founding father of modern Burma, equal only to the assassinated Aung San."[9]

THE MODERNIZING ARMY IN HOLDING THE COUNTRY TOGETHER

At this juncture, it is necessary to review some of the observations, writings, and evaluations of the military rulers of Burma prior to 1988 to highlight the fallacy of *post hoc ergo propter hoc*, a common fallacy made by political scientists and historians who conceive political events in terms of "after this, therefore because of this." In the case of the Union of Burma, the arguments and evaluations in favor of the military coup and the subsequent rule were made on the basis of the "political mess" caused by civilian political leaders and the need for order to be restored by the army which cleaned up and held the country together with stability, efficiency and, benevolence. The classic view of the military as the rational or modernizing agent of the Burmese polity was advanced by Lucien Pye who asserted that: "In societies where traditional habits of mind are still strong one might expect the military to be strongly conservative. Such was largely the case in the West during the preindustrial period. By contrast, in most of the newly emergent countries armies have tended to emphasize a rational outlook and to champion responsible change and national development."[10]

Based upon this theoretical premise, he further enunciated the modernizing role of the Burmese army:

> The virtues of army government [the Caretaker Government of 1958–1960] were essentially the same as those common to any colonial administration. There was a marked improvement in efficiency in public administration. Authority also became far more regulated and predictable, as there was a considerable reduction in the arbitrary use of political power. The focus of government was developing essentially nonpolitical activities which could be seen as improving the economic lot of the population.[11]

These erroneous remarks were based upon his predilection for the efficiency of the British colonial polity, on the one hand, and the misconception of the ostensible rational behavior of Ne Win and his commanders, on the other. These illusive impressions were gained during the political strife of 1958 when U Nu assigned or was forced to assign the task of governing Burma to Ne Win and his army commanders. The same sort of admiration for the military capacity to run the country or conversely dissatisfaction with the incapacity of the civilian political leaders can be discerned in Walinsky's assessments:

> In actuality, the goals of General Ne Win and his chief lieutenants went far beyond these objectives [severe actions against economic insurgents and raising the living standards pledged during the Caretaker period]. Over the years they had been increasingly concerned over the "mess" the politicians had made of the country. Their sense of order had been offended by the slackness, indiscipline, waste, and disorder that pervaded the society. Their patriotism had been outraged by the primacy given to personal and political interests as against the national interests.[12]

The fallacy of this argument lies in the neglect of the growing political and economic interests of the military elites personalized in General Ne Win and his loyal disciples whose privileges were far greater than those of the fragmented civilian politicians since Burma's independence. Both Pye and Walinsky failed in their analyses to see that Burma is "a traditional society in which ways of behavior remained unchanged from generation to generation"[13] with respect to irrationality or authoritarianism, and that both civilian and military personalities were formed in the same traditional socio-cultural mold.

THE MILITARY ROBBER BARONS

Since 1948 various special economic privileges and higher living standards were accorded to or rather claimed by the Burmese army and the military personnel. These were distributed by military managers through immensely powerful economic enterprises such as the Defense Services Institute (D.S.I.) and the Burma Economic Development Corporation (B.E.D.C.). The military commanders and officers not only occupied key managerial positions in the Boards of Directors and Trustees of these enterprises, but also formed a powerful loyal clique with corrupt civilian politicians in sharing the economic cake and special privileges of Pyidawthah Burma. The potential military takeover based upon the economic strength and organizational unity of the Burmese army had been in the making long before 1962.

The Ministry of Defense began its economic ventures as early as 1950–51 when a central organization called "the Defense Services Institute" (D.S.I.) was created and implemented to set up a host of business firms. It was originally set up as a nonprofit association registered under the Burma Companies Act and controlled by a Central Council of twelve members drawn from the armed forces. In the latter part of the 1950s, it began to branch into profit-making business ventures ranging from fisheries, transport, and general stores to trading and tourism. By the end of 1960, there were twenty-five different firms dealing with the internal and external trade of the Union of Burma. The famous Burma Economic Development Corporation under the chairmanship of Brigadier Aung Gyi was created by parliamentary Act 13 of 1961 to coordinate and control the activities of what were called "the Scheduled Companies." The D.S.I. continued to control most of the firms and by the time the military coup occurred in 1962 there were some thirty-eight different firms and five holding companies of the D.S.I. under the control of "the Military Robber Barons" of the Union of Burma.

In a recent speech former Brigadier Aung Gyi, who was the right-hand crony of Ne Win in charge of the powerful B.E.D.C., boasted, "When I was in charge of economics in the country, Myanmar [the new name of Burma after 1989] had foreign exchange reserves totaling about 1,500 million [currency not further specified] every year in addition to 1,200 million [currency not further specified] in gold bullion."[14]

It should be pointed out here that his ostensible claim of managing the economy of Burma is not founded on fact, for he never held a ministerial post in charge of national finance under the civilian government. His only ministerial post of Trade lasted less than a year from March 1962 to February 1963 after the military coup. However, he was the Vice-Chairman of the D.S.I. and the Chairman of the Board of Directors of the B.E.D.C. prior to 1962. The currency which he referred to is the Burmese currency, Kyat, which was worth $.21 at that time. Thus, the above figures would translate to $315 million and $252 million, respectively. They are grossly exaggerated, since from 1952 to 1960 Burma's foreign exchange reserves annually averaged less than $160 million.[15] Be that as it may, the role of military elites in the economic enterprises of the state, especially relating to foreign trade dealing with foreign exchange, was quite strong. Their free access to hard foreign currency in the import and export industries they managed gave them an upper hand in the foreign-exchange-controlled economy of the Union of Burma.

Indeed, the special privileges and power that they cornered in the economy caused the military managers to believe that they were truly efficient and more capable of running the society, polity, and economy of Burma. Their success in running these special monopolistic enterprises, awarded to them by naive civilian political leaders, was the main catalyst for seizing the political reins in the name of cleaning up the so-called "mess" and disorder attributed to the corrupt politicians. The fact of the matter is that the main weakness of U Nu's leadership lay in his inability to manage the mundane world and face the reality of pending dangers from the rising military officers, Boes, under the politically ambitious interregnum Premier of Burma, Ne Win. The managers of the special state-sponsored military business enterprises such as Brigadiers Tin Pe, Aung Gyi, Sein Win, Colonel Khin Nyo, Captain B.O. Barber, Lieutenant Commander A. Bateson, and a host of others (members of the Council of D.S.I.) formed a special group of military elite threatening the political throne of the civilian Thakins throughout the Pyidawthah period.

The economic base of political power was firmly established by recruiting soldiers, cadets, and officers whose relative educational background was rather mediocre. This view is the direct opposite of Lucien Pye's view which contended that military officers had a relatively higher formal education than the civilian politicians.[16] Joining the economically more rewarding armed services, many dropouts from the Rangoon University and other colleges came to form a corps of military personnel loyal to their benefactor, General Ne Win, during the Pyidawthah period. It should also be noted that Ne Win never graduated from Rangoon University.

With the privileges of housing, automobile, and canteen rations, discount stores of the Defense Services Institute, and other implicit wages, the average living standard and privileges of those who served in the Burmese army was much greater than those of equivalent civil servants. The economic incentive and enticement were the main means of building a loyal political base for the rising military elite. For the simple folks and those who did not wish to pursue higher education, the army profession became an avenue for climbing the socio-economic ladder. The titles such as Bo, Bogyi, Bohmu, and Bogyote (ascending ranks of military officers) began to carry far greater prestige, authority, and power than the traditional titles of government civil servants such as Thugyi, Myoeoat, and Wundauk. Against the foil of this socio-economic background of the Burmese army, the ushering in of the military dictatorship over Burma comes into focus as a process of social change, social conflict, and socio-economic mobility during the Pyidawthah period.

Another equally interesting fact of vital importance relates to the nature of and changes in the social structure of the plural society of Burma after its independence. The dominant economic role of the foreign Orientals was reduced due to a series of nationalization measures whereby the land was reclaimed for the native peasants, European enterprises were transferred to state-controlled enterprise, and external trade was governmentally controlled with licensing and foreign exchange controls. The massive withdrawal of foreign and Indian capital from the rural economy and the flight of Indian moneylenders gave rise to a need for and the creation of state ventures. However, in the major urban communities the role of foreign Orientals remained intact in trade, finance, and external trade. The classic case in point was the Open General License which favored the native Burmans in securing licenses for import and export. Lack of knowledge on the part of the natives caused them to sell these licenses to the foreign Orientals and their firms. Thus, one of the reasons for their continued dominance was that the Pyidawthah Government allowed some freedom of private enterprises and tolerance of foreign Orientals.

The majority of the new elites or culture brokers who emerged in the Pyidawthah society were individuals with mixed blood, the Sino-Indo-and-Anglo-Burmans as well as the Karen-Burmese, Mon-Burmese, Shan-Burmese, etc. Both in government and defense services this type of individual tended to dominate the top managerial positions. For example, Brigadier Aung Gyi is an almost full-blooded Chinese, while General Ne Win, General San Yu, and Brigadier Tin Pe are Sino-Burmese. Apart from them, there were many Sino-

Burmese military commanders and prominent political elites with foreign Oriental blood and other mixtures of native bloods. U Nu, U Thant, the infamous Brigadier Sein Lwin known as the "Butcher," and the Military Intelligence Director and the right arm of Ne Win called Mi Tin Oo belonged to the Mon ethnic group or the mixed group of Mon-Burman.

It has been shown earlier that the intermingling of blood that took place historically in Burma, especially in the Delta Region or Lower Burma during the colonial period, made the racial identity of the Burmese amorphous and illusive. Despite the statistical publications of the consecutive governments of Burma claiming that the Burmese population constituted more than 70 percent of the entire population, the reliability of these statistics are as flimsy as the genealogical claim that the Burmese are the descendants of the Sakyan race of India. In trade, finance, and administration as in the technical professions, this special breed of Burmans, especially the Sino-Burmese, stood out as the dominant personalities in postcolonial Burma.

It is a well-known fact that these types of individuals dominated the upper echelon of the political power structure. For example, the four top military leaders of political prominence are Sino-Burmese, Shu Maung (original Chinese name of Ne Win), San Yu (Ne Win's lifelong puppet and President of the Socialist Republic of the Union of Burma in the 1980s), Aung Gyi (second to Ne Win in command, member of the Revolutionary Council up to 1963, and one of the opposition leaders in 1988), and Tin Pe (the Minister of Trade and Development in charge of running the infamous People's Stores or Trade Council replacing Aung Gyi in 1963). Other prominent Sino-Burman military commanders included Tan Yu Saing (member of the Revolutionary Council), Brigadier Thaung Kyi (member of the Revolutionary Council), MI Tin Oo (Director of the Military Intelligence Services and right-hand man of Ne Win up to 1983), and many other inner-circle members of the Ne Win government.

THE TRULY BURMESE SOCIALIST STATE

Given the fact that the economy of Pyidawthah Burma permitted the existence of some private enterprises in the pursuit of a welfare state of democratic socialist type, another view explains the failures of the civilian government as being due to its perpetuation of the non-Burmese colonial institutions, including laissez-faire or capitalism. Although this view contrasted with those of Pye presented earlier, it is a variant of the view that civilian politicians were ineffective and corrupt, while the military leaders were efficient and orderly modernizers. The political argument of this thesis is that Westernized political elites or leaders with colonial mentality created a mythical independent state of the Union of Burma. Thus, Michael Aung Thwin wrote:

> Aside from the immediate historical reasons for the coup of 1962, there was a more fundamental cause: a collective psychological desire

> to establish "real" independence [whatever that may mean], which necessarily included purging one's colonial past. Clearly, the majority of Burmese were more concerned *originally* with a meaningful and ordered society that preserved traditional patterns, and with finding some way to recover a lost identity, than they were with economic development per se, which is a more recent priority.[17]

This erroneous statement betrays the empirical reality of the Pyidawthah polity and its policies of reviving the ancient patterns of culture to purge the colonial past which were endorsed by a great majority of the Buddhist Burmese. It also fails to recognize that a military coup or an illegal seizure of political power is not usually made by a general plebiscite or on the basis of a collective psychological desire.

The fact that U Nu won by a landslide in the 1960 election testified to the social will of the tradition-bound masses in their approval of U Nu's policies and actions during his tenure as a freely elected political leader of the Union of Burma. What went wrong did not go wrong because Burma was not "really independent" but because there was another political contender to the throne, *min lawn*, by the name of General Ne Win who invoked the traditional legacy of the Burmese kingdoms—the dethroning of the ruling monarch by force.

Other similar views of military leaders' actions and policies of a truly Burmanized or rather uniquely "Burmese Way to Socialism" were expressed by John Badgley and Jon Wiant, and by David Steinberg. The former spoke of the ideology of Bama Lo [Burmese Way] and the Ne Win–*Lanzin* Revolution in 1974:

> The Burmese Way to Socialism, the Ne Win–*Lanzin* revolution, is a response to the vexing problem of being modern and yet remaining Burmese. It is a challenge where "modernization" justifies mass mobilization by a military elite. Contemporary Burmese socialism is authoritarianism, frequently tyrannical, yet as a modernizing ideology it attempts to promote such diverse values as equality, mass participation, altruism, scientific knowledge, and Buddhism.[18]

This view also fits squarely with the appraisal of the performance of the Burmese Way to Socialism and the military revolutionary rulers of Burma by Steinberg who assessed the socialist state of Burma as "a highly equitable society" in terms of the existence of a large private sector, income distribution, and economic privileges.[19] His erroneous views will be discussed at length in a later chapter.

It should also be pointed out that these appraisals were made when Ne Win made shrewd economic maneuvers to coax Western aid in the early 1970s. His ostentatious economic reforms initiated in 1972 seemed to have impressed many Western writers and observers, including the United States, Japan, West

Germany, the World Bank, the Asian Development Bank, and the International Monetary Fund which provided billions of dollars in aid to help sustain the military rule over Burma. That is, Ne Win and his military rulers of Burma had successfully fooled a lot of observers, including not only the governments of the Free World but also those of the Sino-Soviet World. Since 1988, however, both Badgley and Steinberg have changed their views.

The essence of their earlier views is representative of another trend of political thought that pervaded the West during the 1950s. During that period, the role of the modernizing military elite or the army, such as the Red Armies of Russia and China along with their "Revolutions" and "Reforms," seemed to have impressed various writers who had witnessed the political chaos and instability in the newly independent states under their respective civilian governments. It was fashionable in the 1950s to write and speak about "a new and novel totalitarianism" in contrast to Nazism, Stalinism, and old authoritarianism which included all previous tyrannies, oligarchies, and despotic governments.[20] The distinction drawn between these two forms of political systems was based primarily upon the efficiency with which the new and novel totalitarian regimes of the Sino-Soviet World mobilized and controlled the masses. The apparent achievements in centralizing political power in a single political party system and in subduing dissidents by force inside the Iron and Bamboo Curtains gave a certain aura of a stable political system capable of modernization and social transformation.

THE TOTALITARIAN SOCIALIST STATE OF BURMA (1962–1990)

Contrary to the above views, negative appraisals of the Burmese Way to Socialism were made by two political scientists, the late Dr. Maung Maung Gyi, and Joseph Silverstein, who consistently argued against the authoritarian rule of force. Even their views were somewhat tempered by a general trend of political thought from the 1950s to the 1970s of not labelling the socialist state of Ne Win as a totalitarian nightmare state in the manner George Orwell had put forth in his novel, *1984*. The basic theme of political thought was to distinguish an authoritarian polity from a totalitarian polity and consequently to consider Ne Win's Burma as an authoritarian state rather than as a nightmare totalitarian state. Maung Maung Gyi wrote: "However, a distinction between authoritarianism and totalitarianism must be kept in mind when referring to communist countries as authoritarian, for communist countries aspire to totalitarianism rather than to be content with authoritarian administration. In Southeast Asia, including Burma, authoritarianism was the way of life best known to the people of the region and is practiced today."[21]

He went on to state further that the Burmese society was or had been authoritarian to explain the emergence of Ne Win's authoritarian rule: "The right soil for the growth of an authoritarian system reminiscent of native Burmese monarchical rule was already there in the society" and "preconditions for the retreat to native authoritarian rule patterns were lying dormant in the minds of the majority of the Burmese public."[22] This is essentially in line with the thesis advanced in this study.

Joseph Silverstein made a historical demarcation between the "constitutional government" (1948–1962) and the "constitutional dictatorship"[?] (1974–1988) with an intervening period of "military rule" (1962–1974)[23] without specifying the authoritarian versus totalitarian nature of the government of Ne Win. Nevertheless, his factual accounts of the policies and actions of the military junta during these periods seemed to indicate that the ***modus operandi*** of the single-party polity of the Socialist Republic of the Union of Burma (the name adopted in 1974) was one of totalitarianism curiously mixed with the ancient despotic system of government.[24] This point of affinity between the traditional despotic system and modern authoritarianism or totalitarianism is in line with Walzer's view of "totalitarianism as the name we give to the most frightening form of authoritarian rule."[25]

Without quibbling over whether or not the Ne Win regime was authoritarian or totalitarian in nature and functions, it will be suggested here that this distinction is one of degree and not of kind. In fact, authoritarianism and totalitarianism share repression of freedom and rule of force by an authoritarian personality in whom the political power is centralized and personalized. This view is consistent with those of Robert C. Tucker who asserted that: "There was, I believe, a fundamental flaw in the theory of totalitarianism [referring to the writings of the 1950s]: however impersonal the institutional workings of the nightmare state may be, the needs being fulfilled by its radically evil behavior are ultimately those of a person—the totalitarian dictator."[26]

Having established the fact that the traditional authoritarian and modern totalitarian forms of governments are not different in belonging to the same nightmare state of "unfreedom," the nature and functioning of the socialist state of Burma under the military dictatorship of Ne Win may be presented on both personal and nonpersonal levels from 1962 to 1972.

THE BURMESE WAY TO SOCIALISM AND THE ROAD TO SINGLE-PARTY DICTATORSHIP (1962–1972)

The Burmese Way to Socialism was adopted and launched with the ideal of establishing what is called a classic "negative utopia"[27] by using modern Marxist revolutionary terms, thoughts, and methods. The method used to create the mythical socialist state of Burma were simultaneously both modern and traditional. They were modern by virtue of the fact that a highly efficient network of political cadres and military intelligence servicemen was deployed to suppress freedom of expression, thought, and information in mass mobilization movements; at the same time they were traditional by virtue of employing the same strategy of invoking Buddhist philosophy, and the hero myth, and of hunting down and purging potential contenders to the political throne, *min lawns*, in the same manner as the Burmese kings had done.

The evidence of creating a utopian socialist state by using both modern as well as traditional values and thoughts can be discerned at once in the *Burmese Way to Socialism: the Proclamation of the Revolutionary Council's Philosophy* (in Burmese) announced on April 30, 1962. It stated that: "The Revolutionary Council of the Union of Burma does not believe that so long as the unjust profit-seeking cut throat economic systems exist in this world, *lawka*, the peoples in societies can be free from social sufferings, *dokkhas*."[28]

After stating this belief reflecting the anticapitalist trauma of the colonial past, it went on to assert that the Revolutionary Council Government (R.C.G.) would create a "new world, *lawka*, of peace and prosperity with a socialist economic system devoid of various *dokkhas*, such as sufferings due to shortages of food, clothing, shelter and inability to meditate because of an empty stomach."[29]

A more sophisticated philosophy was advanced in the official Manifesto of the Burma Socialist Programme Party (B.S.P.P.) called *Ar Nya Ma Nya* (in Burmese) or *The System of Correlation of Man to His Environment: The Philosophy of the Burma Socialist Programme Party* published and disseminated on January 17, 1963. The Marxian philosophy of the supreme importance of man or human society based upon Feurbach's "generic causality of man" or "humanized naturalism"[30] was adopted in stating that human society is, "the most important of all, the most useful of all, the most determinant of all and the noblest of all, for amongst all the living and sentient beings it is only man who has the highest intellect and highest capability to use it."[31]

However, this emphasis on the *sui generis* or supreme importance of man was curiously and contradictorily modified by asserting that man is a combination of "the material body with life, mind and matter in their correlation, and the ceaseless process of mutation."[32] Theoretically, it contradicts the Marxian dialectical materialism and the permanent outcome of its ideal classless society of communism.

Indeed, "the ceaseless process of mutation" is the Buddhist philosophy of *anatesa*, the impermanent nature of things, including the classless society of the Burmese Way to Socialism. In these ontological and epistomological overtures to building a utopian "socialist-Buddhist state," one can detect the same problems confronted by U Nu's ideal "Buddhist-socialist state" of Pyidawthah and the contradictory fusion of Marxian theories and values with the ascetic Buddhist philosophy of life. The only difference between the two seemed to be a reversal of the priority given to spiritual or Buddhist versus secular or socialist aspects in the resurrection of the traditional polity of the Burmese kings.

Using Richard Lowenthal's analysis and evaluation of totalitarian regimes,[33] the actions of the R.C. government of Ne Win may be presented. The first and foremost task in constructing the utopian socialist state was to create a political structure based upon the extreme centralization of the ruling party, (B.S.P.P.), and its political power. Thus, immediately after ousting the constitutional civilian government of U Nu in 1962, three basic monopolies were established within two years: the monopolies of political decision, social organization, and all forms of information. The typical means to achieve this end is the revolutionary destruction of entire social groups (students, press, civilian politicians, pro-Western intellectuals, communists, minorities, etc., in the Burmese case), not only for opposing the regime, but for not fitting into its plans by their very existence. This insight into the process of establishing a typical totalitarian state fits amazingly well with the patterns of behavior and action of the military junta whose intellectual capacity was rather limited in the theoretical formulation and design of programs for creating the "truly Burmese and independent state" of Burma [using Aung Thwin's cliché] or the single-party dictatorship of the B.S.P.P. over Burma.

Indeed, the formulators of the philosophy of the Burmese Way to Socialism were those who fit into the military junta's plans. They were hard-core leftist communists or Marxist-Leninist socialists and former Thakins. They included Colonel Saw Myint, Ko Saw U, and Thakin Chit Hlaing. Thakin Chit Hlaing was the main author of the official philosophy of the Burmese Way to Socialism, a pupil of the Red Flag Communist leader, Thakin Soe and a high-ranking member of the Psychological Warfare Department and the Head of the Central School of Political Science. U Ba Khin was the Head of the Buddhist Meditation Center in Rangoon who was responsible for coining the term *Ar Nya Ma Nya* for the System of Correlation of Man to His Environment. Colonel or Da Meet Ka Ba Than was the Director of the Psychological Warfare Department and the translator of the *System of Correlation of Man to His Environment*, the official Manifesto of B.S.P.P., into English, and U Khin Maung Lat was a leftist socialist and a professor of English who embellished the English translation of the *Ar Nya Ma Nya*.[34]

Apart from these Marxist theoreticians, there were many other Western-educated individuals at home and abroad who helped to shape the philosophy, programs, and implementation of the B.S.P.P. The important but later designers and collaborators were Ba Nyein who was a prominent communist of the National United Front (N.U.F.) with an economics degree from Rangoon University and Yebaw or Comrade Chan Aye alias Sun Suu who was a pupil of the White Flag Communist leader, Than Tun, and wrote several articles on the socialist economy of the Burmese Way to Socialism. The most prominent name among the civilian designers of the socialist republic of Ne Win was Dr. Maung Maung who was a Western-educated lawyer of Utrecht and Yale, an author of several books on Burma, including *Burma and General Ne Win*, the Chief-of-Justice of the B.S.P.P., a lifelong disciple of Ne Win, and the interregnum civilian President during the 1988 political upheavals. Others who came to figure prominently as ministers, *wungyis*, and advisers in the B.S.P.P. Government included Dr. Khin Maung Win (a Yale graduate and Minister of

Education), Dr. Maung Shein (an Oxford graduate in economics), and Dr. Nyi Nyi (a Sino-Burman in charge of the Education Department and a Minister of Mines and Labor).

These individuals of various educational and political backgrounds certainly fit the plans of the B.S.P.P. in having the masses mobilized by the central power-holder, Ne Win. Those who did not fit or rather posed dangerous threats to political power were many prominent military leaders of the Thirty Comrades, well-known communist leaders, such as Than Tun and Thakin Soe, and other prominent civilian socialists. This was immediately obvious in the membership of the R.C. which was made up of only the loyal military commanders close to Ne Win and included not a single military hero of the Thirty Comrades. Despite the claim made by Taylor that there was no personality cult built around Ne Win,[35] the core of the power structure was maintained by the dictator with those who worshipped him like Buddha. Thus, the Chief of Military Intelligence Services and the protégé of Ne Win popularly nicknamed the "Smart Chap" or "MI Tin Oo," who was acknowledged by many Burmese as the next in line to the political throne, *min lawn*, in the Socialist Republic of the Union of Burma, said: "You people may think not highly of me. Even though my parents are devout Buddhists, I myself do not devoutly practice Buddhism. I believe that my 'religion is to do good'... I have only one Buddha and he is *Bogyotekyee* (the Great General) Ne Win."[36]

Unfortunately, he was sacked by Ne Win in 1983 for becoming too smart and popular in threatening the political throne. The strategy of guarding the political throne by breeding a bureaucracy of absolute loyalty is common to both modern totalitarianism and traditional despotism—the absolute centralization of political power in the leader or the Big Brother of Orwell. The basic strategy of Ne Win in protecting his political throne throughout his reign was the repeated emphasis on the political dictum of needing and breeding "loyal" rather than "able" men around him or the deployment of a system called in Burmese *lukawn lutaw*—good man first and smart man second."[37] In effect, this is analogous to Mao's dichotomy discernible in his writings on "red" versus "expert" cadres. The history of Ne Win's purge of the able and smart men within the inner-circle of military commanders will be presented in the following chapters.

THE REVOLUTIONARY COUNCIL'S ACTIONS (1962–1972)

The Revolutionary Council Government of the Union of Burma was established with Ne Win as the Chairman and sixteen other military commanders, the majority of whom were of mixed ethnic blood, including Anglo-Burmans. Apart from Ne Win, other prominent members with Chinese ancestry were Brigadier Aung Gyi who was second in command, Brigadier San Yu, Colonel Tan Yu Saing, Brigadier Thaung Kyi, Colonel Khin Nyo, and Colonel Hla

Han. The well-known Anglo-Burman members were Brigadier T. Clift and Brigadier Sein Win (considered more a minority than an Anglo-Burman since he was a native of Mergui, Baitthar, in the Tennasserim Division). Brigadier Tin Pe, whose name came to fame in managing the infamous People's Stores Corporation, was thought to be an Indo-Burman because of his dark skin but another source indicated that he is what the Burmese called *tayoke mell* or *tayoke ngachate* or *orkalar*—black Chinese. He was married to a Chinese woman, the sister of Tan Yu Saing.

It should also be noted that Ne Win's protégé and the Director of Military Intelligence Services, MI Tin Oo, the nephew of a famous Chinese, Dr. Chan Teik, is a Sino-Mon. From this ethnic background of the members of R.C., it can be affirmed that most of the top military elites came from the social group of mixed blood, especially Sino-Burman, representing the cultural brokers of the colonial past. This is a critical aspect of the Burmese polity which most writers on Burma have missed. It is the root of the ethnocentricity or ostensible Burmese chauvinism and xenophobic attacks on foreigners in general by the policy-makers of the B.S.P.P., especially Ne Win. It may be suggested that the problem of racial identity and the psychological insecurity of not being a mythical "pure Burmese" plagued Ne Win and many other prominent military commanders of mixed blood causing them to undertake ruthless and violent attacks on foreigners and minorities as the Burmese kings had done historically.

Another important point to emphasize is that, despite the fact that the original group of Thirty Comrades or military heroes during the War were supposed to have formed an inseparable bond of blood brothers, Ne Win did not include a single member from that group in his R.C. This, of course, was in line with the traditional method used by the Burmese royalty to guard against a potential threat to the political throne and with the modern totalitarian method of forming an inner-circle of power loyal to the dictator. Most of them left the army after 1948 leaving Ne Win alone as the Chief-of-Staff. However, a few of the Thirty Comrades were given economic opportunities to conduct businesses (Bo Let Yah, who was also a Sino-Burman, and Bo Satkyah, an Anglo-Burman, for example) or given high ranking positions in various government ministries. Some of them joined the communist opposition groups (Bo Kyaw Zaw for example) and other political parties (Bo Yan Naing, son-in-law of Dr. Ba Maw for example).

Immediately after the illegal seizure of political power, R.C. dissolved the Parliament by Proclamation No. 17 on March 8, 1962 and then abolished the Election Commission and the Supreme Court. This reason for the abolishment of the Parliament was given: "Parliament had not worked in the interests of the working people of the Union of Burma. It was, in fact, a bourgeois Parliament which represented the interests of the feudal elements; exploiting landlords; national and foreign capitalists. . . ."[38]

The main explanation for destroying all the democratic institutions of the civilian government was made in terms of Marxian theories as "history will generally record that in the march of man the indigenous peoples of Burma had lagged behind. When the capitalist economic system was in full flower in West European countries, Burma and similar countries slumbered in the shadow of the feudalist social system."[39] Recognizing that these bourgeoisie nationalist leaders made some improvement of Burmese social life, it indicted them as being nourished and infatuated with the educational and spiritual values of the imperialists.[40]

VIOLATIONS OF THE FUNDAMENTAL HUMAN RIGHTS OF THE PEOPLE OF BURMA

By any standard, the violations of the basic human rights of the people of Burma by Ne Win's R.C. Government were either equal to or greater than those of any totalitarian regime in the world. Although in terms of the magnitude of the blood bath these violations may not compare with the bloody massacres of demonstrators that occurred between March and September 1988, they took place continuously with very little international notice for twenty-six years from 1962 to 1988. To begin with, the military coup of March 1962 and the subsequent formation of the R.C. Government were made in direct violation of Article 21 of the *Universal Declaration of Human Rights* by the United Nations. That is, the government of Ne Win was formed not on the basis of the "will of the people" of Burma, but of the "will of the dictator" in the name of "saving the country" or "law and order." Immediately after that violation a series of violations ensued engendering a nightmare state of arbitrary laws and arrests.

During the short period of three years from 1962 to 1965, all forms of "freedom" were annihilated by the R.C. The total centralization of political power in the hands of the R.C. was established by passing hundreds of arbitrary laws, including various laws of sedition against the state, that is against the R.C. In keeping with the colonial legacy of prohibiting acts of sedition, for instance the British Penal Code Section 124 A, the Union of Burma Penal Code Section VIII, which was passed in 1958 and enforced during the Caretaker Government, became the most generic law of arbitrary arrest of anyone actually involved in or suspected of involvement in dissent against the R.C. This law stipulated "Offences Against the Public Tranquility" included among which was the designation of "an assembly of five or more persons" as an "unlawful assembly" with the objective of overawing by criminal force either the government servant or the state.[41]

In 1962, the aforesaid Law, also previously called Law No. 5, Poatma Ngar, during the civilian government, was renamed the Law for Law and Order by the R.C. to enforce the rule of force throughout Burma.[42] It was enforced by using the most feared secret military servicemen called the MIs to intimidate, detain, and arrest anyone at will. The most powerful organization assisting the MIs was the five-man Security and Administration Committee (S.A.C.) made up mostly of military officers. In essence, it was the same old antisedition Penal Code of colonial Burma dating back to 1864 which the British government used to arrest political dissidents. All the other arbitrary laws that were passed and used may be thought of as variations on this generic law with different names and numbers attached by the consecutive military governments of Burma.

Apart from this generic law of sedition, there were many other laws prohibiting activities or sedition against the actions and policies of the R.C., such as the 1963 Law to Protect the Construction of the Socialist Economy, the 1964 Law to Protect National Unity and the Law to Protect the Construction of the Socialist Economy from Opposition, and the 1962 Printer and Publishers Act which repealed all existing press acts starting from the Press Registration Act of 1876, just to name a few.[43] Arbitrary arrests became daily rituals of Burmese life while all writs of the British legal system, *habeas corpus, mandamus, prohibition*, and *quo warranto*, became defunct in the socialist state of Burma.

The most memorable incident of subduing a political dissent occurred on July 7, 1962, when the Rangoon University Students staged a protest initially against the unjust dormitory rules and later against the military government. The incident resulted in the arrest and killing of hundreds of students along with the dynamiting of the Students' Union Building, a citadel of political protests and nationalist movements against the British rule. This incident became the most recalled and guilt-ridden political event for both the critics and the General. Ne Win kept denying his direct responsibility for this affair up to the time of his resignation from the political throne in 1988 and placed the responsibility for this incident on the shoulders of Aung Gyi who also emphatically denied his part. One other name that came to fame with this incident was General Sein Lwin, known as "the Butcher" for his ruthless massacre of students and other dissidents throughout Ne Win's rule. This incident also set the precedent for ruthless repression of youthful students and frequent closing of Rangoon University and other colleges throughout the twenty-six-year tenure of Ne Win as the ruler of Burma. Once again in November 1963, the students of Rangoon University staged another protest which also resulted in the arbitrary arrest and incarceration of their leaders.

In 1962, key leaders opposing Ne Win were quickly arrested, including former Premier U Nu, U Kyaw Nyein, and U Ba Swe. Brigadier Aung Gyi was arrested in 1963 following his personal blunder in making a statement concerning the possible transfer of power back to the civilian politicians while he visited Japan. However, a more serious cause for his downfall was a power struggle with Brigadier Tin Pe and Thakin Ba Nyein of the National United Front who became one of the main civilian political leaders of the B.S.P.P. In fact, Aung Gyi called the model of socialist economy adopted by the B.S.P.P. the Tin Pe–Ba Nyein–NUF model in the forty page letter he wrote and distributed in 1987 prior to the 1988 political upheaval. On March 28, 1964, all political parties were dissolved and their properties confiscated under the Law to

Protect National Unity in the name of national solidarity, and the single-party dictatorship was firmly established. By 1965, all previous civilian political leaders, as well as other dissenters such as the students, monks, journalists, and newspaper owners, had been forcefully put into jails.

The mass mobilization was made by establishing hundreds of thousands of People's Workers Councils, People's Peasant Councils, Security and Administration Councils, and Party Committees all over Burma manned by notorious Military Intelligence Service officers or MIs for short and B.S.P.P.'s political cadres. The formation of the Cadre Party of the B.S.P.P. was quickly made with three top Committees, the Central Organization Committee, the Party Discipline Committee, and the Socialist Economy Planning Committee. The three main organs of the Party were the Six Divisional Supervision Committees, the Divisional Coordination Commissions, and the Party Divisional Coordination Committee. The six Divisional Supervision Committees were set up on the basis of military commands and fifteen Subdivisional Supervision Committees which in turn were set up according to the civil administrative divisions of Burma. The Divisional Coordination Commissions' military commanders coordinated the work of the Party and the S.A.Cs. It should be noted that this model of the B.S.P.P. was patterned after the Communist Cadre Party of Red China. Even the names of its committees and councils adopted the same title of "People's" in all the functionary units of the Party.

In January 1963, a monopoly of information was established by the suppression of the free press and the opening of the powerful state news agency, the *News Agency Burma*, and by government officials giving political classes to journalists. According to U Thaung, the owner of the *Mirror* and a highly-seasoned reporter of the civilian political era who was jailed in 1964, the state lecturer in one of these classes stated that "we cannot afford free press" and "the national development requires subordination of the idea of free press."[44]

On October 1, 1963, the state owned-and-operated *Working People's Daily* was started and began to publish all relevant news and activities of the R.C. The confiscation of the major newspaper-publishing houses began soon after that and, in 1964, major newspaper figures were indicted under the antisedition laws and put into jails. Among them were U Law Yon, U Thaung, U Ohn Khin, U Khin Maung Galay, and U Nyo Mya of the *Nation*, the *Mirror*, the *Thunder*, and the *Voice of Peacock*. By 1965, the only major newspaper of any significance was the R.C.'s mouth-piece, the *Working People's Daily*. U Thaung reported that between 1963 and 1966 there were 30 other writers in his prison wing.[45] By 1969, all private newspapers had ceased to exist in the socialist state of Burma.[46]

This sweeping destruction of the "free press" by Ne Win took Burma back to the dark ages far beyond the days of even the last kings of the Koanbaung Dynasty, especially King Min Doan. According to U Thaung, "Though the newspapers were owned by the King [Min Doan], freedom of writing or press was guaranteed by the monarch with an Act, consisting of 17 Articles."[47] He further described how the king gave permission to write not only about his wrong deeds but also those of his queens, sons, and daughters to the journalists who were allowed to move freely in and out of the palace of the Gem City of Mandalay.[48] This legacy continued in the British colonial period despite its antisedition laws and was kept faithfully by U Nu during his civilian government because of his own belief in the free press. In fact, many prominent newspapers owners such as U Saw and U Ba Cho used the free press as a political weapon to arouse nationalism and anti-British movements in colonial Burma. Recognizing the potential danger of this powerful medium of opposition to the safety of the political throne, the destruction of the free press, domestic and foreign, was the first order of attack in Ne Win's socialist state.

Adopting the methods of communist states, the primary targets of attack were the students, the educated, and the intelligentsia to control public opinion and protest by monopolizing the press. In broadcasting, dissemination of foreign culture, propaganda, and degenerate songs were also terminated by the R.C.[49] By 1965, all foreign missionary and private schools had been taken over by the state. Western newspapers, magazines, and journals ceased to appear in bookstores and newspaper stands. They became as rare as gold in the socialist state of Ne Win. The most poignant account of this was given by U Thaung and his fellow prisoners who paid in gold for a copy of the *Reader's Digest*: "Then one day an American tourist was arrested. Among his belongings was a copy of The Reader's Digest—a rarity in Burma. . . . We had no money at all. Yet resourcefulness is the mark of a good newsman, and one of our band somehow persuaded a fellow inmate, a wealthy merchant, to donate a gold tooth. Thus, The Reader's Digest *was* paid for in gold."[50]

By the mid-1960s even English as a medium of instruction in schools and colleges had been dropped as an undesirable language of foreign influence. Travels in and out of Burma became the special privilege only of the military elite and high-ranking government officials. By stopping the free flow of information and people, Burma was kept as an isolated reclusive country internationally and taken back to the days of absolute obedience under the Burmese kings. The will and opinions of the B.S.P.P. or rather the Big Father (*Ahpai Gyi* in Burmese) were the only news and information provided by the single newspaper, the *Working People's Daily*, which was loaded with what Orwell termed double-negative speeches and thoughts.

THE TRADITIONAL DUAL POLITY RESURRECTED

The last but not least, important monopoly needed to establish and maintain political control was the ownership of everything from land to sea by nationalizing all trade, commerce, and finance and setting up state collective farms, co-operatives, machine-tractor stations, enterprises, and shops. The details of the so-called "planned economy of proportional developments for all" of Ne Win's socialist state will be dealt with in the following chapter. For now, the political aspect of duality between the "center" and the "periphery" will be discussed to suggest that the polity of Burma reverted back to the simple structure of the Burmese kings. Although there were some changes with respect to the composition of the members of the political elite and simple folks, the nature of the socialist polity of Ne Win was such that the gap between the power and privileges of the "center" versus the "periphery" was widened.

Contrary to those who contended that there was political modernization on a national scale of a sort by the modernizing army of Burma, it will be argued that the polity of Burma under military rule reduced its structure to a dual polity reminiscent of the traditional Burmese polity. The political power and privileges resided primarily with the central power-holders, especially with Ne Win, and the peripheral masses subsisted as in the days of the Burmese kings and the colonial period. The intensive and extensive use of force to impose the will of the military elite, personalized in Ne Win, was the central hallmark of the functioning of the socialist state of Burma.

The geopolitical importance of the "center" or central Burma, the valleys of the Chindwin, the Irrawaddy, and the Sittaung, marked out Central and Lower Burma as the seat of political authority throughout the entire history of Burma. This importance of the "center" and the natural isolation of Burma from the undesirable influences of the outer world were reinforced by deliberate actions of the R.C. Rangoon, Mandalay, Moulmein, and a few other central cities form the hub of social life and political power, while the entire eastern and northeastern regions have been dominated by minority insurgents since 1948. In central Burma itself, the political power structure of the military regime is centralized and personalized in Rangoon which is the hub of political control. Rangoon and the famous Ady Road, the well-protected and fortified palace of Ne Win and the villas of his subordinate generals, were the physical core of power from which radiated the resurgence of the political power structure and operations similar to those of the Burmese kings. As Furnivall observed on the ancient polity of Burma:

> At times, the supreme King ruled the country through subordinate kings or vassals governing large provinces, but from a very early period there was a tradition of a more centralized form of government, and this acquired a sharper definition under the dynasty that ruled from the middle seventeenth century. The Crown, with an Advisory Council serving as the High Court, was the center from which there radiated an official organization linking the hereditary petty chieftains with local affairs.[51]

This closely fits the patterns of the dual polity of the socialist state of Burma in which the R.C. represented the Crown, Advisory Council, and High Court simultaneously and the military commanders served as the executioners of the will of this central body from which radiated the official organization called the Burma Socialist Programme Party. This structure was altered slightly when a New Constitution was adopted in 1973 and the new name of the Socialist Republic of the Union of Burma was adopted in 1974 to formalize the dual polity.

PURIFICATION OF BUDDHISM AND SUBJUGATION OF THE CLERGY

Another evidence of Ne Win's invocation of the legacy of the Burmese Kings was the promulgation of the Promotion and Purification of Buddhism on September 5, 1964, which asserted the divine rights of a king over the Buddhist clerical order. Unlike the Sixth Buddhist Synod held by U Nu, Ne Win extolled himself above the Sayahdaws or heads of the clerical order as the omnipotent enactor and enforcer of laws to purify the Buddhist clergymen. The leading Sayahdaws of various associations of the Buddhist monks staged a violent protest against this action. They not only opposed this move but also the Burmese Way to Socialism itself as incompatible with Buddhism. On March 28, 1964, for example, the order of the R.C. requiring monks to register under the National Solidarity of the Union of Burma Law, provoked anger on the part of the monks at Mandalay who not only wrote articles against the R.C. but also directly attacked Ne Win. The Venerable Shin Uttama led the attack on the "Warning on the Purification of the Sasana Law" advertised in the Mandalay *Bahosi* newspaper by destroying the press.[52] Further protest against the registration requirement was launched by Sayahdaw U Kethaya who told a crowd in Mandalay that he considered Ne Win a *talateson*, an animal, a most derogatory remark on any Burmese.[53] It also led to the destruction of government Party offices and shops.

In lower Burma itself, the submission of the Sayahdaws to "the Promotion and Purification of Buddhism" and requiring monks to register met with the same violent protest at Hmawbi Convention on March 17, 1965, when the monks destroyed Party offices and People's Stores Corporations (P.S.C.s).[54] The collapse of this convention led to a massive arrest of Buddhist monks throughout the country. The R.C. explained these actions as due to the instigation of the opposition through the religious orders tainted with party politics. Hundreds of monks met the same fate of arrest, torture, and jail sentences as other dissenters.

An interesting account of one of the arbitrary arrests was given to this writer by a Buddhist monk, Venerable U Wimila of Monywah. He was jailed by Ne Win because of a monk leader involved in the protest movements. The latter signed the former's name to avoid arrest, which resulted in the arrest of the wrong monk. He was jailed without trial or counsel for 30 months from 1965 to 1967. As he sadly told the author, his prison term lasted a period of two and a half years during which the banyan tree, *nyaungpin*, changed fresh leaves three times. Thirty-seven monks from Mandalay and forty-two monks from Monywah were jammed into a small prison cell along with him. The arrested monks also included young ones under age twenty called *koyins*. The treatment inside the jail was harsh and he spoke of prison guards stealing the food allotted to the monks.

According to U Wimala, the arresting army officer with his rifle stuck behind the monk's back boasted that he had the power to arrest even the stone images of Buddha, let alone monks. This was an example of what this venerable monk labelled Ne Win's method of operation, *danna oupel*, signifying passing arbitrary laws and imposing punishments. At the height of the clerical unrest, the rule of force was used to subdue protest of any kind and hundreds of monks were taken away to prisons in blue paddy wagons, *car pyahs*. For example, in Upper Burma at the city of Monywah where the famous abode of Ledi Sayahdaw, the foremost clerical name associated with the nationalist movement against the British rule, is located, the army mounted a ferocious attack on the Buddhist clergy. As the reverend monk described it, the four main monasteries of this sacred place were surrounded by an army squadron armed with 70-millimeter Howitzers ready to demolish the buildings at any sign of trouble under the direct order of Big Father.

INVOCATION OF ETHNO- AND XENOPHOBIA

The major weapon and perhaps the most effective political weapon deployed by Ne Win throughout his tenure as a ruler was the continual invocation of not only the anticapitalist xenophobic traumas of the colonial past but also the basic ethnophobia or mistrust of minorities. The reduction of the Burmese polity to a simple dual structure was done simply by ruthlessly displacing foreign Orientals from the middle layer of the former colonial triple society and replacing them with the military "Robber Barons" in the socialist state. The rapid and massive nationalization of all foreign enterprises, including those of foreign Orientals, was done within three years leading to a massive exodus of Indian, and to a lesser degree Chinese, entrepreneurs as well as laborers.

However, the effectiveness of this destruction of the middle layer of the society occupied by foreign Orientals was only nominal in the sense that the real functioning of both the polity and economy of Ne Win's socialist state remained in the hands of the offspring of this group, particularly the Sino-Burmese. This will be shown later in discussing the giant black market economy which became the real economy of the so-called socialist economy of the Burmese Way to Socialism. Throughout his political reign, Ne Win would stress that foreigners were the real businessmen and the Burmese, including the military commanders, knew very little about running businesses and the economy. As he said at the 1965 Party Seminar: "The men from our Defense Services know only how to wage war. Formerly they ate what the wife cooked for them."[55] In a rhetorical answer to why the military managers undertook such a task with so little knowledge, he explained that "we had to do so because we wished to establish socialist economy."[56]

In order to rebut the rumors about his Chinese blood, he came out to deny it publicly at the Peasant's Day Address on March 2, 1965: "My ears were bored by my grandmother when I was a few days old. . . . Until I became a novice in the monastery I wore top-knot. For at least three generations our family has been pure Burmese. My forebears made offerings to Talaing nats."[57]

This custom of ear-boring is a defunct practice among the Burmese in contemporary Burma. However, the Koanbaung Kings of the nineteenth century, Kings Min Doan and Thibaw for example, and some of the older generation in remote areas of rural Burma had their ears bored and wore top-knot, indicating that Ne Win was attempting to link himself with this ancient Burmese custom.

It is intriguing to note here that this most typical Buddhist Burmese custom of ear-boring is usually associated with a young girl, not with a boy, and the ear-boring ceremony, *narhtwin*, is performed along with the ceremony of her brother's entry into the novicehood, *shin pyu*. The dead giveaway of his Chinese blood seems to be his original name. Many Chinese and their offspring changed their original Chinese names to hide their racial identity, Aung Gyi for example. The names such as Shu and Yu (San Yu and Tan Yu Saing mentioned above) are only found among the Chinese. Not only his original Chinese name, but also his skin color, which is light or yellow in contrast to the commonly acknowledged dark or coffee-brown color of a true Burmese, and his features seem to nullify his claim of being a true Burmese.[58] Whatever claim he made, it was used to establish his political legitimacy as a "pure Burmese" more than anything else.

As late as 1987 at the B.S.P.P. Congress, Ne Win kept up the attack on businessmen of foreign ancestry.[59] Ne Win used remarks and actions against foreigners in general to construct the socialist state and ensure the political longevity of his dictatorship by playing on the traditional xenophobia of the Burmese masses. The clearest example of the use of this potent weapon to gain popular support for his rule occurred in 1967 when the Cultural Revolution of Chairman Mao of Red China spread inside Burma. The rapid nationalization of the economy and the ruthless suppression of private enterprises in the hands of foreign Orientals in the first half of the 1960s had a disastrous economic consequence. The nation-wide development of a black market-ridden economy in the hands of the incompetent military managers of the People's Stores Corporations resulted in a contrived scarcity of goods including the golden fruit—rice. The credibility and popularity of Ne Win and his R.C. was quite low at that time. In order to divert the dissatisfaction of the Burmese masses, Ne Win took advantage of the Sino-Burmese riot of 1967 when Mao's Red Booklets were carried and Badges were worn by the Chinese students. The R.C.'s prohibition against this led to Sino-Burmese riots in Rangoon and elsewhere in which many Chinese were killed and their shops and homes burned and ransacked by the Burmese mobs.

The political success of the R.C. and its military security forces during these riots revived the popularity of Ne Win as a truly patriotic and nationalist hero once more. The clever political stance he took against Mao and China in connection with this incident was an example of using the xenophobia of the Burmese as a weapon for his political legitimacy. Indeed, the infuriated Chinese government launched criticisms and attacks on Ne Win for the persecution of the Chinese minority which acted as a diversion from the failures of his fake Burmese Way to Socialism and the economic chaos that it created for the masses in Burma.[60] Meanwhile, the Russians applauded Ne Win's stance against China reflecting the cleverness with which Ne Win employed his what will be termed "dialectical neutralism"—a simple strategy of playing off hegemonic powers against one another in the international setting of the Cold War. The United States likewise wholeheartedly approved Ne Win's anti-Chinese stance at that time and his anticommunist stance inside Burma throughout his rulership.

The closing of the decade of the 1960s was marked by Sino-Burmese ideological rifts and armed conflicts along the border involving the insurgency of Burmese communists. Ne Win came out triumphant as national hero in standing up against mighty China, the historical threat to Burma, subduing both the White Flag and the Red Flag communists and suppressing the minority insurgency which had the new dimension of deposed Premier U Nu and his rebellious Parliamentary Democracy Party at the end of 1969. The assassination of Thakin Than Tun, the leader of the White Flag Communist Party, by a member of his own Party in late 1968, the capture of Thakin Soe in 1971, and the successful quelling of U Nu's armed challenge with his Patriotic Liberation Army by 1972, all seemed to establish Ne Win as a mighty soldier.

To maintain his political legitimacy as a mighty soldierly ruler, a continual military assault was made against the minority insurgents in the eastern and western peripheral areas of Burma. His ability and success in waging wars against these insurgents were also helped by the very fragmentation among the minorities themselves. There were not only splits among Shans, Karens, Mons, Kachins, and Arakense but also subfactional groups existed within each of these ethnic groups. The inter-and intra-group conflicts cut across the entire spectrum of the Burmese polity, including the so-called majority Burmese group. In a way, it seemed that each of the main minority groups had been waging a separate war against the central Burmese government for nearly forty years reminiscent of the fragmented and warring city states of ancient Burma. It was only in 1976 that a formal united force, the National Democratic Front (N.D.F.), a coalition of ten minority insurgent groups, was formed under the leadership of Bo Mya, a Karen leader of the Republic of Kawthulay.

In the Shan state alone there were several organizations, among which were the Shan United Army of the infamous opium warlord, Khun Sa, the Tai-land Revolutionary Council, a united group between the Shan United Revolutionary Army and the Shan State Army of Mo Heing, and the Burma Communist

Party joined by communist Shans along with other subgroups of "warlords, spooks, narcs, mercenaries and missionaries in the poppyland."[61] Apart from the majority Shans, there were the Was and the Pa-os with their own political organizations in the Shan state. Although Bo Mya and his Karen National Union, with its left wing and right wing factions, seemed to represent the most militant and unified minority opposition, one must also notice that there were many other sublinguistic Karen groups and organizations, the Karen National Defense Organization, for example, in the Delta Region and elsewhere which had never effectively joined forces with Bo Mya's group. The Mons have been waging their separate wars against the central Burmese government with their own organizations of the Mon Freedom League, and its military wing the Mon National Defense Organization since 1948. The latest organization, the New Mon State Party, nominally joined the N.D.F. The same was true of Brang Seng's Kachin Independence Army, the military wing of the Kachin Independence Organization, which waged a separate war on the northeastern frontier of Burma. Apart from these, the Arakanese had their own insurgent groups on the northwestern frontier of Burma.[62]

The history of minority insurgency over the last forty years reflected the nature of the fragmented nation of traditional Burma with splits and temporary coalitions followed by further splits of various groups. At the beginning of 1970, the Burmese opposition to Ne Win was launched by deposed Premier U Nu in a nominal alliance with the minority insurgents, Karen insurgents in particular, to overthrow Ne Win's regime. This attempt also failed due to friction between U Nu and the minority leadership, resulting in the death of Bo Let Yah, one of the Thirty Comrades and commanders of U Nu's "Liberation Army," and the eventual self-exile of U Nu to India. Isolation due to physical geography and fragmentation due to mistrust between the Burmese and the minorities and among the latter themselves, may be thought of as responsible for their inability to overthrow the majority Burmese government of central Burma. Ne Win's continuous invocation of ethno- and xenophobia also worked successfully because of the basic insecurity of the so-called majority Burmese of central Burma with respect to their ethnic and racial identity.

The nightmare socialist state of Burma under Ne Win was best described by a young man with a Ph.D. degree in economics living abroad who wrote to this author recently in Burmese:

> Dear *Akogyi* (Older Brother),
> Before I give comments on your writing, I think that you should know my present status or psychological condition. I began to work for the government the year the Revolutionary Council came to power. Since I grew up working under "the Reign of Terror," my fears are similar to the "conditioned reflexes" of Pavlov's theory. Whatever I do, I am jumpy with panic and fear. *Akogyi* was lucky, ***kankawn-del***, or had a good karma, for experiencing only briefly what we have lived

through, *Kyaut Hkit*, the Era of Fear. I can only envy and feel proud of your and Dr. Maung Maung Gyi's writings. But I cannot dare to write in the same ways as you two have written openly and critically about the truth of military rule.

This letter typifies the state of mind and psychological conditions of many Burmese who have lived under and experienced the "reign of terror" in the nightmare state of Burma for the last thirty years. They all seem to share the fear of repercussions for speaking out against the still reigning Big Father (*Ah-pai Gyi*) and his military commanders.

NOTES

1. Maung Maung, *General Ne Win*, p. 26.
2. Ibid.
3. Ibid.
4. Ibid.
5. Ibid., p. 133.
6. Ten of these deeds of demerit are similar to violations of the ten commandments of Christianity committed by mouth, thought, and bodily conduct. In Burmese Buddhism, the commandments include sexual indulgence or womanization and alcohol consumption.
7. Maung Maung Gyi, *Burmese Political Values: The Socio-Political Roots of Authoritarianism* (New York: Praeger Publishers, 1983), p. 192.
8. Joseph Silverstein, ed., *The Political Legacy of Aung San* (Ithaca: Cornell University, June 1972), p. 2.
9. Taylor, p. 366.
10. Lucien W. Pye, "The Process of Political Modernization," John J. Johnson ed., *The Role of the Military in Underdeveloped Countries* (Princeton: Princeton University Press, 1962), p. 76.
11. Ibid., p. 246.
12. Walinsky, p. 253.
13. Hagen, *The Theory of Social Change*, p. 55.
14. Foreign Broadcasting Information Service, *Burma* (Washington, D.C.: U.S. Government Publication, April 23, 1990), p. 33. From now on, it will be referred to as F.B.I.S.
15. See Walinsky, p. 165.
16. Pye, "The Army in Burmese Politics," p. 234.
17. Thwin, "1948 and Burma's Myth of Independence," pp. 24–25.
18. John Badgley and Jon A. Wiant, "The Ne Win-BSPP Style of Bama Lo," Joseph Silverstein ed., *The Future of Burma in Perspective: A Symposium* (Athens: Ohio University Center of International Studies, 1974), p. 45.
19. David I. Steinberg, *A Socialist Nation of Southeast Asia* (Boulder: Westview Press, 1982), p. 119 and also, p. 93.

20. See Michael Walzer, "On 'Failed Totalitarianism,'" Irving Howe ed., *1984 Revisited: Totalitarianism in Our Century* (Harper & Row Publishers, 1983), pp. 103–105.

21. Maung Maung Gyi, p. v.

22. Ibid.

23. See Joseph Silverstein, *Burma: Military Rule and the Politics of Stagnation* (Ithaca: Cornell University Press, 1977), Chaps. 3–4.

24. Ibid.

25. Walzer, p. 119.

26. Robert C. Tucker, "Does Big Brother Really Exist?", Irving Howe ed., *1984 Revisited*, p. 92.

27. Cf. Richard Lowenthal, "Beyond Totalitarianism," Irving Howe ed., *1984 Revisited*, p. 209.

28. The Revolutionary Council, *The Burmese Way to Socialism: The Proclamation of the Revolutionary Council's Philosophy* (In Burmese) (Rangoon: Ministry of Information: April 30, 1962), p. 1.

29. Ibid.

30. Cf. C.N. McCoy, "Ludwig Feurbach and the Formation of the Marxian Revolution," Laval Theologique et Philosophique, Vol. VII, No. 2 (1951). Also, see E. Cassirer, *The Myth of State* (Garden City: A Doubleday Anchor Co., 1955), Chap. 1.

31. The Burma Socialist Programme Party, *The System of Correlation of Man to His Environment: The Philosophy of the Burma Socialist Programme Party* (Rangoon: Ministry of Information, January 17, 1963), p. 3.

32. Ibid.

33. Lowenthal, p. 212.

34. From the source of Aung Gyi's *40-Page Letter* (In Burmese) dated May 9, 1988.

35. See Taylor, p. 366.

36. From the source of A Retired Burmese Army Officer, *Thuelo Lu* or *That Type of Man* (In Burmese) (Koln: Committee for Restoration of Democracy in Burma, West Germany, 1988), p. 5.

37. Ibid., p. 33.

38. B.S.P.P., Central Organization Committee, *Party Seminar 1965* (Rangoon: Sahpai Beikhman Press, February 1966), p. 33.

39. Ibid., p. 28.

40. Ibid., pp. 29–30.

41. *The 1958 Union of Burma Penal Code, Vol. VIII* (Rangoon: Ministry of Justice, 1958), p. 53.

42. See *A Short History of the Actions of the Revolutionary Council* (In Burmese) (Rangoon: Union of Burma Buddhist Affairs Association, March 2, 1974), p. 374.

43. See for detail U Aung Than Tun, *Four Eras of Burmese Laws* (In Burmese) (Rangoon: Kalaung Pyan Press, 1968), pp. 224–226.

44. U Thaung, "Burma: A Case Study in Press Repression," *Freedom At Issue*, No. 16 (New York: Freedom Foundation, May–June, 1981), p. 19.

45. Ibid., p. 20.

46. Ibid.

47. From the source of U Thaung, "The King's Blessing to a Free Press," *A Tale of Two Journalists* (A Manuscript in Preparation, 1990).

48. Ibid.

49. *Party Seminar 1965*, pp. 102–106.

50. U Thaung, "Paid in Gold," *Reader's Digest*, Vol. 113, No. 676 (New York: The Reader's Digest Association, August 1978).

51. Furnivall, *Colonial Policy*, p. 14.

52. See *Party Seminar*, pp. 62–65.

53. Sterling Seagrave, pp. 64–65.

54. *Party Seminar*, pp. 62–65.

55. Ibid., p. 191.

56. Ibid.

57. Ne Win, "Peasant Day Address," *Forward, Vol. III, No. 15*, Rangoon, March 2, 1965.

58. The most widely acknowledged skin color of a pure Burmese among the natives of Burma is coffee-brown or as the Burmese call it, *athar nyo*. In my own inquiry about the Chinese background of the military commanders and members of the Revolutionary Council, this fact was consistently used by my interviewees to state a particular individual is pure Burmese and not Sino-Burmese.

59. *The Working People's Daily* (Rangoon: Government Press, October 10, 1987), p. 1.

60. See *New China News Agency* (Peking: July 23, 1967), pp. 20–21.

61. Sterling Seagrave, "Burma's Golden Triangle: Warlords, Spooks, Narcs, Mercenaries & Missionaries," *Soldier of Fortune* (Denver: Soldier of Fortune, May, 1984).

62. For details of these groups, see Joseph Silverstein's privately published paper, *Insurgency and Rebellion in Burma* (Hawaii: Defense Intelligence College, United States Pacific Command, March, 1989).

6

The Burma Road to Poverty

The Burma Road to Poverty began soon after the Revolutionary Council (R.C.) took hold of the political reins in the name of "saving Burma" and the "Burmese Way to Socialism." The R.C.'s pattern of strategies and actions was cyclical with respect to tightening and loosening both political and economic controls internally and externally. As was shown before, soon after the military coup of 1962, extreme centralization of political power was rapidly done by total suppression of all opposition and ruthless violations of the fundamental human rights of the people of Burma. However, in the political arena, Ne Win pursued a traditional practice of Burmese kings which involved total subjugation, pacification, and a continual purging of potential contenders for the political throne. The same type of strategy was pursued in the economic arena where tightening, relaxing, and further tightening of controls were used to appease the impoverished masses and guard the political throne.

The exogenous dimension of the above patterns of actions was to deter foreign interest and influence, on the one hand, and gain both political and economic aid from major foreign donors, on the other. For example, the adoption of a single-party political system and the construction of a socialist economy of the Sino-Soviet type gave the military regime of Ne Win favorable relations with Russia and China, while the waging of war against communists inside Burma established the same with the United States and the Free World. Personal and diplomatic visits of Ne Win and officials of China and other Eastern European countries were frequent during 1962 and 1965, followed by Ne Win's visit to the United States in 1966. In fact, President Johnson warmly welcomed the General and hailed him as a truly nationalist leader and a good family man.[1] During the same year, Ne Win also visited Japan and Thailand to convey that his foreign policy was truly neutral. In the international setting of the

Cold War, Ne Win's foreign policy of "dialectical neutralism" seemed to work rather well in maintaining his dictatorship over Burma. By 1974, foreign aid from the West would begin to pour into the Socialist Republic of the Union of Burma.

THE END OF THE REVOLUTIONARY COUNCIL GOVERNMENT

The process of subjugation and pacification of opposition was applied to former civilian politicians most of whom were released by 1968. In 1969, Ne Win convened a talk with all opposition groups for amnesty and participation in the Burmese Way to Socialism without success. To be certain, this kind of token action was taken only after the popular support of the leading political figures reached a state of impotence. Such actions also tended to establish Ne Win as a benevolent ruler rather than a ruthless one in the eyes of various observers. U Nu, U Ba Swe, and others were released from prison in 1966, the former on condition that he leave the country and disavow any intention of reentering politics. Aung Gyi (arrested in late 1963) and U Kyaw Nyein were released in 1968. Of course, U Nu left the country stating that he would go on a religious pilgrimage, but did not abide by this condition and staged his armed challenge in 1970.

The most glaring failures of the Burmese Way to Socialism were in the economic arena. The sweeping nationalization of the economy and the running of state-controlled enterprises by self-admitted unskilled military managers immediately produced economic crises caused by corruption, evasions of controls, and various loopholes in the socialist economy of Burma during the short period of two years. The most notorious disaster developed in the management of the People's Stores Corporation under the directorship of Brigadier Tin Pe. By 1964, it had to be dissolved and replaced by another inefficient government agency called the Trade Council. The net effect of total nationalization and control of procurement and distribution of basic necessities, particularly rice, produced a nation-wide giant black market which came to be known initially as Corporation No. 24 and later as No. 23.

The inner-power struggle and purging by Ne Win within the R.C. began immediately in 1963 and the main casualty was Brigadier Aung Gyi. His resignation or dismissal was due to a policy dispute and direct personal feud with Brigadier Tin Pe who replaced him as the second-in-command of the military junta. Aung Gyi was jailed for four and a half years for his alleged involvement in the dynamiting of the Rangoon University's Student Union Building and his opposition to the economic programs of the B.S.P.P. In any event, this was a political ploy to use a scapegoat for the destruction of the symbol of political freedom and nationalist movements against the British. Brigadier Tin Pe would also be purged from his post as the Minister of the Trade Council in 1968 for his mismanagement of the P.S.C.s and his Ministry. Other casualties of the R.C. included Commander Than Pe (died 1962), Brigadier T. Clift (resigned 1964), Colonel Than Sein (retired), Colonel Kyaw Soe (retired), Colonel Saw Myint (life sentence 1964), Colonel Maung Shwe (retired and arrested in 1972), Colonel Chit Myine (dismissed 1964), Colonel Khin Nyo (dismissed 1965), and Colonel Tan Yu Saing (resigned 1968).

In 1972, when Ne Win and his loyal commanders discarded army uniforms and assumed the civilian title of "U" to become full-fledged politicians, six out of the seventeen original members, San Yu, Sein Win, Than Sein, Kyaw Soe, Hla Han, and Thaung Kyi were left. Some of them retired from the army and later became members of the Council of State in 1974. Apart from one natural death, most of the original members were either forced to retire or resign from the army and the R.C. on charges ranging from mismanagement, money laundering, black marketeering, and corruption to collaboration with the opposition. Some of them were sent abroad as emissaries and others defected or went to prison. Often two or more members met their downfall in association with each other, as in the case of Tan Yu Saing and Tin Pe who were brothers-in-law. This is reminiscent of the royal politics of ancient Burma, verifying the Burmese saying *minhka yaukkyar karnnar thit pin*—those who serve the king are like trees on the precarious bank of a river.

THE ECONOMICS OF PLANNED CHAOS

The end of the Revolutionary Council government was marked by a decade of economic chaos due to mismanagement and corruption unparalleled in the economic history of Burma. The political success of subduing political foes by force was matched by the economic failures of a military command economy leading to the development of a nation-wide black market economy. The most glaring failure occurred in the agricultural sector, rice production and procurement in particular, which was historically the backbone of the Burmese economy. The destruction of the private market economy in the creation of a utopian socialist economy of "planned proportional development" by the R.C. precipitated a vicious circle of controls-evasions-controls during the 1960s. The net effect of the sweeping nationalization of the economy was the first step towards the Burma Road to Poverty.

THE NEW DOUBLE DUAL ECONOMY OF SOCIALIST BURMA

Structurally and functionally, the military command economy of Burma may be looked upon as a double dual economy somewhat similar to, but different from, the double colonial dual economy of Burma. The double dual or triple economy of colonial Burma consisted of the two dual aspects of the coexistence of a small modern sector with modern production function and a large traditional sector with primitive production function along with the third feature of alien dominance of the modern sector. By getting rid of the third element of alien enterprises or trader-financiers, the socialist economy of Burma became a pure double dual economy. In the new socialist economy of Burma under military management, the first duality remained largely intact, and replacing all private enterprises by state enterprises created another dual economy of official versus black market sectors. It is this duality that caused disastrous failures and consequences with respect to economic growth and income distribution in the new double dual economy of socialist Burma.

The construction of a centralized economy fashioned after the Sino-Soviet model was definitely welcomed by the communist world. As a reporter of *Pravda* aptly described the socialist economy of Burma in 1966: "All the foreign companies, all banks, the entire transport system, the entire foreign and domestic and wholesale domestic trade and all the main branches of industry have been nationalized. The creation of any new capitalist enterprises and foreign investment in the national economy have been prohibited. The new power is firmly controlling and channelling the development of the national economy."[2]

The replacement of all foreign and private enterprise by state enterprises produced a dual economy of official versus private black market economies. The nationalization of all foreign enterprises and prohibition of foreign investment formally destroyed the middle layer of foreign Orientals in the colonial and civilian plural society. However, foreign Orientals born in Burma, particularly the Chinese and their offspring, continued to control the real economy, namely, the giant black market.

With respect to its ideal form, the R.C. formally adopted a command centralized economy of the Sino-Soviet type. According to the *System of Correlation of Man to His Environment*, it aspired to build "a socialist economy of the planned porportional development of all national forces" via the state ownership and control of all means of production, trade, finance, and industry to achieve the socialist society envisaged by Marx as "the participation of all for the general well-being of all, deriving the benefits derived therefrom."[3] Unfortunately, the dearth of competent planners, managers, and implementors of such a centralized economy created a nominal and ineffective giant superstructure of congested and disorganized state enterprises run by military commanders with no managerial capacity, knowledge, or experience. The simple replacement of private by state enterprises was a creation of a network of loopholes which eventually became channels for developing not the national economy but the giant black market economy "participated in by all for the general well-being of a few, deriving the benefits therefrom."

A NOMINAL MILITARY COMMAND ECONOMY

The total state monopoly of the economy was formally established by nationalization of all enterprises and creation of a giant superstructure of twenty-three state corporations controlled and managed by military commanders who assumed the titles of *wungyis* or ministers and directorship of former governmental departments. It was a nominal command economy in the sense that most of the former state agencies, departments, and boards remained intact while assuming new names, and the real economy was the unofficial black market economy. Former civil servants continued to function in the actual administration of various state enterprises under the command of the military managers. Most of the twenty-three state corporations of the R.C. were simply the former state boards and departments such as the State Agricultural Marketing Board and the State Timber Board. Various government agencies came to assume the new names of Corporation No. 1, No. 2, etc. The only change made was the replacement of top civilian managers by army officers and B.S.P.P. members.

The sale, distribution, and export of all produce were monopolized by state enterprises under the direct control of the Ministry of Trade, formerly known as the Civil Supply Department under the British government and the Civil Supply Management Board under the U Nu government. The Minister in charge of this powerful state organ was Brigadier Tin Pe who replaced Brigadier Aung Gyi in the power echelon of the Revolutionary Council. All in all, twenty-two People's Stores or Trade Corporations (*Pa Pa Ka*) were created or rather renamed to institute a system of total state capitalism and the entire financial sector of the economy was owned and operated by People's Banks. This surgical transformation of the quasi-private economy of the previous civilian government was made by the simple stroke of abolishing all private enterprises within three years after the military coup of 1962.

Soon after this action was taken, the Burmese economy suffered a dramatic decline in production and export with a concurrent development of loopholes emanating from the state enterprises themselves. The development of a parallel private economy in the form of black markets under the very eyes of the military controllers was immediate and unstoppable. It first occurred domestically, followed by a huge lucrative border trade along the Chinese and Thai borders. The giant black market or Corporation No. 24, as it was called in the 1960s, later known as Corporation No. 23, became the real economy of the nominal military command economy of the Burmese socialist state for the next thirty years.

Before discussing in detail the giant black market of the Burmese economy, two major economic actions with drastic consequences taken by the R.C. deserve attention to highlight the immense inefficiency and planned chaos of the Burmese Way to Socialism. The first one relates to the control of production, procurement, and distribution of rice and other basic necessities associated with the infamous People's Stores Corporation under the management of its infamous Director, Brigadier Tin Pe. The second one relates to the monetary weapon of "demonetization" of various notes, which would become the main ritual of the R.C. in waging war on inflation and black marketeering in the socialist economy of Burma. In the name of fair price, equity, and raising the standard of living of the people of Burma, these two basic measures of state control and other monopolies of internal and external trade were established by confiscating the property, plants, and equipment of all private businesses and factories without fair compensation.

From 1962 to 1964, the R.C. promulgated fourteen major Socialist Economy Laws and created the Socialist Economy Construction Committee (S.E.C.C.), which was empowered to take over the assets of all enterprises, including the former state-sponsored Defence Services businesses such as the Defence Services Institute, Burma Economic Development Corporation, and over thirty-five different military corporations, the Fishery Board, the People's Pearl, Rice Mills, along with all foreign firms and twenty-two foreign banks. Some of the more famous laws were the Tenancy Act (1963), the Agricultural Produce Procurement Act (1962), the People's Stores Corporation Act (1963), the Demonetization Act (1964), the People's Banking Act (1963), and the Law to Protect the Construction of the Socialist Economy (1963). With all of these laws and subsequent amendments, the economy of Burma came to be primarily owned and operated by state agencies and enterprises. By 1964, inefficiency due to mismanagement and corruption ensued, and the functioning of the economy was thrown into a vicious cycle of controls-evasions-controls whereby the infamous P.S.C. had to be overhauled and nominally replaced by another equally inefficient agency called the Trade Council to take over the functions of procurement and distribution of goods. Some case studies will help to highlight the development of the nation-wide black market which ultimately became the economic lifeline of both the military elite and the entire populace of Burma.

THE AGRICULTURAL BLACK MARKET

The most glaring case of the incompetent military managers' inefficiency in managing the centralized command economy of Burma was in the agricultural sector. To begin with, since 1948 the agricultural land of Burma had belonged to the state, which had immediately nationalized land in general to get rid of the Indian land owners under the Two-Year Development Plan and the Land Nationalization Act of 1948. The Two-Year Development Plan was put into effect only in 1951 and the Land Nationalization Act was enforced the same year and renewed again in 1953. These two important economic programs of the civilian government had virtually eliminated alien landlordism by 1958. Close to 3.5 million acres were redistributed to the cultivators by the end of 1961.[4] By the time the R.C. took over the political reins, there was no private landed class in Burma equivalent to the *hacendados* or *latifundistas* of Latin America. The economic programs of the R.C. did not need to seize any farm land which was already in the hands of the native farmers. Instead, by wiping out all private markets, it simply required farmers to sell their produce to the only buyer, namely, the state buying depots. Thus, the ownership of farm lands remained in private hands but the outlets for their livelihood and income now resided with the state.

Having been unable to find a large native landlord class or landed aristocracy (which had never existed throughout the history of Burma with the exception of the Indian money lenders in the colonial period), the R.C. attacked the previous civilian government system of tenancy as the perpetuation of a mythical feudal system. It charged that the renewed Land Nationalization Act and the Tenancy Act of 1953 were not beneficial for the peasants and that they did not free them "from exploitation of the capitalists and landlords."[5] It passed a new Tenancy Act in 1963 putting a ceiling on annual tenancy rent on lands planted with various crops. The fixing of rent was deemed to limit the power of the landlords who previously had been able to demand whatever they wanted for exploitation. However, this arbitrary fixing of rent was accompanied by another system that forced the peasants to sell their output at fixed prices. In 1965, the Law to Amend the 1963 Tenancy Act was passed abolishing all forms of rent and establishing the right of ownership only to the tiller of land.[6]

The rural economy of Burma was flooded with state buying depots, land committees, agricultural banks, multipurpose co-operatives, and a few state collective farms, co-operative villages, and machine-tractor stations designed after the model of the Sino-Soviet command economy. This quantitative push on the agricultural front was a natural political action by the R.C. in an agricultural economy such as Burma's, where the Marxian "mode of production" is typified in "the agricultural reserved army of the tillers of soil" rather than "the industrial reserved army of the unemployed proletariat" as such. The model of the economy designed and adopted was popularly labeled "the three-pronged model" similar to that of the German Democratic Republic made up of the public, the co-operative, and the so-called private sectors. In reality, it was a totally centralized economy of state capitalism in the internal and external sectors of the economy. At this juncture, how a giant black market in both rural and urban sectors of the economy originated from the agricultural sector may be described.

THE ADVANCE PURCHASE OF PADDY SYSTEM

In order to stimulate productivity and create incentives to sell to government depots, the only buyers, the R.C. began to advance agricultural loans at low rates of interest and instituted the Advance Purchase of Paddy System in the name of eradicating the methods of landlords and capitalists. This system was nothing really new since the former government agency of the civilian government, the State Agricultural Marketing Board (S.A.M.B.), had been doing the same since 1948. In the civilian government era, however, there was an alternative outlet for sale of paddy and rice other than the state buying depots, namely, private buyers. In the 1950s, the uniform price of rice offered to the farmers by the S.A.M.B. irrespective of seasonal or regional fluctuations led to economic waste and inefficiency. A Burmese economist, Dr. Hla Myint noted that at times when private demand slackened, the government warehouses would become flooded with rice, leading to waste, and remarked that "Many economists visiting in the 1950s characteristically overlooked this 'simple' but extremely wasteful misallocation of resources in their preoccupation with the more elaborate development plans, including the expansion of investment in 'infrastructure.'"[7]

The R.C. went far beyond the Pyidawthah Government's development endeavors and programs in their preoccupation with revolutionary socialism by completely annihilating the private market mechanism and institutions. The net effect was economic waste and inefficiency unparalleled in the entire economic history of Burma.

The benevolent and novel aspects of the new advance purchase paddy system, the *pintaung*, introduced in the name of the Burmese Way to Socialism, were explained by the designers in this way: "The *pintaung* system of the capitalists was used by them to gain 100 percent profit on their capital within a few months. The capitalists bought the standing crops at half of what they would be worth at the time of harvest. The system of purchase employed by the Revolutionary Council was procurement at the price which would prevail at the time of harvesting."[8] As to how the R.C. arrived at the prevalent price at the time of harvesting, no scientific explanation or econometric model was given. In the absence of the free interplay of market forces and given the state monopsony of paddy and rice, the so-called fair and equitable offered price was meaningless. This was *de facto* exploitation by the new state carpetbaggers or capitalists who had a monopoly of internal and external trade.

Immediately after the new system was installed, farmers found a thriving unofficial market instituted by private market-makers from urban centers who offered prices consistently higher than those of the state buyers. The natural outcome of this system then was the evasion of the forced sale to the state buying depots and the channeling of paddy and rice by the farmers to the more profitable outlet of the black markets. A price spiral in the form of low state procuring prices chasing the runaway black market prices was set into motion. The fixed uniform price of procurement was kept constant for more than a decade between 1962 and 1974. It was changed upward by 50 percent for the first time in 1974 on the advice of potential foreign aid donors from the West with very little success in obtaining a sufficient supply of paddy and rice for distribution by state shops.

THE CASE OF MAUNG PYONE—A BURMESE FARMER

At this juncture, various models of individual cases will be given for the purpose of highlighting the real nature and functioning of the military command economy. All the cases in this chapter and the next one are based upon actual interviews with those who lived through and personally experienced the impact of various programs launched and enforced in the name of the Burmese Way to Socialism by the Revolutionary Council Government between 1962 and 1988. The statistical data used in these cases came directly from private sources rather than the official reports whose reliability is suspect. In fact, the General himself called for revisions of statistical reports by his unreliable Party officials in the early 1980s. The gap between the micro- and macroindicators of the performance of the socialist economy of Burma has been great since the compilers of official statistics are highly vulnerable to persecution for critical reports.

The following is a model of how a Burmese farmer named Maung Pyone or Mr. Smile learned to evade the new system of forced sale to avoid loss, *mashoan aung*, or make profit on what he produced. This is a general process applicable to all Burmese peasants and based upon interviews with an owner and operator of a rice mill and black marketeers in the Delta Region. Maung Pyone has tilled the soil since childhood, planting, reaping, and harvesting of paddy with his parents in his village. He inherited fifteen acres of land (less than the upper limit of twenty acres set by the government for eligibility to receive agricultural loans) from his father and earned his livelihood. Prior to 1962, during the civilian government era, he could sell his paddy in the field (standing rice crop) to the state buyer who visited his village and entered into a contract with him for rice for the state buying depot located in a town some five miles away from his village. He had an option to sell to buyers other than the state buying depots and received an agricultural loan from the village State Agricultural Bank at 6 percent. The repayment of the loan could be made in kind and so he would deal with the state buyer of his rice after he milled the paddy with a private rice mill. Occasionally, he would sell in the private market depending on the price differential between its price and the price offered by the state.

In 1962, everything changed when the government nationalized private mills and the entire private rice market. His option of private sale was virtually wiped out. He had to enter into a contract with the new team of Corporation No. 1, formerly S.A.M.B., under the new system. It seemed attractive at first in terms of receiving lower interest rate loans (3 percent instead of 6 percent repayable in kind) from a new People's Bank and cash from advance sale at a higher price (the maximum of K3.85 per basket) than the maximum price of K3 per basket offered by the former S.A.M.B.'s buying depots of the civilian government. He also saw the formation of a new Land Committee, a village S.A.C., a Peasant Council of the B.S.P.P., and a Multi-purpose Co-operative which were involved in his procurement of cultivation and harvesting loans (K25 and K5 per acre, respectively) as well as his advance sale contract and delivery of paddy after the harvest.

In connection with the economic benefits and education imparted to the peasants by this new system, the R.C. explained:

> Some of the paddy of *ngakywe* and *meedon* variety, being of the long-maturing quality, would not become available in those three months [December, January and February] but only in March, April and May. The prevailing prices in those later months would be higher than the earlier months. But the paddy would be procured at prices calculated on the earlier months and set out in the purchase agreements. Since the peasants already have received the value of sales without interest at an earlier date they would not lose on that account. Education was provided to the peasants in the matter.[9]

However, Maung Pyone learned very early on that this so-called interest-free loan in the form of the advance sale received was substantially less beneficial to him than the higher prices he could have obtained if he had had the option to sell his paddy to private buyers at a later date.

It seemed that the hedging against the risk of a downward slide in price provided by this forced future contract benefited the government, which had a monopoly of internal and external trade, more than Maung Pyone, since the latter had to give up the opportunity of a higher return with no option in case of upward movements of price. This opportunity cost to the farmers underlined the spontaneous development of an unofficial market. In fact, the education he received was that the inefficient rationing system introduced by the government in towns across Burma had created a buoyant market in which the price of rice was several times higher than the price at government shops. In view of the risk-return trade-off and abnormal profit that could be made in unofficial private markets, Maung Pyone found out how to beat the new system.

He found ways to evade the forced sale under the new system by mixing the paddy he had to deliver with sand, pebbles, and other condiments, or selling his *wunsah* paddy to ready buyers, or bribing corrupt officials. An interesting story of how a farmer like Maung Pyone tricked the government buyer relates to selling his paddy at the right time of the day during the harvesting season when the contracts of advanced purchase are due. For instance, the harvesting occurs in rural Burma during the winter months and the harvested paddy weighs heavier when wet with dew at night or in the early morning hours. One should notice here that the Burma winter has no snowfall and only heavy dew gathers on the crops at night and in early morning. Thus, the right time of sale chosen by a clever farmer would be the early morning hours instead of late in the day when a basket of paddy requires more grains of the less heavy dry paddy.

Joining the B.S.P.P. and involvement with the village People's Peasants' Council was almost a must in the life of Maung Pyone in order to secure loans and other favorable treatment from the officers of these institutions. He had never seen so many officials visiting and lecturing on the subject of how benevolent the Burmese Way to Socialism was, and *sitboes*, army officers with green uniforms, replaced the former civilian officials in charge of the new system. In a way, nothing had really changed since he was used to dealing with former state officials, and township and district civil servants, *myoeoats* and *wundauks*. They all symbolized the privileged persons of power and authority, *ahnah* and *awezah*. He had known how to treat and pay respect to gain favor since the days he began to earn his livelihood.

In a normal or bumper crop year, he fulfilled his future contract, either milled or unhusked his paddy by traditional methods for the necessary rice required to feed his own family, *wunsah*, and his economic lot seemed healthy. However, in a bad crop year when he could not repay the loan payable in kind and deliver his future contract, things began to look bad since he was subject to penalty and must appear before the S.A.C. and other government officials of the B.S.P.P. The law of the jungle began to operate, setting off a chain reaction of harsh actions. Higher authority at each layer of the command economy sequentially imposed harsh treatments on the lower authorities or personnel with the net effect of dismissal, replacement, and corruption.

Maung Pyone also learned from the only newspaper, *Working People's Daily*, that in Rangoon and elsewhere many persons, including high military commanders, were occasionally purged, arrested, and jailed for engaging in activities considered as "Opposition to the Construction of the Socialist Economy." He became skillful and educated in how to avoid being caught as well as developing connections with Party members, powerful officials, and private dealers for his economic survival. He also saw, in the river, boats of dealers from the urban centers busily lined up along the side of the government barges buying rice from the state officials who were in charge of hauling rice to the cities. In addition to rice, other crops and basic necessities began to disappear from the shelves of government shops throughout Burma, and the foundation of a parallel economy infested with black marketeering was firmly established. Maung Pyone also found out that he could deal in other commodities such as gems, opium, and foreign products which were many times more lucrative than rice by traveling to the Chinese or Thai border.

He attended the B.S.P.P. Seminar in 1965 and heard the Chairman of the Revolutionary Council, Big Father, speak on the subject close to his heart concerning the causes of the failure of the People's Stores Corporation (P.S.C.): "I should like to talk about the notorious People's Stores Corporation. Like rain on the river they send oil to Magwe [which was the wrong town]. This may be due to dishonest intentions or to lack of skill. Our people handle rice market but they know so little of the trade."[10]

Maung Pyone nodded and cracked a faint smile at the speech which went on at length about how unskilled the military managers from Defense Services, and also former politicians, and former private entrepreneurs and capitalists who were asked to help, were in matters of commodity distribution, transportation, planning, and foreign trade. As Ne Win said:

> We are unskilled people assembled. The skilled people we ask to help are not really skilled. They do not know how to deal in foreign trade. . . . I select one person on hearing good accounts of him. He voiced enthusiasm. . . . At that time we were making arrangements to buy maize and beans. He knew of this from inside. He was aware of the prices. He told his former connections. They went out to buy up the commodities from the peasants at reduced prices. For instance, where prices would be K5 they paid K3 or K4. We were going to procure these commodities for export. When we made arrangements and sent out buyers we found that the commodities were no longer in the hands of the peasants but had been taken by the merchants. I had to have him removed. . . . They may understand to steal but do not know how to handle international trade and are ignorant of international prices.[11]

As to who ultimately and skillfully conducted foreign trade, he intimated that the business of the unskilled native merchants "has to be put in the hands of Chinese, Indian, and English merchants."[12] The xenophobic attack on foreign entrepreneurs for the failures of the system was quite apparent in his speech.

Throughout his military dictatorship, the above theme of blaming the unskilled natives whom he labeled as "lazy bones" and skilled foreign capitalists would become a repeated emphasis in his speeches. These curious explanations of the functioning of the centralized command economy managed by the unskilled military controllers may be full of holes but contained some truth about the nature, origin, and functioning of the giant black market that cut across the entire spectrum of the Burmese economy. He seemed also to underestimate the dexterity with which evasions were made by simple folks, Maung Pyone for instance, in a system of inefficient direct controls. Indeed, this story of Mr. Smile exemplifies how an economy of the Sino-Soviet type spontaneously develops a black market economy when a centralized command economy is forced upon the people from the top in the name of revolutionary socialism. The outcome of this grand design has been a negative utopian state of contrived scarcity and poverty in the case of Burma.

THE CASE OF SHU MAUNG—A RICE MILL OWNER

Shu Maung or Mr. "Handsome to Look at" was a Chinese born in Burma; his grandfather settled in British Burma at the town of Pathain or Bassein as the British called it. His parents gave him a Burmese name to avoid the discrimination and mistreatment of the Chinese by the state. He worked as a part-time manager of the rice mill owned by his uncle during summer vacations and learned the trade while he was attending the Rangoon University. He became the manager and began to operate the rice mill left to him by his uncle in 1960, two years before the military coup. In 1963–64, his mill was confiscated by the R.C. without any compensation whatsoever; he saw military officers take over the mill. The mechanics and laborers continued to work for the new state-owned-and-operated mill under the direct command of the military managers. Within the span of two years, the productivity of the mill declined drastically due to the disincentive effects of forced sale, low pay, corruption, and mismanagement at all levels. Often the mill remained idle and unrepaired in the hands of technically incompetent military managers.

Due to the technical incompetence and corruption of the local military managers, the state found itself unable to procure sufficient rice for internal distribution and export. The R.C. had to denationalize the rice mills in an attempt to increase productivity. To the surprise of Shu Maung, the mill was returned to him in 1966 and the R.C. demanded that he must begin operations with his own capital and enter a milling contract with the state Trade Council, the new name of the reorganized P.S.C. If he refused to operate he would be indicted under the 1964 Law to Protect the Construction of the Socialist Economy from Opposition, which could result in a jail sentence. The new Trade Council provided funds to cover the minimum milling costs of this forced contract which were barely sufficient to run the mill. Thus, the run-down mill was repaired and revived with his own capital and former mill workers were reemployed.

His was a big mill with a capacity of milling 30,000 baskets of paddy or 120 tons of rice output on a maximum fifteen-hour work load, the usual milling work load averaging about ten hours per day. The medium mill has a capacity of milling sixty tons, while the small mill has a capacity under sixty tons. On the basis of the planting and harvesting cycle, the mill would operate at full capacity for approximately six months. Hence, the mill workers had full-time work only half a year and they had to find some other odd jobs to support their families. The minimum daily wage rate was K3.15 or a monthly wage of roughly K63 (assuming five working days per week) for six months. Often, the mill worker had to work overtime on the weekend if he could, which paid a double daily wage. The factory workers also took up black marketeering to supplement their income, involving not only good rice but also broken rice, *san hpwell*, which later became an item for consumption.

Shu Maung also learned that there were two different types of rice for milling: an ordinary quality rice for shipment to Trade Stores of P.S.C.s at urban centers and a high quality rice marked for the consumption of high-ranking military ministers, civilian deputy ministers, directors, and Party officials who were in charge of running the socialist state. The latter was called in Burmese *aindaw san* or "rice for glorious homes" or satirically *bogyi ma-ma san* or "rice taken away by army officers." The high quality rice, such as *ngakywe* and *pathain* for example, was reserved for sale at special shops such as the Padonmah and Myittah Mon in Rangoon, the center of political power. These two shops were set up for the top and middle elites and their families, respectively. They stored goods of all kinds, domestic and foreign, and their shelves were never empty. Not only rice, cooking oil, gasoline, and other basic necessities but also luxury products from foreign lands were sold at discount at these shops to ministers, directors, commanders, and V.I.P.s of the B.S.P.P. They were often directly delivered to the doorsteps of the civilian and military elites by their subordinates. The *aindaw san* was a part of the total contract to which special attention must be paid by the mill owner and the procurement officers alike.

As for the farmers, they could now take their *wunsah* paddy to private small mills and sell them to the owners of the mills at higher prices than those of the state buyers. The owners of the mills in turn would deal directly with the unofficial dealers above their purchase price. The factory workers could also do the same. Not only pure rice but also broken rice began to capture higher prices in the black market. Thus, the majority of good quality rice bought at the very source of production found its way into black markets engulfing the entire economy without ever reaching the distribution shops of the government. Most of the rice that could be bought on a rationed basis per family per week at these shops was low quality rice called *ngasein*, which was never consumed prior to 1962 even by the middle-income urban families.

This was true of some 400 commodities which were nationalized for distribution at one time in the construction of the socialist economy by the R.C. By 1966, corruption and leakages of goods from government shops and factories became so rampant and uncontrollable that thirty-four items other than rice had to be denationalized.[13] These were mostly perishable consumer goods, such as fish and their related products, chillies, and onions, which became rotten and were wasted at government warehouses. The participants in the private black markets included simple folks and elites alike whose wages were also under control. The pay scale of the entire working population, which now worked for state employers in all professions, was kept constant to combat inflation. The supposedly low and fair prices of goods sold by government shops became meaningless in the face of shortages of goods, rationing, and constant wages. The following case of an urban family's economic life will help to illustrate how the Burma Road to Poverty was established.

THE CASE OF HLA MAUNG

Hla Maung or Mr. Handsome was the son of a civilian politician who obtained his high school diploma in 1956 from the famous missionary English Methodist High School where his classmates were the children of both civilian and military elites. At that time he was called Michael Hla Maung by his teachers and peers. He received his B.A. undergraduate degree in economics from the University of Rangoon in 1960 and worked for the civilian government as the manager of the Co-operative Societies Department of the Union of Burma in Rangoon. After 1962, he dropped the English prefix to his name like many others who changed their names to pure Burmese forms for fear of discrimination and assumed the anti-Western posture required by the "Burmese Way to Socialism" of the R.C.

Prior to 1962, he earned a base monthly salary, as a gazetted officer, of K350 (roughly $70) plus a cost of living allowance of K85 more or a total monthly income of K435[14] to support his wife and two young children. The annual increment of his salary was K25 for a fourteen year period. The price of a 16 *pyis* basket (4.68 pounds per *pyi*) of rice in the private market was relatively low at K11 or so. Thus 7.6 percent of his monthly income (assuming the maximum monthly consumption of three baskets for four persons) would purchase more than sufficient to feed his family, since the average monthly consumption of his family was two to three baskets of good quality rice. Thus, the most important item of daily consumption in the monthly cost of living of his family was less than 8 percent of his total monthly income. Similarly, the prices of cooking oil, fish, chicken, onions, chillies, clothing, and other basic necessities were affordable and remained within the means of his income. Education for his children was also free and his economic life was at ease.

Beginning in 1963, his economic life changed drastically even though he retained his job with the same department. The private market for basic necessities vanished and in its place the P.S.C. appeared as the only market distribution center. His section of Rangoon was now demarcated as a special section with a number and his family had to register to secure a government booklet called a Commodity Purchase Book, Konwel Yay Sah-oat, or Oil Certificate, Si Let-hmart, for short. Oil certificate refers to cooking oil, the second most important item of consumption in the Burmese diet, although the booklet may be used to purchase rationed rice and other basic necessities for the household. For those who had an automobile (a state vehicle was provided to a government official with a monthly income of K800 and up), another certificate called *datsi let-hmart*, gasoline certificate, was issued to buy the rationed gasoline per week from the gasoline station owned and operated by the state. He saw residents lining up with these booklets weekly to purchase supplies in front of various government shops at prices set by the government. The prices were quite low and comparable to prices before, although the waiting and queuing for purchase became increasingly cumbersome.

Within a year or so, the supply of goods at these shops relative to the allotment by quota per family per week began to dwindle and sales became irregular. The problem of feeding his family became increasingly difficult. For often, whenever goods were available, they were rationed on the basis of a lottery system by the managers of the P.S.C.s. The majority of the time, the only available rice at these shops was the low quality rice, *nga sein*, which he and his family had never consumed before. The price per basket of good quality rice, *nga kywe*, at these shops also climbed above K12 by 1963. He also witnessed the growth of an unofficial market where he could purchase good quality rice for his family at a price of K28 and more.[15] He could sell his allotment of rice purchased on the spot right in front of these state shops where private dealers would pay a slightly higher price for his rice. The cost of the rice his family consumed had gone up above 20 percent of his income compared with less than 8 percent prior to 1962.

Within the next two years, he no longer had to line up to purchase his basic necessities from government shops. The private dealers would come to his home and provide the service of purchasing goods from the government shops by collecting his booklet. A dealer of this type often advanced cash in *de facto* leasing of booklets. He would collect as many booklets as possible for economies of scale for the purchase of goods announced and distributed by government shops at various times. Dealers peddled goods in the streets and in various sections of Rangoon where both Over-the-Counter and Organized Black Markets for all kinds of goods, domestic and foreign, became institutionalized in the socialist economy of Burma. As time elapsed, the prices in these markets soared several times above those of the P.S.C.s and co-operative shops.

Sometimes, but rarely at the beginning, the dealer might share the profit he made with the leasers of the booklets. It was usually done by citing the price differential between the official and private market prices and offering a booklet-holder a certain percentage of the price spread in cash. However, in most cases the dealer simply advanced cash in exchange for the booklets to the now impoverished families whose cash needs began to exceed their income as their living standard sank below the subsistence level. The Burmese considered this type of transaction as equivalent to "pawning" the booklet for a period ranging from one to three months. The practice of pawning one's possessions for cash at exorbitant rates of interest with the Chinese pawnshops dated back to the colonial days and persisted throughout the independent period. Although private money lending was banned in the socialist economy of Ne Win, the Chinese pawnshops, as well as other private money lenders, continued to function illegally as financial intermediaries to supply the cash needs of poor Burmese families in both urban and rural communities.

As the prices in the private black markets soared at a phenomenal rate, Hla Maung found himself forced to consume low quality rice, or he himself would have had to engage in black market activities or join the B.S.P.P. or the Defense Services to move upward in rank and pay scale. For example, the system of promotion adopted at various government offices was satirically known as "the ten-points system" given to party membership (the top point), loyalty, ability, integrity, performance, education, etc. Educational qualification became the least important or bottom point of the total ten points for promotion. Membership in and loyalty to the B.S.P.P. outweighed any other qualification and meant an automatic ten points and priority in promotion. Those who did not join the Party became targets for discrimination and were subject to persecution. The Burmese satirically termed these misfortunes *"sat-ngar pyars" khan* or *"nget hkar" khan*—suffering, *khan*, of persecution caused by a "fifteen-cent stamp," or a "bitter bird" insignia on that stamp, put on a "hate letter" by an informant and sent to government or Party agents.

In Rangoon and elsewhere, Party elites and military officers usually had the privilege of receiving governmentally distributed goods and other privileges first. In the exclusive and special sections of Rangoon, former habitats of the colonial elite, where the new elite now lived, the lines of queue were shorter and distributions more frequent than those in the ordinary sections of the town inhabited by simple folks. Apart from basic necessities, the luxury products such as gasoline, radios, medicine, and other scarce products of state factories and foreign countries were rationed by applications approved by specialized Corporations with specific numbers, for example No. 3 for canned milk, No. 4 for state liquor, and No. 5 for clothing. For gasoline, the gasoline certificate, *datsi let-hmart*, was allotted by a separate government agency to car owners who were mostly upper-income groups, the military commanders and high-ranking government officials of the B.S.P.P. The black market dealers handled gasoline in the same way as they operated in the basic necessities except that now their operations covered a wider dimension of border trade along the Thai and Chinese borders.

The network of activities created by black market dealers included the "central dealers" called *daings* and "carriers" or couriers who traversed the entire country of Burma and its borders. In the central cities carriers struck contracts with the major kingpins of the black marketeers. The majority of the latter were former foreign Oriental entrepreneurs with foreign connections and large capital for financing and engaging carriers both inside and outside Burma. They either hired the carriers on a commission or a profit-sharing basis to haul foreign products from the Thai and Chinese borders, or to purchase domestic goods which leaked from the government factories, P.S.C.s, co-operative shops, and various households.

THE URBAN BLACK MARKET CENTERS

The aforesaid cases of economic life in the socialist economy of so-called "planned proportional development" and its failures are epitomized in the development of a giant black market economy which operated with efficiency and fluidity to such an extent that the military commanders and controllers themselves had to partake in it and tolerate its existence. The following account of the nature and operations of the black market centers will help to highlight how Burma became one of the poorest countries in the late 1980s. It reflected an economy of what Ludwig von Mises termed "planned chaos" born out of the inefficiencies associated with a centralized command economy managed by unskilled military managers. The basic hypothesis, which I advanced soon after the military coup and the total nationalization of the economy by the R.C., has been confirmed during the last twenty-eight years in the functioning of the economy of Burma. The essence of the hypothesis I advanced was that "a 'simple' transfer of ownership and control of resources from the private to the public sector in the name of equity and justice does not automatically create efficiency or elevate technology."[16]

The origin, growth, and functioning of the urban black markets may be presented in terms of the development of a vicious cycle of controls-evasions-controls which ultimately produced inaction and inefficiencies on the part of the military controllers of the economy.

There were basically two types of black markets in Burma. The distinction resembled somewhat the distinction between the Organized Exchanges and the Over-the-Counter Market in the American securities markets. The Organized Black Market Exchanges in Burma, of course, were not formally instituted as they are in the United States. They originated and developed in Rangoon and other major cities spontaneously out of the process of a vicious circle of controls accompanying the total nationalization of domestic and foreign trade by the R.C. In each of the central cities, they changed physical location like a floating market or a Cheshire cat vanishing and reappearing at various sites in the city at different points in time. They escaped the long arm of the military catchers or enforcers of the Law to Protect the Construction of the Socialist Economy from Opposition with the help of corrupt officials. The Big Father himself had to wear blinders for the existence of these black markets and the technical incompetence of his commanders in controlling them.

Most of the organized markets were located at the very heart of each Burmese city, such as Rangoon, Mandalay, Moulmein, and others. In Rangoon, for example, the famous St. John Bazaar flourished soon after internal trade was nationalized. It originated near the site of a railway station along St. John street where all kinds of contraband goods, domestic and foreign, were unloaded by carriers from trucks and trains bringing them from all sources. In the 1970s, another rival and more important wholesale organized black market appeared at the site of the section of Rangoon called South Oakkalapa and was known as the South Oakkalapa #10 Quarter Bazaar. It came into existence after St. John Bazaar was heavily raided by the military police. In the 1980s, the most famous Mingalah Zay or Bazaar emerged replacing the St. John Market which was destroyed by the government to build a hospital.

In Mandalay, the original organized market flourished in the famous market of Zaycho (the Sweet Bazaar) and later it flourished in the Chinatown section, and thus it was called Tayoattarri Zay (The Chinatown Bazaar). These two markets distributed contraband Chinese products brought from the Chinese borders through the towns mentioned above. In Moulmein, the two respective organized markets were the Karnnar Zay (the Riverbank Bazaar) and the larger market of the Mydah Kwin Zay (the Playground Bazaar). The latter market served as the main distribution center for the contraband Thai products from the previously cited Thai and Burmese border towns. The train conductors and other security personnel would be bribed on the way to the Central Railway Station in Rangoon. The black market carriers would unload their contraband by kicking down bags of goods from the train at various points where they were received by their connections waiting along the side of the rails before the arrival at the Central Station. The security officers were usually stationed at the Central Station or occasionally along the major entry points to check and enforce the laws against black marketeering. However, there were periodic raids under special projects by security forces along the ways to the Central Station. Security officers were bribed either at the transportation unloading points or on the way to the organized exchanges, or in front of these bazaars by major dealers to sustain their operations.

The origin and development of the Over-the-Counter black markets were already given in the cases presented above. They covered rural, urban, and border areas where virtually all kinds of goods were bought and sold in the streets, at small community bazaars, and door to door. The market participants included everyone, housewives, managers and workers at state factories, and children of poor families who were often forced to recycle toilet paper and candy wrappers to supplement their families' incomes. It should be mentioned here that the role of housewives, including the wives of high-ranking government officials and military commanders, and of Burmese women in general in the functioning of the nation-wide black market was of vital importance. The General was quite correct in his speech previously cited that he and his commanders only knew how to wage wars and eat what the wives cooked for them. They had fared very poorly in the management of the utopian socialist economy. Burmese economic life in the chaotic socialist state was supported by the Burmese women who were historically noted to be the able managers of the family's economic life, trade, and businesses in the economy of Burma. In fact, some of the purging of high-ranking government officials and potential rivals for the political throne was made by Ne Win because of their wives' alleged black marketeering.

DEMONETIZATION

Apart from the sweeping nationalization of the economy, the monetary weapon, heavily relied upon to destroy the capitalists in the socialist economy of Burma, was the demonetization of certain currency notes. Sometimes they were replaced by smaller and oddly denominated notes, and other times they were simply taken out of circulation without refunding the original owners of the demonetized notes. The primary economic target of this monetary weapon was the capitalists who were alleged to be obstructing the construction of the socialist economy. Later, they were charged with causing the runaway inflation in the black markets.

The R.C. adopted a variation of the pure-conversion reform with the four basic objectives of its 1964 K100 and K50 Notes Demonetization Law: to destroy the monetary weapon of capitalists who were exploiting the people and opposing the B.S.P.P., to avoid harming the innocent by allowing up to K4,200 redemption, to redeem even for the dishonest savers with large sums, and to grant complete amnesty and light sentences for violation of the law.[17] It was more or less a pure-conversion measure of demonetizing K100 and K50 notes by declaring them illegal on May 17, 1964, and refunding the surrendered notes with smaller-denomination notes up to the maximum of K4,200 value. These notes were to be surrendered to the government by no later than May 24, with the initial promise of redeeming them on the spot up to the value of K500.[18] As for the notes above this maximum limit, the government did not completely demonetize them. Instead they applied a graduated tax rate to put a dampening effect of demonetization for the purpose of confiscating the monetary wealth of the capitalists. However, on May 18, the government redeemed on the spot only up to the value of K200. On May 20, it stopped the redemption completely for reasons which were not officially given.[19]

The B.S.P.P. analysts gave a lengthy statistical account of how the capitalists possessed most of these notes and exploited the economy and poor people of Burma. The evaluators of the demonetization measure based their appraisals of the Burmese economy upon the single premise that the poor did not use these notes and only the rich could redeem the maximum amounts allowed by the government. They further assumed that the unsurrendered notes amounting to some K270 million (K1.2 billion minus the notes worth K930 million surrendered during the redemption period) were in the hands of the capitalists.[20] Unfortunately, such an assumption is untenable, since in a traditional cash economy such as Burma the use of these notes must be deemed universal.

RELATIVE ECONOMIC PERFORMANCES OF THE BURMESE ECONOMY

The above microeconomic case studies may be thought of as the reflections of the mismanagement of the Burmese economy by the R.C. and the consequences of its economic programs of the Burmese Way to Socialism. The regressive performance of the military command economy in terms of gross domestic product, per capita income, and balance of trade may be shown relative to those of the Pyidawthah economy. The economy under the civilian government and its Pyidawthah Plan performed relatively well, although the prewar standards were not reached. The Pyidawthah Plan, launched in 1952 for an eight year period by the U Nu government, had the two phases of the original and the revised plans. It was launched with Western foreign advisers, a group of Oxford economists, United Nations' specialists, and the private American firm of Knappen, Tippets, Abbett, and MacCarthy Engineering Company. A revised Four Year Plan was launched in 1956 with new outlooks, policies, and strategies circumscribed by changes in the international market conditions of Burma's exports, particularly a drop in the price of rice and foreign exchange reserves. The major policy changes were in the areas of desocialization of the economy and the passing of an investment law to encourage private and public foreign investments.

Figure 3

Real Gross Domestic Product (In Billions of Kyats) at 1959-60 Prices

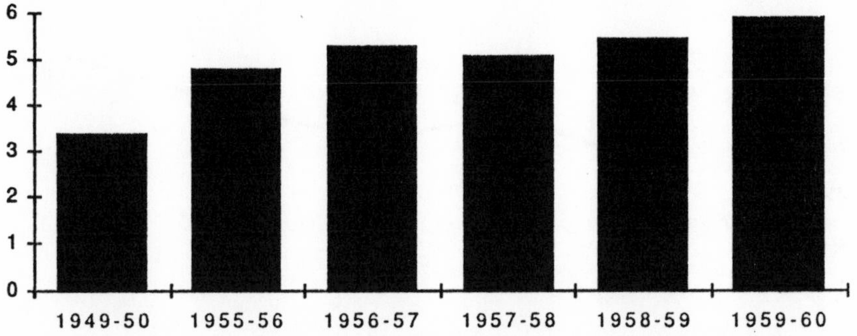

Source: Revolutionary Government of the Union of Burma: Ministry of National Planning, *Economic Survey of Burma 1962* (Rangoon: Government Printing and Stationery, 1962), p. 5. The data were transformed into 1959-60 Prices which are 7.2 percent higher than the 1947-48 Prices.

The overall performance of the Eight-Year Pyidawthah Plan must be assessed as fair in light of the damage suffered by the economy during the Second World War, the massive withdrawal of foreign capital, the gigantic task of restructuring and unifying the socio-political and economic life of Burma after the liquidation of colonial rule, and the dearth of able native administrators, entrepreneurs, and capital. Yet the real gross domestic product of K5.991 billion in 1960 not only reached but also rose above the prewar level (K4.945 billion in 1939) to show the performance of the Burmese economy above the prewar standard. In the 1950s, the relative macroeconomic performance based upon prewar standards was commonly used by many analysts to judge the colonial versus native management of the economy. An examination of Burma's real output from 1950 to 1960 affirms this evaluation (see Figure 3).

The annual growth rate of real gross domestic product averaged almost 6 percent from 1950 to 1960 (from K3.390 billion in 1950 to K5.911 billion in 1960). There was only one negative year of growth (1957–58) during that decade. The per capita growth rate of gross domestic product for the same period was close to 5 percent (K183 in 1950 to K290 in 1960). The annual growth rate of G.D.P. testifies to the fact that the Pyidawthah economy performed relatively well in terms of sustained economic growth (see Figure 4).

Similarly, the per capita real gross output of the Union of Burma showed an increasing trend for the same period, although it did not reach the prewar level of K302. In 1959–60, the per capita G.D.P. was given as K290 (about $65) which was close to 90 percent of the 1938–39 per capita G.D.P.[21] The growth rate of the population from 1948 to 1960 was less than 1.4 percent, a figure true for the period of 1939–1961.[22]

Figure 4

The Growth Rate of Real G.D.P. (1950–60)

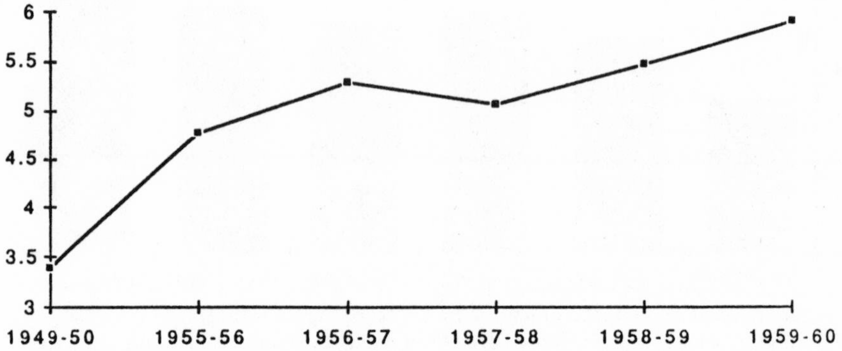

The Eight-Year Pyidawthah Plan also achieved over 80 percent of its planned targets to show that the decade of 1950 was relatively prosperous in terms of macroeconomic performances (see Table 2).

Therefore, the growth rate of real G.D.P. and the per capita G.D.P. were 5.2 percent and 3.8 percent for the eight years of the Pyidawthah period. By contrast, the socialist economy of the R.C. and its performance was regressive relative to those of the Pyidawthah economy in terms of growth. By isolating Burma from the rest of the world both politically and economically, the R.C. succeeded in putting the Burmese economy on the Road to Poverty internally and externally within the span of eight years from 1962 to 1970.

The growth rate of real G.D.P. during the eight years after the military coup in 1962 showed more negative years than positive ones, indicating the disastrous impact of total nationalization and mismanagement of the command economy by military managers. For example, the real output fell from K8.111 in 1963 to K7.962 billion in 1964, while it fell from K8.68 in 1966 to K8.05 billion in 1967.[23] Though reliable statistics for 1967–68 are not available, the government reported a generous estimate of a decline of output from K8.20 to K8.0 billion. This was an underestimated decline since the year 1967–68

Table 2

The Performance of Pyidawthah Plan (1952–60) Gross Domestic Product at 1950–51 Prices

	1951-1952 Planned	Actual	1959-1960 Planned	Actual	% Achieved
G.D.P.(in billions)	K 3.911	K 3.911	K 7.000	K 5.878	84
Per Capita G.D.P.	K 209	K 208	K 340	K 281	83

Source: K.T.A. Reports and F.N. Trager, *Burma: From Kingdom to Republic* (New York: Praeger Publishers, 1966), p. 156.

Figure 5

Growth Rate of G.D.P.

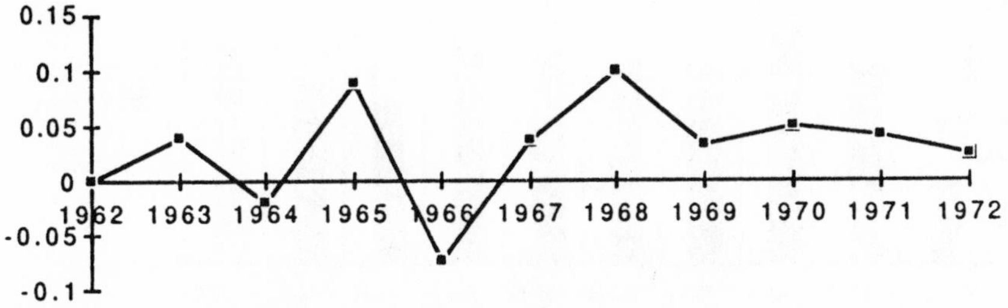

Source: *United Nations Statistical Year Books 1962–75, Reports to the Pyithu Hluttaw 1974–1977* and *Quarterly Bulletin of Statistics, Four Quarters 1966*. (Rangoon: Revolutionary Council Government, Central Press, 1968), p. 132.

witnessed natural disasters such as storm damages on the Arakan coast and bad weather producing a bad harvest, and the Sino-Soviet rift along with rampant black marketeering. The government data on the growth rate of G.D.P. ignoring the negative figure for the year 1967–68 is shown in Figure 5.

This pattern of growth is in line with that shown in the United Nations *Statistical Year Book* which gave the average growth rate for the G.D.P. of Burma during the 1960–70 period as only 2.3 percent and the per capita growth rate as .1 percent.[24] These rates seemed to be nearer the truth than the ones given in the reports of the R.C. The growth rate of per capita output was worse since the annual rate of population growth in the 1960s was 2.3 percent (from 21.527 million in 1960 to 26.806 million in 1970) compared with less than 1.4 percent in the 1950s (from 18.674 million in 1950 to 21.527 million in 1960).[25] It may be inferred from this that the growth rate of real per capita output was either zero or negative to confirm the evidences of poverty in the micro-case studies presented earlier. At any rate, it is conclusive that the Burmese economy under the military government performed less than one half as well as the Pyidawthah economy under the civilian government, showing that Burma was well on the Road to Poverty by 1972.

The foreign sector of the Pyidawthah economy also performed relatively well even though it did not reach the prewar export levels. It suffered from a trade deficit in a number of years, especially in the second half of the 1950s. Yet the average export of rice for the 1948–1960 period was roughly 1.5 million tons which was about 50 percent of the prewar average. The foreign trade fluctuations caused by both external market conditions and the internal managerial inefficiencies of state-controlled enterprises are shown in Figure 6.

For the period 1952–1960, there were more surplus than deficit years to indicate a relatively fair performance by the external sector of the Pyidawthah economy. The balance of trade in the 1960s, shown in Table 3, may be used for

Figure 6

Balance of Trade (in Billions of Kyats)

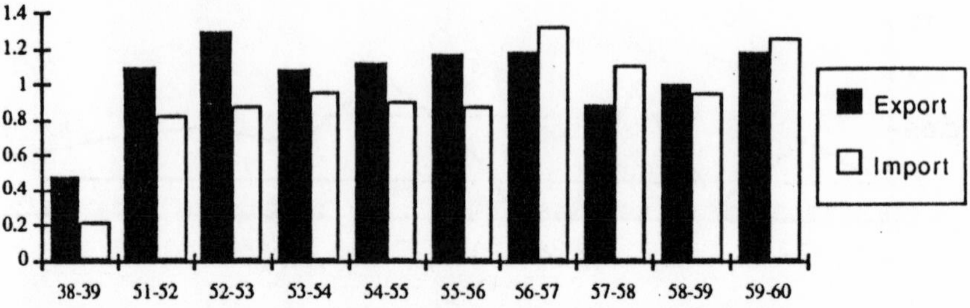

Source: *Economic Surveys of Burma 1956* and *1962* (Rangoon: Government Printing Stationery, 1956 and 1962).

a relative assessment of the performance of the external sector of the Burmese economy under the management of the military government.

It should be pointed out that from 1962 to 1970 every single year suffered from an average trade deficit of over K.2 million. The single most important determinant of the positive or negative trade balance for Burma was and has continued to be the fluctuations in the world price of rice due to market competition and economic conditions. For example, the annual trade deficits of Burma shown in Table 3 were caused by the single most important factor of rice production and export. For example, the average annual volume of rice export fell below 500,000 tons for the 1960s compared with an average of 1.5 million tons in the 1950s. The primary causes for the fall in both production and export of rice was the human factor of mismanagement and the disincentive effect of total nationalization of the economy more than natural factors.

One might argue that the low volumes of rice exports and subsequent trade deficits were due to a higher rate of population growth causing an increase in domestic consumption, and hence less exports. However, statistics on paddy production and procurement, and on the export of rice reported by the R.C. may be used to negate this argument and as direct evidence of the economic mess and disincentive effect generated by the Burmese Way to Socialism (see Table 4).

Table 3

Balance of Trade (In Billions of Kyats)*

	1961-62	1964-65	1967-68	1969-70
Export	K 1.2617	K 1.0178	K .5176	K .5294
Import	K 1.0436	K 1.4129	K .7417	K .8774
Surplus	K .2181	K -.3351	K -.1971	K -.358

Source: *Report to the People by the Union of Burma Revolutionary Council 1969–70* and *Report to the Pyithu Hluttaw 1988–89*. *The figures are in 1959–60 prices.

Table 4

Paddy Production, Procurement, Internal Rice Sale and Rice Export (1964–1969)

	Paddy Production in millions of baskets	Paddy Procurement in millions of baskets	Internal Sale of Rice by Government in millions of tons	Rice Export in millions of tons
1964-65	4.007	1.954	1.09	1.31
1965-66	3.860	1.578	.96	1.11
1966-67	3.180	1.035	.94	.64
1976-68	3.725	1.090	.86	.35
1968-69	3.980	1.421	1.00	.42

Source: *Report to the People by the Union of Burma Revolutionary Council on the Revolutionary Council Government's Budget Estimates for 1969–70* (Rangoon: Revolutionary Council Government, 1969).

The ratio of paddy procurement by government to total production by farmers declined consecutively from 1964 to 1968 reaching the lowest figure of 29.6 percent in 1967–68. For the entire period, it averaged only about 40 percent of the total production. The B.S.P.P. also reported the R.C.'s inability to increase the rate of repayment of agricultural loans advanced to the farmers, and the annual amount of accumulated unpaid loans was almost equal to the newly advanced loans each year during the 1960s.[26] The percent of return of newly advanced loans decreased from 75 percent in the 1950s to 70 percent in the 1960s showing the increased necessity of writing off the arrears of loans.[27]

Throughout the economic history of Burma, the monocultural export-orientation to rice, or what the Burmese called "the golden fruit," *shwe thee*, remained permanent. Despite the import-substitution and other economic self-sufficiency policies pursued by the consecutive governments of Burma, the stark reality of the Burmese economy has been that it is primarily an agrarian economy with 70 percent of its working population engaged in agriculture and extractive industries. The mismanagement of the agricultural sector alone seemed to account for the socio-political and economic decay of Burma which had gone from fair to bad under the military management of the economy. By the end of the 1960s, teak and timber exports began to supersede rice as the major source of earning foreign exchange.

It should be pointed out here that the adoption of the Sino-Soviet model of a centralized command economy encouraged the search for external aid from the Eastern Bloc countries in the 1960s more so than from the West. Before 1962, the major sources of external financing of the public expenditures of

Burma came from Japan in the form of reparation payments, technical and economic cooperation, and international organizations. Soon after 1962, both diplomatic and economic relations between Burma and the Eastern Bloc countries, particularly China, Czechoslovakia, Yugoslavia, East Germany, Rumania, and Russia, increased rapidly. For example, the programs of collectivation of farms and mechanization of agriculture were launched with the economic and technical assistance of these countries. The Czechoslovakian tractors used in introducing the Machine Tractor Stations in rural areas, the Yugoslavian homes built for officers of the Defense Services, and the Russian Hotel in Rangoon were examples of the establishment of close ties with the Eastern Bloc nations. The majority of foreign loans came from China whose share of total foreign loans was more than two-thirds of total loans prior to the 1967 Sino-Burmese rift. It will be shown later that the seeking of foreign aid oscillated between the East and the West circumscribed by the changing tides of world politics.

NOTES

1. See "U.S. and Burma Reaffirms Bonds of Friendship and Cooperation," *Department of State Bulletin No. 55* (Washington, D.C.: Department of State, October 3, 1966), pp. 483–486.

2. Cited in *Far Eastern Economic Review 1966 Year Book* (Hongkong: Far Eastern Economic Review, 1966), p. 98.

3. U Aung Than Tun, *Four Eras of Burmese Laws* (In Burmese) (Rangoon: Kalaung Pyan Publishers, December, 1968), p. 232.

4. Ibid.

5. B.S.P.P., Central Organization Committee, *Party Seminar 1965* (Rangoon: Sahpai Beikman Press, February, 1966), p. 75. Hereafter it will be referred to as *Party Seminar 1965*.

6. Ibid.

7. U Hla Myint, "Economic Theory and Underdeveloped Countries," *The Journal of Political Economy* Vol. LXXIII, No. 4 (1965), p. 486.

8. *Party Seminar 1965*, p. 78.

9. Ibid., p. 79.

10. Ibid., p. 190.

11. Ibid., p. 192.

12. Ibid., p. 191.

13. *Kyay Hmoan Newspaper* (In Burmese) (Rangoon), September 28, 1966. p. 1.

14. This pay scale dated back to the British colonial days. See for details, Hugh Tinker, *The Union of Burma*, p. 154.

15. *The Working People's Daily* (Rangoon), March 17, 1969, p. 3.

16. Mya Maung, "Burmese Way to Socialism Beyond," pp. 533–534.

17. See B.S.P.P., Central Organization Committee, *The Economic Affairs of the Burma Socialist Programme Party, Newsletter No. 1* (In Burmese) (Rangoon: Sirpai Beikman Press, 1965), pp. 65–66.

18. Ibid., p. 54.
19. *Working People's Daily* (Rangoon) March 7, 1969, p. 3.
20. For a detailed study, See Mya Maung, *Burma and Pakistan*, pp. 147.
21. Ibid.
22. From the source of United Nations, *Demographic Year Books 1951–1962*.
23. See International Monetary Fund, *International Financial Statistics Yearbooks 1966–68*.
24. See United Nations, *Statistical Year Book 1974* (New York: United Nations, 1974).
25. B.S.P.P., *The Newsletter on Party's Affairs, No. 1, 1966* (In Burmese) Rangoon: Central Organization Committee, 1966), p. 10.
26. Ibid.
27. Ibid.

7

The Socialist Republic of the Union of Burma (1974–1988)

After close to a decade of total subjugation of political foes and opposition, the Revolutionary Council took another step towards the establishment of a totalitarian state. By the end of 1970, the Big Father seemed to have successfully removed all potential threats to his political throne and established a nationwide political base of loyalty with thousands of B.S.P.P. political cadres. In June 1971, the R.C. convened the First Congress of the B.S.P.P. and formed a Constitution Commission headed by Dr. Maung Maung, a Western-educated constitutional lawyer and lifelong disciple of Ne Win. On April 20, 1972, General Ne Win and his military commanders discarded their army uniforms and assumed the civilian title of "Us" or "Oos" to engage in full-time politics and govern the new state modeled after the polity of the communist countries. The new Constitution, after being drafted for the third time, was approved by National Referendum on December 15, 1973, and came into force on January 3, 1974. The Union of Burma was then named the Socialist Republic of the Union of Burma and the Revolutionary Council was dissolved.

THE POLITY OF A TOTALITARIAN STATE EMULATED

At the very outset, it must be pointed out that the polity of the Socialist Republic of the Union of Burma was nominally structured after the model of a

Table 5

The Party Setup	The State Setup
I. *Chairman of the Party*	*President of the State*
II. *Party Advisers* (Central Executive Committee) (Usually the Three Secretaries of the Party:Ideology, Foreign Affairs and Agriculture)	*Council of State* (Central Committee)
III. *Different Committees or Councils* (People's, Peasants, Workers, Youth etc.)	*Council of Ministers* (Cabinet with Prime Minister and Others)

communist state along the single-party line, although it was really a traditional polity resurrected in terms of absolute dictatorial rule by Ne Win and his hand-picked inner-circle of military commanders. It should be pointed out that by the time the First Congress was held in 1971, Ne Win had successfully removed most of the original members of the R.C. and added seven more new recruits. Among them were Thakin Ba Nyein, a staunch communist and one of the formulators of the Burmese Way to Socialism in 1962, who had temporarily lost grace in connection with the sacking of Brigadier Tin Pe in 1968, Dr. Maung Maung who later became Chief of Justice, and Colonel Tin Oo, promoted to General, who became Chief of Staff and Defense Minister in 1974.

The so-called Pyithu Hluttaw or People's Assembly was nominally elected and vested with the sole legislative power to elect and form various organs of the State such as the Council of State, the Council of Ministers, the Council of People's Justices, the Council of People's Inspectors, and the People's Councils.[1] In reality, all the top elite of each of these Councils were elected according to the wish, caprice, and will of the Chairman of the B.S.P.P., Ne Win. It will be shown later that any deviation from the wish of Chairman Ne Win in electing the wrong candidates to these organs was ruthlessly and abruptly halted whereby a new election had to be held.

With respect to the real nature and power structure of the polity of the newly named socialist republic, Burma had all the trappings of the one-party "people's democracies" of Eastern Europe. Despite the claim that the elections were devised to satisfy "the people's long-cherished aspirations for freedom, equality and socialism," there was no freedom of options for the people.[2] The nominal structure of this polity of the Socialist Republic of the Union of Burma may be presented in terms of a typical organizational setup of a communist polity of the Sino-Soviet type (see Table 5).

The political organizational structure of the Socialist Republic of the Union of Burma in 1974 was set up duplicating the model shown in Table 5 primarily along the "Party Setup" line similar to what is known as the single-party working system of the Volkskamer (German Democratic Republic) or the Pyithu Hluttaw in Burmese case. The Pyithu Hluttaw or People's Assembly was nominally the highest legislative organ of the State with 451 elected representatives of the B.S.P.P. The members of this Unicameral People's Assembly were elected by secret ballots on the basis of former British administrative divisions and states of Burma. The inner-circle of power rested with the Central Executive Committee whose members were chosen by the Party's Chairman out of the outer-circle of power, the Central Committee of the B.S.P.P. The People's Assembly was nominally empowered to establish a Council of State of twenty-nine members (one member each from fourteen states and divisions, fourteen members of the People's Assembly and the Prime Minister) whose Chairman was the President of the Socialist Republic of the Union of Burma.

The "State Setup" was also adopted representing the administrative machinery with very little or no political decision-making power of major importance. The Council of Ministers or the Cabinet was made up of eighteen ministers, *wungyis*, with a Prime Minister nominally elected by the Pyithu Hluttaw. As Perakumbar correctly pointed out:

> The Revolutionary Council, predominantly of generals and top Army officers, continues as the decision-maker. Council of Ministers, headed by Premier U Sein Win, is really what in British and South Asian bureaucratic practice is called Permanent Secretaries—the heads of the executive arm. The congressmen and local councilors at all levels are party *apparatichiks*, the instruments of policy implementation and surveillance. . . . All that has happened is that the generals slipped out of their uniforms and changed into civilian clothes.[3]

The majority of these Ministers were actually chosen by the Chairman from among his loyal military commanders. For example, during the fourteen years of the Socialist Republic of the Union of Burma from 1974 to 1988, the position of the Prime Minister of that Council (Brigadier Sein Win in 1974), or for that matter any vital ministerial position, was never filled by a civilian. The deputy ministers were mostly made up of former high-ranking military commanders and civilian administrators serving directly under the military ministers, *sitbo wungyis*.

The only two civilian ministers appointed in 1974 were Dr. Khin Maung Win and Dr. Nyi Nyi to run the minor ministries of Education and Mines. All the other ministerial positions of Finance, Trade, Industry, Agriculture and Forest, Foreign Affairs, Information, Culture, Labor, etc., were filled by active and retired military commanders. However, many civilian administrators of both the colonial and civilian government eras were given the positions of deputy directors and general managers of various ministries. Each and every minister of the Council as well as all the high-ranking administrators had to be full-fledged cadre members, *tin pyits*, as opposed to peripheral members, *a-yans*, and friends, *mateswes* of the B.S.P.P. indicating the absolute power wielded by the B.S.P.P. and its Chairman in particular.

Ne Win held a dual position of power as the Chairman of both the Party and the Council of State (President) in each Congress or Election held every four years from 1973 to 1981. During the same period, his lifelong crony, San Yu, held the important position of the Secretary of the B.S.P.P. The Second Congress was held in 1973, while the Third and Fourth Congresses were convened in 1977 and 1981. Each Congress simply automatically elected the two leaders by secret ballots, with the exception of the Third Congress when the B.S.P.P. did not elect Ne Win as the Chairman to the surprise of the dictator himself. This was quickly mended by holding a brand new Congress and Ne Win retained his political throne. This was indicative of the absolute dictatorial power of Ne Win and the nominal nature of the elaborate and ostensible governmental structure of the socialist republic. At the Fourth Congress of 1981, Ne Win voluntarily stepped down from his position as the President and his puppet, San Yu, was nominally installed as the new President. However, Ne Win remained as the Chairman of the Party and the absolute ruler of Burma up to 1988. This also confirmed the fact that it is not the political office but the person who occupies it who represents the "center" of political power.

THE TRADITIONAL LEGACIES OF BURMESE KINGS REVIVED

Under the charades of a socialist republic of people's democracy and an economy devoid of "exploitation of man by man," the state was proclaimed as the ultimate owner of everything similar to a Burmese king's ownership. As Article 18 of the New Constitution of Burma asserted: "The State is the ultimate owner of all natural resources, above and underground, above or under water, or in the atmosphere, as well as all land; and in the interests of the working people of all national groups, is to develop, extract, exploit, and utilize these natural resources."[4] This clause of absolute state ownership did not seem to differ drastically from the 1947 Constitution of the civilian government with respect to the traditional heritage of the Burmese Kings who had owned virtually everything in their kingdoms. However, the New Constitution stipulated that all means of production would be nationalized and that "suitable enterprise" are to be owned and operated by co-operatives (Article 19).[5] Ostensibly, it also stated that in accordance with law some private ownership of enterprises would be allowed if it did not undermine the socialist economic system (Article 20).[6] In fact, all these omnipotent privileges and powers of the State were already fully claimed and utilized in the 1960s by the military rulers.

Further provisions of the Constitution contained socialist type guarantees of equality and justice and the promise that "no penalty is to be imposed which would be incompatible with human dignity" (Article 24)[7]—a promise continuously violated throughout the tenure of Ne Win as the ruler of Burma. However, as was pointed out earlier, the most generic antisedition law, passed in 1974, was the Law for Law and Order which superseded any other law in getting rid of all the citizens' rights or legal writs. This Law and its variants were continuously promulgated to violate the nominal promises of justice and equality for all citizens. In effect, Burma was taken back to the dark ages of the ruthless Burmese kings and became a nightmare state governed according to the wish and will of the Big Father.

The changes made in the enforcement of the provisions of the new Constitution and its subsequent laws were mainly in giving new names to the old B.S.P.P. units and organizations, of which the emergence of centrally controlled "Seven-Man People's Councils" on Regional, District, Township, and Village Tract levels was most conspicuous. In the running of the socio-political and economic life of Burma, these councils and their members became the most powerful arms of the State in the urban and rural communities. They, with the help of the greatly feared MIS, governed the Socialist Republic of Burma, bringing out the worst socio-political character of rulers and ruled alike. They replaced in name the former infamous military "Five-Man Security and Administration Committees (S.A.Cs.)" of the R.C., while the important heads of these new People's Councils remained active or retired officers.

THE ERA OF PROTESTS AND PERMANENT PURGE (1974–1983)

The political saga of this newly formed socialist republic during the period from 1971 to 1984 may be viewed as a period of absolute centralization and permanent purge which characterized many totalitarian states. Immediately following the 1974 establishment of the new socialist state of Burma, inner-power struggles and a series of protests ensued for a potential downfall of the Big Brother. The rest of the decade of 1970 was marked by pervasive poverty of the masses and relentless purges of challengers to the political throne of Ne Win. The most internationally noticed incident related to the return and burial of the body of the deceased U Thant, who died of cancer in New York on November 25, 1974. He was the former Secretary General of the United Nations and a close friend of the deposed Premier U Nu. The international fame of this highly esteemed civilian diplomat never set very well with the General who had ruled Burma with an iron fist for more than a decade at that time.

THE U THANT AFFAIR AND THE STUDENT PROTEST (DECEMBER 1–11, 1974)

At the very outset, it must be noticed that the events surrounding the death of U Thant and the issue of his burial site in Rangoon represented a chance or opening for the Burmese students and the masses to release their anger, frustration, and resentment against the unjust rule of the military dictatorship of Ne Win. His death and the return of his body in December 1974 to be buried in his native land invoked the legacy of political protest against the British colonial rule left by General Aung San, U Nu, and U Thant himself while they were Rangoon University students. It touched off a defiant protest by the students of Rangoon University and led to a major revolt against the unjust subjugation of the student body in the same manner as the July 7 Protest of 1962 when the Rangoon University Student Union Building was annihilated by Ne Win and his army.

Throughout the 1960s, the primary target of attack and the potential source of protest had been the college and university students. To the university students, Ne Win and his military commanders represented a group of anti-intellectual and uneducated power-holders by virtue of their military strength. The anti-intellectual position of Ne Win and his relentless strategy of subduing college students stemmed from his own personal educational background. He was a university dropout who had more than once failed the Intermediate or Second Year examination at the University of Rangoon. Most of the loyal military commanders of his Revolutionary Council and the subsequent military juntas of the Socialist Republic never finished their college educations.

Against this personal background of the dictator and his military commanders, it is fairly clear that U Thant, a highly educated civil servant, a teacher and headmaster of a national high school of the colonial past, and an internationally known diplomat who represented the civilian government of U Nu and Burma at the United Nations prior to becoming the Secretary General of the same organization in 1961, always posed a symbolic threat to Ne Win's dictatorship. The basic psychological insecurity of the General regarding the potential threat of the educated and the intellectual to his power and prestige was more than apparent in his policy of total suppression of the freedom of expression and thought which was presented in detail earlier. With the exception of a handful of Western-educated personal disciples, every person of importance in the power structure and echelon of authority running from top to bottom was what he deemed "a good or more correctly loyal person first and a smart one second." From soldiers, civil servants, and party officials to generals, the main pool of human resources from which he drew his political strength was mostly made up of the loyal uneducated first and the educated second.

The resentment against the position and symbol of U Thant, an educated civilian political figure, on the part of the General began even before the military coup of 1962 when the former was elected the Secretary General of the United Nations in 1961. According to Burmese diplomats and journalists, U Nu's acclamation of the prestigious position attained by U Thant was shrugged at by Ne Win. Indeed, when Ne Win visited President Johnson in 1968 he reluctantly visited U Thant and met with him for lunch only after his diplomatic team urged him to do so. An additional grudge Ne Win held against the late Secretary General related to the permission given to U Nu to address the U.N. in 1969 while he visited the United States in his campaign to overthrow the Ne Win regime. U Thant visited Burma twice, in 1964 and 1967, while he was preoccupied with finding a solution to the Vietnam War.

According to a former army officer of the inner-circle of Ne Win, one of these visits by U Thant was for the purpose of paying homage to his mother and during it he sought to greet and meet with the President of the Socialist Republic. The General avoided seeing the famed international diplomat by taking a trip to the famous Ngapali Beach on the Arakan coast of Western Burma. U Thant himself went to the Beach to meet the General who deliberately left the area to avoid the meeting between the two. Instead, Colonel Tin Oo (promoted to General and Chief of Staff in 1974 and purged by Ne Win in 1976) met with U Thant.[8] Another visit made by U Thant in 1971 culminated in the same manner without any official reception, indicating Ne Win's resentment against the late Secretary General of the United Nations.

The following account of the incident is based upon a direct interview with the immediate members of the family of U Thant, one of the student leaders (Bo Bo Kyaw Nyein), and the written eyewitness testimonies of five students who were directly involved in the affair. U Thant resigned from his U.N. position in 1971 and died of cancer at age sixty-five on November 25, 1974, in New York. Ne Win refused to validate his and his family's Burmese passports prior to his death. However, the wish of the deceased requesting burial of his body in his homeland was granted and the body was flown to Rangoon on December 1 with no official reception by the military government or Ne Win at the airport. A Deputy Minister of Education came privately on his own to the airport to receive the family and was sacked shortly after from his post. Thus, it seemed that from the very beginning the signs of resentment and disrespect towards U Thant's reputation by Ne Win were quite apparent and noticed by the students. Hence, the eventual outburst of violent protest against the military regime's indifference was in the making.

U Thant and his body symbolically represented the memory of democracy and freedom under civilian rule. It is not coincidental that the troubles and violence occurred once again on the campus of Rangoon University and centered at the site of the old Student Union Building blown up by the army. The central issue of the protest related to the burial site which, according to the government, the family of U Thant had supposedly initially agreed would be at the relatively obscure public cemetery of Kyandaw where the deceased body of one of the wives of the General, Katy Ba Than, was buried. The following statement was issued on behalf of the students of all the Universities and Colleges of Burma and signed by the Committee to Establish U Thant's Mausoleum:

> We wish to respond to the government statement broadcasted at 8 p.m. on December 8, 1974 by the government-controlled radio, Burma Broadcasting Service. Our motive in protecting U Thant remains was not to thwart the wishes of his family and relatives. Were U Thant's body to be buried in the obscurity of Kandawmin Park as his enemies intended, they would have succeeded in their design to elim-

> inate the memory of U Thant by such furtive burial. For that reason, we buried him with befitting honor in the Mausoleum we built on the ground where the old Students' Union building stood. Our sole purpose was to confer dignity worthy of his stature and establish Peace throughout the land. We had no reason or ulterior motive. Accordingly, we trust the people will harbor no misunderstanding and we trust in the wholehearted support and help and unity of the entire people throughout the land.[9]

Despite this formal response to the government's broadcast and the statement of their purpose, the deliberate choice of the site of the old Student Union Building blown up by the army was *de facto* a defiant move against the military rulers. After the arrival of the body on December 1, it was laid to rest in a temporary pavilion erected by the family in the middle of the former race course grounds of Kyiakkasan or Rangoon Turf Club. Thousands of people visited and paid their respects. The military regime planned to bury the coffin by giving a tiny plot of land in a local public cemetery, Kyandaw, on Thursday, December 5. With respect to this burial site, a student wrote: "A group of animals, a minority group of inhuman people, in their bitter jealousy of U Thant's international stature, refused to allow a proper and befitting resting place for U Thant remains. Instead they allocated a tiny plot of land at the foot of the prostitute's grave [referring to Katy Ba Than, one of the wives of the General, buried at Kyandaw]."[10]

These bitter and abusive words used against Ne Win and his military commanders on the part of a Rangoon University student reflected the mood and the sufferings of many dissident students during the 1960s. That afternoon, the crowd lined up along the route to the cemetery was slowly replaced by young people, mostly students of the Rangoon Institute of Technology (R.I.T.) joined later by Rangoon University Arts and Science (R.A.S.U.) students who had previously marched to Kyiakkasan from their campuses. The race course ground was eventually swallowed up by their increasing numbers. By about 3 p.m., the students moved in to take the coffin away from the Red Cross guards posted to watch it and hoisted it on their shoulders at which a thunderous cry went up to the sky from the crowd.

Thousands of chanting students marched in a procession, following the bearers of the coffin, along the ten miles or so from the race court to the Rangoon University campus where they laid the coffin on a funeral bier in the Convocation Hall. Buddhist monks in saffron robes were seated in a row in front of the bier, waiting to say prayers for U Thant in the Buddhist tradition. Students with red head bands stood guard, ready to defend the coffin and the monks with their lives. The government closed schools and colleges immediately and for three days no action was taken; thousands of people visited the site and paid respect as well as brought donations and food to the students and monks. Among the visitors were spying B.S.P.P. members and government agents whom the students recognized and successfully locked up or stoned away from the campus. The students were braced for murderous assault by the army based upon their previous experiences. At this point, the Rangoon University campus became a political rallying ground for denouncing all the atrocities and miseries imposed upon the people of Burma by the illegitimate military regime of Ne Win. People came and listened to the youthful students give speeches of sedition against the state openly and freely—an exercise of the freedom of expression which had been suppressed with an iron fist since 1962.

The government gave a deadline for returning the coffin to the family by noon December 8. Meanwhile, out of several student groups with their own leaders there emerged two basic student groups: the Convocation Group and the Mandalay Hostel Group. The former was represented mostly by law and economics students of the R.A.S.U. in charge of the bier at the Convocation, while the latter, especially the R.I.T. engineering students, was preparing and already constructing the mausoleum at the site of the old Student Union. The family of U Thant came to the campus seeking a talk with the leaders to resolve the problem. They met first with a student group at the Convocation Hall. Upon the suggestion of one of the student leaders representing the Medical School, Tun Kyaw Nyein, the son of U Kyaw Nyein who was a former minister of civilian government, to meet with all the student groups, they met at the Mandalay Hostel. It should be noted that only at that time at the Mandalay Hostel did many students groups meet for the first time; from this meeting there emerged eleven leaders, among whom were the two sons of U Kyaw Nyein, Bo Bo Kyaw Nyein of R.I.T. and his older brother Tun Kyaw Nyein of Rangoon Medical College and Goshel.

The student leaders cast votes on the issue of surrendering the body to the family and the votes of the eleven leaders were seven to four in favor. The four negative votes were cast by the two brothers and two other R.I.T. student leaders. A meeting was held at the Town Hall attended by the student leaders, the family, and government officials. The students leaders and the monks made a three-point proposal of building a mausoleum in Kandawmin Park (Cantonment Park) at the foot of the famed Shwe Dagon Pagoda upon the return of the coffin, holding a state funeral befitting U Thant's stature, and granting amnesty to all students and citizens involved in the demonstration. The government agreed to the first and the third points of the proposal and refused the second. The family also did not endorse the second point of the proposal for fear of conflict and reprisal.

Meanwhile, the mausoleum had already been constructed on the ground of the old Student Union Building by the engineering students of R.I.T. using the construction materials readily available on the campus because of a construction project. The public had also donated some K200,000 which was used mainly to feed and support the student demonstrators on the campus. On December 10, the family made a proposal to have the coffin placed at that site temporarily for the purpose of paying final homage before the ultimate burial at Kandawmin Park. Accordingly, it was placed that day at the historic site of political protest against unjust rule. Various student leaders began to give speeches against the military government, once more causing the student body to be in a state of frenzy and defiance. Sensing the danger of a mass riot, the family was forced to leave the site and the body wrapped in the flag of the United Nations, was interred in the mausoleum by the students. Another three days of uncertainty and potential trouble passed, while hundreds of students stood encircling and guarding the new mausoleum. By that time, however, the army had already surrounded the entire campus with tanks and armored trucks ready to crush the students.

The government broadcasted a report on the unruly conduct of the students, accusing them of stealing the public donation and acting against the wishes of U Thant's family by burying him at a site it did not approve. The students responded with two statements repudiating the accusation (one of which was cited above) and an appeal to the Burmese populace as well as the outside world for their support. On December 10, as night fell, the student leaders headed now by Bo Bo Kyaw Nyein and his brother asked and got volunteers numbering close to two thousand men and women to stand watch over the new mausoleum. The following is an eyewitness account of the ensuing massacre of students by the army:

> It was 2 a.m. Wednesday before dawn, December 11, when the attack came. The Army government had sent troops from outside the city to storm the University; they feared that troops stationed in Rangoon would be sympathetic and refuse to kill students. A crane ripped off the iron gates as the troops fired a blanket of tear gas. Armored units rolled into the campus, crushing the students who were sitting behind flimsy wooden benches. The crane was used to hit and maim, while the students standing guard in a circle around the mausoleum were bayoneted. As they fell in a bloody heap, an Army engineering team rushed up to the mausoleum, smashed it, and brought the coffin out amidst the carnage. Those not killed were rounded up and taken away in Army trucks.[11]

It went on to state that "the blood of the dead students flowed in a river on campus and when it congealed, it was taken in bags and pockets by the people."[12] The coffin itself was quickly taken away and the U Thant family summoned. It was buried that morning at 6 a.m. by the Army pouring cement over it in the Kandawmin Park. Thus, U Thant was ultimately unceremoniously buried at the foot of Shwe Dagon Pagoda near the site where another famed political leader of the colonial past, Thakin Kodaw Hmine, was buried.

The above atrocious scenes of massacre do not seem to differ much from the ones that took place a century and a quarter earlier in the Royal Courtyard of King Thibaw except for the fact that the army of Ne Win was equipped in 1974 with modern lethal weapons. Following the massacre, students, monks, and ordinary folks took to the streets demonstrating, and burning and destroying government offices and shops whereby Rangoon became a war zone of arrests, shootings, killings, and the hauling away of bodies in army trucks. The accounts given by the eyewitness gave the casualties of the incident as thousands of dead and wounded, while the government acknowledged only 15 rioters killed and 81 wounded. According to the 34-page Interim Report of the Government, it acknowledged the arrest of 2,887 persons 1,000 of whom were released, and damages to 38 offices, 4 police stations, 11 cinemas, 65 cars, 4 motorcycles, a diesel train, and 15 traffic posts.[13]

Most of the student leaders, with the exception of the two sons of U Kyaw Nyein and their followers, were rounded up the same day and put under detention. The two sons escaped that morning but were captured at their father's home the next day. The following is an account of the arrest, trial, sentencing, and life inside the prison given by Bo Bo Kyaw Nyein in a direct interview:

> Most of the events surrounding the U Thant Affair were spontaneous and actions were taken by students on an *ad hoc* basis. Up until December 8, there was no single leader or a group of leaders totally in charge. There were basically two separate groups at the Convocation Hall and the Mandalay Hostel. Only after the government issued an ultimatum, the eleven leaders finally emerged out of an emergency meeting representing various departments of the R.I.T., the R.A.S.U. and the Medical College of Rangoon. They voted 7 to 4 in favor of meeting the ultimatum and my group (3 R.I.T. students and my brother representing the Medical College) lost. We abided by the majority decision. Only during the night of December 10, I and my brother formed an emergency committee to organize and await the imminent assault of the army which we knew before hand. Most of the other student leaders did not agree with our proposal to go underground without surrendering the donation fund of about K100,000 to the authority. That night the army slaughtered, shot and hauled away thousands of unarmed students who defended the mausoleum with their lives.

This statement reveals that the riots and protests by the students against the highly organized, efficient, and ruthless military regime arose out of anger and frustration without organizational efficiency and able leadership. This point was also made by Andrew Sleth in his detailed account and assessment of the incident:

> The U Thant disturbances revealed, however, that there was no viable alternative leadership able to replace Ne Win and his supporters. While the students, monks and others were generally able to conduct

> their initial protest coherently and according to the popular will, they did so in conditions almost of anarchy. . . . Few natural leaders emerged from among the students and the monks, and those that played any significant role were immediately identified and compromised.[14]

It should be added here that his observations are largely true except for the fact that the lack of natural leadership among the youthful students was also a result of the highly efficient and systematic hunting down and destroying of various potential successors to the throne, *min lawns*, by Ne Win. This was in accordance with the traditional legacy and legend of an insecure Burmese monarch, King Anorya-htah, who even sought out and killed unborn children to destroy a potential *min lawn* as was described earlier.

The evidence of this traditional legacy was further testified to by Bo Bo Kyaw Nyein in his account of his experiences:

> By December 11, all the student leaders were arrested except the two of us who managed to escape. We could have gone underground, but we did not for fear of possible repercussions on our father. We remained at our father's home and the next day we were captured. Thousands of students arrested were categorized into three groups. The first was immediately released and the second was given jail sentences of 3 to 5 years without counsel but were also released. The third group of 52 students were detained and put into Insein Jail after four months of interrogation involving physical and mental torture. As for me, I was not physically tortured but went through a process of unbearable mental torture for four consecutive months at a government quarter. I was interrogated non-stop daily by two abusive army officers taking turns and forced to write confessions and reports of our actions. At the same time, I was not allowed to bathe and forced to eat meals at constantly changing hours. I became disoriented both physically and mentally. In fact, there were altogether six of us who went through this type of torture. One went mad, another died of ill health and two others turned state witnesses during the four months. Eventually, I, my brother and fifty others were taken to a court house in front of the Insein Jail and was quickly tried without counsel and sentenced on the testimony of state fake witnesses to 7 years jail term. I was incarcerated for four years and ten months and released after receiving what is called remission. Most of my jail term was served in isolation cells. Inside the jail, two separate groups emerged out of the hundreds of arrested students between 1974 and 1975: the communist and the pro-democracy. We belonged to the latter. Many riots broke out during that period and many students, including very young ones, were beaten and you can hear their painful cry.

The entire year of 1975 following this incident saw the shutting down of all colleges, shops, and markets, ruthless raiding of the black markets in Rangoon, and the sending of thousands of people to "Moscow"—a satirical Burmese term for "jail" used by the victims of the Burmese Way to Socialism. Major cities were put under martial law tightening the control over the political and economic life of Burma. This incident demonstrated the fact that a native Burmese ruler can be hundreds of times more cruel and atrocious in killing his own people than any other past foreign ruler of Burma. For, during the foreign colonial rule of the British and the Japanese, the only significant life lost on the part of the students was that of Bo or Ko Aung Kyaw, a Rangoon University student killed during Student Strike in the 1930s.

THE ECONOMIC CRISES AND PROTESTS

This incident just described of major unrest among students joined by monks, workers, and ordinary folks on the fateful day of December 11, 1974, was a manifestation of the anger and frustration against the economic stagnation brought about by the Ne Win regime during the previous twelve years. It represented the final outburst of the smoldering dissatisfaction of the masses with the gross mismanagement of the economy and the ruthless rule of force imposed by the military commanders. As a Swiss reporter wrote in 1975: "Time seems to have stood still in this oasis. . . . As a clever Burmese interpreter comments, moats and high walls today remain apt symbols for Burma under the Ne Win regime; they serve the double purpose of protection against external threat and hermetic insulation of the encapsulated population against any influences from the outside world."[15]

This general depiction of the traditional state of Burmese society and its resurrected ancient polity under the military kingdom of Ne Win is largely accurate. One of the embittered students involved in the U Thant affair gave an assessment of the economic impact of the military rule: "It quickly became apparent how ill-equipped General Ne Win and his Army officers were to handle the economy; in 12 years of Army rule, Burma which was a developing, growing political democracy before 1962, has slid backward into a deteriorating economy. . . ."[16]

He went on further to indict the General who had initially boasted and promised that his regime would bring about prosperity under "the Burmese Way to Socialism." For example, in 1966, the General briefly described his purpose to the people: "Before the war a man could buy three *longyis* (a sarong-like garment or a traditional native garment for men) a year. In the years after independence [referring to the civilian government era] he could buy two at the most. I would like to see that he can buy at least four."[17] That he had failed in his promise is clear from the fact that "Burmese in the lower income groups in 1974—nearly 80% of the population—thought they were lucky if they could afford one *longyi* a year, even the coarsest cloth, at current prices."[18]

The socio-economic decay generated by the Burmese Way to Socialism was commonly observed by foreign journalists one of whom observed in the *Far Eastern Economic Review* in 1975 that "it may have been 12 years since Ne Win and his army administrators took over the running of the country for the second time, but the mongrels and the dirt were back on the streets.... It was a scruffy setting for an economy in rags and a far cry from the promises of Burmese politicians [should be military rulers]."[19] Such types of observations and critiques of the Burmese Way to Socialism began to appear frequently and commonly in many Western newspapers and journals following the U Thant affair in the mid-1970s when a slight opening of the country was made by the ruling military government. Journalists and tourists were allowed to enter Burma with a week visa. Some observed Burma at breaking point and forecasted a possible downfall of the dictator, while others noticed the ostentatious reforms cleverly undertaken by Ne Win to fool the West and forecasted a brighter future for Burma. As usual, there were dichotomous views of the dictator and the impact of his rule and actions.

THE WORKER AND STUDENT STRIKES (1974–1976)

The year 1974 was an inauspicious year for the inauguration of the establishment of the Socialist Republic of the Union of Burma. It was marred by workers' strikes in May and June, the natural disaster of floods in August and September, and the U Thant affair in December. The labor unrest of major strikes at various State-owned factories in May and June began in Upper Burma at Mandalay, Sagaing, and a dozen central towns and eventually spread to the Delta and Rangoon itself. It was a reflection of the "rice politics" of Burma, since the scarcity of rice at government shops and its skyrocketing prices in the black markets underlined the workers' protest throughout the land. In Akyab and elsewhere, dockers "downed their tools and refused to load rice for export, saying that it was needed to feed the people at home."[20] On July 7 workers at Simma-like dockyard in Rangoon went on strike violently by locking up managers, *gheroas*, downing tools, and staging sit-ins. The Army crushed these protests of May, June, and July with bullets as it had done before against any political dissident group. The casualties of the ruthless suppression reported by the eyewitnesses and the government again differed greatly. The latter reported only twenty-two killed and seventy-three wounded.[21] while the former gave the numbers of dead and wounded in hundreds.

The workers' unrest and protests, followed by the natural disaster of the worst floods in the history of independent Burma in August and September of 1974, further aggravated the acute rice shortage that had been artificially created by mismanagement of the military managers. The *Working People's Daily* reported that the floods of August 8 and September 7 caused 1.4 million homeless, 270,000 homes lost and 1.1 million acres of paddy inundated in the Delta and Chindwin regions.[22] Thus, the entire year of 1974 saw political unrest, death, and destruction caused by both natural disasters and military executioners unparalleled in the history of independent Burma. There is a traditional Burmese belief that natural disasters, such as earthquake, flood, fire, food shortage, or drought, are signs of punishment by higher spiritual beings put upon a bad and malevolent king, *mingso* and his kingdom. Perhaps they might have been right in believing in these signs and happenings of 1974 in the same way Westerners believe in aphorisms such as "bad things come in threes" or "troubles come in bunches." It will be shown later that not only common Burmese folks, but also the dictator and other prominent leaders wholeheartedly believed in such things and performed rituals to counter bad omens and deeds of atonement for their sins.

In June 1975, barely a month after colleges and universities were reopened, another student protest broke out when the students of the Institute of Economics seized the Natural Science College at Tha Hmine located in a northern suburb of Rangoon. The leaders urged the students to boycott the forthcoming examination and go on strike against the Education Ministry and its Minister, Dr. Khin Maung Win. Their main complaint centered on the lack of gainful employment for college graduates under the Burmese Way to Socialism. On June 7, they marched to Sule Pagoda in central Rangoon where their number grew to 3,000 strong and burned effigies of Ne Win and San Yu in front of the Independence Monument.[23] Their complaints and demands included the skyrocketing prices, the mounting unemployment for the educated, and an end to the military rule. For the next four days they set up a strike camp at the famed Shwe Dagon Pagoda—the site where U Thant and Thakin Kodaw Hmine were buried. The troops moved in once again to kill, arrest, and dole out jail sentences of four to five years. Some railroad and state factory workers joined this student strike and met the same fate. The year 1975 was virtually beset with violent protests, strikes, and an earthquake on July 17 which damaged many pagodas of great architectural merit at the famous ancient capital of Pagan.

Colleges and universities were shut down once again for six months following this strike and reopened in January 1976. One month later on March 23, student trouble flared up again on the birth centenary of Thakin Kodaw Hmine. Some 2,000 students marched once more to the foot of the Shwe Dagon Pagoda to peacefully commemorate the birth centenary of Thakin Ko Daw Hmine at the site of his grave. Apart from the Student Union Building of Rangoon University, this most famous Pagoda in Burma had symbolized the center of protest since the days when General Aung San delivered his fiery freedom speeches against the British rule there. It may be thought of as the "Tiananmen Square of Burma" for inciting major political rallies. The initial peaceful march developed into another violent protest against the military regime when the students returned to the Rangoon University campus and seized the Convocation Hall. Colleges and universities were closed down once again. By March 24, the strike had lost all its momentum due to internal strife and the capture of the student leader, Tin Maung Oo, a former Rangoon University sociology student, by the MIS. He was found to be an agent of the insurgents and sentenced to death on March 26.

THE OSTENSIBLE REFORMS AND PURGES

Beginning in 1974, with the purpose of quelling the mounting protests of the students, workers, and the masses, Ne Win began to initiate some ostensible economic reforms such as partial decontrol of the rice trade, raising the procurement price of paddy, adjusting the pay scale of all state employees upward, allowing limited foreign ventures in oil exploration, and reconnecting with the West to receive economic and technical assistance. It should also be pointed out that these nominal measures of reform were made simultaneously with harsh and tight measures of political and economic controls. For example, the partial liberalization of the rice trade was accompanied by the introduction of a compulsory quota system imposed upon the peasants for production and delivery of paddy to the state. Failures to fulfill these quotas were punishable by jail sentences or confiscation of farms by the vigilantes of the People's Councils which became the most powerful arbitrary law enforcers in the rural society of Burma. The impact of these actions will be discussed later in the case studies.

The political strife emanating from the students and workers was also matched by dissent in the rank and file of the military junta and the civilian Party echelon of power, leading the General, who renamed himself U Ne Win, to invoke the traditional method of safeguarding the political throne. The first sign of inner-power struggles became apparent by 1976 when the rapidly rising star, General Tin Oo, seemed to have amassed respect and followers within the Defense Services. He was promoted to the rank of General in 1974 and became the Chief of Staff and the Minister of Defense. The U Thant affair itself must have touched off some dissension among some of the ministers who began to show dissatisfaction with the Big Brother's policies of isolation of Burma and the Burmese Way to Socialism.

The casualties in 1975 were Dr. Nyi Nyi, the Minister of Mines, and Tha Gyaw, the Minister of Transport and Communication. The former was removed from his post on the racial grounds of his Chinese ancestry, while the latter was forced to resign on grounds of ill health. Both of them were sent abroad as ambassadors to Australia and Great Britain later. This practice of banishing ministers from the royal city and simultaneously rewarding them was in line with the traditional practice of the Burmese kings and the modern practice of removing the danger from the center of political control. For example, many of the purged members of the Revolutionary Council were sent abroad as emissaries and those who remained inside Burma received special economic privileges. A particularly illustrative case in point is former Brigadier Aung Gyi who became a millionaire from his capitalist ventures in Indian bread, *palatah*, coffee, pastry, and Burmese noodle shops in the central cities of

Rangoon, Mandalay, Moulmein, Maymyo, Myitkyina, and Taunggyi. Although he was arrested twice prior to 1988, he was allowed to become a rich private business man with special access to imports of sugar, canned milk, and other commodities in the socialist economy which supposedly does not tolerate "exploitation of man by man" in any shape or form.

THE GREAT PURGES OF 1976, 1977, AND 1983

The 1974 partial demilitarization of the power structure of the B.S.P.P., the U Thant affair, and various strikes in 1975 and 1976 seemed to have touched off political dissent and a break in the ranks among the inner-circle of the military power-holders in the Socialist Republic of the Union of Burma. The first to meet the downfall were the prominent civilian Marxist-Leninists who were responsible for the formulation and implementation of the official philosophy of the Burmese Way to Socialism, *Ar Nya Ma Nya*, such as U Chit Hlaing, Thakin Tin Mya, Thakin Ba Nyein, and Yebaw Chan Aye. All of them opposed the ostensible liberalization measures of trade decontrol, receiving Western foreign aid, and foreign direct investments in oil. It should also be pointed out that they were purged by pensioning them off rather than a total subjugation in terms of arrest or jail sentence.

The year 1975 also saw a determined drive against black marketeers, corrupt officials, and insurgents. Hundreds of officials from various government agencies and departments were removed and over a thousand so-called criminals, mainly black marketeers, were tried by special courts and given sentences ranging from four to sixteen years. This tightening of political screws on both government officials and civilians went on for the next two years under various arbitrary laws among which were the Vanguard Party Safeguarding Law and the Law to Protect the State from Subversive Elements. These two laws were passed at the January extraordinary meeting of the National Congress which met three times in 1975 alone following the U Thant affair.[24] An interesting example of arbitrarily removing an official was the sacking of the Trade Minister, U San Win, in January 1976 for letting Western pop music play at the Inya Lake Hotel which is located across from Ne Win's residence. He was dismissed for not enforcing the Prime Minister's [rather Ne Win's] directive of banning "the decadent alien bourgeois culture."[25]

THE PURGE OF A *MIN LAWN*—GENERAL TIN OO

General Tin Oo, the President of the National League for Democracy, who is in jail today, began his rapid rise to fame and power in 1971 when he was only a colonel. By 1974, he had been promoted to the rank of General by Ne Win and appointed the Chief of Staff and the Minister of Defense. He was a professional soldier representing one of the field commanders of Ne Win's army and did not figure prominently in the political scenes in the era of the

Revolutionary Council government. His popularity and the respect he commanded from the young officers, soldiers, and the public were the main causes of his potential downfall under the watchful eyes of an insecure ruler in a situation reminiscent of ancient royal politics. His popularity with the general public was also connected with the U Thant affair. He was credited by the public with exercising restraint during the U Thant affair before the final massacre of December 11, 1974. Indeed, such a rapid rise in rank and popularity certainly spelled potential trouble in the life of those close to the ruler. As a former army officer wrote concerning what another high-ranking army commander said: "As we become a high-ranking officer, we have to be careful of what we say and do: cannot make mistake. If one is an officer of other lower ranks, Bogyoke [General] only scolds and curses and very rarely penalizes. If a high-ranking officer makes mistakes, punishment is immediate with higher the rank the higher the penalty."[26]

Certainly, General Tin Oo in 1976 was very high in rank since he was one of the two full Generals in the entire country apart from General Ne Win, the other General being General San Yu. Thus, he was standing on the precarious bank of a ferociously running river ready for a fall at any moment he made a mistake.

At the same time, another Tin Oo nicknamed the "MI Tin Oo" or "the Smart Chap," who was considered Number One and a Half in running the totalitarian polity of Burma, was the well-groomed right hand man of Ne Win and commonly recognized as the next contender for the political throne, *min lawn*. His position, as the Director of the infamous National Intelligence Board and the Chief of the Military Intelligence Service at various times, was the most important next to the position of the dictatorial ruler of Burma. Hence, General Tin Oo represented a rival contender to the throne on the part of MI Tin Oo and both of them represented a potential danger to the safety of Ne Win's throne. The trio of General San Yu, General Tin Oo, and MI Tin Oo represented potential *min lawns* in the new socialist state of Burma. The latter two were the most able and likely successors to Ne Win's throne in the eyes of the public, although General San Yu seemed to have gained popularity within the B.S.P.P. during the latter part of the 1970s.

Against the foil of this background, the forced resignation of General Tin Oo in March 1976, under an indictment for his wife's alleged black market activities, was a simple maneuver reminiscent of the royal politics of ancient Burma in which a *min lawn* was removed by an insecure monarch. For that purpose, he was implicated further in an assassination plot by a group of young officers under the leadership of Captain Ohn Kyaw Myint announced by the regime in July. It involved some fourteen military officers (eleven captains and three majors) plotting to assassinate General Ne Win, San Yu, and MI Tin Oo. The trial of General Tin Oo, along with Colonel Hla Pe, the commander of the northwest division, Captain Ohn Kyaw Myint, and five others, was held in September at a civilian court with two of the captains involved in the plot turning state prosecution witnesses. All of them except General Tin Oo were indicted for treason or encouragement of treason. General Tin Oo was charged with a complex term of "misprison of treason," an offense carrying a sentence of imprisonment up to seven years. It means the negligence of duty befitting a high-ranking officer or the failure to hold high standards of conduct. It ultimately means that he had the knowledge and failed to report the plot of the above assassination attempt or treason against the state. It ended in February 1977 with Captain Ohn Kyaw Myint receiving the death sentence, the second captain, Win Thein, a life sentence, the others jail sentences, and General Tin Oo a jail sentence for seven years. Others were convicted under the Vanguard Party Safeguarding Law of 1975.

During the trial purging General Tin Oo, thousands of party members and government officials were also removed and replaced by the loyal followers of Ne Win. In October 1976, while the trial was in progress, the B.S.P.P. convened an extraordinary congress to end the four-year term of the Second Congress eight months earlier than scheduled to "arrest the country's continuing deterioration in the political, economic and social fields."[27] In November, the B.S.P.P. under the ostensible leadership of San Yu, quietly removed 54,193 of its members by withdrawing their membership cards under the command of the General who spoke of changes and revisions needed at the extraordinary congress. All of them were accused of being "unworthy of continued party membership."[28] Meanwhile, another trial of the Opium King, Lo Hsin Han, which had been dragging on for three years, was also held. He, U Thwin, and two other government officials had been indicted in 1974. U Thwin, who had joined Bo Mya and the Karen rebels since that time, was sentenced *in absentia* to life imprisonment for treason in 1974. Lo Hsin Han's trial ended in September 1976; he was charged with and found guilty of treason and subversion. He was sentenced to death for the first offense and to life imprisonment for the second in November. However, he served only five years and was released in 1981 when Ne Win offered amnesty to various insurgents.

The year 1976 was also beset with problems caused by ethnic minority insurgency and the underground Burma Communist Party (B.C.P.). In the beginning of 1976, the military regime mounted a vigorous campaign against the B.C.P. and the ethnic Shan rebels on the northeastern frontier. The most important psychological victory for the B.C.P. was the defection of Brigadier Kyaw Zaw, a well-known retired army commander who was one of the Thirty Heroes. He joined the B.C.P. and made a public announcement calling upon the people, the students, and the military to overthrow the Ne Win regime. The insurgent exiles kept up their raids throughout 1976 and engineered several bomb blasts in Rangoon itself. Hence, it seemed that for the three consecutive years following the U Thant affair, the political throne of Ne Win was at jeopardy from within the B.S.P.P. and the army and from without.

THE GREAT PURGE OF 1977

The rapidly declining popularity of General Ne Win during the three years after his establishment of the Socialist Republic of the Union of Burma was caused by a number of events and by actions taken by the dictator himself. Between 1974 and 1977, Ne Win was beset with personal crises in which he exhibited irrational behavior. These included his handling of the U Thant affair; the involvement of his wife's elder sister, Htay Htay Myint, in black marketeering resulting in a separation and divorce from his wife; the scandal surrounding his marriage to June Rose Bellamy or Yadanah Nat Mei, a direct descendant of King Thibaw's brother; and the violent physical assault on diplomats, including a Norwegian U.N. expert, at Inya Lake Hotel where a Western-style party was held and attended by his daughter in defiance of her father's order. All this violent and irrational behavior reflected the authoritarian personality of Ne Win who began to rely more and more on astrology, numerology, and the occult in times of personal and national crises as he got older.

These personality traits of Ne Win are explained by the Burmese zodiac chart and planetary system based upon numerology. The numbers which have played dominant roles in Ne Win's life seemed to be "eight" and "nine." The number "eight" is considered a bad omen for the General who was born on Wednesday after 12 noon, and was accordingly named Shu Maung, his original name which he never resumed after the Japanese occupation of Burma. According to the Burmese zodiac sign, a person born on Wednesday after 12 noon is symbolized by a rogue elephant, *yah-hoot sin*—a loner with violent temperament and antisocial character. It seems to fit his personality and behavior quite well. For example, Ne Win's fear of the number "eight" was supposedly known to the students who deliberately chose the date of 8 August, 1988, to demonstrate against the seventeen-day presidency of General Sein Lwin, known as the "Butcher" for all his atrocious killings, causing a rapid decline in Ne Win's popularity and power. Hence, 8/8/88 became one of the most famous incidents of the democracy movement of the 1980s.

The year 1977 was a bad year for the General whose political fortune and popularity were at their lowest. His crony, San Yu, began the second purge on March 1, 1977, when the Prime Minister, Brigadier Sein Win, was removed and his entire Council of Ministers was dissolved with the single exception of Colonel Maung Maung Kha, the Minister of Mines. The Prime Minister and three other ministers of his eighteen-man Council of Ministers were accused by San Yu of arbitrarily reversing the directives of the Second Congress and were forced to resign. However, the Prime Minister and two of his ministers were immediately elected to the twenty-eight-man Council of State, while the third minister, Ko Ko, was sent to Canada as ambassador. A new Council of Ministers was formed with Maung Maung Kha as the Prime Minister who retained this position until 1988.

Altogether a gang of 113 members of the Central Committee was removed in this second purge. The purge was made after the first meeting of the Third Party Congress was held in February. The voting results of the People's Assembly at that meeting in electing the Chairman of the Party and the President of the Council of State showed San Yu as the most popular leader of the Party with 1,266 votes against Colonel Kyaw Soe's 1,265 votes and Ne Win's 1,246 votes.[29] Although it looked as though Ne Win had suffered a defeat and a new leader was rising in the person of San Yu, the reality of the dictatorship of Ne Win quickly became apparent. Under his order, new elections were held in November 1977 at another extraordinary Congress headed by San Yu and Ne Win was reelected as the Chairman of the Party and the President of Burma. Eighty percent of the Central Committee of 250 newly elected or rather installed members were either serving or retired army officers replacing what was called "a gang of 113 former members." The purged members were branded as "anti-party" and "anti-people" elements."[30] This indicated who really held the central power and political reins in the Socialist Republic of the Union of Burma.

In September 1977, the second attempt to assassinate Ne Win, involving members of ethnic minorities, was uncovered and announced by the regime. The two main defendants were Mahn Ngwe Aung, a Karen,and U Htein Lin, an Arakanese, both of whom were former B.S.P.P. officials. The other two defendants were Mahn Da Waik and U Kyaw Htoo. Their plot began in July involving Karen and Arakanese insurgents who were to assassinate Ne Win and other leaders at a state reception in a concerted effort between the two minority leaders and the military attaché of Bangladesh, Colonel Amin Choudhury. Their trial ended in May 1978 with all four receiving death sentences, while Colonel Choudhury was quickly recalled to his homeland. Ne Win once again invoked ethnophobia to gain popularity by attacking the minorities of Christian Karens and Muslim Arakanese as destructionists of his republic in connection with this incident.

The decade of the 1970s ended with Ne Win's political success in subduing fragmented civilian political dissidents and insurgency, and in purging the military commanders and ministers in the inner-circle of the power structure. Towards the end of the decade, civilian and student political dissidents were either arrested, killed, or exiled from central Burma to the borders, especially the Thai border. For example, the leaders of the five different rebellion groups, Bo Let Yah (the People's Patriotic Party), Tin Maung Win (the Union Solidarity Party), Bohmu Aung (A.F.P.F.L.), Bo Yan Naing (the National Liberation Army), and Mahn Ba Saing (the Karen National Union) were stranded on their last legs in Thailand. It was from there that U Nu and his Democracy Party had staged an unsuccessful armed rebellion in 1970. In 1978, however, a coalition of some eight ethnic minority groups called the National Democratic Front (N.D.F.) was formed representing a formal united attempt to overthrow the central Burmese government, but it was not successful. The inability of the opposition groups to form a united and effective force to overthrow the Ne Win regime reflects the traditional legacy of a historically fragmented polity and power struggles among various contenders to the political throne. This legacy persisted in the 1980s and has remained intact up to the present.

A PERIOD OF APPEASEMENT AND THE FINAL PURGE (1981–1983)

With this political turmoil and the inner-power struggles between 1974 and 1978, the new socialist republic of Burma witnesses fragmentation, disorder, and ruthless purging of various contenders for the political throne of Ne Win. This successful process of eliminating political rivals was followed by another clever move of Ne Win in 1981 to appease the opposition leaders. At the Fourth Congress held in August 1981, Ne Win was reelected to the chairmanship of the B.S.P.P. On the last day of the Congress, August 8, he announced his resignation from the Presidency of his Republic by stating that he would not run for that position for the next four-year term for reasons of old age, disease, and impending death speaking in a Buddhistic philosophical vein. However, he retained the most powerful position, the Chairmanship of the B.S.P.P., thus remaining the real ruler, while San Yu was nominally elected as the President and would retain that position until 1988 serving the dictator as he had done all his life.

After making certain that all the forces of opposition desiring to overthrow him had subsided, Ne Win made a clever move to appease the opposition by awarding them medals and pensions in 1981. In January, Ne Win's disciple, Maung Maung Kha, the Prime Minister who replaced Sein Win who was purged in 1977, invited many prominent opposition leaders and former military commanders to be awarded patriotic medals and pensions. The Council of State chaired by him awarded "the State Medal of Honor" to sixty-six "patriots" for their role in the Thakin nationalist political movement against the British. Among those who accepted the Medal were the deposed premier U Nu who quietly and willingly returned to Burma and Thakin Soe, a former leader of the Red Communist Party. The medal carried a lump sum gratuity of US $4,200 and a monthly life pension of US $85. In February, seven Japanese World War II veterans were decorated with the Banner of Aung San. All of these awards and the fact that the opposition leaders accepted them reflected the traditional nature of the Burmese polity, the need to be dominated by and to submit to a traditional authoritarian personality, and the successful invocation of the traditional practice of appeasement by Ne Win to sustain his reign.

By 1981, the entire power echelon of the government and the B.S.P.P. was in the hands of serving or retired military commanders. Indeed, the partial "civilianization" of the power structure made in the early 1970s was too dangerous for the dictator. Consequently, the former military junta of the Revolutionary Council type was methodically reinstituted to safeguard the political throne.

In 1983, another potential danger to his throne was removed to the surprise of many observers. The retired Brigadier-General or MI Tin Oo, who had faithfully worshiped and served Ne Win like a god all his life, was sacked and sentenced to life imprisonment. Apparently, the so-called "Smart Chap" became too smart for the dictator. He had been considered an adopted son of Ne Win since his youthful days as a soldier in the Burmese Army when he was taken under the wing and tutelage of the General. He was the personal aide and chief of the security force for Ne Win and his family throughout his entire life. He was slowly and thoroughly trained in the art of military intelligence services by Western-trained Burmese military intelligence commanders as well as by the U.S. Central Intelligence Agency on the Pacific Island of Saipan in the late 1950s.[31]

During the late 1970s, as the Chief of the Military Intelligence Services in the Socialist Republic of the Union of Burma, he became the second most powerful and feared figure after the dictator. In 1983, he occupied the key positions of overall chief of intelligence, a military adviser to President San Yu, right security arm of Ne Win, and joint secretary of the B.S.P.P., which was the key position in the Executive Central Committee and the most powerful one next to that of the Chairman. After all the previous potential military *min lawns* were removed in the 1970s, he stood alone in the inner-circle of power as the most dangerous threat to Ne Win's throne. He and his own protégé, Bo Ni, who had succeeded him as the Chief of the National Intelligence Bureau in 1983 and who became the Minister of Home and Religious Affairs in control of the infamous security police called the Lon Htein, formed a formidable and dangerous team with followers capable of ousting the General. The two of them represented the last remaining source of internal dissent within the army which Ne Win could not afford to ignore.

Thus, in 1983 MI Tin Oo was purged in a surprise move for offenses far less serious than the ones with which the other General Tin Oo, the Chief of Staff and Defense Minister, was charged and purged in 1976–1977. On May 17, 1983, an official announcement was made giving him the "permission to resign" from the Council of State and the People's Assembly. On the same day, the suspension of Bo Ni from his post was announced separately. This dual dismissal was made by accusing and indicting them for misappropriations of funds. Tin Oo was indicted for the withdrawal of funds from the National Intelligence Bureau, for sending his newlywed son and daughter-in-law on a honeymoon trip to Thailand, for authorizing Bo Ni's misappropriation of funds and knowingly ignoring it. Bo Ni was charged with a habit of withdrawing funds for personal purposes and particularly with using them for his wife's black marketeering in gold and foreign currency on a medical trip to London involving an Indian gold and gems merchant.

All of these charges were made in terms of the abuse of the high official positions they held. These offenses were usually punishable by jail sentences of seven to sixteen years or more given to those who had committed similar crimes in the past. In November, MI Tin Oo was given five consecutive life terms imprisonment. His powerful position of joint secretary of the Party was given to the infamous Butcher, General Sein Lwin, a lifelong executioner for Ne Win. Bo Ni was also given life imprisonment with an additional ten years added later. These extremely harsh sentences themselves showed that it was a deliberate act of permanent purge on the part of the dictatorial ruler. Along with these two prominent military intelligence commanders, many other staff members of the Military Intelligence Service were removed. In October, 1983, the entire National Bureau of Intelligence was overhauled and reshuffled by the Big Father after the famous incident of an attempt to assassinate the visiting Premier of South Korea, Chun Doo Hwan, in Rangoon, which was attributed to North Korean saboteurs. Although the visiting Premier escaped the bomb blast by luck, four of his Cabinet ministers were killed. It infuriated the dictator immensely and another era of the Reign of Terror dawned in the nightmare state of Burma.

NOTES

1. See for detail, Daw Mya Saw Shin (translator), *The Constitutions (Fundamental Law) of the Socialist Republic of the Union of Burma* (Washington, D.C.: The Library of Congress, June 1975), Chap. IV.

2. Ashok, Perakumbar, "Burma's Signboard Socialism," *Orientations*, February 1975, pp. 7–8.

3. Ibid., p. 8.

4. Mya Saw Shin, pp. 8–9.

5. Ibid., p. 9.

6. Ibid.

7. Ibid.

8. See A Retired . . . Officer, *Thulo Lu*, pp. 24–25. Also see Andrew Sleth, *Death of a Hero: The U Thant Disturbances in Burma, December 1974* (Nathan: Griffith University, April 1989), p. 10.

9. *Committee to Establish U Thant's Mausoleum's Statement, Account A* (Rangoon: Students of All the Universities and Colleges, December 1974).

10. *Account B of a Student Eyewitness*, Rangoon, December 13, 1974.

11. *Account A*, p. 8.

12. *Account B*, p. 3.

13. Far Eastern Economic Review, *1976 Asia Year Book*, (Hongkong: Far Eastern Economic Review, 1977), p. 122. From now on it will be referred to as FEER.

14. Sleth, p. 24.

15. Christian Muller, "Burma's Splendid Isolation," *Swiss Review of World Affairs* (Zurich: Swiss Review of World Affairs, May 1975), p. 16.

16. *Account A, Epilogue*, p. 11.

17. FEER, *1975 Asia Year Book*, p. 136.

18. Ibid.
19. Ibid.
20. See for detail, Ibid., p. 137.
21. Ibid.
22. See *Working People's Daily*, Rangoon, August 8 and September 7.
23. See FEER *1976 Asia Year Book*, p. 123.
24. Ibid., p. 124.
25. FEER, *1977 Asia Year Book*, p. 130.
26. A Retired . . . Officer, *Thulo Lu*, p. 16.
27. FEER, *1978 Asia Year Book*, p. 145.
28. FEER, *1979 Asia Year Book*, p. 155.
29. *1978 Asia Year Book*, p. 146.
30. *1979 Asia Year Book*, pp. 154–155.
31. See Bertil Lintner, *Outrage: Burma's Struggle for Democracy* (Hongkong: Far Eastern Review Publishing Company, June 1989), p. 89.

8

Socio-Economic Life in the Socialist Republic of the Union of Burma

The political saga of the Socialist Republic of the Union of Burma during its first decade from 1974 to 1984 may be thought of as essentially the same as that of any other communist state with respect to the dialectics of contradictions. The same contradictions or problems of all the communist regimes of the underdeveloped countries plagued the Ne Win regime. Among them, the two most conspicuous contradictions were the pursuit of and failure to achieve the dual goals of a socialist utopian society and a modern industrial state; and the absence of "unambiguous procedural rules for decision making and leadership succession."[1] The inability to resolve the first contradiction calls for recurring revolutionary changes from the top, while the second contradiction necessitates a continual purge. With respect to this dialectical feature of communist regimes, Lowenthal observed:

> Communist regimes have in fact been compelled to pursue dual goals—the achievement of the Communist utopia on the one side, and of modernizing on the other. While harmonizing the two goals proved possible initially with regards to some measures, such as the ex-appropriation of pre-modern landowners, recurring revolutionary upheavals became increasingly "counterproductive," first in Russia and later in China, as economic development advanced, resulting fi-

> nally in a running down of the institutionalized revolution and bitter conflicts among leadership.[2]

This closely fits the political patterns of development in Burma with the exception of the name of Ne Win's Burmese Way to Socialism and his battle against the communists inside Burma. Furthermore, there was no significant economic advancement or modernization after he and his military commanders seized political power. As for the second contradiction, the process of a permanent purge presented in the previous chapter testifies to its validity in the socialist state of Burma since 1962.

A series of recurrent and ineffective reforms were made to combat the economic ills and failures of the Burmese Way to Socialism in the 1970s including upward scaling of wages and procurement prices of rice, negotiations for and acceptance of Western economic aid and to a lesser degree foreign investments in oil, a slight opening of the country to the outside world, and partial liberalization of internal trade controls. The impact of these measures and their consequences may best be presented in terms of the following micro-cases based upon direct interviews with those who experienced it in the 1970s and 1980s prior to the 1988 political upheaval.

THE CASES OF DISPROPORTIONATE INCOME, WEALTH, AND SOCIO-ECONOMIC DEVELOPMENT

At this juncture, it is useful to continue the case studies presented in the last chapter and present additional cases for the purpose of analyzing and evaluating the socio-political development and the economic plight of the Burmese in the new Socialist Republic of the Union of Burma. They will serve to highlight the continued journey on the Burma Road to Poverty, the impact of new policies and the inequality of income, privileges, and power between the "center" and the "periphery," on the one hand, and the methods by which the General and his military commanders maintained the political throne and power, on the other.

The new Constitution, the People's Assembly, the Congresses, and the nominal "civilianization" or rather demilitarization of the political structure in 1974 were designed to sustain the dictatorial political power and at the same time reestablish outside economic aid badly needed for recovery and for launching a series of haphazard short-term Four-Year Plans and a long-term Twenty-Year Plan. These Plans, unlike the Pyidawthah Plan of the civilian government, were never formally announced and launched with specific machinery of administration, implementation, and planning boards. Except in name, the so-called Socialist Economy Planning Committee of the previous R.C. formed in 1963 remained an idle organ of the state for more than a decade. All economic actions and policy changes were made on an *ad hoc* basis according to the wish and will of the General executed by the Ministry of Planning and Finance.

THE CASE OF MAUNG PYONE CONTINUED IN THE 1970s

Maung Pyone, the farmer, was forced to deal with a new system of quota or "compulsory delivery system"[3] in 1973. The name of the state procurement agency, Corporation No. 1, was now changed to the Agricultural and Farm Produce Trade Corporation (A.F.P.T.C.) under the control of the same Ministry of Trade. The new enforcers of the system were now called the People's Councils and structured along the village tract, township, and district lines. Instead of five members of the Security Administration Committee, there were now seven members in these Councils. As far as the personnel of these new units of state control were concerned, the top positions of Chairman and Secretary were filled by the same military commanders and ex-military officers who now assumed the civilian title of "Oo." These mostly ex-military officials drew double salary from the military pension and the civilian administrator pay plus all the fringe benefits that accompanied the official title and power. The system of advance purchase of paddy remained intact and so also did his methods of evasion and black marketeering. However, the punishment for not meeting the quota ascribed to him became severe; he was now subject to jail sentences or confiscation of his farm land.

The procurement price was raised by the government 19.4 percent in 1972 (from K144 in 1965 to K172 per ton in 1972), 22 percent in 1973 (from K172 to K210 per ton), and there was a phenomenal change of 105 percent in 1974 (from K210 to K431 per ton). In 1980, the procurement price of paddy was raised to K446 per ton, the maximum figure for the decade of the 1980s, representing an increase of over 212 percent between 1974 and 1980. However, the spread between the government procurement price and the black market price for paddy widened a great deal more in 1980. The ratio of the latter to the former was recorded as 2.71 in that year relative to 1.4 in 1970, for instance.[4] This reflects the ineffectiveness of the sequential raising of the procurement price as an incentive to sell the paddy to the state. Inability to meet the quotas was more rampant among the small farmers owning and cultivating less than ten acres rather than among the large ones with over fifteen acres. Maung Pyone had to sadly watch the unfortunate fate and poverty of smaller farmers in his village throughout the 1970s and 1980s who were often forced to sell the paddy reserved for the consumption of their own family, *wunsah*, to the state forcing their living standard below subsistence.[5]

All in all, the socio-economic life of a Burmese farmer like Maung Pyone did not change dramatically under the benevolent Burmese Way to Socialism and the rural society of Burma remained traditional. The sequential actions of raising the procurement price were neither effective in increasing productivity nor in achieving equity for the benefit of the small farmers. Large farmers were relatively better off by being able to meet the quotas and conduct lucrative black market trade with urban dealers. With respect to the impact of state actions on the economic life of a farmer in the rural economy of socialist Burma, Dr. Mya Than and N. Nishizawa reported:

> After 1976, the picture was not rosy for farmers, especially those with small holdings. Since the prices of essential consumer goods had also increased, real income did not rise. Sometimes, in case of a bad harvest, small farmers had to sell all of their harvest including the *wunza* to the government because the quota was set very high, at a flat rate for them. Thus, in the long run only those farmers with large holdings (that is, above 10 acres) benefitted from the system [compulsory delivery system] for they had enough surplus to sell in the free market [black market], after selling their quota to the government.[6]

Socio-economic life in the rural society of Burma underwent very little change with respect to its traditional ways of behavior and its primarily agricultural nature despite various programs and policies launched by the military regime under the Burmese Way to Socialism. Dr. Mya Than in one of his very rare empirical studies of a Burmese village observed that:

> The dominance of agriculture in the village economy has not changed at all and is not expected to change in the near future .... The village population has increased by 49 percent during the period [1960 to 1980] and as a result per capita production declined .... While household incomes have increased due to increases in agricultural production, average per capita income has decreased while the dependency ratio has become higher. Cottage industries have not taken root in the village. Due to the higher cost of cultivation and higher prices of basic inputs, real income has not improved.[7]

It should also be pointed out that procurement prices for paddy were dramatically raised to the maximum in 1980 upon the advice of the World Bank and the IMF along with the Burma Aid Group, a consortium of Western industrial countries including Japan, all of which Ne Win was able to coax into helping him to revive the dying economy of Burma.

THE CASE OF MAUNG MAUNG—A NEW COLLEGE GRADUATE TURNED ARMY OFFICER

Hla Maung, a college graduate prior to 1962 and a gazetted government officer whose story was presented in the last chapter, was rather fortunate in comparison to a new graduate from Rangoon University in 1974, Maung Maung, who could not find gainful employment. Even though Maung Maung graduated as a Bachelor of Science, the job opportunities were as scarce as the basic necessities at government shops. His was a degree which could be obtained only by those who had scored the high grade in science and mathematics in the national examination given to eighth graders. The state separated two groups of students according to the score they made in that test. He and those who scored the high grade belonged to the "science student group" as opposed to the "arts student group" made up of those students who did not score the required grade to pursue science subjects in that examination. In the tenth grade, two separate entrance examinations into university, or matriculation examinations, were given to these two groups. He successfully passed the University's entrance examination with good grades and finished his undergraduate studies and obtained the degree of B.Sc. (Bachelor of Science) in physics.

In the post-1972 period, the pay scale of civil servants was revised for all levels of jobs. For example, a former gazetted officer's monthly base salary was increased from K350 to a flat K435 without the cost of living adjustments. Relative to the K435 (base salary of K350 plus cost of living allowance) starting pay of a gazetted officer prior to 1962, this represented a zero increase. In 1980, another upward adjustment was made by raising the starting monthly pay of a gazetted officer to K450. This represented an increase of K15 or 3.5 percent over a period of 18 years (1962 to 1980). Likewise, a high school graduate theoretically could earn K125 per month (the new pay of a Lower Division Clerk at government offices) or a maximum total of K150 after five yearly increments of K5 (less than one US dollar) annually added on to this base salary. If he was extremely lucky, he could earn a base salary of K185 per month (the new pay of a Higher Division Clerk at government offices) and a maximum total of K260 after 15 years of annual increments of K5. These government pay scales, along with others, were kept virtually frozen from 1980 to 1988.[8]

These jobs could be secured only if one was lucky enough to find employment or had connections. College graduates were forced to look unsuccessfully for Lower Division or Higher Division Clerk positions as job opportunities deteriorated rapidly in the new socialist state under the Burmese Way to Socialism. They might also find employment as cab drivers, black market dealers, or workers in a government factory and receive a new minimum daily wage introduced in 1972 of K5.40 or a monthly wage of about K112. By contrast, a soldier without a high school diploma could earn the same base salary as a high school graduate, K126 per month. He also obtained the additional privileges of housing in the barracks, military supplies, and easy access to basic necessities from military discount shops whose shelves were not empty as in the case of civilian government shops. This implicit income would give him a real income well above any office clerk or state factory worker of around K200. All in all, the monthly income of a civilian worker at a government office and or state factory declined both in pecuniary and real terms in light of the scarcity of basic necessities and rigid pay scales without sufficient cost of living adjustments.

The jobs necessary to earn the most comfortable livelihood included joining the army, becoming a high-ranking Party official, working as a carrier engaged in illegal internal and border trade, or becoming a sailor on a foreign ship, which Maung Maung learned was one of the best jobs available in town. For a youngster who did not wish to finish high school and pursue a higher education, military service became the most attractive economic profession requiring more loyalty than ability or educational qualification. From a good living standard to prestige, the profession of soldiering became tenfold more preferable as employment and easier to find than other professions.

After having exhausted energy and evaluated alternative opportunities of employment, Maung Maung decided to join the Army and applied for the cadet training program of the Officer Training Service (O.T.S.). For three days and nights, he had to take the physical and psychological tests given by the Officer Testing Team of the O.T.S., which he passed successfully. After nine months of cadet training, he was commissioned as a Second Lieutenant. The next required step was to undergo a three month in-service ideological training by taking special courses on the political ideology of the Burmese Way to Socialism. He then became what is called *ayan party-win*, a peripheral member of the B.S.P.P. After he became a commissioned officer of Second Lieutenant, Du Bo, he earned a monthly salary of K350 along with special privileges of military supplies and housing facilities. After two years or so, he had to apply for and undergo additional advanced in-service political training to become a full-fledged member of the political cadre, a *tin-pyit party-win*, who was given the highest priority in terms of promotion and rank.

He met many commissioned officers who had never graduated from the colleges and universities. Prior to 1962, many Rangoon University students dropped out after completing the first two or intermediate years to join the Army. They became commissioned officers after undergoing the O.T.S. training for a short period of six to nine months depending upon the demand condition for new officers or the political situation of the country. He also met his old classmates from primary school, Saw Maung and Sein Lwin, who had never even finished high school and had risen through the ranks to become top-ranking officers. There were also some other officers who did not matriculate with a grade good enough to enter regular degree colleges and universities and became officers like him after completing what was called the OUT—Officer Under Training program.

This special program was set up to recruit students with low grades who could not enter regular degree colleges by the matriculation examination. After enlisting in the Army, these new recruits had to undergo roughly one and a half years of military training at Burma Army Training Depots (B.A.T.D.s.), together with regular soldiers and other low-ranking officers, at Maymyo and Ba Htu in Upper Burma. They then received further training at the O.T.S. headquarters in Hmawbi in Rangoon and were given the title of O.U.T. or Officer Under Training. After they completed the training at Hmawbi, they would be assigned to their respective divisions. After a period of time, they might obtain the rank of Second Lieutenant upon the recommendation of their supervising officers. On the average, it took about two and a half to three years to be commissioned for those who went through the OUT program. In the 1970s and 1980s, as the job opportunities deteriorated rapidly for new college graduates, bachelor degrees became a requirement to be able to become a commissioned officer. The O.T.S. became harder which required college graduates to take a competitive examination.

There were other officers who were graduates of the Defense Services Academy (D.S.A.) at Maymyo, the West Point of Burma founded in the 1950s. These D.S.A. officers were students who matriculated with good grades and opted to join the military academy. They studied for four years and were commissioned as Second Lieutenants after graduation. In contrast, there were other high-ranking officers who obtained their positions on the basis of years of military service or personal connections without ever finishing high school after undergoing the Officer Training Service (O.T.S.) before 1974. He also noticed that most of the top high-powered Lieutenant Colonels and Colonels in the central cities of Rangoon, Mandalay, Moulmein, etc., came from the in-service O.T.S. program rather than from the groups of D.S.A. students and university graduates with professional degrees.

For example, in the late 1980s there were only three important divisional commanders who were graduates of the D.S.A. (Tun Kyi, Nyan Linn, and Maung Aye). This standard upward mobility in ranks and power positions was a well-known fact among the officers of the Defense Services. It was dictated by the General's belief in and practice of promoting or conferring power according to his famous aphorism—"good or loyal men first and smart ones second," or *lukawn lutaw* rather than *lutaw lukawn*. It is obvious from this composition of the power structure within the Burmese Army that the young and educated officers were deliberately discriminated against by the dictator to guard against the rise of potential rivals to his political throne. His bureaucracy was carefully structured according to his famous motto of placing the good above the bright in the power echelon.

He was now addressed as Du Bo Maung Maung with prestige, power, and privileges surpassing any other civilian gazetted officers. Within two years after obtaining this rank, he became well acquainted with the functioning of the inner-circle of power-holders and worked his way through the B.S.P.P. echelon by taking advanced ideological training to become a full-fledged member of the Party cadre or political officer. This was a must for him to show absolute loyalty to the Big Father and belief in the philosophy of the Party. He also married the daughter of a powerful Colonel, Bo Hmuegyi, during that period. He was promoted quickly and sequentially to the ranks of Lieutenant, Bo, Captain, Bogyi, and Major, Bo Hmue, within the short span of 6 years. Normally, it took ten years to become a Major under a system called 2-3-5; two years as Second Lieutenant, three years as Lieutenant, and five years as Captain.

The corresponding monthly pay scales of each of these ranks were K450, K525 and K800. By the time he was promoted to the rank of Major, special housing, real estate, automobile, and other luxurious facilities were bestowed upon him. After ten years of establishing personal contacts and political positions within the military Party structure, he was ultimately promoted to the rank of full Colonel. The monthly pay for that rank was K1,300 with free home, automobile, and special privileges. With this implicit income and these privileges, his monthly income was several times above his regular pay. He was also appointed as the Chairman of the People's Council in one of the prosperous townships in the Prome District where the General came from.

The most important power or privilege that accompanied this position was access to all state economic and black market activities which came under his direct control. All those who were involved in the network of corruption must pay tributes in cash or kind to him for their operations. Within the four years of his tenure as the Chairman of that Township People's Council, Colonel Maung Maung had amassed enough savings and wealth to last for the rest of his life. The satirical term used by the Burmese for this was to "become a rich man within four years"—*laynit tha-htay hpyit*. It means that either an active or a retired military officer or, very rarely, an exceptional civilian nucleus Party member, who secured the position of either a chairman or secretary in the administrative People's Councils of a prosperous township or district, could be rich within four years of his tenure before another Congress or Election was held. Thus, by 1984, Colonel Maung Maung became a *bona fide* member of the new military elite or top upper income class of the new socialist republic of Burma with access to better economic opportunities and life styles.

THE CASE OF HLA MAUNG CONTINUED IN THE 1970s

By 1972, Hla Maung's monthly income had gone up to K450, a flat monthly salary paid after 1972 to a gazetted officer. However, after two years of K25 annual increments that he was given according to the new pay scale, his monthly income was K500 (K700 being the maximum attainable at that rate for his rank according to the formula of a base-annual increment-maximum pay scale set up as K450-25-700 in 1974). He could have earned a higher salary or rank but his refusal to become a member of the B.S.P.P. had kept him from promotion to a higher rank. Meanwhile, individuals with relatively less education, experience, and knowledge, who had joined the B.S.P.P. and became full-fledged cadre members, had moved up in rank above him in his department. However, none of them became top directors, positions which were reserved only for active or retired military commanders.

His lifelong friend and college classmate, Win Maung, who unlike him became a full-fledged member of the B.S.P.P., also seemed to be in the same predicament in not being able to secure the top management position in a state-owned and -operated factory. For, in all state departments, ministries, and factories, no civilian could become a top manager irrespective of his affiliation with the Party. However, in terms of privileges and implicit income, such as easy access to scarce goods, housing facilities, and opportunity to trade in the black market to augment Win Maung's base salary, his real income was far greater than that of Hla Maung.

For instance, Win Maung was given an apartment by the state in the central section of Rangoon without having to pay the current rate of rent like other civil servants who were nonparty members such as Hla Maung. The monthly utility bill for his living quarters might have run up to a maximum of K50 compared with K85 to K100 which a nonparty member civil servant had to pay in a similar facility located at the outskirts of Rangoon. These living quarters were known as *pyidaw-pyan tite-kharns*—the rooms of brick homes taken over by the state from the Indians and Chinese who had either left or been expelled from Burma. These quarters were now owned by the state and their keys were privately sold by government officials at the multiple values of K10,000 for requisition (called key money).

The cost of living of Hla Maung and his family had gone up several times above his increments in monthly income in the 1970s, since most of his consumption needs were bought outside the official shops and markets. In 1975, the price per *pyi* of rice at government shops had gone up to K1.75, while in the black market where he had to buy most of the time it had gone up to K3.50 per *pyi*.[9] Relative to the K1.75 or so per *pyi* that prevailed in the black market in 1963, this new price represented a 100 percent increase. His two children were now teenagers and consumed rice as adults. Assuming three baskets of rice as the average monthly consumption of four adults, the monthly consumption of rice alone now cost him K168 accounting for over one-third of his monthly income (168/500). Cooking oil, clothing, meat, kerosene, medicine, and other basic necessities had also gone up by 5 to 10 times, depending upon the product, since 1963. The annual rate of inflation was averaging around 30 percent. For example, the black market price of a *longyi* of the coarsest cloth alone cost K35–40 (officially priced at K20) relative to an average price of less than K10 in the 1960s, while a high-quality Dacron shirt with an Arrow label would sell for as high as K60 in the black market.[10]

The scarcity of goods reached its peak during the crises of the mid-1970s at the People's Stores and thousands of newly formed Co-operative Shops which received a great quantitative push by the state beginning in 1974 in the name of privatization of the economy. These newly formed co-operatives simply replaced the distributive function of some of the People's Stores with the same result of leakages of goods and corruption in the hands of the new co-operative managers as before. In fact, the new co-operative shops were satirically called *tharwa mayarwa* by the Burmese, which means fattening the son and the wife of the co-operative manager, instead of its true name *thama wahyama*—a Burmese term for a co-operative society. This is not really a new phenomenon in Burma. In the civilian government era, Con-Cos (Consumers Co-operatives) were also satirically called Kon Hkoes which means "stealers or stealing of goods" distributed by the state.

Between 1973 and 1975, B.S.P.P. vigilantes from various township Councils were appointed to oversee the state distribution without being able to stop the flow of goods from the official to the black markets. These vigilantes themselves would claim the scarce goods for themselves or their relatives and engage in black market trafficking. Corruption was rampant and thoroughly entrenched in the functioning of the economy of the newly established socialist republic. The supposed enforcers of the famous Law to Protect the Construction of the Socialist Economy from Opposition themselves became black marketeers. Perakumbar described the prevalent ring of corruption that cut across the entire spectrum of the elite, party members, and simple folks:

> Corruption seeps from the top down to the bottom lowest levels of economic activity. One of the main channels is the assignment of commodity distribution to wives of ministers, high-ranking Army officers and party men. There is a hierarchy in corruption. For instance, the wife of a top executive gets a carton of 10,000 cigarettes daily; a former colonel gets a carton of 10,000 [cigarettes] weekly. The official selling price would be 100 kyats for a carton. The carton is passed on to a trader, who pays 350 kyats for each. Permits are issued to party functionaries for sugar. The sugar is sold in the black market at seven times the official price.[11]

It should be further added that not only foreign goods but also domestically produced goods of all kinds found their ways from the top elite's privileged possession downward through lower ranks via a network of corruption to the black markets. For instance, if the cigarettes mentioned above were foreign products, they would only be available at special shops such as the Padonmah and Myittah Mon set up for the top elites in Rangoon. They would be purchased by the wives at K6.60 (about $1) a package and directly delivered to their homes by the household servants or managers of these shops. They then sold them to a black market peddler at K33 ($5) a package. These peddlers in turn sold them to the black market shop owners who in turn would sell each cigarette out of a package, say U.S. Marlboro or U.K. Triple Fives, at a price as high as K4 each (roughly US $.60) or K80 ($12) a package in the 1980s. There were also stories of co-operative shop keepers selling imported canned sardines piece by piece in the black market.

Based upon this case of Hla Maung, it can be inferred that "but for the black market and the rapaciously expensive free market, Burma's consumer economy would have collapsed."[12] It did not because the government wore blinders, on the one hand, as a safety valve to ensure its survival and, on the other, because of the impossibility of controlling the natural functioning of the market mechanism to meet the needs of the impoverished masses which the centrally controlled economy failed to fulfill. In such an economic climate of shortage of basic necessities and frozen pay scales, the economic well-being of Hla Maung and his family was pushed to a standard of living below the subsistence level. He now had to find a way to supplement his insufficient regular monthly income for the economic survival of his family.

HLA MAUNG TURNED A PRIVATE ENTREPRENEURIAL SCHOOLMASTER

Hla Maung found a spare job to feed his family which the government overtly prohibited in the name of socialism but privately permitted. One of these jobs was to open up a private school to teach the subjects allowed under certain restrictions by the government, such as English which was abolished as a medium of instruction in colleges, or the ones that the state schools did not prepare adequately for higher education such as science and mathematics. He set up a private evening school, which offered the maximum two subjects of English and Mathematics permitted by the government for private schools, to supplement his family income. The license fee for registering his school was K10 and the fee for the teaching license, *sayah kyay*, was K25. He was allowed to charge a monthly maximum tuition fee of K10 per subject per student or K15 per two subjects per student. These license fees and maximum tuition fees had been fixed by the state since 1965 after all private schools were nationalized.

He set up the school at his own home in 1974 to avoid overhead costs. Within a year, he had thirty students taking courses, half of whom took two subjects. After a period of observing the number enrolled and charging the legal maximum tuition fees, he began to charge tuition fees above the legal ceilings on a yearly basis. His own tuition fees were now K20 for one subject and K30 for two subjects per student, representing an illegal markup of 100 percent above the legal limits. Thus, he came to earn the total monthly gross income of K750. Deducting the maximum of 10 percent of gross income for operating expenses, his monthly net income from this operation generated K675 additional monthly income. The new monthly total income of K1,175 (K500 plus K675) was more than double his regular monthly income of K500. This black market operation, charging illegal tuition fees in the private sector of education, functioned the same as other black market operations in that the corrupt enforcers of laws could be easily bribed for a sustained operation.

Within five years of starting his operation, the number of students at his school had expanded rapidly to over 1,000 requiring him to move the school from his home to a regular office building. By 1984, he had close to 5,000 students taking courses taught by hired teachers, some of whom were full-time teachers and some part-time teachers who were forced to seek out second jobs for the economic survival of their families. These teachers would earn a monthly salary two to three times more than their regular pay as a teacher in government schools. U Hla Maung's monthly income likewise had grown by leaps and bounds from meager hundreds of kyats in the mid-1970s to tens of thousands of kyats before the end of that decade. His private school now offered instruction not only in the evening but also in the early morning hours before the public schools began during the week as well as full days during the weekend. In effect, he became one of the most affluent persons with an income several times higher than that of any top government official in the impoverished socialist state of Burma.

EDUCATIONAL BLACK MARKET AND QUALITY OF EDUCATION

The period from 1961 to 1974 in the socialist state of Burma saw the development of an educational system parallel to the low-quality mass educational system of the state created spontaneously by individuals like Hla Maung. From 1974 to 1984, this semi-black market private tutorial educational system was in a state of boom. The low quality of education at state schools forced most educated and able families to obtain a better education for their children from these schools which also provided a higher income for the teachers. The following account was written to the author by a young Burmese lady after she read the case of U Hla Maung:

> U Hla Maung was one of the fortunate few who hit it big. Many teachers, mostly women, who could not start an establishment like U Hla Maung, went from house to house to tutor small groups of students. They made good money [rather more money than the low pay of government schools] too. Some teachers quit government schools to devote to full time tutoring. With this "tuition boom," the attendance at public schools dropped and teachers left class rooms. The students spent their time at private homes, where they gathered inconspicuously avoiding the watchful eyes of the ward People's Council Committee members, and took private lessons from highly paid teachers. My two children were privately taught by these tutors when they began middle school (7th standard or grade) to prepare for the matriculation. I myself privately hosted and provided the place for such tutorial class to two groups of students in my apartment. This type of offering private "illegal classes" was called "round table tuition," ***wine kyushin*** in Burmese. [Notice here that they were illegal because the tuition fees charged were above the legal limits and they were conducted without a proper license.] Students came from far away places as far north as Myitkyina to Rangoon. There were also cases of swindlers

> cheating the country kids out of their parents' hard-earned money. I spent K600 a month on my son's private tuition for matriculation class of 1984, while I earned K825 a month from my government job as a medical officer. My daughter's tuition fee was about the same. That year, just a few weeks before the final matriculation examination, the government outlawed all private tuition schools. The consequence was, as naturally with our Burmese way of getting around, the private tuition schools and its system went underground and the fees went up exorbitantly. For the law stipulated that if one was ever caught either conducting or hosting a private tutorial class, the penalty was 3 years imprisonment plus K30,000 fine. Many teachers could not afford the high risk and the students the high cost.

Another source from a Rangoon University professor and a tutor also pointed out that many of these private teachers were tutors or instructors from colleges and universities whose monthly pay scale of K260-10-350 was kept frozen between 1972 and 1980. After 1980 this pay scale was revised upward to K350-10-450. Promotion to the assistant lecturer rank, which paid a gazetted officer's monthly salary, was also very difficult for most tutors, especially those who had no party contact and affiliation. These college tutors participated in this private tutorial system to earn additional income by what may be termed "stealing the time," *achain khoe*, assigned to the regular job. For example, college tutors were assigned to tutor certain sections of tutorial classes such as English, Economics, History, Geography, etc. A tutor would free up his required tutorial time by asking his fellow tutor to take over his section, who in turn would combine the two tutorial sections. He would do the same for his colleague. In this way both of them benefitted from the time swapped and stolen to engage in private tutoring outside the university.

For those tutors who could not or did not wish to "steal time," the option was to work overtime as a wandering tutor from place to place where there were *wine kyushins*. As he became well-known, the respective host families would even send a car and provide transportation for his service. Most of these families were very well-to-do and he could make a monthly income several times above his low monthly income paid by the University. The only problem he confronted was the possibility of being caught by the military intelligence servicemen, the infamous MIs. To avoid that danger, he had to establish personal connections. This was done by offering free tutorial services to the children of powerful military ministers, directors, and commanders who also participated in this educational black market. His work was seasonal and about six months prior to the matriculation examination was the busiest. All of this educational black marketeering reflected how the quality of education as well as the living standards of the teachers in the socialist state had deteriorated.

After 1984, when the government declared the private tutorial schools altogether illegal, Hla Maung and others like him had to shut down their lucrative private licensed-schools and go underground to avoid penalty and risk. The underground tutorial education continued in the socialist state whose mass state educational system failed to meet the required professional standards it set for precollege students to matriculate with good grades. The practice of offering private tuition dated back to the civilian government era when many high school students preparing for the matriculation examination attended private schools offering English and other hard subjects which were not adequately prepared at government schools. In the new socialist state, the monthly base pay of a Junior Assistant Teacher with a Bachelor's degree at government schools was K185, the same salary earned by an Upper Division Clerk with a high school diploma at government offices. The dearth of qualified teachers, combined with this low monthly pay scale for a teacher, caused the quality of education to deteriorate rapidly under the Burmese Way to Socialism. It should be pointed out that if one looks simply at the number of students attending various levels of public schools and the data on mass education provided by the government, as Robert Taylor and others have done, it would suggest that the literacy rate and education in the socialist state of Burma improved greatly relative to the past.[13]

They tend to forget that there was a large gap in good educational facilities between the elites and the simple folks in the socialist state. For example, the best schools were located in the exclusive residential areas of the elites and their families. In Rangoon, the former English Methodist High School, the Myoma National High School, and other missionary schools of high quality were renamed as Basic Educational High Schools (B.E.H.S.), Achaigan Pyinnyahyay Ahtetturn Kyawns, with numbers attached such as B.E.H.S. Rangoon No. 1, No. 2, etc. Children of ordinary folks had tremendous difficulties in entering these schools, while the children of the elite could not only enter these schools but also received private lessons at home. The best qualified or well-known teachers were either commanded to teach them privately at their homes or paid exorbitant wages for their private instruction. This was a *de facto* black market operation in education except that the lawmakers themselves practiced it. Likewise, the few students who were sent abroad for foreign education belonged to the privileged class, mostly children of the military elite.

Furthermore, the continual brain drain of Western-educated and highly competent teachers since the military government seized power has had a damaging impact on the quality of education. The disruption of education caused by the recurrent closing of schools and colleges to stamp out political unrest also magnified this downward trend in the educational quality of the graduates. For example, between 1974 and 1977 alone, schools and colleges were closed down three separate times with an average of a six-month duration each. It forced the state to graduate the students without taking proper examinations. The same was true of the late 1980s up to the present. Since the political upheaval of 1988, colleges and universities have remained closed, although the children of the military commanders have been receiving education without interruption at their own private schools. From these cases, it may be inferred that there was a relative decline in the quality of education received by the masses in a socio-political system of rewarding loyalty, connections, and brethren rather than ability or education.

THE CASE OF MA YE YE—A MEDICAL DOCTOR

The case of Ma Ye Ye or Miss Laughter exemplifies the limited opportunity for a brilliant student of medicine who refused to join the B.S.P.P., and the practice of medicine in a country whose ratio of doctors, nurses, and medics to population has been among the lowest in the world. At the outset, it should be pointed out that the General in his youthful college days aspired to be a medical doctor and his own daughter, the infamous Sanda Win, held the degree of M.B.B.S. (Medicine Bachelor and Bachelor of Surgery). It would seem that the field of medicine or the medical profession should be the highest priority in terms of privileges and rewards in the Socialist Republic of the Union of Burma. The following case testifies to the contrary.

Ma Ye Ye passed her eighth grade nationwide state examination with flying colors by scoring in all subjects above 60 points or 60 percent out of 100 possible total points. She was classified as a science student as opposed to an arts student by the state. This screening or weeding out of the brighter students at the high school level to pursue the field of science versus the arts was at first highly promising for those brighter students with respect to a future career and gainful employment. In the tenth grade, two separate sets of matriculation examinations were given for entry into a degree college or university. A science student must score 40 percent or more of the total grade in the subjects tested to successfully enter the Rangoon University and other regional colleges. Ma Ye Ye matriculated in 1978 by scoring more than 70 percent (420 out of possible 600 points) of the combined grade of the six science subjects examined required by the state for a science student to be eligible for the study of medicine. The state also required that both of her parents must be Burmese citizens. She studied for two years at the Regional College No. 2 at Hlaing in Rangoon during which she had to take a course every year in the political history and philosophy of both the Burmese and Marxist-Leninist socialism. She could not miss the attendance of this course more than three times during a year or faced reprimand. This compulsory requirement for all students to study the Burmese Way to Socialism was enforced under two laws passed in 1973. A student who failed in these courses would not be allowed to graduate or pursue his or her degree in science.

She finished her two years of course work by ranking in the top 1 percent of her class. However, she did not join the B.S.P.P. and was marked as a potential student dissident under the surveillance of the students who were Party Youth Organization or Lanzin Youth Organization members. Based on the average grade of the matriculation and the first two years of college examinations, some

500 out of 10,000 or so science students were declared eligible to pursue the field of medicine. These 500 students were further broken up according to grades and places of residency into three groups to attend the three medical schools of Medical Institute 1, Medical Institute 2, and Mandalay Institute of Medicine. Medical Institute 1 was the former School of Medicine located in the central section of Rangoon near the old General Hospital set up for the general public, while Medical Institute 2 was a new Institute of Medicine located near the Mingaladon Airport, Rangoon, set up for the Defense Services personnel where major army bases were located. The split of 500 medical students was 250 for Medical 1, 100 for Medical 2, and the rest for the Mandalay Institute of Medicine.

To obtain her M.B.B.S. degree, Ma Ye Ye had to study and finish five more years of course work in medicine or seven years altogether including the two years she completed at Rangoon Regional College. In the seventh year, she became an intern earning a monthly salary of K250 for one year which was the same as an Upper Division Clerk's monthly salary. After receiving her degree in 1980, she had to look for a position working for the state, and for the state only, since there were no private hospitals. If she had been the daughter of a high-ranking military commander or Party official, there would have been no need to hunt for potential employment. She could also have enlisted in the armed services and would have been directly commissioned as Second Lieutenant which she did not wish to do.

Thus, she had to secure a position through another infamous state agency called P.S.C., which was not the People's Stores Corporation discussed earlier, but the Public Service Commission. The state occasionally recruited medical student graduates as the need arose. They put an advertisement of openings for state medical officer positions without specifying numbers or locations. A new medical graduate like Ye Ye could apply and was required to take an examination on politics or rather the Burmese Way to Socialism and general knowledge given by the P.S.C. Failure in this examination meant automatic unemployment or saying good-bye to the prospective job. After passing this examination, Party officials interviewed her and urged her to join the Party, which she no longer could afford to refuse to do if she wanted to work. Finally, she obtained a position and was paid a gazetted officer's monthly pay of K450 and she was lucky enough to find a position in Rangoon. Others like her might be sent away to work anywhere in a village or town located in remote districts in Burma. If they refused to comply with this arbitrary order, they could be persecuted for insubordination or have their medical practice licenses revoked. Those who abided by the order had to undergo a month of orientation training and an additional eighteen-week political indoctrination conducted by the Department of Health.

The cost of living had gone up at an annual inflation rate of 30 percent since the mid-1970s and, by 1980, her K450 monthly income was not sufficient to meet even her basic needs. Like Hla Maung, she was forced to find a second job which she found in a private medical service group run by a group of doctors in the central section of Rangoon. She worked for this group in the evening after her regular job at the public hospital to supplement her income. After two to three years, she made better connections and became the personal physician of a high-ranking military commander and her monthly salary and standard of living improved by leaps and bounds. This case of Ma Ye Ye is essentially not different from that of any other educated person in the socialist state of Burma where employment opportunities and a better living standard could be obtained only through the institutionalized network of corruption, connections, and party politics.

As in the case of education, there was a tremendous gap between the medical care received by the elite and the ordinary folks. In fact, pharmaceutical products topped the list for exorbitant black market prices and their availability was virtually nonexistent at the government distribution shops. Foreign drugs and medical products, like the imported luxury products, were only available at the special shops set up for the military and political elites who usually had their own personal physicians. For the general public, aspirin products, like Anacin and Bufferin, and antibiotics had to be purchased piece by piece in the black market like cigarettes. The bettle shops, *kunyah saings*, formerly run by Indians and now by everybody, became the private distribution centers for these drugs.

For example, in the 1980s a bottle of 100 *analgesin* pills (a pain killing drug for oral consumption similar to the defunct U.S. Dipyrone drug) manufactured by the state enterprise, the Burma Pharmaceutical Industry (B.P.I.), at a government shop was rationed and sold at K12 or 12 *pyars* (cents) per pill, while in the black market it was sold at K150 per bottle or K1.50 per pill, or 12.5 times above the government price. In the 1960s, the same drug was priced at K60 per bottle at government shops. This also represented a phenomenal rise of the government price by 250 percent (K150/K60) during the two decades.

In the 1980s, a bottle of 100 ordinary aspirins of B.P.I. was distributed at K6 or .06 *pyar* per pill, whereas it was sold at K25 a bottle or 25 *pyars* per pill in the black market, which is over 400 percent above the official price. A penicillin bottle for injection was priced at K1 to K.75 or 75 *pyars* at government shops, while a doctor might sell it for K4 and a black market dealer for K5. Western pharmaceutical products became as rare as gold like the *Reader's Digest* and most of the medical supplies came from government factories, Thailand, and Red China. The medical products from Thailand and Red China were often low in quality relative to most of the drugs manufactured by the state. This was primarily due to the fact that the state factories simply recycled the imported Western pharmaceutical products by repackaging them into capsules or bottles with B.P.I. labels rather than producing them on their own using domestic inputs.

The government rationed the pharmaceutical products of the state-owned-and-operated B.P.I. to doctors and hospitals in the same way they distributed the basic necessities. Like ordinary folks, doctors had to line up in front of government distribution shops to purchase the needed medical supplies. They would also engage in black marketeering. The result was the same in creating black marketeering and empty shelves at the government distribution shops. Hence, the general public needing medical care and medicine had to purchase most of their needs in the black market after consultation with the doctors at hospitals which supposedly provided free medical care. The shortage of medical supplies at the hospitals got to be so bad that the patients themselves had to bring with them the necessary medical supplies such as bandages, plasters, rubbing alcohol, and gauze. The shortage of hospital beds was so severe that two to three patients might be assigned to a bed. There was also a rampant faking of foreign medical products for profit, resulting in ill health for the unfortunate patients who had to purchase them in the black markets. To many outside observers, the government statistical data on hospitals, doctors, and medical facilities gave an impression of a great leap forward in public health.[14] In reality, however, there was a large gap between what the elite and the masses received with respect to medical supplies, personal health services, and care throughout Burma.

THE GLARING INEQUALITY OF WEALTH AND INCOME DISTRIBUTION

In major cities, such as Rangoon and elsewhere, the best homes and sections of the city became the exclusive habitats of the new elite. Indeed, General Ne Win and his family reside at the famous Ady Road, while San Yu and other active or retired military commanders and ministers occupy special residences in the exclusive sections of Rangoon with great affluence. This view is the direct opposite of what Steinberg claimed in 1982: "Burma has now probably the most favorable income distribution of any non-Communist country in Asia. Poverty is widespread, and indeed the vast majority of the population can be considered poor. Great affluence, however, is rare. The elite live at modest levels compared with other developing societies."[15]

He contradictorily went on to remark that farmers were hard pressed, workers underpaid, and inequities still existed. However, "they [the military rulers] had eliminated the great income disparities of some other countries."[16] What this contradictory statement missed is that the Burmese economy shared in common with all communist states the relative inequality of income, privilege, and wealth between the elite and the masses. Even his implicit statement of Burma as a noncommunist country is suspect. Neither the polity nor the economy of socialist Burma differs essentially from a communist country of the Sino-Soviet world. The conclusion of a favorable income distribution in Burma relative to other noncommunist nations of Asia on the basis of the elite living at modest levels only reflects the relative poverty of Burma as a nation among other developing countries of the world. It does not necessarily reflect a favorable or equal income distribution between the elite and simple folks in Burma.

In contrast to the incorrect observation made by Steinberg and others on the egalitarian distribution of income in Burma, a relatively more correct assessment was given by the European Intelligence Unit (EIU) in 1990: "Income distribution is by no means egalitarian; although the disparities are less marked than in neighboring Thailand there are obvious differences, especially between town and country side. The distribution of wealth is probably much less even than income. Corruption and black marketeering among the ruling elite was a cause of the 1988 upheavals."[17]

Even this assessment misses the fact that corruption and black marketeering were not confined to the elite and that the 1988 upheavals may be directly attributed to the great disparities of wealth and privileges between the elite and simple folks.

In fact, during the years of political protests, turmoil, and purges of various military ministers in the mid-1970s, the People's Deputies' Emoluments Law was passed in October 1975 fixing new salaries at high levels, especially those of the President and the Ministers who were also given special residential buildings, automobiles, and entertainment allowances at state expense. The President received a tax-free monthly honorarium of K3,500, the Secretary of the Council of State and the Prime Minister K3,000, members of the 28-man Council of State K2,500, a Deputy Prime Minister K2,300, ministers K2,000, and deputy ministers K1,800.[18] For example, the Prime Minister and the Secretary of the Council of State were given free residences and could use three different cars with chauffeurs for personal and official uses. The others were also provided with special housing facilities, cars, and easy access to scarce goods and services. It shows that power and privilege go hand and hand in Ne Win's socialist state as in most communist totalitarian states. These pay scales were structured in the same way as those received by the Chief Justice of the Union of Burma, Supreme Court Judge, Chief Justice, Pusine Justice, Attorney General, etc. of the civilian government.

Indeed, great affluence is not rare among the new Burmese military elite, black market kingpins, and corrupt civilian officials. Apart from basic necessities, their access to a modern standard of living included better housing, the best health care with private physicians, the best domestic and foreign education for their children with private tutors, foreign travel, golf, tennis, foreign liquor, television, stereos, and other privileges. The life styles, wealth, and comfortable modern homes of the military elite and their families living in former colonial residential quarters and newly constructed modern quarters in Rangoon, all conspicuously symbolized the abodes of what the Burmese called Lawki Nateban or modern Nirvana. Examples of these heavenly quarters are the very famous Ady Road, the well-fortified palace of Ne Win, the Golden Valley or Shwetaung Kyar, the luxurious home of Sein Lwin, and the homes of other rich folks with political connections, the Chinchawn Chan and the adjacent Kanbawza and the villas of San Yu and former Revolutionary Council members, the Windamere Road and modern homes of retired ministers, rich civilian elites, and black marketeers, and the Inyar Myaing and homes of rich Party officials and civilians and the Parami and the comfortable homes of former military commanders.

All these modern living quarters and real estate claimed or rewarded as appendages to his loyal servants by the Big Father were satirically called *warsai* by the Burmese, which is transformed into *waisar* by a rhythmical reversal of the two words to mean distribute, *wai*, and eat, *sar*, the wealth among the military officers. One should recall that this customary practice dated back to the days of the Burmese kings who rewarded their loyal bureaucracy by giving appendages of villages and townships known as *myoesar* and *ywah-sar*. Meanwhile, simple folks in Rangoon continued to live and subsist in shabby homes with honey buckets and poor utility facilities under unsanitary conditions as they had done in the past.

This gap of living standards and homes between the military elite and the masses was not confined to major cities but could also be found in the rural areas. Like the practice of the ancient Burmese kings, Ne Win awarded appendages to the military commanders of various districts whose real estate and homes were secured through the power and control they wielded over the lower-ranking officers and soldiers. They controlled the whole network of the state distribution system as well as the private black markets. The financing and construction of their better living quarters were provided by the junior officers and soldiers through the manipulation of the already corrupt system of government distribution of goods and materials. These district military commanders, *tine hmues*, were in effect the same as the royal governors of the Burmese kings known as *ywahsars*, "the village eaters," and *myoesars*, "town eaters," who were given taxing power over the villages and towns. Indeed, there has been a tremendous inequality of real income distribution and living standards between the central military elites and peripheral simple folks in the negative utopian state of socialist Burma for nearly thirty years.

The deterioration of physical conditions and the infrastructure in Rangoon and Mandalay for the ordinary folks was aptly described by Henry Kamm of the *New York Times* in 1975:

> As Burmese wealth is drained renewal and maintenance suffer. Rangoon, once a gleaming city, shows the effects of decades of monsoon seasons and the absence of plaster and paint. Mildew and rot proliferate on the houses that line its major streets and crumble the fronts of once-thriving shops closed through nationalization or for lack of merchandise. Pavement stones are tilted, tripping pedestrians. Gaping holes dot roadways. Uncollected garbage is shoved into them by boys cleaning the street for soccer games; they need not worry about heavy traffic. Mandalay, a city of 400,000 still has no sewage system and

> draws its drinking water from the open moat where its castle stood until World War II. The Government declared the water unsafe 18 years ago, but there is no plan to improve it. The last public housing was built in 1957.[19]

He went on further to point out that in Rangoon with some two million residents "there seems to be hardly any recent construction. But on the outskirts, army officers are building villas."[20] The shortage of housing facilities was so severe that even certain sections of a monastery compound, *kyawn tite*, were rented out as living quarters in urban communities for profit by some Buddhist monks to reap the benefit of the nation-wide black market. This process of retrogression of living conditions for ordinary folks continued into the decade of the 1980s when a number of Burmese civil servants visiting the United States in 1987 told the author about the rats and mosquitoes thriving in the homes, the mongrels and stray cats roaming the streets of Rangoon along with the poor children recycling and selling used bottles, candy wrappers, and toilet paper.

The glaring inequality of real income and living conditions between the elite and simple folks is not unique to Burma since the political elite of every totalitarian polity and centrally controlled economy wound up being the top privileged class. Power and privileges go hand in hand in a political and economic system of central controls where corruption and loopholes permeate to negate the benevolent goals of equality and justice for all. It has been the common feature of the so-called revolutionary socialism imposed from the top. In a way, the state capitalism and ownership of everything in Ne Win's Burma does not differ essentially from the state monopoly of everything in the Burmese Kingdoms of the Koanbaung Dynasty. In short, Burma became a poor nation for the masses and a rich one for the military "Robber Barons" whose homes, wealth, and life styles are reminiscent of the royalty of the ancient Burmese Kingdoms and former British colonial rulers.

MACROECONOMIC PERFORMANCE

In contrast to the above cases of pervasive poverty of the masses and inequality of income distribution, many studies on the economic performance of the Socialist Republic of the Union of Burma showed a favorable trend of development towards the end of the 1970s. The main reasons for the rosy picture of the Burmese economy during that period are twofold: the use of highly unreliable statistical data provided by the *Reports to the Pyithu Hluttaw*, which tend to distort and hide the real life and quantitative performances of the various sectors of the economy, and the massive external pump priming which helped temporarily to revive the dying economy in the late 1970s. For example, if one relies on the statistical data on Gross Domestic Product (G.D.P.) of the Pyithu Hluttaw, the average annual rate of growth for the 1970–1980 period would be 3.4 percent (from K10.388 billions to K14.562 billions). However, for the 1974–1984 period it was recorded at 5.1 percent (from K11.101 billions to K18.429 billions).

An example of exaggerated growth rates based upon government statistical data was given by a Burmese economist in his assessment of the economic performance of Burma: "The growth in the gross domestic product (GDP) which achieved an average (compound) growth rate of 6.5 percent during the Third Four-Year Plan period (fiscal year 1978/79 to 1981/82) declined to an average of 5 percent in the Fourth Four-Year Plan period (1982/83 to 1985/86) and further dropped to 1 percent for the fiscal year 1986/87 (which ended on 31 March 1987)."[21]

With the exception of the year 1986/87, these impressive rates of growth of the G.D.P. certainly do not indicate the dismal state of the economy up until 1987. The major reason for this is that the first half of the 1970s as well as the early 1980s were not representative years and the government data show only one negative year of growth with G.D.P. declining by 1 percent between 1972 and 1973. It also recorded a phenomenal average growth rate of over 6 percent from 1977 to 1982 (from K12.265 billions to K16.717 billions). From the case studies of the politico-economic crises presented in this study, it was shown that from 1974 to 1977 Burma was governed under martial law in a state of emergency and that the period was filled with consecutive stagnant years of natural and political disasters across Burma. The years from 1979 to 1985 were also years when massive foreign aid was received, exaggerating the growth rates.

With respect to the unreliability of aggregate statistical data, Henry Kamm gave a more realistic assessment in 1975: "Official statistics, which are not considered a reliable guide, indicated a growth rate of 3 percent last year after a rise of 1 percent in the previous year. But the high birth rate causes the significant per-capita growth rate to hover around zero."[22]

This is in agreement with what this study has shown with respect to the growth rate for the decades of the 1960s and 1970s. Further assessments made by Kamm on the economic performance of Burma under military management may be deemed as closer to the truth than the later assessments made by some willing donors of aid to Burma:

> Before General Ne Win's military take-over of 1962, Burma exported 1.9 million tons [rice]. Last year's output was 8.4 million tons. The population has risen about 30 percent since the years just before World War II; of the 8.4 million tons, 104,000 were left for export. At the present pace of annual population growth—2.2 percent—and increase of rice production 1.8 percent—the world's one-time leading exporter will be importing the staple of its diet early in the next decade.[23]

This export figure of 104,000 tons may be contrasted with the annual rice export a century ago of 811,106 tons by British Burma (Lower Burma) between 1868 and 1874.[24] Kamm was not too far off the mark except for the fact that the rescue of the dying economy in the mid-1970s was made by the outside world. The so-called reversing of the trend or the phenomenal recovery of the economy by 1980 was highly exaggerated based upon government statistical data rather than microanalyses of the economy as was done in this study. However, it may be conceded that the economy was revived to a certain extent in the early eighties by huge external pump priming in the form of massive foreign aid and assistance from the West.

REVERSING THE TREND OF STAGNATION

During the height of political strife in the mid-1970s, the military regime invited and negotiated various foreign investments in offshore oil exploration and mining. The partial decontrol of the internal rice trade and consecutive raising of procurement prices for paddy beginning in 1973, the publication of a list of 268 industries which could be operated by the previously nationalized private sector in 1974,[25] a massive push on the co-operative movement in 1974 in the name of privatization, and the devaluation of or rather floating the *kyat* in 1976 created a somewhat conducive environment for the positive reception of foreign aid from the Western world. As was pointed out before, these measures were taken out of the necessity to appease the growing political unrest of the impoverished masses, on the one hand, and to replenish the rapidly declining foreign exchange reserves born out of the continuous trade deficit in the 1970s, on the other.

Even the international organizations such as the World Bank and the International Monetary Fund (IMF), which were called upon to help, failed to notice the real nature of the ostensible economic reforms and political suppression by the dictatorial regime of Ne Win. Indeed, in 1978 both of them observed the positive impact of the reform measures that were nominally taken by the Ne Win regime in an attempt to woo the international and national donors from the West. Many studies on the macroeconomic performance of Burma in the late 1970s and early 1980s shared an observation captioned with the cliché of "reversing the trend"[26] or "recovery period" on the basis of government statistical reports. The implication of this cliché was the beneficial effect of the ostensible reform measures of the Ne Win regime. One of the classic examples of such an accolade was made by Steinberg (while he was a U.S. AID official) on the state of the Burmese economy in 1982:

> The other hall mark of the Burmese socialist state is economic and social egalitarianism. It was only in 1976, after the economic reforms approved in 1972 began to be felt, that the Burmese standard of living, finally reached the prewar level. In addition, Burma has less maldistri-

> bution of income among economic classes than most non-Communist societies. The highest 20 percent of the population controls 40 percent of the national income, whereas the lowest 20 percent has 8 percent. Land reform has been effective. The average farm size is 5.4 acres, and 86.8 percent of all farms are under 10 acres.[27]

These observations certainly were not supported by a few empirical socio-economic studies of a Burmese village made by Burmese economists which are exemplified in the works of Dr. Mya Than, Dr. Win, and Dr. Khin Maung Kyi. According to their findings, neither the real income nor the socio-economic life had significantly improved or changed since the days of the civilian government.[28]

Steinberg's observations of the income distribution in terms of unreliable and unavailable data on the Lorenz curve are suspect. Indeed, it will be suggested that the reduction of farm size in the name of socialist equality and justice was the major cause for the decline in productivity as well as inequality of real income distribution. The diseconomies of scale and waste contributed greatly to the widening gap of real income between a small percentage of the population, made up of a few remaining large landholders, money lenders, black marketeers, and military party officials, and the large percentage of the population which are small farmers in the socialist state of Burma. However, he went on to state that, although ruthless foreign landlords were gone, the state landlord "could be as unsympathetic as any Chettyar"[29] and that the development plans were financed with an indirect tax on the farmer. It is precisely this unsympathetic, nonegalitarian, and ruthless policy of the state capitalist landlord towards the farmers that reduced Burma from its historical status as the largest exporter of rice in the world to the least developed country in the next decade.

The same kind of positive remarks as Steinberg's were made by both the IMF and the World Bank. The IMF's enthusiastic appraisal of Burma's potential economic growth was observed by Ho Kwon Ping, a reporter: "In recent years, the accolades for Burma's economic growth have been numerous. One of the most enthusiastic was from the International Monetary Fund (IMF), which noted in a confidential report early in 1978 that the Burmese economy 'experienced a remarkable improvement, reversing the stagnation that prevailed during most of the past quarter-century.' "[30]

Two other confidential reports of similar enthusiasm, made by the World Bank in 1979 and the U.S. Agency for International Development (AID) in May 1978, were also cited by him. According to his citations, the World Bank's assessment of the macroeconomic performance of Burma in 1979 under the reform measures of the military government was: " 'Noteworthy success,' " but at the cost of dismal " 'economic deterioration' " [which] has been arrested and the process to resuscitate the economy is now underway. . . . Tenancy and agricultural rents were abolished, and land holdings made more equal."[31]

Contrary to the analyses and evaluations given in the previous chapter of this study, The Bank also assessed the economic performance of Burma in the 1960s as:

> The government was well within the reach of its objective to provide universal basic education. Malnutrition was largely eliminated. By the end of the period, the presence in many villages of banks, tractor stations, co-operatives, state buying depots, local administration bodies, schools, and health clinics suggested that a far smaller dichotomy existed between the rural and urban life in Burma than is found in most developing countries.[32]

However, the Bank charged the government with committing "a cardinal sin of neglecting agriculture."[33] Contrary to this charge, it will be argued here that it was not the neglect of the agricultural sector but the wasteful expenditures, programs, and overemphasis on agriculture that caused the poor performance of that sector. As a matter of fact, the congestion of thousands of inefficient state banks, tractor stations, state buying depots, etc., in the same sector was the very cause of the decline in agricultural productivity. It will be emphatically argued here that the Bank did not make correct assessments of the nature of the tremendous inefficiency of a totally state-controlled agricultural economy, on the one hand, and of the enormous gap of wealth and privileges between the "center" and "the periphery" in the dual economy of Burma under the military rule and the Burmese Way to Socialism, on the other.

It should be noticed also that the historical relationship of Burma with the United Nations and its Agencies such as the IMF and the World Bank has been quite intimate and smooth due to important personal ties Burma had with these organizations. For example, two economists with Harvard and Yale Ph.D. degrees, Dr. Tun Thin and Dr. Tun Wai, have worked for the IMF as prominent directors since the late 1950s. Apart from them, two other prominent economists who worked for the IMF and the World Bank in the 1970s were the late I.C.S. U San Lin, a former General Manager of the Union Bank of Burma, and a highly well-known former teacher, Dr. Sundrum of the Economics Department of Rangoon University. To what extent they might be responsible for the observations made in the above reports, specifically the IMF's, cannot be ascertained. However, the legacy of the late U.N. Secretary General U Thant together with their positions in these specialized agencies of the United Nations certainly helped in Burma's successful negotiations with these agencies for receiving development loans and assistance.

MULTINATIONAL AID

The main factor in the prolongation of the military dictatorship of Ne Win and the short-lived remission period for the dying economy in the first half of the 1980s was primarily exogenous, namely, external financial assistance and lending received multinationally and bilaterally by Burma from both the Western and the Eastern Bloc countries. Ne Win's success in extracting external funds lies in what will be termed a use of "dialectical neutralism" as opposed to what most writers tended to emphasize as the "truly non-aligned neutralism" pursued by the dictator. By "dialectical neutralism" is meant a foreign policy of riding the changing tides of international politics and reaping advantages by playing off the hegemonial powers against one another. For example, while Ne Win was launching the so-called economic reforms and negotiating loans with the West, he visited China for the ninth time in 1977 to establish political and economic ties. In 1976,the Soviet delegation led by Nazar Matchanov, the Vice-President of the Supreme Soviet, paid a visit to Burma. In the 1980s, President San Yu followed the same strategy.

THE ASIAN DEVELOPMENT BANK AID

Of all the international organizations, the Asian Development Bank consistently and continuously provided project loans and technical assistance to the Ne Win regime from 1973 up until 1986. The total loans of this Bank from the Asian Development Fund given to the Socialist Republic of the Union of Burma amounted to $524.60 millions. These loans were given with a grace period of forty years at an interest service charge of 1 percent. From December 6, 1973, to December 8, 1983, a total of twenty-seven different project loans were advanced amounting to roughly $500 million averaging $50 million a year. These loans covered a wide range of funding for various development projects in agriculture, fishery, mines and infrastructure. This annual loan figure of $50 millions represents close to 60 percent (50/87) of the annual total merchandise export of Burma between 1973 and 1983.[34] It should be noticed that these loans were entitled by the Bank as "Loan, Technical Assistance and Private Sector Operations Approval,"[35] although all the loans given to Burma were for state projects.

Beginning in 1974, the Ne Win regime called for private foreign investments in offshore petroleum exploration and entered into formal agreements with firms from the United States (Exxon), Australia and others. "Eight different foreign companies were given proceeds-sharing service contracts for oil exploration and production in 13 off-shore areas"[36] bringing in substantial sums of foreign exchange which the regime needed badly to finance its trade deficits. However, most private multinational firms soon found out that this slight opening of the economy was a charade and that their contracts were caught up in red tape and tight state controls. By 1977, most of them had either canceled or pulled out of the socialist republic of Burma. The only willing rescuers left were the two lifelong aid donors, Japan and West Germany, and the international organizations.

THE UN AND THE BURMA AID GROUP AID

The effort to extract external funding began as early as 1976. Ne Win and his ministers "decided to seek large-scale "capitalist" investment for the ailing economy by means of joint-ventures with the private sector and by borrowing up to $2 billion during a five-year period from what became the World Bank's Aid Consultative Group."[37] This Group met in Tokyo in November 1976 and was made up of Australia, Canada, France, the Federal Republic of Germany, Japan, the United Kingdom, and the United States as well as the United Nations Development Program, the Asian Development Bank, and the IMF. After the positive appraisals of the ostentatious economic reform measures of the Ne Win regime and the performance of the economy by the visiting teams of the aforesaid countries, the U.S. AID, the IMF, and the World Bank between 1976 and 1978, this giant consortium of aid donors met again in Paris in 1979 and began pouring in billions in loans and assistance.

In 1979 alone the United Nations Development Program, the IMF, the World Bank's Burma Aid Group, plus other countries such as China, Italy, and Denmark entered into fourteen separate transactions to provide external financing for Burma of close to two billion in U.S. dollars and other hard currencies. The Asian Development Bank, the World Bank, the U.N. Development Program, and the Burma Aid Group together provided $1.169 billion worth of loans and assistance. The last two were the largest donors with $684.4 million and $400 million respectively in aid, soft loans, and assistance. Chinese aid amounted to $80 million, West German aid to 114.5 million DM, and Japanese aid to 3.3 billion yen. The GDP of Burma in 1979 was $5.31 billion and thus the total aid package of the multinational and national donors of over $2 billion in 1979 accounted for roughly 40 percent of Burma's GDP. From 1983 to 1986, the average annual multinational aid to Burma was given as $106.58 million, over 90 percent of which came from the United Nations and its specialized agencies.[38] The International Development Association of the World Bank Group alone provided annual average aid of over $50 million or close to 50 percent of the total multinational aid to Burma during the same period.

U.S. AID

By far the most important, United States leadership was responsible for reestablishing financial relations between the West and the Ne Win regime thus generating a brief remission period from 1980 to 1984 for the cancerous economy of Ne Win's Burmese Way to Socialism. The two basic factors responsible for the willingness of the United States to lead in this multinational venture were "anticommunism" and "the opium." The latter dominated the U.S. aid program in the 1970s. The opening of the economy or rather the quest to reconnect financially with the West began as early as 1974 when the U.S. entered into an agreement with Ne Win to provide aid in the form of military hardware under the International Narcotic Control (INC) Program. As the U.S. State Department Report stated: "In general, U.S. and Burmese interests in narcotics control coincide. During the early 1970s, a growing domestic narcotics abuse problem here focused the attention of the highest levels of the Burmese Government on the need to reduce poppy cultivation and opium trafficking. Furthermore, Burmese criminal and insurgent groups turned increasingly to opium traffic to finance their operations."[39]

Of course, this assessment of the narcotic and opium trafficking by Burmese criminals and insurgents, mostly attributed to the Shan minority insurgents, ignored the fact that the Burmese army itself has been closely tied up with these traffickers in sharing the profit from this extremely lucrative trade emanating from the famous Golden Triangle under the control of the Opium Kings, Khun Sa and Lo Hsin Han. For example, in the 1960s, both of these Opium Kings were assigned as commanders to aid and cooperate with the Ne Win regime when it launched a military campaign called K.K.Y. (Kar Kwe Yay) against the Shan rebels and communists in the Shan state. Khun Sa gained an informal status as the head of all K.K.Y. forces. In 1970, Khun Sa's authority was challenged by Lo Hsin Han and the Burmese government also began to fear his growing power. He was sought and imprisoned by the Burmese government. However, in 1976 he was released when his followers kidnapped two Russian doctors after some covert deals.[40] The case of Lo Hsin Han's trial and release was presented earlier (see Chapter 7).

In any event, beginning in 1974 with an Exchange of Notes, "the United States has supported Burmese Government narcotics control efforts by providing 27 helicopters and 5 fixed-wing aircraft (plus replacement, telecommunication equipment, and associated training and equipment maintenance support)."[41] The INC funding level for 1982 was given as $5.95 million for aviation support and maintenance, telecommunication, income/crop substitution, enforcement, and demand reduction. This military aid to the Burmese government strengthened the military arsenal to wage war against not only the narcotic and opium smugglers but also the minority insurgency in general. The equation of U.S. policies seems to be that the minority insurgents are leftist communists and drug traffickers with whom contact is to be avoided in order not to antagonize the majority Burmese government. Many observers, the majority being minority insurgents, noticed that the military hardware provided by the United States was deployed not to wipe out the poppy fields and refineries of drug kingpins but to suppress minority insurgency. Overholt correctly assessed the U.S. antidrug policy and its results in Burma:

> Yet U.S. antidrug policy in Burma in effect has allied Washington with one of the world's most antidemocratic and vicious regimes. That government's economic policies have forced segments of the population into the drug trade and have eliminated any alternatives to the

> drug economy for some tribal groups. Moreover, the Burmese government did not employ the helicopters and herbicides provided only against the drug trade: It used them primarily as weapons in an extensive war against tribal groups that favor democracy and freer trade rather than the Burmese Way to Socialism.[42]

It must be added further that not only the tribal groups but also the corrupt Burmese military commanders in charge of controlling drugs at the borders as well as the Burmese black market dealers were forced to participate in the highly lucrative drug trade. Furthermore, the provision of American military technology under the U.S. Security Assistance Program, made up of Foreign Military Sales (FMS) and International Military Education and Training (IMET), has helped the military intelligence services of the totalitarian government of Ne Win not only to suppress the minorities but also the entire population of Burma since 1962. It should be pointed out that the basic foundation and arsenal of Ne Win's military intelligence service has been built upon Western sources, mainly the United States and Great Britain, since the civilian government era.

The U.S. economic assistance program under the auspices of the Agency for International Development (AID) resumed in 1980, providing $2 million in that year and jumping to $12.6 million in 1983. Altogether it gave out assistance of over $28 million in dollars and local currency in 1983 alone. Additional funding was given to various development projects such as maize and oil seeds ($8.6 million for fertilizer and equipment) and health and medical care ($5.1 million) along with the reactivation of the 1956–62 PL-480 aid program by transferring K129 million between 1981 and 1983.[43] The average annual total of U.S. loans and assistance between 1983 and 1988 was around $20 million. One other factor responsible for this renewed program of American assistance was the presence of Japanese private enterprises, technical teams, and a strong business footing that had been established in Burma since 1974.

JAPANESE AID

The two most important bilateral donors of aid to Ne Win's Burma were Japan and West Germany which had a long history of personal ties with the dictator. His personal connection with the Japanese veterans of the Second World War dated back to the days of the Thirty Comrades, while his Western German connection dated back to the days of the civilian government of U Nu while he was the Chief of Staff and the Defense Minister. Japanese aid to Burma dated back to the era of the civilian government when the war reparation payments were made. In fact, Brigadier Aung Gyi was intimately involved in the managing of these payments and Japanese assistance when he was running the famous Burma Economic Development Corporation in the early 1960s. His feud with Brigadier Tin Pe and Thankin Ba Nyein of the B.S.P.P. and eventual downfall from the inner-circle of power centered around the policy issue of private capitalist ventures involving Japan and the West.[44] Prior to 1979, Japanese bilateral foreign aid was the primary source supporting the limping economy of Burma.

Japan topped the list of bilateral donors of aid and assistance to the Ne Win regime in the 1980s. From 1982 to 1986, the average annual aid given by Japan to Burma was $140.1 million (net receipts) which was more than 55 percent of the annual average of the total bilateral foreign aid ($255.92 million) to Burma from seventeen different countries of the Western Bloc. This amount was consistently higher than the annual average of the total multinational aid to Burma which amounted to $106.58 million during the same period. That is, Japan provided close to 40 percent of the annual average of the combined bilateral and multinational aid ($362.5 million) in the 1980s.[45] The Japanese played a major role in financing the state Heavy Industries Corporation called Ka Sa La of the Ministry of Industry No. 2 of Burma. Throughout the entire history of the socialist state of Burma, Japanese companies such as Mazda helped set up and finance major installations and factories for producing automobiles and electric appliances for civilian use, although these supposedly civilian factories were very often easily transformed into Defense Products Industries or Factories, Ka Pa Sa, to produce military trucks and other military needs for the Defense Services.

WEST GERMAN AID

The Burmese connection with West Germany, like that with Japan, was firmly established in the 1950s during the civilian government period. In the late 1950s, when Ne Win was the Chief of Staff and the interim Premier of the Union of Burma, the West German firm of Fritz Werner helped set up a Rangoon rifle factory. Throughout the 1970s, West German aid was next to that of Japan in importance in providing the Ne Win regime with economic, technical, and military assistance. West German economic and technical assistance figured prominently in the infamous failure of the state venture to construct a modern textile factory (satirically called the White Elephant Factory) at the town of Paleik located across the Irrawaddy river from Sagaing in Upper Burma. It was begun in the late 1960s with Chinese help for producing modern textiles and was taken over in the 1970s by West German technicians under the directorship of Colonel Maung Lwin, the Minister of Trade who was removed in 1977.

The Fritz Werner private firm, partly owned by the West German government, played a vital role in modernizing the army of Ne Win. Its historical ties with the military regime became apparent when in 1984 for the first time in the history of the Socialist Republic of the Union of Burma, this firm formed a joint-venture company with the military regime known as the Myanma-Fritz Werner Ltd. It was the first foreign joint-venture firm legally allowed to invest and operate in the Burmese socialist state since 1962. This venture was supposedly formed to develop heavy industries under the civilian Heavy Industries Corporation, Ka Sa La, but the Burmese people and the foreign diplomats knew that the real effort was to construct army supply and weapon factories.

In the early 1970s, Fritz Werner also took over the stamps, currency notes, and securities printing factory at Wasi near the city of Chauk, a project initially developed with the help of the East German government. Later, it financed and helped set up weapon and ammunition factories under another state enterprise called Ka Pa Sa, the Defense Products Industries or Factories under the direct control of the Ministry of Defense. With the help of Fritz Werner, many weapon and supply factories labeled as Ka Pa Sa No. 1, 2, 3, etc., were set up in various towns: the largest weapon factory at Sindell in the Prome District, military supplies factories at Inndaing in the Pegu District, and at Htonebo and Nyaung Chidauk (an ammunition factory) in the Prome District of Lower Burma under the management of the Ka Pa Sa. Other major weapon and ammunition factories were Ka Pa Sa No. 1 and three other Ka Pa Sas built near the Inya Lake Hotel along the Peace Pagoda Road in the suburb of Rangoon. From 1983 to 1986, the average annual aid of West Germany to Burma was around $52 million, the second largest bilateral assistance to Burma. As of July 1988, the grand net total grant committed by West Germany stood at DM 242.45 million or over $360 million. The total gross intended or projected aid stood at over DM 1.25 billion, showing West Germany's long-term commitment to assist Burma at that time.[46]

The above external capital inflows into Burma in the 1980s were more than twenty times higher than that of the previous two decades combined. For example, as of 1970 "Burma's net-medium and long-term loans totaled $50.1 million; by 1975 this figure had passed $1 billion and by the end of FY-83/84 it exceeded $2 billion,"[47] representing an increase of forty times between 1970 and 1984. Of course, this phenomenal increase in the debt burden put further strain on the rapidly declining foreign exchange reserves of Burma stemming from its inability to expand its exports or cure the continual trade deficits under the worsening terms of trade in the 1980s. This clearly shows that, but for this massive external pump priming, the Burmese economy would have collapsed long before it attained the least developed country status in 1987.

EASTERN BLOC AID

Of all the Eastern Bloc nations that provided financial and technical aid, the People's Republic of China stood out as the closest and the largest donor to the Ne Win regime. From the very inception of the socialist state under the Burmese Way to Socialism in 1962 up to the present, the Sino-Burmese relationship in terms of diplomatic visits and exchanges of educational and cultural groups may be considered as the most frequent. Although Ne Win fought continuously against the Burma Communist Party which Red China supported and discriminated severely against the Chinese inside Burma, there never was a total diplomatic severance between the two countries. With the exception of the 1967 Sino-Burmese rift, Ne Win was able to employ his "dialectical neutralism" most effectively in the changing climate of world politics. More importantly, Sino-Burmese economic relations centered on the huge informal or black market trade that flourished during nearly thirty years of military rule over Burma. The governments of China and Burma wore blinders to its existence for both political and economic reasons. It will be discussed at length in the next chapter.

Foreign relations with the Soviet Union and the Eastern European countries, Yugoslavia, Czechoslovakia, and East Germany, in the 1960s, as has already been shown, were cordial and close in terms of both political and economic support. The Russian Hotel (Inya Lake Hotel) and the Rangoon Institute of Technology in Rangoon, the Yugoslavian Myauknawin Dam Project and homes built for army officers at the Defense Services Academy at Maymyo, the machine tractors and their stations set up in the rural economy were some of the examples of the Burmese-Eastern Bloc connections. The East German aid given in the 1960s for the construction of a printing factory for Burmese currency notes and securities at the town of Wasi near the city of Chauk stood as a testimony to Ne Win's ability to extract help from around the globe. Both the economy and polity of the Socialist Republic of the Union of Burma were based upon the East German model. The training for both socialist education and military intelligence services was also provided by East Germany when Ne Win sent hundreds of students and army officers to East Germany after the state scholarship to the West was terminated in the 1960s. In the post-1974 period, these relationships cooled somewhat due to liberalization measures and turning towards the West. Yet some of the Eastern Bloc economic and technical assistance remained intact.

NOTES

1. Cf. Richard Lowenthal, "Beyond Totalitarianism," Irving Howe ed., *1984 Revisited*, pp. 212–213.

2. Ibid., p. 213.

3. See for detail Mya Than and Nobuyoshi Nishizawa, "Agricultural Policy Reforms and Agricultural Development in Myanmar," Mya Than and Joseph L.H. Tan, eds., *Myanmar Dilemmas and Options: The Challenge of Economic Transition in the 1990s* (Singapore: Institute of Southeast Asian Studies, 1990), pp. 96–98.

4. Ibid., p. 97.

5. Ibid., p. 103.

6. Ibid., p. 106

7. Mya Than, "Little Change in Rural Burma: A Case Study of a Burmese Village (1960–1980)," SOURJOURN Vol. 2, No. 1, p. 84.

8. The 1972 pay scale was kept frozen until March 1989 when the Saw Maung regime revised the rates upward. See *The Working People's Daily*, Rangoon, March 4, 1989.

9. See Ashok Perakumbar, p. 6.

10. Ibid.

11. Ibid., p. 9.

12. Ibid.

13. See Robert Taylor, p. 359.

14. See J. Steinberg, pp. 92–93.

15. Ibid., p. 93.

16. Ibid.

17. European Intelligence Unit (EIU), EIU Country Profile 1989–90: Burma (London: EIU, 1990), p. 40.

18. FEER, *1977 Asia Year Book*, p. 131.

19. Henry Kamm, "'Socialist Burma': Pervasive Poverty, Indifferent Military Rule," *The New York Times*, New York, June 25, 1975.

20. Ibid.

21. Tin Maung Maung Than, "Burma in 1987: Twenty-Five Years after the Revolution." *Southeast Asian Affairs* (Singapore: Institute of Southeast Asian Studies, Spring 1988), p. 73.

22. Kamm, *New York Times* June 25, 1975.

23. Ibid.

24. C.J.F.S. Forbes, p. 5.

25. See Frank N. Trager, "Democratic and Authoritarian Rule in a Not So Newly Independent Country," in Joseph Silverstein ed., *The Future of Burma in Perspective*, p. 71.

26. Cf. William L. Scully and Frank N. Trager, "Burma 1979: Reversing the Trend," *Asian Survey* (Berkeley: University of California, February, 1980).

27. Steinberg, p. 119.

28. See Mya Than.

29. Steinberg, pp. 92–93.

30. Ho Kwon Ping, "The Cautious Search for Success," *Far Eastern Economic Review* (Hongkong: Far Eastern Economic Review, January 18, 1980), p. 36.

31. Ibid.

32. Ibid.

33. Ibid.

34. Asian Development Bank, *Loan, Technical Assistance and Private Sector Operations Approval, No. 89/09* (Manila: Asian Development Bank, September 1989), pp. 12–13.

35. Ibid.

36. FEER, *1975 Asia Year Book*, p. 140.

37. See Frank N. Trager and William L. Scully, "The Third Congress of the Burma Socialist Programme Party: The Need to Create Continuity and Dy-

namism of Leadership," *Asian Survey* (Berkeley: University of California, 1978), p. 831.

38. From Scully and Trager, "Burma 1979: Reversing the Trend," pp. 170–171.

39. The U.S. State Department, *U.S. Programs—Burma* (Washington, D.C.: Privately Published Report, October 1982), p. 3.

40. An excellent account of the relationships between Khun Sa and Lo Hsin Han and the Burmese government was given by C.T. Yawnghwe (Eugene Thaike) in his, *The Shan of Burma*, pp. 189–190 and pp. 204–205.

41. From the U.S. State Department, (see note 39), pp. 1–3.

42. William H. Overholt, "Dateline Drug Wars: Burma: The Wrong Enemy," *Foreign Policy* (Washington, D.C.: Foreign Policy, Winter 1989), p. 177.

43. U.S. State Department, (see note 39), p. 1.

44. See Aung Gyi, *40-Page Letter to Ne Win* (In Burmese), Rangoon, May, 9, 1988, pp. 30–34.

45. From the sources of OEDC, *Geographical Distribution of Financial Flows to Developing Countries, 1985/86* and EIU, *Country Profile (Thailand and Burma)*, 1988–89.

46. From the source of West German Government, *Landerkurbericht: Birma* (Bundesministerium Fur Wirtschafliche Zusammennarbeit, January 7, 1988), pp. IX–X.

47. From the source of U.S. State Department and the Embassy in Rangoon, *1984 CERP 004: The Foreign Economic Trends Report for Burma* (Rangoon: U.S. Embassy, June 18, 1984), p. 7.

9

The Collapse of the Socialist Economy and Failed Totalitarianism

The collapse of Ne Win's single-party socialist state in 1988 began as early as 1983, when a brief remission period for its cancerous economy ended with the resurgence of galloping inflation and a shortage of goods and services far greater in degree and dimension than any in the previous two decades. The political success in subduing potential contenders for the political throne was matched by the economic failure to cripple the invisible force of a giant black market. The basic foundation and the functioning of this real economy of the socialist republic were so firmly institutionalized and thoroughly entrenched that they could not be altered by ostensible and contradictory reform measures. The same unskilled and corrupt military managers manned the inefficient economy with its vicious circle of controls-evasions-controls which finally got out of control by 1987.

THE COLLAPSE OF THE SOCIALIST ECONOMY—THE NOMINAL OFFICIAL ECONOMY

Before dealing with the nationwide black market representing the real economy of socialist Burma and the disruptive effects of Ne Win's contradictory policies of reform upon its functioning, it is necessary to recall the new double dual economy of Burma created by the Burmese Way to Socialism. As pointed out before, the political and economic survival of both the military elite and the simple folks depended heavily upon the nation-wide unofficial or black market economy. The growth of this market was fueled by the inefficiency of the nominal official economy in meeting the economic wants of the society at large. The glaring inefficiency of the giant superstructure of more than fifty State Economic Enterprises (S.E.E.s) and thousands of state-owned-and-operated factories was reflected in the continuous scarcity of goods at government distribution shops and official trade deficits throughout the 1970s which reached the crisis level by 1983. That is, the collapse of the socialist economy was not sudden but had been in the making for more than two decades of massive neglect of efficiency in the construction of a utopian socialist economy.

Since the state with its more than fifty enterprises monopolized the internal and external trade of Burma and declared all private business activities outside the official market illegal, it is safe to assume that the size of the illegal market was much larger than that of the official one. The case studies and the functioning of the dual command economy presented in this study support this assumption. The indirect indicator of the leakages of goods from the official to the illegal black markets inside and outside Burma can be discerned in the continuous trade deficits of the socialist republic from 1974 to 1984 with the exception of 1979, the year in which Burma received a massive foreign aid. The government reports of phenomenal 6.5 percent and over 5 percent growth rates of G.D.P. in the late 1970s and early 1980s may be contrasted with the equally phenomenal annual trade deficits for the same period. The data in Figure 7 may be used to indirectly confirm the importance of the nation-wide illegal market.

The annual trade deficit from 1970 to 1980 averaged around $40 million compared to the annual average trade deficit of over $380 million between 1980 and 1983. It certainly indicates the inability of the monocultural export-oriented economy of Burma to reverse the trend of retrogression it had suffered for nearly two decades under the gross mismanagement of military rulers. The single most important parameter of Burma's stagnation and trade deficits remains its dependency on rice production and export. A young Burmese graduate student at the University of Michigan aptly evaluated the economic stagnation by providing the data in Table 6 on the comparative shares of Burma and Thailand in the total rice export of the world.[1]

The dramatic drop in Burma's share of rice export in the world total from 26.9 and 30.5 percent in the 1950s and early 1960s to an average of a little over 5 percent in the 1970s drives home the fact that Burma was well on its Road to Poverty by 1980.

In order to be fair, the huge annual trade deficit of more than $380 million during the first three years of the 1980s was due to simultaneous downturns in two independent trade cycles: the rice cycle and the overall world trade cycle. The U.S. Embassy assessed the impact of these two cycles on Burma:

With both the rice market and the world economy in cyclical declines, Burma could not maintain its foreign exchange earnings and was forced to draw down its reserves. The decline in the rice market has resulted from two factors; (a) the small size of the world market; and (b) the implementation of high yield variety (HYV) programs by many of Burma's potential rice customers. The small size of the world market makes it volatile because relatively small shifts in supply or demand can cause major swings in prices. When most of Burma's trading partners successfully adopted HYV programs, it was only a matter of time before prices declined. Burma's rice earnings fell from $219 million in CY-81 [Current Year] to $169.8 million in CY-83.[2]

Figure 7

Exports and Imports in Millions of Dollars

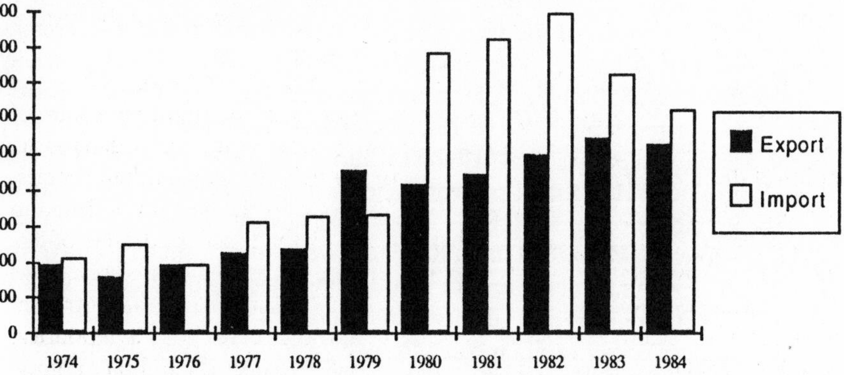

Source: IMF, *Direction of Trade Statistics, Year Books* from 1977 to 1987.

Table 6

Rice Export in Millions of Metric Tons

	1950	1960	1970	1976	1979
Burma	1.231	1.627	.5708	.4282	.6070
% of World	**26.9**	**30.5**	**6.5**	**4.6**	**5.1**
Thailand	1.294	1.255	1.372	1.685	2.723
% of World	**28.2**	**23.5**	**15.0**	**17.9**	**22.9**
World	4.584	5.338	8.794	9.400	11.887

Source: FAO, *Trade Yearbooks from 1950 to 1980*
Note: Figures are in five-year average except 1979.

The significance of this assessment also indicates that the military management had not paid serious attention to the changing structure and conditions of the world market and the international competitive factor in the rice market. More than two decades of creating a hermit state testifies to this negligence. The net effect of this neglect necessitated borrowing from international sources and financing the domestic deficit by pumping more money into the economy and adding more fuel to the already skyrocketing prices in the unofficial black market.

The estimated annual bilateral and multinational capital inflows into Burma during the 1980s were given as $250 to $400 million. By the end of 1984, the debt service ratio, measured relative to merchandise exports, including the IMF repayments, reached over 40 percent. It increased to more than 50 percent by 1987. The long-term debt service ratio, measured relative to the GNP, increased from 1.2 percent in 1970 to 2.8 percent in 1985[3] indicating the growing burden of external debt being used to rescue the dying economy of the Socialist Republic of the Union of Burma. Although the annual average trade deficit of around $136 million from 1984 to 1987 was substantially smaller than the $380 million of the previous three years, the rate of inflation and scarcity of goods increased at an accelerated rate unparalleled in the history of the Socialist Republic of the Union of Burma. By 1987, the growth rate of G.D.P. dropped to less than 1 percent to yield a negative per capita growth rate and the imminent collapse of the economy was realized.

The historical path of the Burma Road to Poverty may be presented in terms of the real growth rate of net output (goods and services plus trade) or G.N.P. from 1969–70 to 1986–87 as depicted in Figure 8.

Growth rates of per capita income from 1973 to 1987 show the incredible journey of the Golden Land to poverty (see Figure 9).

Although the figures on the growth rates of both real net output and real per capita income based upon the government data are grossly exaggerated with respect to their phenomenal rises in 1980–81 and 1984–85, they cannot hide the sudden colossal collapse after 1985–86 when the growth rate of per capita income became negative. By 1987, the bottom of the economy seemed to fall out without any major war or natural catastrophe of any kind to discredit the great rises given in the official reports. On December 11, 1987, the Socialist Republic of the Union of Burma under the military dictatorship of Ne Win officially gained the economically degrading status of one of the 41 least developed countries in the world. The three criteria of the United Nations for granting this unenviable status were a country with less than $200 per capita income, less than 10 percent contribution of manufacturing to G.D.P. and less than 20 percent national literacy. The last criterion was not met by Burma. Hence, although Burma in 1987 remained a literate country, as it had been for many generations, it had become one of the very poorest nations in the world.

Figure 8

The Real Growth of Net Output(%) (1968–87)

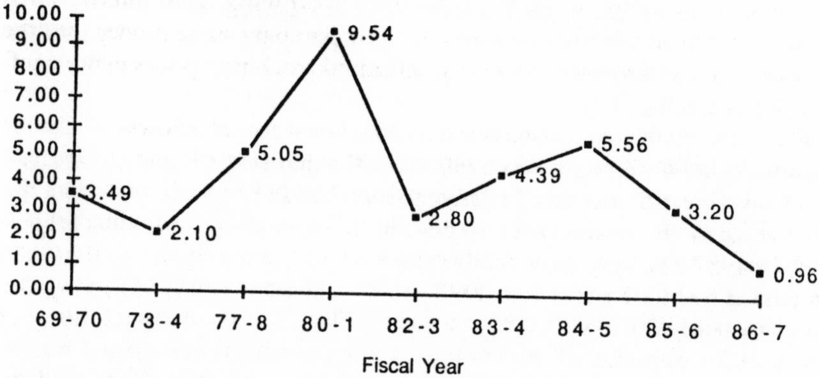

Source: Ministry of Planning and Finance, *The Union of Burma: Review of the Financial, Economic and Social Conditions for 1989–90* (Rangoon: Ministry of Planning and Finance, 1989), pp. 7–8. The adjustment was made to these data by calculating various implicit deflators for these years.

*Net ouptput in the above *Report* refers to the value of goods and services net of inter-industry use plus trade.

Figure 9

Growth in Real per Capita Income 1973–87

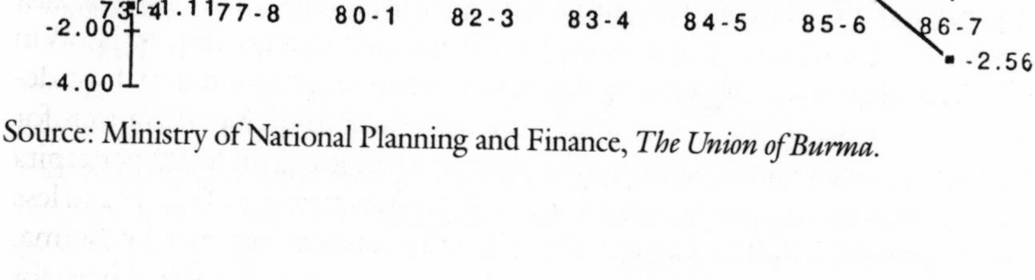

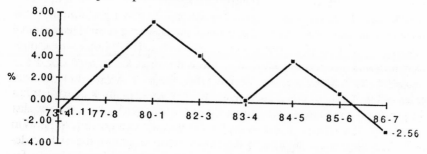

Source: Ministry of National Planning and Finance, *The Union of Burma.*

THE REAL ECONOMY OF BURMA—THE GIANT BLACK MARKET

It has been shown before that the real economy of the dual economy of socialist Burma was the nation-wide black market. As the official economy deteriorated, the size and functioning of this market expanded rapidly in the 1980s. The black market trade flourished along the Sino-Thai-Indo-Burmese borders, which served as the major outlets for exports of Chinese, Thai, Indian, as well as other foreign products to Burma, and conversely, for the export of Burmese jades, gems, minerals, and agricultural, forest, and fish products to Thailand, China, India, and others. There were altogether ten different major black market routes between Burma and its three neighbors of China, Thailand, and India. Six of them were located in Lower Burma connecting the trading posts at the Thai-Burmese border along the southeastern frontier. In terms of size and volume, these routes were the most travelled and important ones for the giant black market. Two others were located in the Shan State connecting the trading posts at the Sino-Thai-Burmese border along the northeastern and eastern frontiers. They represented the second most important routes for the illegal border trade. The other two routes traversed the western coastal state of Arakan and the northwestern frontier along India and Bangladesh.[4]

Of all the black market trade, the Thai-Burmese border trade was the largest. It covered several hundred miles running from Chaing Rai to Ranong. The largest trade points were border market centers in Mae Sot, Phop Phra, Mae Ramat, and Tha Song Yang district. In Lower Burma, the city of Moulmein was the hub of the huge illegal border trade with Thailand throughout the military rule. The most active illegal border trade between Burma and Thailand was conducted along the Thai river of Moei involving more than fifty different Thai market centers or custom outposts. However, the six main outposts of Mae Sai, Mae Sot, Mae Hong Song, Mae Sariang, Kra Buri, and Ranong dominated the entire border trade. Mai Sai was the largest of these Thai outposts in terms of trade volume.[5] From Moulmein to the Thai border alone, there were four different routes connecting various Burmese, Karen, and Mon towns toward the east, northeast, and southeast directions: (1) **Moulmein-Kyondo-Kawkareik-Thanganyin-and-Myawaddy,** (2) **Moulmein-Zathabya-Kaya-Thanlae-Jai-Dawlan-and-Wangka,** (3) **Moulmein-Kawbane-Kawpauk-Angkong-Myohaung-and-Palu,** and (4) **Moulmein-Mudon-Thanbyuzayat-and-the Three Pagodas Pass.**[6] Most of these routes were the ancient trails used by the Burmese kings when they invaded Thailand. The first route of Moulmein to Myawaddy was the most famous one among them. The Burmese border trading post of Myawaddy is located across the Moei River from the major Thai border outpost of Mae Sot.

There were five different outposts in the township of Mae Sot alone. The largest daily trade was observed to occur at the border bridge of Moei Li Chai, one of the five outposts, which connected Thailand and the border region of

Burma under the control of the Karen National Union rebels. As Khin Maung Nyunt reported: "We understand that from Mae Sod 30 pick-up cars arrive per day at the bridge. The value of the goods on each pick-up is believed to be an average of 200,000 baht [around K256,000 at the black market exchange rate of 1 kyat = .78 baht in 1983]. The value of the goods, however, will depend on the type of the goods."[7]

The Thai exports from Mae Sot were mostly basic necessities needed by a Burmese family such as garments, footwear, household appliances, paper towels, powders, pastes, soap, etc. Thailand imported precious and semiprecious stones, livestock, woods, crustaceans, etc.

The next important black market route between Burma and Thailand connected the two respective trading posts of Kawthaung or Victoria Point and Ranong at the southernmost tip of the Tenasserim Peninsula of Burma. The Burmese border city of Kawthaung is connected northward by sea with a series of Burmese cities **Boatpyin-Mergui-Palaw-and-Tavoy**. The major products exported by the Burmese at Ranong were mostly natural rubber, wood, fish, seeds, beans, and pulses, while the Thai goods imported by the Burmese smugglers were mostly manufactured products such as sugar, garments, cosmetics, cement, rubber tires, kerosine, lubricating oil, pastry, biscuits, preserved fish, fish sauce, canned milk, etc. It should be added further that the goods from the countries of the Association of the Southeast Asian Nations (A.S.E.A.N.), particularly Singapore and Malaysia, were also smuggled along this coastal route.

It was reported that in the 1970s Thailand's major exports through the border outposts were "pharmaceutical products, aluminum, wadding rope-coated fabric, boiler machinery, synthetic rubber and man-made fibre," while in the 1980s, the dominant exports of Thailand were "edible preparations, organic chemicals, iron and steel, manufacturing articles and wadding rope."[8] The dominant imports of Thailand from Burma have been wood and wood articles, especially teak, and gems. This economic interest of Thailand in Burmese teak and gems was reminiscent of the British and French interest in the nineteenth century which ultimately led to British colonization of Burma. The rapid depletion of Thailand's forest reserves under modernization programs led to the striking of deals with the Karen insurgents to extract the rich Burmese forests along the border.[9]

The composition of the Burma-Thailand border trade by categories of goods was observed by two Japanese empirical researchers, Takamuri and Mouri, in 1982–83 (Tables 7, 8).

The dominant types of goods traded between Burma and Thailand during the 1970s and 1980s clearly show that Thailand was relatively more modern and economically developed than Burma on the basis of its specialization in and export of manufacturing products. It certainly enjoyed a comparative advantage over Burma in industry and even in agriculture in terms of its relatively more advanced technology. The types of goods exported by Thailand further

Table 7

The Export of Burma to Thailand (in thousands of kyats)

Fish, Food and Others	2,328,750	46%
Opium and Drug	1,950,000	39%
Gems	411,000	8.2%
Timber and Wood	243,250	6%
Livestock	52,500	.5%
Minerals	15,000	.3%
Total	5,000,000	100%

Source: Saburo Takamuri and Suguru Mouri, *Border Trade: the Southeast Asian Black Market (in Japanese)* (Tokyo: Koubundo Publishers, 1984), p. 134.

reflect the shortages of basic necessities in the socialist economy of Burma generated by the inept economic policies of total nationalization and forced rationing of goods by the military regime of Ne Win.

The central city of Mandalay, the hub of the black markets for Upper Burma, was connected with the Chinese mainland by the major route of the famous Burma Road crossing northeastward via the Shan towns of **Hsipaw (Thibaw)-Lashio-Hsenwi (Theinini)-Kutkhai-Muse-Namkham-and-Kyu-hkok**

Table 8

The Export of Thailand to Burma (in thousands of kyats)

Auto Parts and Bicycles	189,750	20.7%
Pastes and Sauces	120,000	13%
Textiles	92,000	10%
Chemical and Watches	61,800	6.8%
Plastic	8,500	1%
Pharmaceutical	45,000	4.9%
Food Products	44,000	4.8%
Electrical Appliances	15,800	1.8%
Miscellaneous	343,000	37%
Total	919,850	100%

Source: S. Takamuri and T. Mouri, *Border Trade*, p. 135.

(Wanting). The last two cities are the Shan trading posts located at the Chinese border along the Shweli River, which connects with the Chinese city of Rui-li (Shweli) in the Yunan Province of China. This route and the majority of the Shan towns were not really new, their existence dating back to the days of the Burmese kings. For example, the last king of the Koanbaung Dynasty, Thibaw, came from the Shan province and the town of Hsipaw. As early as the thirteenth century, the Chinese trading caravans and the invading army of Kublai Khan from China travelled that route.

In the socialist state, this ancient route became one of the busiest roads travelled by illegal native and Chinese traders. The ancient Shan towns served as the major entry points for the inflow of contraband Chinese silk, textiles, ceramics, medicine, tools, bicycles, electrical appliances, stationery, and other items. These imports were either traded on a cash basis or bartered in exchange for the Burmese goods traded illegally by the ethnic minority groups, Shans, Kachins, Pa-os and Was, the Burma Communist Party rebels, and the Burmese, including the army officials, for their economic survival. Trade with China, and also with Thailand, was conducted along two other routes, one located in the Kachin state and another in the Shan state. The route in the Kachin state was less well-known since most of its traffic was located inside Burma. It linked jade and other gem mines in the Kachin state with Mandalay via the Kachin cities of Bahmo and Myitkyina to the Kachin border outpost of **Na Hpaw**. It was the main route for smuggling famous Burmese jade and gems, an activity primarily attributed to the Kachin Independence Army (K.I.A.) and its leader Brang Seng. However, merchants from all the above cities, the K.I.A., Burma Army officials, and other minority tribes also participated in this trade.

The more important second route in the Shan state connected the city of Taunggyi with Mandalay, and to a lesser degree with Rangoon, for border trade with Thailand. The Shan towns of **Taunggyi-Hopone-Loilem-Namsan-Kwanhein-Maibyin-Kentung-and-Tachilek** mapped out this second route southeastward to the Thai border. This route has been the vital outlet for the two most important contrabands of socialist Burma—jade and opium. The Burmese jade known as "jadeite" is the most valued jade next to "nephrite." The Chinese demand for Burmese jadeite began in the late seventeenth century when the emperors of the Ming Dynasty were exposed to Burmese jadeite. Since then the Chinese merchants from Yunan have historically established the Yunan-Burma trade along the old Burma Road, described above, which connected the Kachins and Chinese traders from mainland China for many generations. The link between the merchants of Yunan and the Kachins who owned and mined most of the jade mines was not broken throughout the British rule. Only after the Second World War did the route shift to the Thai border outposts via the second route in Shan State due to the Communist Revolution of Red China and the Burma Communist rebels who controlled the old Burma Road route. Thus, the route was changed and the major base of the jade trade also shifted to Hong Kong.

In the socialist state, the control of the Burmese jadeite trade was almost entirely in the hands of the Kachin rebels since the military regime of Ne Win was never able to subdue the Kachin rebels. Only two of the deposits were under the control of the central Burmese government, which has held an annual state Gems, Jade, and Pearl Emporium representing only a quarter of the total jadeite supply of Burma. The rest of Burmese jadeite found its way to Chiang Mai in Thailand, which is linked with the Kachin mines located between the Uyu and Chindwin rivers not far from the small Kachin town of Hpakan. From this small town the jade mined was carried by bullock carts to the larger town of Mogaung, a trading center for jade for 200 years. The Chinese merchants or their agents came down regularly to bid for the jade. After Mogaung a long journey of some 400 miles marked out the black market trail southeastward travelled with mules by couriers either belonging to various hill tribes or under the protection of the Shan United Army, the Karen National Union, the Wa National Army, or the Kuomintang, the remnants of Chiang Kai-shek's army.

In the socialist state, the politics of jade became the most important power struggle between the central Burmese government and the Kachin Independence Organization (K.I.O.). As Timothy Green observed, "this clandestine trail exists because the socialist government has never been successful in subduing the Kachin people of northern Burma in whose territory the best deposits are located. The Kachin regard the jade mines as their inheritance, and the revenue produced by smuggling provides the main income for the Kachin Independence Organization."[10] It is also the major route for opium trafficking emanating from the famous Golden Triangle under the control of the infamous Khun Sa and his pocket army. Not only opium but also jade, rubies, sapphires, and other famous gems of Burma found their way to Thailand via this route. The main participants included not only Khun Sa but also other Sino-Shan and Sino-Burmese warlords, Burma Army officials, Burma Communist Party rebels, and merchants from Mandalay, Mogok, Taunggyi, Lashio, Tangyan, and Kentung.

The border trade with Bangladesh and India was conducted by two basic routes. The first one connects Mandalay with Monywah along the Chindwin River northwestward through the towns of **Monywah-Ye Oo-Kalewa-and-Tamu** (the Indian border trading outpost). Opium and Burmese gems were smuggled via this route. The larger and more important second route traversed the Arakan state stretching southward from the border town of Maungdaw in the far northern frontier through the cities of **Maungdaw-Buthidaung-Rathedaung-Sittwe(Akyab)-Ramree-Taungup-and-Prome** (the famous Burmese city in Lower Burma) which supplied the illegally imported Indian products to Rangoon and Mandalay. In terms of volume, these two routes were relatively not as important as the other routes.

The exact volume of the total black market border trade of Burma is not known, but some estimates gave the volume to be even higher than the official external trade. However, the *Europa* estimated in 1987 that "the economy of Burma continues to suffer from extensive trading of goods in the black market: in 1985, about two-thirds of such goods were smuggled in from Thailand, and total illegal trade was thought to have a turnover of up to 50 percent of official trading."[11] This generous underestimation may be contrasted with other estimates which gave the illegal turnover trade ratio either equal to or greater than the official one. Two Japanese empirical researchers, S. Takamuri and S. Mouri, gave the figure of K1.810 billion or 85 percent of total official trade in 1983. Of this amount the share of goods smuggled in from Thailand was K920 million or 51 percent of total border trade, with Malaysia and Singapore combined 33 percent, China 8 percent, India 4 percent, Bangladesh 3 percent, and Indonesia and Laos accounting for the rest of total border trade.[12]

By contrast, Harry Kramer estimated the size of Burma's black market in the *Wall Street Journal* on August 3, 1976, as "smugglers move from $100 to $150 million worth of goods between Burma and its neighbors each year. Burma official external trade, at the official exchange rate of 6.7 kyats to the U.S. dollar, amounts to $450 million. At the more realistic open-market rate, 25 kyats to $1, Burma official trade is worth about $120 million."[13] Hence, the size and value of the black market trade was equal to or greater than the official external trade. He further reported that despite its riches in natural resources, Burma exported "less than any place in Asia except tiny Macao, the Portuguese enclave near Hong Kong, and war-ravaged South Vietnam, Cambodia and Laos."[14] In the 1980s, the value of Burmese currency deteriorated rapidly with an 100 percent increase in the black market price for U.S. dollars at the exchange rate K50 to $1. This increased the value of black market trade well above that of the official foreign trade.

THE IMMEDIATE CAUSES AND THE COLLAPSE OF A TOTALITARIAN STATE

The immediate causes of the collapse of the socialist republic of Burma are to be found in the contradictory economic reform measures and ineffective actions taken to dismantle the giant black market by Ne Win, on the one hand, and in the irrational behavior not sanctioned by the traditional culture of Burma, on the other. The contradictory reform measures and their impact have already been discussed. The most important and devastating measure taken by the dictator related to a series of financial actions in introducing new oddly-denominated currency notes and at the same time demonetizing old ones during the period of 1985–1987. The intent of the demonetization measures undertaken during that period was not essentially different from that of the 1964 demonetization measure in that all of them were aimed at destroying the destructive elements in the construction of the socialist economy, namely, capitalists, who were declared to be the main culprits causing economic havoc in the socialist state.

THE 1985 DEMONETIZATION AND THE FIFTH CONGRESS OF THE B.S.P.P.

The year 1985 marked the end of the fourth Four-Year Plan and the beginning of the fifth Four-Year Plan. The Fifth Congress of the B.S.P.P. was held beginning on August 1 at which the Chairman emphasized the importance of fulfilling the economic target of the Twenty-Year Plan launched in 1974 and cautioned the members not to abandon their tasks and work for the achievement of the goal each and every year of the various plans. A review of the past four Four-Year Plans was made and the future targets for the fifth and the sixth Plans were set. The target average growth rate of 5.9 percent for the Twenty-Year Plan was rededicated and the ambitious target of a 7 percent growth rate for the fifth Four-Year Plan was set by admitting the failures of the first two Four-Year Plans to achieve their respective targets of 4 percent while acclaiming the achievement above the target rates of the third and the fourth Plans.[15] The Congress elected some 280 members of the Central Committee, only five of whom were female, at the fifth session of the meeting. Ne Win and San Yu retained their respective positions as the Chairman and the President with the Council of State and the Council of Ministers dominated entirely by military commanders.

During the same year of this ambitious undertaking, the rate of inflation accelerated in the rapidly deteriorating economy. To halt the inflationary pressure, Ne Win resorted to the easy measure of demonetization once again. The state authorized the Council of Ministers to demonetize K100, K50, and K20 notes effective on November 3, 1985, under the Notification No. 1, Special / 85. The people were allowed to exchange these notes for legal tender between November 11 and December 31, 1985. The main targets of attack were the destroyers of the socialist economy labeled as the greedy "black money holders," "black money hoarders," and tax evaders who were responsible for the hyperinflation and scarcity of goods. The only thing new in these clichés in 1985 was the invention of "black money and black moneyed people" in the socialist economy of state capitalism.

On the basis of the cases presented in this study, these so-called black money holders included all wage earners in the black-market-ridden socialist economy of Burma. However, the state newspaper, *Working People's Daily*, still spoke of capitalists by stating that the announcement of the Demonetization Bill was made "to uncover the black money in the hands of the capitalists."[16] In a way, it seemed to have admitted the failure of the Burmese Way to Socialism to free Burma from the yoke of "capitalists" vis-a-vis black money holders who happened to include not only common folks but also corrupt officials.

In a different vein, the purpose of the Demonetization Bill of 1985 was explained by the Deputy Prime Minister and Minister for Planning & Finance, Tun Tin, as: "The K100, K50 and K20 Currency Notes Demonetization Bill was introduced to collect taxes from those who engaged in the unscrupulous economic activities and to prevent the rising prices of foodstuffs and personal goods brought by those who, holding black money, were manipulating the market."[17]

The maximum amount of the demonetized notes allowed to be deposited in exchange for the legal notes was interpreted by one of the members of the Pyithu Hluttaw, Daw Kyi Kyi Sein, of Thingangyun Township in Rangoon as:

> According to the Bill, only one person from each household or organization shall make a single deposit. Should more than one deposit be made only the minimum amount deposited shall be recognized and the remainder of the deposited money shall be confiscated as State property. Likewise, should more than one person from a household or organization make deposits, only the minimum amount deposited shall be recognized and the remainder of the deposited money shall be confiscated.[18]

This zealous interpretation was more ideological than technical. The actual stipulated maximum that a person or organization could deposit to exchange for legal tender was K5,000 and one-half of any deposit in excess. These would be exchanged provided that the depositor could prove its legality. Assuming that a person legally obtained the money, this demonetization measure was tantamount to a 50 percent confiscation of money saved or earned above K5,000. It was a *de facto* imposition of progressive income taxes on all income saved or earned legally. Additional provisions of the Bill included handing out jail sentences of six months to three years for dishonest depositors, tax evaders, and black marketeers.

Like the 1964 demonetization of the same notes (apparently they were reintroduced sometime after 1964), the 1985 Demonetization Bill was hastily passed and haphazardly implemented with flaws which were soon discovered and had to be amended. To begin with, the meaning and the amount of "black money" are extremely difficult to determine in a cash economy of defective statistical and accounting records. In any event, the two basic flaws of the Bill were the first flaw of punishing only the agent depositors and not the "moneyed people" who hired them and the second flaw of not exempting the diplomatic community.[19] This forced the government to amend the Bill quickly by passing two additional ordinances which mandated that only 25 percent of the value of the demonetized notes surrendered be refunded and shortened the period of refund similar to the 1964 demonetization case.

Another equally defective and self-defeating effort to control inflation was the simultaneous issue of K75 new notes with the picture of General Aung San, dressed in traditional Burmese attire, by the Union Bank of Burma on November 10, 1985, during the same period of demonetizing the above notes.[20] Two other notes with K35 and K25 were also introduced into circulation in the same period. Neither the quantity of money, due to the introduc-

Figure 10

The Annual Rate of Inflation

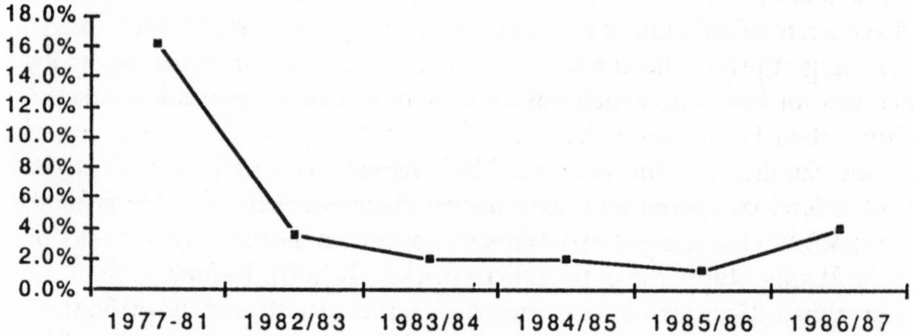

Source: Ministry of National Planning and Finance, *Reports to the Pyithu Hlu Haw (1987–1989)*.

tion of new notes, nor the average velocity of circulation, due to refunding the demonetized notes with notes of smaller denomination, was reduced to curb the inflationary pressure. These contradictory and ineffective monetary weapons used to control inflation seemed to indicate a lack of systematic planning and technical competency in financial management on the part of the military managers of the economy.

The ineffectiveness of these measures to control inflation and stamp out black market activities was more than apparent in 1986 when "the consumer price index, which stood at 136.60 (1978 = 100) at the time of demonetization, showed a slight decline in the first few months, but began to rise in May and reached 141.55 in June."[21] Yet, if one uses the official data on the rate of inflation between 1977 and 1987, it would show an amazing trend of price stability suggesting the enormous success of the military managers' monetary policy in arresting inflation. Data on the annual rate of inflation shown in Figure 10 exemplify the total unreliability of government statistics. These rates of inflation are derived by calculating the relative percentage changes between the G.N.P. at current prices and constant prices of 1979–80 given in the government reports. It shows the government's ostensible success in bringing down the mounting double digit inflation of the late 1970s to an average of less than 2.6 percent in the 1980s.

However, if one looks at the real rates of inflation based upon the price differentials between the official and the black market and the changes in the black market prices themselves, this bright picture turns into darkness engulfed by hyperinflation and triple digit rises in the consumer price indices in the 1980s. The single most important determinant of the cost of living for a Burmese family is rice consumption. The ratio of black market to official price for two qualities of rice, *Nga Sein* (low quality) and *Nga Kywe* (high quality) in January 1985 was given as 2.10 and 3.4 compared with 1.57 and 2.95 in January 1984. The official prices were set at K1.90 and K2.20 per *pyi* during that period.

Hence the rates of inflation in the black market between 1984 and 1985 for these two qualities of rice were 33 percent and 15 percent. Within five months, from January to June 1985 alone, the above two ratios increased to 2.26 and 3.86 or a rate of inflation of 7.6 percent and 13.5 percent, respectively.[22]

The largest price differential between the black market price and the official price was for kerosine, which was used by most urban and rural families for lighting their homes since electricity like everything else was in short supply for most families. In June 1985, the black market price per gallon of kerosine stood at K54 compared with almost unavailable kerosine distributed by the state at K2.6. That is, a gallon of kerosine was sold in the black market at a price almost 21 times higher than the official market (K2.60). In June, 1984, it was sold at a price 11 times higher in the black market than the official price, showing an inflation rate of close to 100 percent. The next item was gasoline whose black market price in 1985 was K17.8 per gallon which was 510 percent above the officially rationed price of K3.50 per gallon.[23]

The consumer price index called the "Rice Bowl Index" may be used to show the rising cost of living based upon black market prices in the urban centers of Burma. This is a simple index made up of three basic items, rice, cooking oil, and charcoal, for moderate and poor urban families. The average size of these two families was five adults and two children for the moderate, and four adults and one child for the poor. Using 1984 as the base, the moderate and the poor family's annual budgets for the "Rice Bowl" in 1985 went up from K3,694 and K1,878 to K4,590 and K2,484, respectively.[24] This represented a 24 percent and a 32 percent rise in the cost of living for the two families. Even using the top pay scale of a gazetted officer with a monthly income of K450 or annual income of K5,400, the cost of the rice bowl alone represented 85 percent of the cost of living in 1985 (4,590/5,400). Since most moderate families did not earn a gazetted pay, the level of poverty for even the moderate family would be at bare subsistence. Using 1985 as the base year, consumer prices rose by some 9.3 percent in 1986 and 36 percent in 1987, while the Rangoon Consumer Price Index rose by 23 percent in 1987 according to the European Intelligence Unit (EIU).[25] To combat these rising prices and cost of living, Ne Win undertook short-term stopgap measures with very little success.

THE 1987 DECONTROL AND DEMONETIZATION MEASURES

The year 1987 marked the silver jubilee of the so-called "socialist revolution" initiated by the Revolutionary Council Government of Ne Win under the banner of the Burmese Way to Socialism in 1962. The failing economy in the relentless grip of the giant black market did not give reason for jubilation and celebration of this failed revolution. Ne Win began to demand "full and frank reports" and candid appraisals of the economy which he had overlooked for a quarter of a century. On September 1, 1987, after hinting to his loyal bureaucracy of some policy changes he wished to make, the dictator made a surprise announcement of decontrolling domestic trade in rice, maize, pulse, and beans. This was done under Notification No. 6/87 of the Council of Ministers which passed the Private Enterprises Rights Law with a provision that all those who wished to establish private firms must register with the local People's Council Executive Committees. This gave a short-lived relief to the farmers and traders.

XENOPHOBIC ASSAULTS

Even this move was made with threats and warnings given to various private businessmen. At the October 9th meeting of the B.S.P.P., he delivered a lengthy concluding speech dealing with the economy, the untrustworthiness of foreign advisers, the selfishness of the private entrepreneurs, and the laziness of the Burmese in general. This was nothing new in regards to the strategy of invoking xenophobia which he had repeatedly employed whenever his programs and policies failed. He stated that:

> After we had gained independence, our Burmese government was patriotic. However, since we had no experience we did not know how to go about in economic matters, we had to ask for advice from others [foreigners].... When we heard that there will be a fall in the pound sterling, we informed London because some of the pound sterlings we had was in London. We instructed the then trading bank—the Burma's Trading Bank—to sell our pound sterling. The adviser who was a foreigner was at the bank. What did he do? He mixed up the word "buy" with the word "sell." Therefore "to sell" became "to buy." If we could have sold the pound sterling, we would not be affected by the fall in the value of the pound sterling, but instead of selling, they bought more pound sterling and we were twice affected because the value of the pound sterling we bought also fell.[26]

This incredible story, with so many holes in blaming the foreigner engaged by the Burma Trading Bank as an adviser, hides behind its smoke screen the self-confessed technical incompetence and lack of knowledge on the part of "the ultimate owner and controller of the pound sterling" itself, the dictator. Putting the blame on a foreigner was the easiest and quickest way of finding a scapegoat for the mistake made by the political ruler in his simple attempt to hedge against the foreign exchange rate risk.

He went on to comment in the same vein on his program of decontrol by accusing the Burmese of being ignorant and lazy, and at the same time giving a stiff warning to greedy businessmen, especially those with foreign blood:

> The Burmese government controlled the hands of the foreigners [after 1962] and gave free rein to the Burmese nationals with a view to en-

> abling them to learn to do business. However, our people are rather lazy, and they also had no experience and so they did what others [military managers or foreigners?] told them to do. In the end, they did everything for their own selfish ends without paying any heed to the interests of the State and the interests of the majority of the people. . . . Now we have given free rein to private hands in the short-term. From here I would like to speak to the private entrepreneurs. We have declared that private entrepreneurs can do business after getting themselves duly registered if they are citizens.[27]

He went on at length to explain his meaning of a Burmese citizen according to the 1982 Burma Citizenship Law which he passed to weed out and discriminate against foreigners, undesirable alien Asian residents of Burma in particular.

The details of this Law need not be presented except that according to this arbitrary law true "Burma citizens" were defined as "nationals such as the Kachin, Kayah, Karen, Chin, Burman, Rakhine or Shan and ethnic groups who have settled in any of the territories within the State as their permanent home from a period prior to 1185 B.E. [Burmese Era], 1823 A.D."[28] The year 1823 A.D. was the year preceding the outbreak of the First Anglo-Burmese War when the Koanbaung King Bagyidaw reigned over Burma. According to this incredible criterion of requiring proof of permanent residency from some 159 years ago, no one in Burma today, particularly Ne Win and San Yu with Chinese blood, will be a true citizen of Burma. The Burmese custom of not using family names or keeping systematic genealogical records is sufficient to show how irrational and lunatic this criterion was. It further specified second-class citizens, "associate citizens" and "naturalized citizens," relative to true citizens. It also did not confer citizenship on foreigners who married a Burmese citizen. He warned those whose ancestors came from foreign countries to settle and do business in Burma that: "What I would like to say to such persons is that they have come to our country, live here, and earn their living here and so, they should make up their minds once and for all to live together with us in weal and woe and through thick and thin. They are the ones who do business most. Take what they should get and enjoy the rights they should enjoy, but if they do business only serving their selfish ends too much, there will be problems."[29]

He focused his whole speech on the incoherent permission for private enterprise to conduct business in the interests of the state and loaded it with xenophobic remarks without explaining the nature and purpose of the privatization that was to help the dying economy.

The nominal character of this ostentatious decontrol measure can be discerned in the passing of two orders which called for tightening the supervision and control of farmers' economic activities, representing the classic Marxist-Leninist strategy of one step forward and two steps backward. On October 6, an order was issued requiring farmers to undertake all operations such as planting, harvesting, storage, milling, and marketing on their own under the direct supervision of the local People's Councils. On November 11, the Council of Ministers issued an order under Notification No. 15/87 forcing farmers and private entrepreneurs dealing in decontrolled crops to pay revenue or taxes in kind instead of cash by stipulating so many baskets per acre. The new laws were called the *Private Enterprises Rights Law* and the *Profit Tax Law*. This was a way of ensuring the delivery of sufficient paddy, rice, and other agricultural produce for state export, which had been decreasing fast. The "Catch 22" of these two orders was the forced extraction of a large enough supply of rice and other agricultural produce for the state co-operative shops and the Myanma Export Import Corporation. In 1986–87, the farmers across the country protested against these measures and the inadequate procurement price increase of paddy and rice, which was well below the black market price, and looted various government warehouses.

CAPRICIOUS EDUCATIONAL POLICY CHANGES

At this juncture, it is relevant to point out another inconsistent and capricious action of Ne Win. In 1980 the English language was reintroduced in the school curriculum as a medium of instruction. Since 1962, not only the English language but also English journals, magazines, dancing, and music had been barred in the socialist state as representative of "degenerate and decadent bourgeois culture," although Ne Win himself was an avid golfer and a regular tourist to London, Switzerland, and Western Europe. Indeed, throughout the 1980s, Ne Win and his aging revolutionary leaders continued to prohibit Western cultural influences such as dancing, rock music, and movies among the youth with very little success. For, like everything else, black markets provided outlets for importing "bootleg" cassettes and posters of Madonna and Bruce Springsteen. The children of military commanders, especially, could not be isolated from this decadent cultural influence. The state-approved tapes of foreign films included Terminator, Commando, Air Wolf, and Rambo, reflecting the military elite's view of what was appropriate for a Burmese audience. In reintroducing English as a medium of instruction and inviting English professors to Burma to teach in colleges in the 1980s, Ne Win contradicted the overt antiwestern cultural policies he had imposed upon the people. This action may be thought of as a betrayal of his personal integrity and philosophy not befitting a ruler.

A policy change of such national significance was made for purely personal reasons rather than to uplift the educational standard. In 1979, his daughter, Sanda Win, reportedly took an entrance examination in English to study at a British medical school, which she failed badly due to her lack of proficiency in the English language, hence the policy change. It was not the first time such a change of national policies was made according to the impetuous whim and wish of the dictator. For example, in 1981, the famous Burma Research Society of Rangoon University was abolished at once under his personal command. It was done immediately after his visit to the University to attend the 70-Year Anniversary of the Society and listen to the symposium. As usual, he indicted this prestigious research institution which had existed for seventy years as an undesirable remnant of the colonial past. All of these contradictory and capricious actions taken by the impulsive authoritarian personality confirm the dictatorial nature of the Burmese polity epitomized in the person of Ne Win.

He also made changes in the educational system, abolishing former faculties or departments of medicine, arts, sciences, and teacher education in the colleges and universities according to his wish to destroy the civilian government's educational institutions. They were simply renamed "Institutes," such as the Rangoon Institute of Technology, the Institute of Economics, the Medical Institute, etc. He also set up regional two-year colleges and so-called General Technical Institutes in the 1970s and later de-emphasized them due to a tremendous surge of grade inflation at these schools caused by the corrupt faculty. The teachers took bribes and inflated the grades for the students who must make good grades to pursue professional fields in the universities. Also, the belated establishment of an Institute of Computer Science at Tha Hmine in the suburb of Rangoon was supposedly set up directly upon his personal wish in 1986 after he saw a modern computer at work. All in all, these capricious actions simply indicate that Ne Win ruled Burma like an ancient despotic Burmese king.

THE DEMONETIZATION OF SEPTEMBER 5, 1987

Four days after the September 1 Announcement of the Decontrol of Rice and Other Crops, the unexpected demonetization of K75, K35, and K25 notes was announced. Notice here that these notes had been introduced only two years before simultaneously with the demonetization of 1985. Unlike the previous two demonetizations of 1964 and 1985, this one was undertaken with no provisions whatsoever for refund enraging the masses. It was tantamount to a forced confiscation of the monetary savings and wealth of the people in general. This unjustified move was the most damaging not only to the masses but also to the dictator himself. To relieve the hardship of the people due to this action, the government gave an extra month's salary to government employees which included workers at state factories and enterprises. A demonstration by Rangoon Institute of Technology students ensued, destroying a cooperative hairdressing salon, hurling stones at riot police, and burning a government jeep near the campus. There were also some minor demonstrations of students in some other colleges across Burma. As before, colleges and universities were shut down and the demonstrators were dealt with by force.

The impact of this action was directly felt first along the Thai-Burmese border where the black markets thrived and later inside Burma whose real economy depended heavily upon the border trade in general. The contagious repercussion of demonetization from the border to central Burma was not as immediately damaging as it was for the border trade. Yet it impacted soon after emptying the already half-empty stomachs of the Burmese people and hurting the limping economy to the point of collapse. It will be suggested here that this action and its damaging repercussions on both the border and internal black markets were the direct and immediate cause for the mass movement downing the single-party dictatorship of Ne Win in 1988.

The immediate impact of the 1987 demonetization on the Thai-Burmese border trade was assessed by Pon Praphanphon in his October 25, 1987, article, "Mae Sot: the Day That City Fell Silent":

> Almost all the consumer goods traded in Burma and the Karen state came from Thailand. . . . It is estimated that at least 10 million baht [20 million kyats or $400,000 at the black market exchange rates] a day flowed into Mae Sot. The value of the goods exported from Mae Sot was at least 5–6 billion baht a year. When the Burmese government demonetized the 25, 35 and 75 kyat notes, those who held millions of kyats complained loudly, because the money had suddenly become worthless scraps of paper. . . . Ever since then, trade in Burma has been very depressed. The old kyat notes were demonetized and new 45- and 90-kyat notes were issued. But merchants have refused to accept the new notes. . . . Large scale trading has come to a halt. . . . As a result, Thai merchants who engage in trade along the Thai-Burmese border are afraid to accept payment in kyats.[30]

Indeed, the depressed state of trade inside Burma and along the border intensified the scarcity of goods and inflationary pressure in 1988 to a degree unparalleled in the entire history of the socialist republic of Burma. As the border trade declined, the value of the Burmese kyat fell at an accelerated rate reaching the low of 5 to 10 kyats to 1 baht, depending on the types of goods traded, compared with the nominal official exchange rate of .34 kyat to 1 baht. Likewise, the black market exchange rate for 1 U.S. dollar soared to K50 compared with K25 in the early 1980s. Hurting both the Thai and Burmese traders and the Karen insurgents who benefitted from the Thai-Burmese border trade, the stage for the political protest of 1988 was set as the economic lifeblood of the black-market-ridden socialist economy was drained.

IRRATIONAL ACTS OF A DICTATOR AND THE INVOCATION OF TRADITIONAL RITES

The most intriguing measure coupled with the September 5 demonetization was the introduction of oddly-denominated K90 and K45 notes effective on September 22, 1987. This simultaneous demonetization of old notes and introduction of new notes into circulation was a common pattern employed previously by the dictator. What was new in 1987 was the outright confiscation of old notes with no refund and the introduction of oddly-denominated K90 and K45 notes. Notice that the cumulative digital value of each of these notes adds up to "9" (9 + 0 = 9 and 4 + 5 = 9). As incredible as it may seem to a modernized Westerner, the Burmese belief in the mystic power of "9," which was shown before in this study to be a common belief in both Eastern and Western ancient cultures, is an unshakable Burmese cultural trait. The belief in the luckiness of this number can also be discerned in the playing of a Burmese card game similar to Blackjack which places number "9" as the highest winning number and "10" as the losing one or burst, *bu*. Ne Win shared this belief which a modern man would term irrational.

To most Burmese, the choice by the dictator of 90 and 45 for the denominations of the new notes indicated the performance of a traditional ritual based upon the mystic power of "9" to counteract misfortune or ensure success for an important venture. The Burmese term for this act is *koenawin chai*, the term "koe" signifying number "9." As was shown in detail in an earlier chapter, the belief in numerology, astrology, and the occult dated back to the days of the Burmese kings. Like most traditional people of the world, the Burmese in general tend to look for help in times of crises from providence or the unseen spiritual power beyond the mundane world. Ne Win is no exception to this cultural trait. With respect to this national Burmese cultural trait, an astute native writer named U Saw Tun wrote in 1942:

> The Burman is a great believer in omens, portents and signs. Hardly a thing happens before he begins to interpret it either as good or bad. . . . It is difficult to knock this trait out of the Burmese people. I have met many Burmans brought up in England, with high academic degrees from Oxford and Cambridge, so thoroughly Anglicized that they hardly speak the Burmese language on their return to their mother-land, who visit fortune-tellers and ask them to interpret certain signs that heralded their birth. Yes, it would be well-nigh impossible to get the Burman out of this habit. He has been born with it, and it has grown with him.[31]

Indeed, the consulting of astrologers, *baidin sayahs*, and the heeding of their advice are an integral part of the life of a Burman. Not only Ne Win but also his high-ranking commanders, the butcher Sein Lwin who is known to be highly versed in astrology for example, were known for their interest in astrology and consultation with their own private professional astrologers whom they kept as advisers. This again is nothing new since a Burmese monarch gave a prestigious status to his royal Brahman astrologer known as *ponnar* in his royal court. Consultation with a *ponnar* for advice was an integral part of performing his kingly duties or waging wars against enemies. As for ordinary folks, they could not afford private *baidin sayahs* in Ne Win's socialist state.

The custom of reliance on soothsayers and spirits, *nats*, reportedly picked up momentum in the socialist republic of Burma as both elites and simple folks were caught in the vicious circle of misfortune and fear. In the streets of major cities as well as in rural communities across Burma, the traditional customs of consulting various native soothsayers and performing animistic rites have been as buoyant as the black market activities themselves. One humorous Burmese remarked that, "the astrologers, *baidin sayahs*, are doing business like hell" and observed that a small and thin female child spirit named Ma Nell Lay had become Ma Nell Gyi—she got big and fat since many sacrifices were made to her by the Burmese. In Upper Burma near Mandalay, the annual festival of worshipping a pair of spirits named Shwe Hpyin Nyi Naung or Taung Byone Nats has been held with a level of attendance never seen before in the history of independent Burma.

Ne Win's reliance on traditional practices, astrological rituals, and supernatural spirits for good luck under the advice of his own personal soothsayer, Sayah Myaing, began to pick up frequency as early as 1980 as his political kingdom showed signs of potential downfall. There are several accounts of his acts, details of which are known only among the Burmese inner-circles, although some of them surfaced occasionally to the outside world.

One other number which represents a danger or a bad omen to the Burmese is the number "8." As the story goes, it is based upon the legend of the Fall of the Tagaung Dynasty in A.D. 888. Ne Win is believed to be afraid of this number. For example, the massive demonstration against Ne Win's puppet President, the butcher Sein Lwin, was deliberately held on 8/8/88 by its leaders who supposedly knew Ne Win's fear of that number. It seemed that they also believed in this number for the successful downing of the military dictatorship. It has also been suggested that the final demise of the dictator may take place when he is "80" years old in 1991.

The prediction of future events or rather wishes based upon certain signs on the pagodas and statues of Buddha is commonly found throughout the political history of Burma. For example, the end of the British rule was supposedly heralded by similar signs at various pagodas. U Saw Tun told this story: "I remembered clearly in 1940, just before I left Burma for the United States, there was a stir because "Os" were supposed to have appeared on the pagodas, on the statues of Buddha and the sacred banyan trees. The Burman interpreted this as a sign of approaching freedom from British domination."[32]

All of these incidents simply confirm the central thesis of this study that Burma has been a traditional society with few changes in belief and behavior for generations and that the reign of terror under Ne Win and his military commanders for nearly thirty years has reinforced the traditional belief system and barriers to modernization.

NE WIN'S PAGODA—MAHAH WIZAYA

Real evidence of Ne Win's reliance on traditional customs and the ritualistic aping of the ancient Burmese kings can be found in the construction of his infamous pagoda, Mahah Wizaya, which stands today as a testimony in Rangoon at the foot of the famous Shwe Dagon Pagoda. The story of this pagoda is common knowledge among the Burmese, especially government workers in Rangoon, who were forced by local People's Councils to contribute donations out of their hard-earned pay during the 1980s. The following is the inside story told to me by the Venerable U Wimala who was personally involved in the project:

> It began in 1980 when the King of Nepal, Mehendra, gave a small statue of Buddha about a foot tall called Pinsa Lawha Hpayar as a gift to Ne Win along with other relics of Buddha. The statue was made of five different metals, *kyay ngarmyo*, and was brought back to Burma. In 1981, the construction of a pagoda to enshrine the statue and the relics began in Rangoon when Ne Win deliberately chose the site near the famous World Peace Pagoda, Kabah Aye Zaidi, and the Great Cave constructed by U Nu during his premiership. The original name of the pagoda was Mahah Zaidi. The builders and construction workers neither approved the site nor wished to see a rival pagoda opposite the famed World Peace Pagoda of U Nu. As the ground was prepared and the brick foundation for the pagoda was being laid, a group of clever persons put a family of strayed dogs at the site to signal a bad omen, *namate*. The construction was halted immediately and the new site was chosen by the dictator. In 1982, upon the advice of his astrologer, the new site was chosen near the Kandawmin Park at the foot of the Shwe Dagon Pagoda where U Thant and Thakin Kodaw Hmine were buried. Thus, the new pagoda of Ne Win named Mahah Wizaya was born.

During the period of constructing this pagoda, a Burmese poem or song with futuristic omens floated among the people of Rangoon and goes as follows:

> **Kalar Hpayar Htee Tin;**
> (When the Umbrella is crowned on the Indian Pagoda);
> **Nai Winloej;**
> (The Sun shall certainly disappear);
> **La Ma-htwet;**
> (And the Moon will not rise up);
> **Sanai Min Pyet.**
> (The Saturday-born King shall self-destruct).

It was called the Indian Pagoda, Kalar Hpayar, because of the gift given by the King of Nepal. Although Ne Win is not really a Saturday-born person because of his original name Shu Maung (a Thursday-born person), he used the name Ne Win and the omen seemed to be directed against the ostensible Saturday-born ruler of Burma. Afraid of this dark omen, Ne Win reportedly postponed the crowning of the umbrella on his pagoda for a few years. This tradition goes back to the Burmese kings who kept the construction of their pagodas incomplete upon bad omens or signs, *atate* or *namate*. With respect to the faithful practice of a Burmese of interpreting signs and acting accordingly, U Saw Tun wrote: "He practices it every day, and if things do not come true, it is not the signs but his interpretations that were wrong. For did not his master the learned monk [more correctly the soothsayer] tell him that all events, either great or small, are heralded by signs?"[33]

Regarding the traditional political and cultural significance of a pagoda built by a Burmese king for the atonement of sins committed during his reign, a Burmese writer using the pseudonym of Moksha Yitri wrote: "In this category is the massive and brooding Dhammayangyi Temple (built in 1170 A.D. but never completed) at Pagan. It had been commissioned by the patricide-king Narathu (1167–1170) before he was murdered and seems to embody the "dark horror of his soul." It should be interesting to see how later generations regard the Maha Wizaya."[34]

The crowning of the umbrella on the Mahah Wizaya was done before 1988, the year Ne Win resigned from his official rulership of Burma. According to the Buddhist custom, the umbrella-crowning of a pagoda is considered to be the final act of completion. Perhaps the omen came true after all. However, unlike the pagodas built by previous famous rulers of Burma, gold sheets have yet to be laid upon it and other shrines have not been completely constructed, making one wonder whether or not the pagoda is completely finished. Hence, the brooding Pagoda of Ne Win stands today naked in Rangoon with no glittering of gold. The estimated cost of this pagoda was K20 lakhs or 2 million most of which was extracted from the people without choice.

Despite the lack of empirical proof with respect to the validity of these omens and actions, it is certain that Ne Win like many other prominent civilian rulers of Burma adopted the traditional customs and practices of Burmese kings. The very name of Mahah Wizaya was borrowed from the name of the famous pagoda built by Bayintnaung of the Toungoo Dynasty in the sixteenth century. From a modern perspective, these archaic acts represent authoritarian personality traits, described by Hagen in this way: "Rather than rely on his own analysis to solve problems of the physical world or his relations to other individuals, he avoids pain by falling back on traditional ways of behavior."[35]

VISIT TO MONYWA AND PERFORMANCE OF NUMEROLOGICAL RITES

One of the less well-known rituals performed by Ne Win to safeguard his power and political throne related to his 1986 visit to Monywa in Upper Burma to celebrate the birth centenary of the renowned Buddhist clergyman, the most Venerable Ledi Sayahdaw. This prominent leader of the Buddhist clergy was the second Ledi Sayahdaw to reside in Monywa and came to political fame during the British colonial period. The first was born and lived in Monywa during the reign of King Min Doan. The ostensible purpose of the visit was to repair and rebuild the famed Ledi Monasterial Abode, Ledi Kyawntite, together with the wish of Ne Win's wife, Ni Ni Myint, who was appointed the Head of the History Department of the Rangoon University without a Ph.D., to study the archives of over one hundred Buddhist stone inscriptions, preachings, and writings compiled by the two Ledi Sayahdaws. According to Venerable U Wimala, the real purpose of Ne Win's visit was to perform certain rituals to sustain his power and counter omens. U Wimala described some of the acts he undertook upon the advice of his astrologer:

> In order to counter the potential loss of power, he entered the famous abode of Ledi Sayadaw from the northern gate or entrance after ordering his subordinates to dig up an artificial ditch to build a bridge which he was required to cross for the successful act of countering potential danger, *yadayah chai*. The use of a northern gate instead of a southern gate symbolizes a bad luck, *ar-min-galah*, to the Burmese. Customarily, it is the northern gate through which the body of the dead is carried for burial in a cemetery. In the performance of the ritual, the deliberate act of using the bad gate is required to preterminate the future bad happening. During the same period, Ne Win also performed the rituals based upon the mystical power of "9" by ordering his soldiers to plant 27 (2 + 7 = 9) flower plants called diamond plants in Burmese, *seinpan pins*, on a Thursday. In terms of Burmese numerology, Thursday has 18 (1 + 8 = 9) astrological planets, *gyos*. He also gave alms and "9" different medical products of the state Burma Pharmaceutical Industry to the monks.

The sacred ground of the abode of Ledi Sayahdaw symbolized the winner circle or the "winning earth," *aung myay*, upon which the General must stand to perform the traditional rituals. All of these known acts since 1980 seemed to reflect the behavioral pattern of a ruthless monarch in times of personal and national crises.

There were many stories told among the Burmese with the common denominator being how Ne Win believed himself to be the descendant of the Koanbaung Kings and emulated their behavior. The belief in the occult and the supernatural cuts across the entire spectrum of Burmese society and the ritualistic aping of the Burmese kings by Ne Win reflects an aspect of the unchanging behavior and belief system of a traditional society. At any rate, all the political leaders of independent Burma invoked the past heritage of the Burmese kings as was shown earlier. Unlike relatively more passive and religious Burmese political leaders such as U Nu, General Tin Oo, and Aung Gyi who sought refuge in religion by becoming Buddhist monks as political misfortunes struck, Ne Win relied upon the oldest of all customs by practicing occult rituals. In a way, this seems to fit the behavior patterns of many authoritarian rulers and dictators in both traditional and modern societies around the world.

NOTES

1. Stanley Tun Thwin, *Agrarianism; The Burmese Context—Past, Present and Future*, Unpublished Term Paper (Ann Arbor: University of Michigan, Urban Planning 658, November 21, 1989), p. 18.

2. U.S. Embassy, *1984 Foreign Economic Trends Report for Burma, CERP 004* (Rangoon: U.S. Embassy, June 18, 1984), p. 5.

3. Ibid.

4. See Saburo Takamuri and Suguru Mouri, *Border Trade: Southeast Asian Black Market* (In Japanese) (Tokyo: Kobundo Publishers, 1984), pp. 145–157.

5. See Khin Maung Nyunt, *Market Research of Principal Exports and Imports of Burma with Special Reference to Thailand (1970/71 to 1985/86)* (Bangkok: Chulalongkorn University, March, 1988), p. 106.

6. See Takamuri and Mouri, pp. 145–150.

7. Khin Maung Nyunt, p. 98.

8. Ibid., p. 92.

9. Ibid., p. 93.

10. Timothy Green, "Jade Is Special, As Are the Risks in Bringing It from Mine to Market," *Smithsonian Magazine* (Washington, D.C.: Smithsonian Institute, July 1986), p. 30. Chao Tzang Yawnghwe, a Shan rebel who served in the Shan State Independence Army and travelled this route, also provided relevant information about this route and the jade trade.

11. Cited by Khin Maung Nyunt, p. 94.

12. Takamuri and Mouri, pp. 131–135.

13. Harry Krammer, " Poor Rich Land," *Wall Street Journal*, August 3, 1976.

14. Ibid.

15. See B.S.P.P., *Lanzin Thating*, (In Burmese) Rangoon, August 8, 1985, pp. 6–7.

16. *The Working People's Daily*, Rangoon, November 6, 1985.

17. *The Guardian*, Rangoon, November 6, 1985.

18. Ibid.

19. FEER, *1987 Asia Year Book*, p. 118.

20. *The Guardian*, Rangoon, November 4, 1985.

21. FEER, *1987 Asia Year Book*, p. 118.

22. The U.S. Embassy, *The Rice Bowl Index* (Rangoon: The U.S. Embassy, 1985).

23. Ibid.

24. Ibid.

25. European Intelligence Unit, *EIU Country Profile* 1990, p. 47.

26. "Ne Win's Speech At Socialist Program Party Meeting," *Working People's Daily*, (Rangoon, October 10, 1987), pp. 1–2.

27. Ibid., p. 2.

28. See *Working People's Daily, Special Supplement* (Rangoon, Saturday, 16 October, 1982), pp. A–B.

29. "Ne Win's Speech . . . ", (see note 26).

30. Joint Publication Research Service (JPRS), *Kyats Demonetization, International Trade Competition* (Washington, D.C.: JPRS, January 6, 1988), p. 2.

31. U Saw Tun, "Tales of a Burmese Soothsayer," Hiram Haydn and John Cournos eds., *A World of Great Stories* (U.S.A.: Crown Publishers, 1961), pp. 838–839.

32. Ibid., p. 838.

33. Ibid., p. 839.

34. Moksha Yitri, from his original draft of the published paper, "Burma: Back from the Heart of Darkness," *Asian Survey* (Berkeley: University of California, 1989).

35. Hagen, *The Theory of Social Change*, p. 97.

10

From the Union of Burma to Myanmar

All the drastic action taken towards the end of 1987 and its immediate impact on the economic life of the people of Burma set the stage for the outburst of political turmoil beginning in March 1988. The violence and intensity of the confrontation between the Burmese army and the demonstrators from March to September 1988 were far greater than that of the Chinese revolt at Tiananmen Square a year later, which received greater and wider coverage in the Western news media. In terms of death and destruction, the massacre of 1988 was unparalleled in the entire history of modern Burma. The scenes and stories of killing and violations of human rights were reminiscent of some of the stories of brutal massacres of ethnic minorities committed by the Burmese kings. The only difference between the two was the naked and indiscriminate slaughtering of unarmed demonstrators by the Burmese army equipped with modern lethal weapons.

The political drama of Burma since March 1988 has mirrored some of the brutal images of the past and reflected the rule of force imposed by the Burmese kings—the owners of the life, head, and hair of their subjects. It also brought out some of the basic characteristics and weaknesses of the Burmese polity. It will be suggested that the dictatorial regime of Ne Win and other totalitarian regimes share a common problem of disorderly succession to the political throne due to their basic political power structure which is personalized and centralized in the Big Father. The success of the Praetorian Army of Ne Win in subduing the opposition has been due to the two interrelated factors of its unity or rather organizational efficiency and the very disorganization of the opposition itself.

THE ECONOMIC ROOTS OF THE POLITICAL PROTESTS OF 1988

The political upheavals of 1988 were deeply rooted in the economic immiserization of the masses which reached its breaking point under the direct impact of the irrational socio-economic actions taken by the dictator in 1987. A brief account of the heightened scarcity of goods and escalated inflation at the beginning of 1988 will help to highlight the bursting forth in 1988 of the accumulated economic miseries and political frustrations suffered by the people of Burma for more than a quarter of a century. The major causes of this economic crisis have already been given in detail. To recapitulate, by the end of 1987, the economic chaos created by the assault on the nation-wide black market which formed the economic life line of the masses was already apparent in the accelerated drop in per capita output and rise in the cost of living in the urban centers.

In terms of aggregate data, the growth rate of per capita output in 1988 was negative 11 percent relative to negative 4 percent in 1987. The rise in the consumer price index of Rangoon between 1987 and 1988 was given as 32.1 percent, while consumer prices in general rose by some 16 percent for the entire country.[1] Relative to those monthly pay scales of urban workers, schoolteachers, professionals, and civil servants discussed in the case studies, these rises in the cost of living represented a below subsistence level of existence. The average rate of inflation between 1987 and 1988 was commonly estimated at 30 percent which means that the real income of most urban workers was cut in half in major urban centers.

For example, the minimum daily wage of a state factory worker increased from K5.40 in 1980 to a high of K8.50 in 1988. This was an annual rate of increment of about 15 percent. Hence, an urban blue-collar worker would earn only K204 (6 working days a week) a month in 1988 at the minimum daily wage of K8.50. The black market price of the low quality rice in August 1988 was K15 per *pyi* (4.69 pounds). Assuming the worker was single and consumed about 1 basket of rice (16 *pyis*) per month, the cost of rice consumption alone at that price would be K240 showing that he could not afford to buy rice, which was his main diet. As a matter of fact during the seventeen-day presidency of Butcher Sein Lwin, the rioters in Rangoon shouted the slogan, "since the price of one *pyi* of rice is K15, let's behead Sein Lwin" in Burmese—*san da-pyi- setngar kyat*, Sein Lwin *gonggo hpyat*.

As for the peasantry across Burma, a relatively lower rise in the cost of living, together with the consecutive increments in the state paddy procurement prices between 1972 and 1988, had not affected their subsistence level of living standard as much as the escalated inflation had the urban workers. This relative disparity of economic hardship between the urban center and the rural periphery explains why the political protests of 1988 began at the political center, namely, Rangoon. Indeed, throughout the twenty-eight years of the Burmese Way to Socialism the heaviest economic and political price was paid by the urban dwellers, especially the proletariat, rather than the peasantry. It also explains why Ne Win was successful in retaining his political crown for so long since the peasants which constitute more than two-thirds of the Burmese population were relatively less poor than the minority urban population.

This by no means suggests that the farmers were economically and politically better off under the benevolent Burmese Way to Socialism, but rather points out that the breaking point or the tolerance level of economic misery imposed by the state was somewhat higher among the rural population. For, as in most underdeveloped economies, they have not been acculturated to modern luxuries and ways of life as the urban dwellers have and their simple and traditional socio-economic life has remained unchanged for many generations. The gap between the center and the periphery with respect to economic privileges, life styles, and wealth has always been wide throughout the history of Burma, but the gap between the urban elite and urban ordinary folks has widened to such an extent that the majority of urban workers for the state could no longer tolerate it as their living standards sank rapidly below subsistence level.

The basic index of urban economic poverty in the socialist economy was the price differential between the prices of goods rationed and sold by the state shops and those sold by the black marketeers. The ratio of black market prices to official prices in 1987 and 1988 may be used to show the state of urban poverty in Rangoon and other major cities for the purpose of explaining the mass movement for downing the single-party dictatorship of Ne Win first and the later demand for democracy in 1988. The ratios of prices for food, medicine, gasoline, and personal care as of October 1987 are shown in Figure 11.

It should be recalled that the end of 1987 had already been marked by the collapse of the socialist economy due to the wars waged by Ne Win with a number of irrational economic measures whereby the prices in the black market skyrocketed. This economic crisis continued as 1988 began with shortages of goods and political unrest. Black market prices rose at an accelerated rate, by October 1988 reaching an unbearable breaking point for the urban dwellers (see Figure 12).

The three categories of food, medicine, and personal care are a composite of various essential products which were controlled and had listed official prices, while gasoline is a single item. From the data in Figures 11 and 12, it can be seen that food prices went up by close to 28 percent, medicine by 50 percent, and personal care by 290 percent, while gasoline prices had risen by some 136 percent in October 1988. The rise in gasoline was not really as significant as the other categories since most of the urban population could not afford an automobile. However, it indirectly reflected the tremendous shortage of energy for the country as a whole.

The most devastating rise in food prices was that of rice: black market prices for the two good qualities, Nga Kywe and Emata, were K320 and K272 per basket compared with the official prices of K56 and K37.60 per basket in October 1988. Thus these two qualities of rice were sold in the black market at prices 571 percent and 723 percent higher than the official prices. It should be pointed out that most of the time these two good qualities of rice were unavailable at the government shops due to both government mismanagement and corruption. Most families were forced to buy low quality rice such as Nga Sein, which also began to disappear from the shelves of state co-operative shops and was sold in the black market at prices several times higher than the official prices. At these black market prices, even a high-ranking government executive

Figure 11

Ratio of Black Market Prices to Official Prices—October 1987

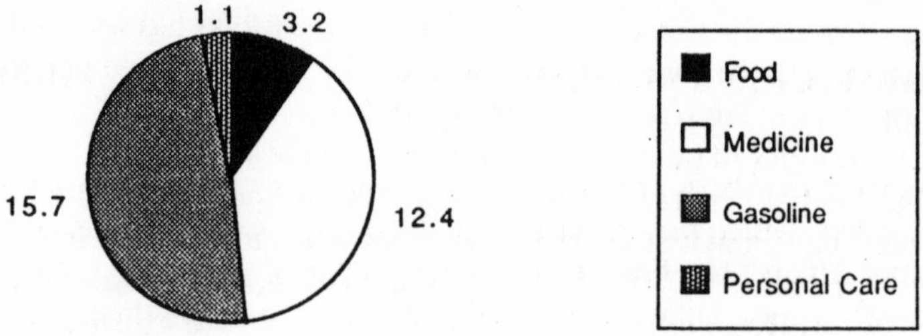

Source: U.S. Embassy, *Shadow Survey*, October 1987.

Figure 12

Ratio of Black Market Prices to Official Prices—October 1988

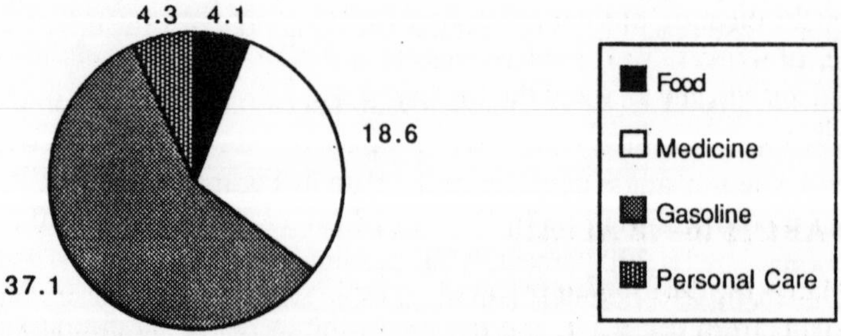

Source: U.S. Embassy, *Shadow Survey*, October 1988.

with a K800 monthly income could no longer feed good quality rice to his family of four who consumed roughly three baskets of rice per month.[2]

Against this background of economic crisis, the political upheavals of 1988 come into focus as the rupture of the economic miseries suffered by the urban population. Particularly important was the fact that for several years the new generation of college graduates could not find jobs, the socialist economy of Burma being under siege by stagflation. The students' political consciousness and anger at the military dictatorship were born out of the rampant unemployment of the newly educated caused by the mass education movement as well as the discriminatory policy of the military rulers against the educated relative to the uneducated in the socialist state. Consequently, their economic miseries reached the breaking point first and exploded into violent political protests precipitating a nation-wide movement. Thus, the violent protests and massacres of 1988 began with a seemingly innocent quarrel between a couple of Rangoon Institute of Technology (R.I.T.) students and the owner of the Sanda Win tea shop in the suburbs of Rangoon in March.

THE DEMOCRACY MOVEMENT AND THE KILLING FIELDS OF 1988

There were four basic confrontations between the outraged masses and the military rulers, which may be termed the March, the June, the August, and the September Affairs. The first two incidents were mild relative to the latter two in terms of violence, killing, death, and destruction, yet all of them represented the ruthless violation of the fundamental human rights of the people of Burma by the military rulers in a way which had never before been seen in either colonial or independent Burma. These incidents brought out the worst socio-political character on both sides of the confrontation with the oppressor taking a very low death toll in the process of annihilating the unarmed demonstrators in the streets of the cities across Burma. They also revealed the traditional weakness of fragmentation among the highly disorganized opposition groups and the chaotic problem of succession to the political throne ostensibly left empty by the dictator. Since the details of each incident have been described by a number of writers,[3] only the basic nature and essence of these affairs will be presented analytically to show the backward and forward linkages of the Burmese polities.

THE MARCH 16–18 AFFAIR

The March 18, 1988, Affair began as a random incident of a quarrel between two students from the R.I.T. and the son of the owner of the Sanda Win tea shop on March 12. A fight broke out and a student named Win Myint received a severe head wound inflicted by *dar*, the Burmese sword. On the evening of March 13, a gang of one hundred or so RIT students went back to the suburb and a violent confrontation broke out between them and the gang of Gyogoan residents. The students were pushed back to the RIT campus and the confrontation grew larger in size and violence. Later that evening, the Security Unit, *Lon Htein*, of Butcher Sein Lwin moved in to break up the confrontation using fire hoses with little success. Later, tear gas, batons and guns were used and students were brutally subdued and forced to confine to their hostels. During that crack down, Maung Hpone Kyaw, a student Red Cross worker and leader of the BSPP Youth Organization, was shot and killed, while another student, Soe Naing, was critically injured and later died at the Rangon General Hospital on April 16. The burial of Hpone Maw at the designated cemetery of Kyandaw by the students was not allowed by the police who took the coffin away and cremated the body at Tamwe Crematorium on March 16. This ignited a rampage of student protests across various college campuses and in the central sections of Rangoon between March 16 and 18 calling for the end of the fascist military regime. It resulted in the arrest, beating, and violent killing of students, which were revealed to the outside world for the first time in the history of the Socialist Republic of the Union of Burma.[4]

It was not accidental that the incident occurred at a tea shop. The total suppression of freedom of expression and thought in the nightmare state of Ne Win had made tea shops relatively safe havens for enjoying forbidden music, political discussions, and debates for the students in the major urban centers. These tea shops were regularly visited by Burmese for the custom of drinking tea and eating an Indian pastry called *samusah* or the Burmese dessert of fermented tea leaves, *la hpet*, in the evening. In fact, Aung Gyi owned several of these in Rangoon and elsewhere, becoming a millionaire as a private entrepreneur. He also became politically active covertly using these shops as a political base for popular support. His views and opinions against the military regime seemed to have spread among the students and other visitors prior to the 1988 upheavals. Thus, the incident at the Sanda Win Tea Shop came to light as a natural starting point for the March Affair.

The March 16–18 massacre led to the charge of human rights violation by former Brigadier Aung Gyi who began to write a series of letters to Ne Win and his associates. This is the first time that the issue of human rights violations was raised publicly and received some international attention. During the twenty-six previous years, human rights violations were regularly made by the military regime of Ne Win, yet they had never surfaced and received serious attention inside or outside the nightmare state. The explanation for this lies in the relative degree of openness of Burma in the mid-1980s because of Ne Win's need to keep depending upon Western foreign aid in order to appease the impoverished masses. Although Aung Gyi's writing was rather timid, carefully avoiding a direct attack on his former boss, it was the first of its kind written by a Burmese political figure detailing the brutal massacre of students and human rights violations. The following is an excerpt from his letter dated June 6, 1988:

> Bogyoke [General] Sir,
> You have now attained a ripe old age and even I am 70 years old. You have done what you believed was best for the country and naturally the results are mixed, some good and some bad; some mistakes have also been made. But this is only to be expected and experienced by all leaders of countries. . . . However, there is one thing which I wish to say, and the fact is that you alone are being held responsible for unrealized aims, goals and improvement of the country.[5]

It is apparent from these introductory remarks that Aung Gyi dared not charge and put the blame squarely on the shoulder of the dictator for he would have been arrested immediately. He went on to assert that he did not wish the General to become the scapegoat for the 1988 student demonstration and its aftermath which had been dubbed "the March Affair." The ugliest sights of the student massacre at Inya Lake were described by him as follows:

> The normal methods of dispersing crowds were not employed. Instead, the students were first trapped and then beaten to death. . . . Most of the beaten on the embankment were girls. Some of the girls were dragged by the hair and kicked into the lake. Those who attempted to swim ashore were again beaten, including those who knelt in postures of prayer and supplication. Those who ran away and lost their longyis [lower garments] in the process were pulled back by the hair and beaten. They were kicked into the water in broad daylight. There were many who died in Insein Jail that night, and the bodies were cremated at Kyandaw Cemetery from 9 p.m. to 3 a.m. the same night. . . . In cremating the body no attempt was made at identification and no records were kept. They were quietly cremated and disposed of without the next of kin being informed. . . . This is a Human Right matter for the world record. . . . The families were forbidden to display any sign of grief in public and no rites of any kind were allowed in the home; instead they had to be done covertly at a monastery.[6]

He went on to say that "my shop is a tea shop to which all manner of people come. Some talked of ordeal they have been through and some have the courage to mention their names and places of residence. . . . For them, the "March Affair" is unforgettable . . . and our children and grandchildren will be able to read the records of "The Day Blood Flowed on the Inya Embankment."[7] He further reported what his family saw on April 4: "My family looked up and saw that the truck [army truck] was piled high with corpses. Afterwards, this convoy turned into the mortuary compound. I found out after making some enquiries that some 20 corpses, of which 4 had died of suffocation."[8] He concluded by pleading with the dictator "not to insert his arm for his left-hand

and right-hand men"[9] to indicate that his indictment was mainly against Ne Win's subordinates rather than the fearful Big Brother.

The following eyewitness account given by a student, who was directly involved in the March incident, more lucidly portrays the atrocities committed by Ne Win's death squad, the Lon Htein:

> On March 16, the students from Rangoon Arts and Sciences University began a peaceful demonstration. There must have been some 1,500 of us gathered. We had no weapons, not even sticks in our hands. Suddenly, at approximately 2 p.m., about six TE 11 trucks (large military trucks supplied to the Rangoon government by the Japanese) manned by the infamous Lon Htein [Security Unit] speeded towards us with their horns blaring. Many did not know what to do and were driven over by these trucks.
>
> Other students tried to escape by running up the steep embankment which holds back the water from the Inya Lake. The soldiers from the Security Unit pursued them, and forced many of them to jump into the lake. Many of the women students could not swim and drowned. Others, who could swim, tried to come back to the shore, but the soldiers forcibly took off all their jewelry and then beat them back with sticks. Many of them drowned. At least forty women students drowned in the lake that day. Later, when their bodies floated back to the surface, the soldiers came and took the bodies away to be cremated.
>
> The Security Unit also began firing into the students with all kinds of weapons, including large machine guns. When the students were hit by these big weapons, the bullets would rip out a huge hole in their bodies as they exited. Many students died on the spot. At least 280 students died on that day on Prome Road. When the shooting finally ended on that day, the military took away at least ten truckloads of students to Insein Jail. There they were tortured, and many more died. At least two hundred more students died in the prison. Each truck holds about twenty people, but the military forced about eighty students into each truck. When they reached the prison and opened the truck doors, many of the students had suffocated to death.

The number of deaths reported by the government was forty-one or so, although the exact number was not known. However, the United States Senate Report on Human Rights Practices for 1988 gave the following account and estimates:

> The regime admitted that in March 41 student demonstrators died by suffocation after being forced by police into an overcrowded paddy wagon. Government effort to cover up this incident failed in the face

> of eyewitness accounts, photographs, and public pressures. Other students were killed or wounded by police or died in jail during the March disturbances, but government secrecy makes it impossible to arrive at a reliable estimate of casualties. Some responsible observers place the March death in the hundreds.[10]

This problem of reliable estimates of death tolls is not unusual in light of the total suppression of information in a totalitarian state. The dates, the scenes, and the number of deaths of these slaughters may be different, but they were not essentially different from those of many dictatorial and totalitarian regimes around the world. As time elapses and freedom is restored, the real death tolls and graveyards will eventually be discovered as in the case of Stalinist Russia.

Despite the timidness of Aung Gyi's letter, it may be taken as one of the most important impetuses responsible for the subsequent demand for an end to military dictatorship and the restoration of democracy by the students and the masses across Burma. His timidity and lack of courage were only natural considering his personal military background, the jail sentences he received, and the nature of the nightmare state which did not allow any dissent or potential contender to the political throne, *min lawn*, to emerge. It also reflected the need for submission by a traditional authoritarian personality loyal to the Big Father and the Army he had served. It will be shown later that his political downfall in the post-1988 period was precisely due to this weakness. The reign of terror and fear cuts across the entire spectrum of the socialist state of Burma, a state which seems to be continuing without an end up to the present.

It should also be pointed out that these violations were made by the notorious riot police force called the Lon Htein and by army squadrons under the command of the present military ruler, General Saw Maung, who was then the Chief of Staff. He was also considered to be close to the Butcher who appointed him as the Defense Minister during his seventeen-day presidency. He, like Sein Lwin, has very little educational background and is a career military man who gradually rose through the ranks. In his speech on the Armed Forces Day of March 27, he urged soldiers to carry out the task of "eradicating all the subversive elements in the country . . . while constructive tasks were being carried out under the BSPP leadership to develop the socio-economic conditions of the people, destructive elements, above ground and under ground, are resorting to all sorts of disruptive acts to hamper progress."[11]

The months of April and May were relatively calm on the surface with the diplomatic visits of General Chaovalit Yongchaiyut, the supreme commander of the Royal Armed Forces of Thailand hosted by his Burmese counterpart, General Saw Maung, and of Mr. Hussain Mohammad Ershad, the President of the People's Republic of Bangladesh. The April 21 visit of the Thai General was strategically significant to the military regime of Burma for future political development. On the same day, the Thai proposal of a joint development project of five border rivers and dams at a cost of $6.579 million was accepted by the

Burmese government. The Thai Chief of Staff was hosted by the Burmese Armed Forces Chief of Staff, General Saw Maung, whose name began to emerge on the political scenes. Besides this project, the issues of rebel minority groups along the Thai border, trade cooperation, timber trade, border problems, narcotic traffic, and other exchanges were discussed between the two Generals. Hence, at the very outset of the 1988 political upheavals, the foundation for Thai-Burmese military cooperation seemed to have been firmly established.[12]

During the same month, the proposal of peace talks by the rebel National Democratic Front (NDF), a coalition of ten guerrilla groups including the ethnic minorities of the Kachin, Wa, Palaung, Karenni, Arakanese, Lahu, and Shan rebels, was emphatically rejected by Saw Maung.[13] Meanwhile, the Report on the March Affair by the Enquiry Commission was cleverly delayed to May 17. It should be noted here that at the very outset of Saw Maung's emergence in the political arena, the relationship between the Thai and Burmese chiefs of staff seemed to be symbiotic with respect to their common interest in the border trade and their opposition to the minority insurgents of Burma who controlled the Thai-Burmese border trade. The economic interest of Thailand in Burmese teak was clearly discernible at that time.

THE JUNE AFFAIR

The report on the March Affair by the government Enquiry Commission headed by Ba Maw, Hla Tint, and Dr. Maung Shein, blaming the unruly conduct of students and implicating the Muslim minority, led to a demonstration by students and monks in the third week of June. On June 21, the confrontation between some 1,000 R.A.S.U. student demonstrators and the riot police in Rangoon resulted in ten deaths, five of which were reported as policemen. The students demanded the release of the students, reinstatement of those involved in the March Affair, and legalization of the student unions. The momentum of anger, frustration, and dissent had now spread to all campuses and streets of Rangoon, Taunggyi, Prome, and other cities. It forced the military regime to close down all colleges and schools and to impose a 6 p.m. to 6 a.m. dusk to dawn curfew on June 23, which lasted until August 19. The army crushed the June demonstration with greater violence in arresting and killing unarmed protestors enraging the masses across the country.

The most intriguing and important aspect of the June Affair was the invocation of xenophobia similar to that in the Sino-Burmese riot of 1967. Although the provocateurs of the racial riot against the minority Muslims in Rangoon, Taunggyi, Prome, Moulmein, and other cities were not exactly known, it had all the trappings of the previous racial riots of both the colonial and independent periods.[14] The diversion of attention from the March massacre of students and the anger of the Buddhist population to the Muslim population was made by the government Report of the Enquiry Commission on the March Affair. It implicated the Muslim students as responsible for the riot. Many Muslims were rounded up and put into Insein Jail during that Affair.

Following the student demonstration of June 21, the enraged Burmese looted, burned, and ransacked the businesses, homes, and mosques of Muslims in various cities. However, this time the riots failed to quell the anger and frustration of the masses against the military rulers. Unlike the case of the 1967 Sino-Burmese riot, the campaign against the Muslim minority failed to extol the xenophobic dictator as a nationalist hero. The mounting anger against the military regime persisted and the month of July was filled with the imminent eruption of the collective psyche of the masses which had been abused and tortured for more than a quarter of a century. This racial aspect of the June Affair may be taken as an indicator of the nature of the post-1988 democracy movement, which seemed to have overcome somewhat the age-old xeno- and ethnophobias among the masses in Burma. Indeed, all the people of Burma, whether Buddhists, Muslims, Christians, or majority or minority ethnic groups, have been indiscriminately attacked and killed since March 1988.

THE OSTENSIBLE ABDICATION OF NE WIN

Sensing the danger of losing face and power, Ne Win convened an extraordinary B.S.P.P. Congress on July 23 at the Saya San Hall in Kyiakkasan ground in Rangoon. Even the choice of the meeting site had some symbolic significance, since most of the other Congresses were held at the Mingaladon Central Political Science School. This new site was where the body of U Thant was placed in 1974. According to an inner source, Ne Win slept at the Saya San Hall the night before the meeting was convened upon the advice of his astrologer. Saya San was one of the folk heroes who rose up against the British rule in the 1930s, which was the reason for choosing the Hall named after him. In any event, Ne Win made a surprise move, announcing his resignation from the chairmanship of the Party at that meeting for reasons of old age and mistakes he had made.

He delivered a lengthy speech almost half of which dwelled upon the guilt-ridden July 7 Affair of 1962 which resulted in the destruction of the Rangoon University Student Union Building. He denied his responsibility for that Affair and put the blame squarely on Aung Gyi who had been writing letters touching upon the same subject and denying his responsibility. The important aspects of his speech of resignation were (1) the assumption of an indirect responsibility for the bloody March and June Affairs, (2) the admission of a lack of trust by the people in the ruling government based upon these two affairs, (3) the suggestion of holding elections and a national referendum for the people to choose between the single and the multiparty political system of government, and (4) the unchangeable role of the army in overseeing the process and maintaining power to control civil disturbances until the new or future organizations can assume full responsibility.

Some excerpts of his speech will help to highlight these points and the real intent of the dictator to control and shape the future destiny of Burma:

> If a multiparty system is chosen, we [Army] shall have to continue working as I have stated earlier to create the conditions for a multi-party system. . . . I am retiring from politics. However, we shall have to continue the control until the future organizations can assume full responsibility. This is to ensure that no chaos ensues and to keep the country from ruin. Regarding the control of civil disturbance, I must inform the people throughout the country that when **the Army shoots, it shoots to hit; it does not fire in the air to scare**. Therefore, I warn those causing disturbances that they will not be spared if in the future the Army is brought in to control disturbances.[15]

The political overtones of this speech clearly indicated that the Army would continue to command authority and power over the people of Burma. It also mandated that the decision to create conditions for a multiparty system or government rested mainly with the Army, and not with the people or any winning party in the elections which were to be held by the Army. Indeed, it will be shown later that these pledges have been kept since his resignation by the consecutive puppet governments of Ne Win. Using the excuse of civil disturbances, the consecutively installed rulers of Burma faithfully subdued all disturbances, including any sedition against the Army, following the mandates made by the retired dictator in his resignation speech.

THE AUGUST AFFAIR—8/8/88

The August Affair or the date of 8/8/88 is the incident of a killing field most recalled by the people of Burma. It has been pointed out before that this date was deliberately and numerologically chosen by the student leaders for a good omen of success in accordance with the historical fall of the Tagaung Dynasty in A.D. 888. It was the most brutal and violent confrontation between the Army and the demonstrators ever seen in Burma. It also marked the crumbling of the single-party rule of the B.S.P.P. and the starting point of a full-blown democracy movement among the people of Burma. At the end of the extraordinary Congress on July 25, the Party accepted the resignation of the General and his lifelong crony San Yu, while those of the remaining inner-circle members, Sein Lwin, Aye Ko, Kyaw Htin, and Tun Tin, were rejected. The suggestion of a multiparty system and referendum was also pushed aside by the Party. Meanwhile, the people were outraged over the General's speech saying "the Army shoots to hit" and began demanding the end of fascist military rule over Burma.

It should also be pointed out here that there was wide speculation about the next successor to the political throne of Ne Win for two to three days, involving the names of Aung Gyi, Aye Ko (the Secretary of the Party), and Maung Maung Kha (the Prime Minister of longest tenure). This reflected the basic problem of a dictatorial totalitarian polity which lacks an orderly succession of political leadership just as the ancient Burmese kingship system did. To the surprise and anger of many, none of these names appeared on a ballot; rather, that most despised lifelong executioner and disciple of Ne Win, Sein Lwin known as the "Butcher," was named the new Chairman of the Party and the President of Burma on July 26. The Prime Minister Maung Maung Kha and the Attorney General Myint Maung were simultaneously dismissed. This in effect showed that Ne Win's abdication was a farce and that his wish and will continue to dictate the political fate of Burma.

Sein Lwin's appointment to rule Burma ignited a violent protest by thousands of masked students who were joined by monks and the people of Rangoon. They once more marched to the famed political rallying point of Shwe Dagon Pagoda, only to be subdued by the Butcher on August 3. One day prior to this event, Sein Lwin was reportedly shot and wounded by a trusted private secretary, which was never really confirmed. On the same day, Rangoon was placed under martial law and Sein Lwin started a massive roundup of all political dissidents. Various sections of Rangoon were labeled as "black sections" #1, 2, 3, etc. and the crackdown was in full swing. On July 30, Brigadier Aung Gyi, the famous journalist U Sein Win, and seven other dissidents were arrested. Of the seven, five were former military commanders among whom was one of the leaders of the National League for Democracy, former Colonel Kyi Maung.[16] At this point, the demand to down the Butcher and the military government in the name of democracy became the focal point of demonstrations across Burma.

The final breaking point of violence took place when "the Butcher" lived up to his reputation by butchering thousands of unarmed demonstrators, including monks and children, following a peaceful demonstration staged by students, monks, and others on August 8. For the following three days up to August 11, the Army met the demonstrators head on and went berserk with killing and decapitating, producing a blood bath unparalleled in the history of Burma. Since the famed Shwe Dagon Pagoda's ground, the Tiananmen Square of Burma, was sealed off by the Army, the main killing fields in Rangoon were at the Sule Pagoda, the U.S. Embassy, the Rangoon General Hospital, and the North Oakkalapa. The last site was the largest of them all and the local people have erected a memorial monument for those who died during the 8/8/88 Affair. As Bertil Lintner aptly wrote: "In North Oakkalapa, where large numbers had been killed, the local people built a concrete pillar to commemorate their dead friends and relatives. In consonance with historic date 8.8.88, the pillar measured 8 feet 8.8 inches in height."[17]

The mass revolt against Sein Lwin became a nation-wide confrontation between the army and people from all walks of life and various signs of breaks in the ranks of the armed forces began to emerge. The people fought the armored cars and machine guns of the Butcher with primitive weapons of clubs, swords, spears, and jinglees—sharpened umbrellas and bicycle spokes fired from catapults. The potential downfall of the military regime became apparent as the enraged mobs continued to raid government shops, offices, and police stations throughout the major cities. Sein Lwin was forced to resign on August 26 and thus he ruled Burma for only seventeen days from July 26 to August 12. As usual, the exact death toll of the August 8–11 massacre is not known, but some estimates run between 1,000 and 3,000 in Rangoon alone[18] and thousands more jailed, wounded, and killed across Burma.

THE CIVILIAN PRESIDENCY OF MAUNG MAUNG—AUGUST 19–SEPTEMBER 18

The violence subsided only for one day with the triumphant jubilation of the students for the downing of the most hated President Sein Lwin—the Butcher. Their cry and fight for the end of single-party military rule and the establishment of a democratic government resurged immediately, demanding an answer from the Party by August 19. The danger of a total collapse of the military stranglehold of power was more than possible because of certain retired military commanders and soldiers siding with the public demonstrators during the August Affair. On August 19, sensing the danger of losing political control and power, Ne Win installed another one of his cronies, Dr. Maung Maung, a western-educated lawyer who figured prominently as the legal mind and Chief of Justice in the BSPP's power echelon.

This move was at first welcomed by certain older segments of the population, since Maung Maung was not a serving or retired military commander. But to most young and educated protestors, he represented the worst kind of political enemy. Despite his intellectual and scholarly background of Western education, he had collaborated all his life with the dictator as a sycophantic biographer, lawyer, and historian of the Burmese Way to Socialism. He lifted martial law after five days of his presidency. In an apparent move to appease the enraged masses, he released Aung Gyi, U Sein Win, and others on July 29. All of these actions failed to placate the incensed public.

He gave a speech saying that "power corrupts and absolute power corrupts absolutely" as though he intended to restore democracy. However, he kept on talking about the need to maintain law and order and the important role of the army, resounding the same notes as his mentor, General Ne Win. Many young student leaders and political comics, the famous one being Zagana, began to doubt and openly challenged his sincerity and ability to uphold the belated empty promises to hold a national referendum for a multiparty system and dissolve the B.S.P.P. His name had been inseparable from the 1974 Constitution of the Socialist Republic of the Union of Burma and he had helped pass thousands of the arbitrary laws by which Burma was so ruthlessly governed for more than a quarter of a century. The vigor of the protest did not wane but rather solidified and turned violent toward the end of August. On August 22, a general national strike was called for by the student leaders who had hastily formed the All-Burma Students Union with their own leaders, among whom Ming Ko Naing and Mo Thi Zun (both pseudonyms) were the most prominent. This was the forerunner of the All Burma Student Democratic Front (A.B.S.D.F.) which eventually had to be moved to the Thai border.

THE EMERGENCE OF OPPOSITION LEADERS AND A *MIN LAWN*—DAW AUNG SAN SUU KYI

The last week of August saw the consecutive emergence of four basic opposition leaders, three of whom were former purged leaders, while the new one was Daw Aung San Suu Kyi, the daughter of the legendary hero and liberator of Burma from the British rule, General Aung San. His symbolic leadership was clearly discernible during all these riots led by unknown names in the Burmese political arena. His picture was hoisted high as a banner by the student demonstrators in their frantic and violent confrontations with Ne Win's army from March through August. From August 24 to 28, students, monks, and dissidents saw the sequential emergence of former Brigadier Aung Gyi, Daw Aung San Suu Kyi, former General Tin U, and U Nu to challenge the puppet President, Maung Maung, and his ruling B.S.P.P.

These four leaders delivered speeches at various political rallying points, including the Shwe Dagon Pagoda, where Daw Aung San Suu Kyi delivered her first speech on August 26 captivating thousands of listeners; thus a new *min lawn* was born with charisma and courage unmatched by the other three older opposition leaders. She was truly an accidental tourist political figure who came into political prominence on a visit to her native land from England to take care of her ailing mother during the political uprising. In the legendary image and shadow of her father, Daw Aung San Suu Kyi at the young age of forty-five symbolized a savior of a sort or her father reincarnated to save the oppressed people of Burma once again from an unjust rule. With time her own courage and outspoken personality captured the hope and imagination of the people amidst the carnage of killings and struggles against the guns of Ne Win's Army.

Unlike the defeated old political leaders who were staging a comeback against the reigning king, she was a new challenger with the vitality and dauntless courage to overthrow the military regime. She herself explained her lack of fear of the reign of terror as being due to her not being brought up in the nightmare state, since she spent most of her life abroad and graduated from Oxford in England. She, like many other children of prominent political leaders of the civilian government era, was the product of a missionary school, English Methodist High School in Rangoon, and married an Englishman named Michael Aris. Ordinarily, such a Westernized background would have been a deterrent to her political leadership in the eyes of the xenophobic traditional people of Burma.

She was, however, eventually accepted as the legitimate successor to the political throne. Her fluency in the Burmese language and her native manners shown in her political speeches and campaigns across Burma won over the majority of the Buddhist Burmese. Her own military linkage by blood to General Aung San also seemed to partially fulfill the myth of the soldierly hero, even though she was a woman. For example, her statement in one of her speeches that it was possible for anyone to become Buddha was attacked by the military rulers as sacrilegious to discredit her. The famed reverend Buddhist monk from London, U Yaywada, and other Buddhist clergymen came to her aid by supporting her statement to nullify this charge. Throughout the political upheavals of 1988 and her political campaigns in 1989, the military rulers attempted in vain to discredit her by invoking xenophobia and slandering her foreign marriage. They failed badly and she became the only leading symbol of power and hope for the tradition-bound Burmese masses who is capable of ending the military dictatorship over Burma today.

The cautious and timid challenge of the old leaders contrasted with that of Suu Kyi who gradually amassed all the support of the youthful students and the old alike. For example, on August 25, Aung Gyi first appeared and gave a speech attended by some well-known former military commanders at Sanchaung township in Rangoon. His return to politics was welcomed at first but when he started to talk about his faith in the Army, the crowd was turned off. This marked the beginning of his decline in popularity and disrespect on the part of the people who had lost respect for the Burmese Army after the killings of March, June, and August. On August 28, U Nu with his own followers from the older generation of Thakins formed an organization initially called the League for Democracy and Peace, and later the League for Democracy, and eventually set up an interim government claiming his political legitimacy. Former General Tin Oo temporarily joined U Nu's original Party; however, within a week he parted company with U Nu when he declared the formation of an interim government on September 9.

THE RESURGENCE OF FRAGMENTED OPPOSITION

The first week of September saw signs of the resurgence of the basic weakness of fragmentation among opposition leaders vying for power and prominence. On September 2, the general strike committee of Rangoon issued an ultimatum to the Maung Maung government demanding the formation of an interim government. On September 6, the forgotten surviving members of the Thirty Comrades with the exception of Brigadier Kyaw Zaw and Ne Win called on the soldiers to support the uprising. President Maung Maung ignored the ultimatum but hastily announced that the second extraordinary Congress of the B.S.P.P. would be held on September 12 to discuss the issue of multiparty elections. It was held two days earlier on September 10 as the political unrest intensified.

Meanwhile, U Nu went ahead on his own and formed an interim government, apparently without discussing it with the other three opposition leaders. This caused a confusion and lack of unity among the leading opposition leaders which was revealed in the direct interviews conducted by U Oung Myint Tun of the British Broadcasting Corporation (B.B.C.) between August 30 and September 10, 1988. The details of these interviews will not be given, but the following excerpts of interviews with U Nu and Daw Aung San Suu Kyi will highlight the problem:

INTERVIEW WITH DAW AUNG SAN SUU KYI

U Oung Myint Tun: Concerning the announcement of the interim government by U Nu, did he discuss and consult with you before it was announced?

Daw Aung San Suu Kyi: No, there was no discussion or consultation with me.

U Oung Myint Tun: In connection with this, why do you think that there was no discussion with you and others before the announcement?

Daw Aung San Suu Kyi: I don't know. As far as I understand, even the members of his Party, the League for Democracy and Peace, were not informed and did not know before the announcement.

U Oung Myint Tun: Daw Aung San Suu Kyi, I have been told that before the announcement of the formation of an interim government by U Nu, he sent General Tin U to meet with you and invite you to join and work together with him and his League for Democracy and Peace. Is it true?

Daw Aung San Suu Kyi: No it is not true.

U Oung Myint Tun: When General Tin U sent by U Nu came and asked you the above question, you replied that if their Party included Brigadier Aung Gyi you could not work with them. Is it true?

Daw Aung San Suu Kyi: No, since there was no communication and nobody came to ask me that question, I had no reason to give such an answer.

INTERVIEW WITH U NU

U Oung Myint Tun: Uncle Nu, before your announcement of the formation of an interim government, did you discuss or consult with the Daw Aung San Suu Kyi and Brigadier Aung Gyi Groups?

U Nu: Why do you think that we need to consult with them? You give me the answer. Do you consider that we owe an obligation to consult with them? They have their own organizations and if Bo Aung Gyi or Suu Kyi wants to do what he or she wants, he or she does not need to consult with me. Theirs are different organizations and mine is a separate one from theirs.

U Oung Myint Tun: The reason for my asking this question was should or should not those who are working together in the democracy movement consult one another.

U Nu: As far as I know based upon my experience of about thirty years of Burmese politics—mind you I am not referring to the politics of other countries—if the people with different views work together, they debate a lot, quarrel, and later split. This kind of affair, I do not wish to present to the country at this time. Therefore, they can do what they want, I will not object and I will do what I want. It is not necessary to have a total unity or what is called a general consensus which is only needed sometimes. When the League for Democracy and Peace was formed, I sent General Tin U to go and invite Suu Kyi to join and work together with us. As you know, I am an elderly statesman and much older than they are. The answer she gave was that if Bo Aung Gyi was included, she did not want to join. I did not meet with her but my representative General Tin U told me about her reply. So, I got mad.[19]

He went on to state that he also invited Brigadier Aung Gyi to join him since he had known him for a long time and desired to work with him if he ever decided to enter politics again. Aung Gyi answered that he wished to wait until September 12 when the B.S.P.P. met to decide on the holding of a multiparty election. In any event, when the same interviewer interviewed General Tin U asking a direct question of whether or not he visited and invited Suu Kyi, the answer given was totally vague. All of these confusions and rhetorical answers indicated the nature of the fragmented opposition leadership amidst the carnage of killings and the urgent need to overthrow the military regime. The "thin skin" and the ego-focused character of the opposition leadership were more than apparent in the answers and statements given in the above interviews.

Each opposition leader seemed to be occupied with establishing his or her own political base with very little interest in a truly united effort to depose the military regime, despite their verbal emphasis on unity. Young Daw Aung San Suu Kyi who was 45 years old was drawing political strength from the youthful students and younger generation of followers, while the other older politicians who were over 60 years of age, U Nu at 83, Aung Gyi at 71, and Tin U at 63, were forming their own respective political bases among the older generations. U Nu's followers were older politicians and Thakins of the past, while General Tin U and Brigadier Aung Gyi were vying for the support of the former military commanders and defectors from the Army. All of them, including Suu Kyi, were restrained and cautious not to attack the Army. Thus, the resurgence of a power struggle for leadership among the opposition set the stage for the fake military coup by General Saw Maung.

THE SEPTEMBER MASSACRE AND THE FAKE MILITARY COUP OF SAW MAUNG

By the end of August, it became apparent that Maung Maung's reign was ineffective in restoring order and the credibility of the Army, while various civilian and ex-military challengers to the political throne emerged. For example, on August 30, some eighty-five ex-military commanders under the leadership of former Brigadier Aung Shwe issued a statement calling for "the support of people's wish to end the single-party system and restore democracy, since the Army was formed to serve the interest and benefit of the people."[20] At the same time, mass rallies by students, teachers, monks, and workers at various strategic locations in Rangoon and other cities were in full swing. On August 31, hundreds of prisoners at Insein Jail were also released in Rangoon and the power held by the dictator and his civilian and military cronies seemed to be about to crumble.

In reality, the basic strategy of Ne Win and his loyal military commanders was similar to that of the Nazi German gestapo operations to create both political and psychological anarchism among the masses for the final takeover of power. From March through August, the Army's methodical approach to crushing the democracy movement was known to the Burmese as "a 3-step counter-intelligence revolutionary movement" of diversion-anarchy-salvation. The first step was the installation of puppet heads of state to divert the hate and guilt away from the Big Father by unsuccessfully implicating the Muslim minority for the March and June riots, while the second and third were deliberate magnification of the prevalent state of anarchy by using agent saboteurs to cause fear, mistrust, death, and destruction for the ultimate seizure of power in the name of saving the country. The first was already presented in terms of mob violence and protest against the Butcher Sein Lwin, Maung Maung, and the ruling B.S.P.P., rather than Ne Win who had ostensibly abdicated the political throne.

The second step was the magnification of the lawlessness and chaos in major urban centers. The looting of government shops along with the violent capture, sentencing, and execution of the government agents by enraged mobs occurred all over Rangoon during the month of August. The economic and political aspect of this mass hysteria and chaos was reflected in the satirical Burmese sayings of "Sein Lwin Bazaar, Maung Maung Bazaar and Saw Maung Bazaar." They referred to the deliberate opening of government warehouses and shops by soldiers and government agents who took the goods first and left them open for the public. When the public came to take the goods, they were shot and killed by the waiting soldiers and government agents. Many jails, Insein in particular, were opened up, releasing thousands of prisoners to participate in the political chaos in Rangoon. Not only these released prisoners but also many homeless people were paid and allowed to participate in these lootings to stage the "Food Riots."

Another strategy to intimidate the demonstrators and cripple the democracy movement was the use of the psychological weapon of food and water poisoned by government agents associated with the name of Sanda Win, Ne Win's infamous daughter. These agents, some of whom were homeless vagrants and soldiers, were supposedly drugged to do their jobs. They poisoned food and water given by the supporting public to the demonstrators to instill fear among them. The final epilogue of this drama was similar to the Hitlerian accusation of communists burning down the Reichstag in that the Big Father indicted the Burma Communist Party instigators for causing all the disorder and political agitation to overthrow the government. All of these strategies were the work of the military intelligence and the Army which stood in the wings waiting for the final assault to crush the unarmed, scared, and highly disorganized demonstrators with their multiple leadership. Rangoon and the other major cities stood vulnerable to the assault of the Army equipped as it was with modern weapons and intelligence.

By September 10, the Maung Maung presidency was ready to fall when, in a last ditch effort, the announcement to end the single-party system and the promise of holding a multiparty referendum were made at the second extraordinary Congress held two days before its scheduled date. These actions temporarily stopped the riots and violent demonstrations and the people paused with jubilation to await the promised elections. The danger of the downfall of the Maung Maung regime seemed imminent at that point. To avert that danger, General Saw Maung, who considered Ne Win as his own father, staged the fake bloody coup on September 18 slaughtering thousands more Burmese across the country in the name of saving Burma. Indeed, he stated that "I saved Burma" and created a body of government with the appropriate name of the State Law and Order Restoration Council.

Highly disorganized opposition leaders, dissidents, and strikers were no match for the modern killing machine of the Army whose battalions struck each and every center across Burma with quickness and efficiency. Within two weeks after the so-called coup, most resistance was subdued enough to make Saw Maung issue an order to all civil servants and state workers to report back to work by September 26. The intensity and dimension of the killing field during that coup surpassed any of the previous three encounters between the Army and the masses. The following is an eyewitness account given by Lin Neumann, a foreign reporter for *The Independent*:

> Looking for the orgy of violence that erupted on that Monday, September 19, in Rangoon was like grasping at shadows.... A man was shot through the heart as he sat in a tea shop. A 10-year old boy was

> killed by a bullet between the eyes. A stray shot killed a man asleep in his bed. A medical student wearing Red Cross markings was shot as he tried to rescue the wounded near Sule Pagoda. Two students were taken from their homes in the slum district of Okkalapa and ordered to turn around. They were shot in the back and left as an example to others. The crematorium in the municipal cemetery was said to be working 24 hours a day as soldiers were seen in downtown Rangoon piling bodies in trucks and carting them away.[21]

This is a modern version of the killings in the royal courtyard of Thibaw described by Tennyson Jesse a century before. She went on further to give a vivid account of the results of the inhumane slaughter in the Rangoon General Hospital.[22] The reports on these killings were not as widely available as those on the previous massacres of March, June, and August due to an immediate closing of Burma to foreign reporters and the outside world. There were also stories of soldiers demanding payments from the parents according to the number of bullet holes in the dead bodies of their children when they tried to retrieve the bodies.

The weapons used were modern but the methods of killing and disposing of the bodies were traditional. The stories of atrocities committed by the Army similar to those of the ruthless Burmese kings included the ancient Burmese customs of clubbing, beheading, cremating the wounded alive, and putting the bodies of the dead and the half-dead victims in gunnysacks, instead of velvet sacks as used by King Thibaw's executioners for royal members, filled with stones to be thrown by policemen from their boats into the Rangoon River. As usual, the number of deaths acknowledged by the government differed greatly from the private estimates. The government admitted "to the killing of 400. The Burmese, who have seen their government murder opponents for 26 years, say you must always multiply the official figure by 10."[23] The death toll paid by the people was reported by a foreign journalist as "the number killed was more like 8,000 to 10,000."[24]

THE FORMATION AND FRAGMENTATION OF THE NATIONAL LEAGUE FOR DEMOCRACY

Aung Gyi, Tin U, and Aung San Suu Kyi seemed to be temporarily united when they formed a coalition party by the name of the National League for Democracy (NLD) on September 24 which was to become the strongest political party to oppose the present military regime of Saw Maung. The unity was short-lived when Brigadier Aung Gyi left the NLD soon after its formation in a personal feud with Aung San Suu Kyi over the issue of communist membership. Meanwhile, U Nu formed his own Democracy Party and set up an interim government. Aung Gyi went on to form his own Union National Democratic Party and has insisted that he is the real president of the NLD up to the end of 1989. These fragmentations are a reflection of one of the main obstacles in the functioning of the Burmese polity dating back to the time of political splits among tens of parties when U Nu was the Premier of Burma in the 1950s.

The personal feud between Suu Kyi and Aung Gyi began long before this split, as was evident in the interviews presented earlier. Aung Gyi's indictment of the NLD as infected with communists was not far off the mark, although it was the same old strategy used by Ne Win of the pot calling the kettle black. The portfolio of membership in the NLD naturally included some of the defectors from the ruling BSPP Party who were communists aboveground to begin with and young militant students who were the followers of Daw Aung Sun Suu Kyi, the Secretary of the NLD. It also included the old ex-military commanders and followers of former General Tin U, the President of the NLD. This informal split between the followers of the two leaders of the NLD itself posed the age-old problem of fragmentation.

As for the students, the same fragmentation can be discerned among the three major organizations, the All Burma Federation of Students' Union (ABFSU), the Democratic Party for New Society (DPNS), and the Committee for the Reformation of the Students' Union under the leadership of Min Ko Naing, Mo Thi Zun, and Min Zeya, respectively. It should be noted here that these names are pseudonyms reflecting the fear of arrest by the military intelligence service. At the same time, the political refugees escaping pursuit by Saw Maung's army took refuge in Karen and Mon insurgent camps joining a giant coalition group called the Democratic Alliance of Burma (DAB). The DAB is made up of the National Democratic Front (NDF), a coalition of eleven minority groups, and ten other political organizations under the leadership of the Karen rebel leader, Bo Mya. It is housed along the southeastern Burmese-Thai borderland. On the northeastern frontier, the Kachin Independence Army (KIA) under the command of Brang Seng has been waging wars against the Burmese governments for more than forty years. The Shans have their own separate armies and political organizations such as the Shan United Army of the famous opium warlord, Khun Sa, the Tai-land Revolutionary Army of Mo Heing, and the Shan State Army. Last but not the least important is the Burma Communist Party which operated in the Shan state. All of these multi-ethnic and political opposition groups have thus far not succeeded in forming an effective united force to overthrow the central Burmese government.

THE STATE LAW AND ORDER RESTORATION COUNCIL GOVERNMENT—SLORC

Given this background of opposition, the present military regime of Saw Maung called the State Law and Order Restoration Council (SLORC) comes into focus as a resurrection of the Revolutionary Council of Government of

1962. The single most outstanding feature of the present regime's operations and policies has been to maintain the military stranglehold of power by means of the legacies and methods left by Ne Win. The polity of the land now renamed Myanmar by the Saw Maung regime is a pure military dictatorship with no specific revolutionary ideals or philosophy. In a way, it may be thought of as the traditional Burmese despotic system resurrected with the modern trappings of the rule of force executed by nineteen military commanders assuming the functions of the legislature, judiciary, and executive all at once.

Ten of the SLORC members never matriculated or finished high school, while only three had an equivalent college degree, namely the three Defense Services Academy (DSA) graduates, Brigadier Generals Nyunt Linn, Tun Kyi, and Maung Aye, and only three attended the university (Major Generals Phone Myint, Khin Nyunt, and Chit Swe). All nineteen members were above fifty years of age. In effect, the ages and educational background of the present military rulers of Burma confirm Ne Win's unswerving policy of breeding loyal rather than smart or educated followers to protect his political throne. The real power-holder behind this military bureaucracy, then, is the same old dictator, Ne Win. The indirect evidence of this is reflected in the same policies and strategies used by Ne Win being employed by the SLORC in the governance of Burma.

The original military council governing body, which may be termed the original SLORC or SLORC 1, was made up of seventeen active military commanders of the Defense Services with General Saw Maung as the Chief of Staff. Of these seventeen, eleven were Army divisional commanders, excluding General Saw Maung, two were from military intelligence and the police force (Khin Nyunt and Thura Pe Maung), three from navy and air force. On September 18, it was called the Organization for Building Law and Order in the State (OBLOS) and two more members, Brigadier-General Khin Nyunt as Secretary 1 and Colonel Tin U as Secretary 2, were added by Order No. 1/88. Neither Khin Nyunt (Director of Military Intelligence) or Tin U were military divisional commanders and thus the original military council was still made up of seventeen active military commanders. Two days later on September 20, the present SLORC government (SLORC 2) was formed by assigning one or more ministerial positions to the original members of OBLOS. The number of members of this new body now called SLORC remained the same but the Cabinet of 9 Ministers that arose in this new government included two new members: one civilian member, Dr. Pe Thein, as the Minister of Health, and Colonel Abel as the Minister of Trade as well as Finance and Planning. These two were not members of the SLORC. Dr. Pe Thein was later given the titles of Colonel and Brigadier General in charge of the nonexistent Rangoon University cadet regiment to make the present SLORC a pure military governing body reminiscent of the Revolutionary Council of 1962. Out of the nineteen members of the present SLORC, only seven were Cabinet ministers.

The Cabinet of the SLORC

General Saw Maung
Minister of Defence; Foreign Affairs
Major-General Hpone Myint
Minister of Home & Religious Affairs; Information & Culture
Rear Admiral Maung Maung Khin
Minister of Energy and Mines
Major General Chit Swe
Minister of Agriculture & Forest; Livestock & Fishery
Major General Aung Ye Kyaw
Minister of Construction; Co-operatives
Major General Tin Tun
Minister of Transport & Communication; Social Welfare; Labor
Colonel David Abel
Minister of Trade; Finance & Planning
Colonel Pe Thein
Minister of Health
Major General Sein Aung
Minister of Industry (1) and Industry (2)

It should be pointed out that all these ministers are the product of in-service OTS and not a single DSA commander is included, although there are three DSA commanders in the SLORC itself. The two basic personalities who have dominated the SLORC government, not the Cabinet, since the military coup are Saw Maung and Khin Nyunt. Saw Maung was born in 1928 and represented the type of person Ne Win employed to sustain his political reign. He was what Ne Win labeled *lu kawn* which means literally a good person and politically a loyal one with a low educational background. Indeed, he was a career military man with an eighth grade education who joined the Army in 1942. He rose through the ranks during his thirty-six years of service to become the Chief of Staff in 1988 by being loyal to key military commanders, Butcher Sein Lwin, for example. He holds the multiple positions of the Chairman of the SLORC, Chief of Staff, and the Minister of Defence and Foreign Affairs reminding us of a many-titled Burmese monarch.

In contrast, Khin Nyunt is neither a Minister nor a divisional military commander but the powerful Director of the Directorate of Defence Service Intelligence (DDSI) who became Secretary 1 of the SLORC without being a divisional commander. He was a high school graduate and went to Rangoon University, a somewhat more educated and intelligent person whom Ne Win used to run his military intelligence services. He was born in 1940 and became commander of the 44th Light Infantry Division in the 1970s. He rose through the ranks rather quickly to become the Chief of the Directorate of Defence Service Intelligence in 1983 when the infamous military intelligence service chief, MI Tin Oo, was purged by Ne Win. He was the same type of person as

MI Tin Oo and like him, a university dropout. They both are what the Burmese call *lu taws* or "smart chaps" who were carefully groomed to serve the dictator with absolute loyalty and devotion. Although it cannot be empirically confirmed, inner-Burmese circles intimated that Khin Nyunt like MI Tin Oo is a Sino-Burman. Both Saw Maung and Khin Nyunt went through the in-service Officer Training Service at Hmawbi to rise up to the top echelon of military command. As pointed out before in the case study of Maung Maung, these types of persons occupied the top positions in the chain of command in the Army of Ne Win.

One other person that came to fame is Colonel David Abel, a descendant of Portuguese ancestors named Abereu. He, like Khin Nyunt, is not a divisional commander and may be considered not a member of the real SLORC. He was appointed as the Minister of Trade as well as the Minister of Finance and Planning in the SLORC government's cabinet. He was also the personal assistant of San Yu and a Sandurst-trained army officer. His appointment as a minister shocked most Burmese, since none of the ministers in the Ne Win socialist state for twenty-six years was ever a person with a foreign name as conspicuous as David Abel. It should be recalled that in 1982 the dictator declared all persons with such alien blood to be second class citizens in his socialist state. However, in technical and professional matters, Ne Win always relied upon this type of individual. For example, his lifelong personal physician was a Chinese doctor named Lao, his personal cook an Indian, and his psychotherapist an Austrian.

Apart from this formal structure of the SLORC, the governance of Burma is totally controlled by nine main military commanders of Central, Eastern, North-East, North-West, Northern, Rangoon, South-East, South-West, and Western commands: Brigadier Generals Aye Thoung, Maung Aye, Maung Tint, Tun Kyi, Kyaw Ba, Myo Nyunt, Nyan Lin, Myint Aung, and Mya Thinn. For the administrative governance of States and Divisions, there were altogether fourteen military commanders serving and enforcing law and order by assuming the Chairmanships of the State/Division Law and Order Restoration Councils (LORCs).[25] The further division of this total military control of the country followed the former Party apparatus of People's Councils now renamed as district, township, and village LORCs totally manned by uniformed officers. In short, the government of Burma (Myanmar) is totally military in power structure and administration.

In essence, the structure and functioning of the SLORC is a duplicate of both the Revolutionary Council Government and the B.S.P.P. of the Socialist Republic of the Union of Burma, whose violation of basic human rights continues by passing and enforcing laws with new numbers and names. Freedom of opinion and expression is not allowed as is evident in the fact that the only newspaper reporting all events is the same governmentally-owned-and-operated *Working People's Daily*. The state maintains absolute and complete control of information and all news media by using and invoking various press registration laws of Ne Win's socialist republic. As for foreign press and journalists, they have been restricted most of the time inside Burma since 1988. The same policy of only allowing tourists in a guided group tour has been used to suppress news and observations.

THE MYANMAR ROAD TO DEMOCRACY

Soon after the coup the Saw Maung regime began to drop the prefix of Socialist Republic from the name of Burma and unofficially began to call it simply the Union of Burma. On May 24, 1989, the country known as Burma for many generations was officially renamed Myanmar. Not only the name of the country but also names of cities and places were decreed to change on June 18, and the changes were officially accepted by the United Nations on June 23. It is also important here to recognize that the United Nations itself seemed to recognize the authority and legitimacy of the military regime of Saw Maung by this acceptance. This very changing of the name was done without a general plebiscite or the approval of the people of Burma. Many wrote and protested in various international magazines and newspapers about this name change. As was presented at the very beginning of the book, in naming the country Myanmar the regime also proclaimed political suzerainty of the majority Burmese, the Myanmahs, over the ethnic minority in general.

Since then, the so-called Myanmar Road to Democracy has been marred by continual violations of the fundamental human rights of the people of Burma under the charades of holding a multiparty democratic election and legalization of trade. Immediately after the coup, Saw Maung's regime under the name of the Organization for Building Law and Order in the State ordered all public service personnel to continue work and ordered those who had stopped work to report back to work by September 26 or they would be suspended. Many who returned to work were forced to sign confessions and promises not to engage in any further political activities. Former Party members and new Army sympathizers were recruited by the new regime with food and transportation tickets to establish the political base. As before, the reign of terror was methodically restored to control the political power.

On September 19, the Army took over six state-run newspapers after shooting four people dead. It abrogated the 1964 Law to Safeguard the National Unity, the 1974 Law Safeguarding the Burma Socialist Programme Party, banned foreigners and reporters, and declared martial law. The abrogation of the first two laws set the stage for allowing political organizations to be formed and the dissolution of the single-party political system which had already crumbled anyway. In the first week of October, massive overhauling of the entire civil service was done by suspending all those who were involved in the demonstrations.

The army nominally dissolved the BSPP by giving it another name, the National Unity Party. It also set up the Commission for Holding Democratic Multiparty General Elections or Election Commission and passed the Political Party Registration Law on October 26, allowing political parties to register with the Election Commission. Indeed, hundreds of parties registered at an accelerated rate. By the time the Commission closed the registration on February 28, 1989, there were 233 registered. The number was finally reduced to 200 or so after some of them had deregistered. In March, the Commission issued a fourteen-month long timetable for holding the multiparty elections with a three-month campaigning period. This clever political maneuver of allowing civilian political parties to form and register, followed by a long timetable of holding the free democratic election by May 1990, was made more to appease the masses than anything else. The basic strategy was to delay as much as possible to prepare for the subduing of the leading opposition parties and dissidents, especially the NLD of Suu Kyi. For the intimidation, detention, and arrest of student leaders and other dissenters continued with no interruption by the local "Law and Order Councils" throughout the land.

The primary targets of assault by the SLORC have been the student rebels above and underground, the minority insurgents, and prominent opposition leaders, particularly Aung San Suu Kyi. The first two targets, which are located primarily along the southeastern borderland at various insurgent camps of the Karen National Union (KNU), have been under assault and almost totally subdued. The military assault of the Burmese army, with new divisions and the cooperation of the Thai government, has successfully wiped out most of the major KNU bases such as Klerday, Mae Tha Waw, Mawpokay, and Mae La. The last stronghold of the KNU at Manerplaw has been under seige, casting a dark shadow over the future prospects for the survival of the DAB. The role of the Thai army in helping Saw Maung to subdue the ethnic minority rebels and the student refugees along the border became obvious when, on December 14, General Chaovalit once again paid a visit to Burma with a thirty-four-member delegation and forty-seven journalists. Addressing General Saw Maung as brother and eulogizing him with the many titles of esteemed President, Chairman, Prime Minister, Minister of Defense and Foreign Affairs, the Thai General pledged to cooperate and help to solve the problem of student refugees at the Thai-Burmese border.

Since that December 14, 1988, visit of General Chaovalit of Thailand, some 7,000 students who had taken refuge at these camps have been sought by the regime. On December 21, the infamous Tak Repatriation Center was opened with some twenty-seven reception camps in a repatriation agreement with the Thai government. It was staffed by the Thai and the Burmese Red Cross whose chief was reportedly under the control of the Saw Maung regime. In fact, the Burmese Embassy at Bangkok offered a bounty reward of 5,000 bahts for bringing in or informing on the whereabouts of any student refugee.[26] On January 5, 1989, the United States State Department spoke of the questioning, torture, arrest, and death of fifty or more student returnees, causing vociferous denials by both the Thai and Burmese governments.[27] In central Burma, the famous student leader of the ABFSU, Min Ko Naing, was apprehended and jailed, while Mo Thi Zun had fled to the Karen insurgent camp of Thay Baw Bo. In the Thai border area the student rebels formed the All Burma Students Democratic Front (ABSDF) and joined the DAB to resist the regime.

THE SUBJUGATION OF *MIN LAWN*

Having successfully subdued the student rebels and their leaders in central and peripheral Burma, the SLORC deployed a methodical and effective strategy to stop the foremost political challenger to its legitimacy, namely Daw Aung San Suu Kyi and her NLD. To prepare for destroying the main contender to the political throne and her followers, Order 2/88 and Notification No. 8/88 were mandated on September 18 and October 10, 1988.[28] These two arbitrary pieces of legislation are in essence the same as the 1958 Union of Burma Penal Code and the British Law of Sedition. Order 2/88 restipulated Section 141 of the former's prohibition of the unlawful assembly of five or more persons, while Notification No. 8/88 redefined sedition as "organizational activities, speeches, propaganda, and subversive literature aimed at dividing the Defense Forces."[29] From September 1988 to June 1989, these two laws were not fully invoked to arrest Suu Kyi by playing a waiting game of letting the mass hysteria simmer down to a state of inertia. However, she and her NLD members were continuously slandered, harassed, and detained throughout that period by various law and order councils set up all over the country.

On April 5, the first sign of confronting Suu Kyi occurred at the town of Danubyu when an army captain ordered his soldiers to load their guns and aim them at her with no violent results. After March 27, 1989, when Ne Win resurfaced at the side of general Saw Maung on Armed Forces Day, Suu Kyi took a steadily more aggressive stance against the dictator, holding him responsible for the past and present violations of human rights by the army. Her defiance and direct attack on the dictator set the stage for her eventual house arrest. At the press conference which she gave on July 8 attended by many foreign and domestic reporters, she held Ne Win directly responsible for the division between the Army and the people. The following is the gist of her indictments of Ne Win:

> First of all, I have been charged with dividing the army which is not true. I have repeatedly stated that if the army disintegrates, the country will suffer. This charge by SLORC against the NLD at press conferences is false and groundless. I do not wish for the Army to disintegrate. The reason for the division between the Army and the people is due to U Ne Win. For 26 years, the real goal of instituting and building the strength of the Ma Sa La [B.S.P.P.] was to establish and maintain his dictatorship. In so doing, he used the Army as his handy cane. The reason for the division between the Army and the people is

> because U Ne Win deployed it as his instrument to maintain his power. The respect for the Army declines. I said that. It is true and I will say it again.[30]

Indeed, such a bold sedition against and direct attack on the Big Father had never before been publicly expressed by any political leader inside Burma in twenty-six years. This led to the systematic subduing of this young and courageous political leader.

To prepare for this assault on her popularity and on the threat she posed which had been rising rapidly, two martial Law Orders No. 1/89 and No. 2/89 were issued on July 17 and 18 to curb the potential mass demonstrations in memory of the fallen demonstrators of the 1988 political uprisings. Suu Kyi had already been detained for an hour or so on June 21 to warn her and the final house arrest was made on July 20, along with Tin Oo, the president of NLD. The law invoked for their arrest was the old 1975 Law to Protect the State from Destructionists. Suu Kyi went on a hunger strike for about two weeks without stirring any mass political rally behind her and the subjugation of *min lawn* was complete. Myanmar was put under martial law and military tribunals were created throughout the country to detain, arrest, and sentence any dissenter. Massive crackdowns and arrests ensued; the government emptied crowded jail cells to make room for the new wave of political prisoners.

Meanwhile, the other two prominent leaders, U Nu and Aung Gyi, did not come out directly to protest the actions taken by the SLORC. U Nu made some mild statements against these actions, while Aung Gyi sided openly with the SLORC by stating that he "trusted the army."[31] None of the hundreds of political parties nor the masses rallied behind Suu Kyi, a reflection on the political impotence of the opposition. Since the house arrest of Suu Kyi, the SLORC has launched a nation-wide campaign of discrediting all opposition groups, including foreign embassies unsympathetic to the regime, foreign reporters, Burmese abroad, and foreign broadcasting services. To again provoke xenophobia, a number of billboards with antiforeign slogans, targeted mainly at the United States, have been posted in Yangon (Rangoon).

The same old charge of communist infiltration, infection, and influence among the opposition, particularly the NLD, was laboriously made by Khin Nyunt at a marathon press conference on August 5, 1989.[32] Khin Nyunt attempted to discredit the NLD with letters, photographs, and documents of contact between the Burma Communist Party (B.C.P.) and the NLD. He began his main indictment by narrating the history of the B.C.P. and claiming that the B.C.P.'s leaders, Bo Kyaw Zaw and Thein Tin, had direct communication with the late Daw Khin Kyi, the mother of Suu Kyi, and other political leaders. He further indicted the politburo of the B.C.P. for aiming to overthrow the B.S.P.P. government and install Daw Khin Kyi as the new leader to govern Burma.[33]

Aung San Suu Kyi's connections with the underground B.C.P. were laboriously shown with direct charges of communist infiltration into the NLD and instigation of the entire democracy movement of 1988–89. He further claimed that during the mass riots and confrontations with the Army, the communist-oriented student leaders such as U Win Tin and Daw Myint Myint Khin approached Suu Kyi and made her the leader of NLD for the purpose of not being shot by the Army. The main reason was that Suu Kyi was the daughter of the late General Aung San. The entire theme of his marathon statements and charges was that Suu Kyi apparently fell victim to the political manipulation and influence of communist agitators seeking to overthrow the government.[34] This is the same strategy that Ne Win used throughout his reign to justify his political legitimacy and woo the West. All these strategies implicitly indicate that Ne Win still presides over the central throne of political power and control.

The term of house arrest for both Suu Kyi and Tin Oo extends far beyond the May 1990 elections, ensuring that the two will not be candidates. For any intelligent political observer, the fate of Suu Kyi was sealed back in 1988 when the election rules were announced. They contained a clause which could possibly prohibit the candidacy of anyone enjoying citizenship privileges in a foreign country; Suu Kyi's husband is British. Moreover, despite Suu Kyi's immense popularity, courage, and charisma, the historically limited role accorded to women in the Burmese polity must be a drawback in her efforts to become a leader. This is a crucial point to reckon with when speculating about the political future of Suu Kyi.

THE "FREE AND FAIR" ELECTION

On November 10, 1989, after methodically arresting and jailing thousands of political dissidents and placing the two leaders of the NLD, Daw Aung San Suu Kyi and U Tin U, under house arrest, Announcement No. 326 was issued by the Election Commission fixing May 27, 1990, as the date for holding a "free and fair" election. At this juncture, it must be mentioned that the mystical number 9 seemed to be reflected in the choice of the election date on May 27 (2 + 7 = 9). The issuance of K45 and K90 notes back in 1987, his appearance by the side of General Saw Maung on the Armed Forces Day of March 27, 1989, the changing of the name of Burma to Myanmar on June 18, 1989, and the latest announcement of not transferring power to the NLD on July 27, 1990, all seemed to confirm Ne Win's obsession with that number. It also serves as indirect evidence of Ne Win's dictating all the actions taken by the Saw Maung regime. There was also another story of Ne Win's performance of one of the most talked about rituals in 1988 involving the three acts of shooting his own image in the mirror, bathing in human blood, and marrying a young maiden from Arakan.[35] Whether or not he actually performed all of these acts is uncertain, but the fact that he married or rather had an affair with a young twenty-five-year old girl is confirmed by various writers and Burmese observers.

Political parties were informed on November 13, 1989 that they must indicate how many candidates and in how many constituencies they wished to contest by December 11. In February 1990, three more orders Nos. 1, 2 and 3/90 were issued involving the dissolution of registered parties which did not apply to run in the forthcoming election, the number of candidates, and the rules of campaign. Of these, Order 3/90 gave "The Right to Assembly and Campaign" according to the SLORC's arbitrary rules as follows:

> Political parties shall have the right to campaign in the following manner:
> A. Right to assemble and deliver speeches at a prescribed place with permission from the Law and Order Restoration Council concerned;
> B. Right to present writings, printings, and publications;
> C. Right to deliver speeches through the medium of the Voice of Myanmar [Burma] or the Myanmar Television Service.

These so-called rights to campaign were ultimately restricted by various requirements imposed by the SLORC as follows:

> In delivering speeches and presenting writings pertaining to the policies, concepts, and programs, the political parties and independent candidates shall be subject to existing laws, prohibitions and stipulations or conditions mentioned in this order;
> Application for permit: Political parties and independent candidates desiring to assemble and deliver speeches for campaigning in a prescribed place shall apply to the Law and Order Restoration Council concerned for a permit at least seven days in advance.[36]

Several detailed requirements and restrictions were imposed on this main order of freedom to campaign and deliver speeches. All of these arbitrary restrictions on the right to assemble and have free expression indicated that the May 27 election was a farce violating beforehand the fundamental human rights as prescribed by Articles 19 and 20 of the United Nations Universal Declaration of Human Rights which state that: "Every one has the right to freedom of opinion and expression; this right includes freedom to hold opinions without interference and to seek, receive and impart information and ideas through **any media** [emphasis added] and regardless of frontier."[37]

The details of the gross violations of fundamental human rights and international standards were given in the *Report on the Myanmar Election* conducted by the International Human Rights Law Group on May 19, 1990. The basic conclusion of the Report states that:

> The Myanmar government has grossly breached the minimum campaigning freedoms necessary for a free and fair election in Myanmar. Those freedoms, as stated in the Introduction, include the ability of all eligible citizens to participate actively in the political process and to exercise freedom of association, assembly, and expression for a period adequate to allow political organizing and campaigning and to inform citizens about the candidates and the issues.[38]

By the end of December 1989, the right of all prominent opposition leaders to participate with the exception of former Brigadier Aung Gyi was denied. Daw Aung San Suu Kyi and U Tin U, who had been under house arrest since July 20, were declared ineligible to run. On December 22, the military tribunal further sentenced U Tin U to three years at hard labor. On December 29, U Nu was put under house arrest for not obeying the order to dissolve his interim government which he had formed back on September 9, 1988. The eighty-three-year old former Premier took his last bold stance against the SLORC by defying the order to dissolve his interim government. He defiantly stated that: "If Bogyoke [General] Ne Win first publish a letter to the effect that he had done wrong in seizing power from the Prime Minister [U Nu] on 2/3/62, that he is sorry for it, and that he will never again do such thing, I will announce in writing that the new government formed 9/9/88 is dissolved as Bogyokegyi and your associates desire."[39]

The natural outcome of this defiance was his house arrest along with fourteen other members of his interim government, putting out the last dying fire of the democracy movement. It should also be noticed that six of the members of his parallel government resigned from fear of arrest in January 1990. Thus, the so-called free and fair multiparty election was held on the scheduled date with every conceivable human rights abuse and odds stacked against all dangerous opposition, especially the main opposition party of the NLD, whose prominent leaders were not able to run in the election.

THE MISCALCULATED OUTCOME OF THE ELECTION AND RENEGING ON ITS RESULT

The election was held by the SLORC with great confidence that its unofficially-backed National Unity Party could defeat the NLD and the Democracy Party, without their respective leaders running in the election, and the not too dangerous opposition party of Aung Gyi. The military rulers apparently underestimated the symbolic power of the young and courageous Suu Kyi, whose charisma and popularity were enhanced rather than reduced by her house arrest. Most analysts and observers, including this author, assumed that the election was a farce and that the chance of the NLD winning the election was very remote in view of the extensive restrictions imposed by the SLORC on the NLD and its remaining unknown candidates.

Some ninety-three political parties and thirty-three independent candidates contested for 486 electoral seats of fourteen major districts for the nonexistent Constituent Assembly or Parliament. Initially, 2,311 candidates of some 97 parties and 87 independents registered to contest for the 492 seats of 14 major districts in the nonexistent Hluttaw or General Assembly. When the elections were held on May 27, only 2,296 candidates of 93 parties and 87 independents contested for 485 seats where elections were held after the disqualifications and deregistration of candidates by the Election Commission. They were prohibited from engaging in eight illegal activities subject to the penalty of a three-year jail term or K5,000 fine or both. These so-called illegal speeches, writings, and activities included "sedition against the independence and sovereignty of the state, the destruction of the unity of the country and ethnic groups, the disturbance of peace and tranquility by degrading the government, the division of the army, security and prosperity, the racial and religious provocation, the disturbance of the peaceful educational process, and the provocation of the personnel of the army, police and civil service to oppose the government."[40] All of these simply boiled down to the imposition of the same arbitrary antisedition laws inherited from the colonial ruler and Ne Win's generic Law for Law and Order of 1964 mentioned earlier.

THE DISPERSAL OF VOTERS AND OPPOSITION

In order to disorient the voters and insure against the possible loss of its National Unity Party, the military regime launched a massive eviction of the urban population in major cities during March, 1990, two months prior to the May election. This so-called relocation had been going on since the late 1980s forcefully moving people from the central sections of the cities to shabby satellite towns. The estimated number of the urban population evicted was as high as one million. According to the government, the evicted were squatters and the homeless, but private and diplomatic sources reported that most of them were regular homeowners whose residences were located in the key sections of the city where opposition parties had their strongest bases.

In certain key sections of Rangoon, regular houses and buildings were leveled by the Army to construct new buildings for shopping plazas and living quarters. The spaces for shops were sold at a phenomenal price of K800,000 to K1,200,000 per unit. For relocation of the evicted, there were at least six satellite towns around Yangon [Rangoon], which the evicted people were supposed to settle by requiring them to buy land and secure permits. They were Shwepyithah, Dagon Myothit (New Rangoon), Waibahgi, Pauktalaw, Hlaing Thahyah, and Shwe Pyithah. The basic objective of the eviction and relocation was for security reasons to remove the residents from locations near the defense services offices or army bases. For example, the largest and quickest eviction was made near the Rangoon Zoo where the Defense Services Headquarter Office is located. This central office of the military commanders is a well-fortified brick fortress painted in red with gun-holes on its walls. The Burmese satirically called this building Zoo Number 2.

People were ordered to tear down their homes quickly and the army trucks loaded them and dumped them in these new towns where they had to build their new homes on their own on allotted plots of land. Some token materials were given for that purpose. Most of these towns have no utilities and people themselves have to provide on their own whatever they need for living. If a person is a government worker, he gets the permit and a loan from the state bank. The time period given to finish building a home, prescribed exactly as to style and size by the military commanders, is six months. If a person fails to complete the construction and meet the requirements within the prescribed time, the land is confiscated and a penalty imposed. Those who had no income or savings to cover the cost of homes became homeless in these new satellite towns.

The relocation program was a part of the nation-wide urban beautification drive which came into prominence after the military coup, although it had been going on for a period of time. This is more an aspect of the control of urban centers for political security and dispersing political dissidents than real urbanization. The new satellite towns are anything but modern and the residents of these new towns are physically and economically less well-off than they were before.[41] The majority of them are far away from their jobs in the central sections of the city and the cost of transportation, physical dislocation, and poor facilities may eventually take a physical and economic toll on the new settlers. Perhaps this is the exact objective of the military rulers in order to weaken potential political unrest. It may be thought of as a mild variant of the Khmer Rouge's undertaking to restructure the Cambodian society.[42] On March 13, General Chaovalit and his good-will delegation visited once again promising to "stand by Burma forever" and applauded Saw Maung's national development efforts including the mass eviction measure and the "emergence of new buildings in the capital and relocation of slum dwellers to satellite towns."[43]

The following political rap by the young Burmese high school students of Rangoon sent to this author shows their penetrating awareness of the real nature and impact of the actions of the present military regime. By a play on words, they changed the Burmese term for the army, ***tartma-daw***, to ***tartma-taw*** (*taw* means clever) and wrote political satire entitled "What the Heck Has Been Happening?":

> The one who loves the country is *tartma-**taw*** (clever army); the one who is patriotic is *tartma-**taw***; the one who defends is *tartma-**taw***; the one who saves Burma is *tartma-**taw***; the one who repairs pagodas, builds roads, bridges, gardens at a cost of one kyat, and puts nine kyats into the pocket and shows the total cost as ten kyats is *tartma-**taw***; the one who robs alms is *tartma- **taw***. Every lip is sounding the word *taw*, *taw*, (clever, clever)—what a hell of a clever Army, *tama- **taw***?

> Look! The homeless were provided with plenty of "water," *yay*, and "fire," *mee*, by relocating them [to shabby satellite towns]. Yes, indeed there are plenty of water and fire; torrential flood in the rainy season and innumerable fire in the summer. That is the bountifulness of "water" and "fire" provided by the ***tartma-taw*** for the people of Burma.

THE CONTEST AND RESULTS

There were ten main parties of political significance and four of them, which were associated with the names of Daw Aung San Suu Kyi, U Nu, Aung Gyi, and the army-backed National Unity Party, topped the list to win the election. The remaining six parties included the Coalition League for Democratic Multi-Party Unity, the Democracy Party, the Union of Burma Main AFPFL Party led by the children of former Premier U Ba Swe, the Democratic Front for National Reconstruction led by Thakin Chit Maung, a former leftist NUF group, the Graduates and Old Students Democratic Association, and the Original Anti-Fascist People's Freedom League led by Cho Cho Kyaw Nyein, the daughter of the late U Kyaw Nyein.[44] It can be easily seen that there was a continued fragmentation among the major opposition parties. For example, the age-old split of the Anti-Fascist People's Freedom League which occurred when U Nu was the premier of Burma remained intact; U Nu's own original opposition party, the League for Democracy and Peace, split into two separate parties, the split party being the Democracy Party led by former retired or purged military commanders, fielding two separate groups of candidates in the elections.

The multiparty democracy election was held on May 27, 1990, under various restrictions and orders concerning campaigning activities. Altogether 93 parties fielding 2,209 candidates and 87 independent candidates or a total of 2,296 Hluttaw candidates contested for 485 electoral constituencies out of the total of 492 constituencies designated for holding elections. The 7 constituencies where designated elections were not held or were canceled represented mostly the ethnic minority states of insurgency. Only five parties fielded over 100 candidates; the National League for Democracy (NLD) of Daw Aung San Suu Kyi (447), the National Unity Party (NUP) backed by the SLORC (413), the League for Democracy and Peace (LDP) of U Nu (309), the Union Nationals Democracy Party (UNDP) of Aung Gyi (247), and the Democracy Party (105).

Just two days before the elections, the confident SLORC decided to allow some fifty foreign reporters to enter and observe the elections. The reporters observed the election to be quite fair at the polls where for three days thousands of Burmese cast votes primarily for the NLD whose insignia was a farmer's hat and a bundle of "golden fruit"—paddy. As usual, Aung Gyi gave a belated political speech for his party with a mild criticism against the military rulers in a vain attempt to capture the votes of the people. He even attempted to raise funds and support for his candidacy in the United States through agents. His loss of political credibility had occurred long before the elections, when the Burmese began to label him as *samusah*, the Indian pastry with three sides, to satirically describe him as foxy and cunning in three ways: working for the Army, ostensibly for the people, and for himself.

To the surprise of many observers, particularly the SLORC, the unofficial returns of the elections showed that the candidates of the Party of Daw Aung San Suu Kyi (NLD) won in almost every constituency in which they competed. Saw Maung himself unofficially admitted this victory in the public media. However, the official "Catch 22" of this unexpected backfiring of the election outcome was the delay in counting and verifying the votes which took over a month instead of the three weeks initially promised. It should also be pointed out that the SLORC itself never officially mentioned, confirmed, or admitted the landslide victory of the NLD in the elections. Instead, they kept on hinting at possible frauds committed by the NLD based upon the charges made by the badly beaten National Unity Party.

The official result of the May 27 elections was announced by the Election Commission on July 1 in the *Working People's Daily*. According to its Announcement No. 895 dated June 30th, 1990, the candidates elected were 392 out of 447 fielded or 87.7% by the NLD, 10 out of 413 fielded or 2.4% by the NUP, 1 out of 247 fielded or .4% by the UNDP, 1 out of 105 or .95% fielded by the Democracy Party, and 0 out of 309 fielded by the LDP.[45] Thus, the NLD candidates of Suu Kyi's Party won the elections by a landslide capturing more than 80 percent of the total electoral seats, 392 out of 485 constituencies where elections were held.

THE DELAY OF POWER TRANSFER AND BROKEN PROMISES

The first evidence that the military regime was not about to transfer power came when Saw Maung spoke on June 18 at the meeting held by the SLORC and the Commission for Compiling Authentic Facts on Myanmar History. After the remarks on Burma's independence from the British colonial rule, he talked about the drafting of a new constitution and the legitimacy of successive military governments as follows:

> Just as the election results have come out, our nation has changed from a one-party system to a multiparty one. From the points I have stated earlier, it is evident that the 1947 constitution was drafted according to the wish of the British. . . . The Revolutionary Council is in fact a legal government. It is also true that the 1974 Constitution was drafted through a national referendum. . . . The SLORC government today can also be said to be a legal government, a government recognized by the world. It is also an indisputable fact that we are a member

> state of the United Nations. The fact is that the government in charge today, or the SLORC, does not abide by any constitution.[46]

This contradictory statement that Myanmar's polity had automatically changed from a one-party to a multiparty system under the dictatorship of the SLORC which is recognized as the legitimate government set the political overtone for not transferring power to the winner of the election. Although it may seem incoherent, his emphasis on the recognition of his regime as a legal government by the world and the United Nations was not too far from the truth. For Japan recognized the regime in February 1989, while Thailand's recognition was implicit in the numerous diplomatic exchanges and various trade concessions and deals struck between the two nations. Indeed, the United Nations has shown that it recognized Myanmar and considered it as a member up to the present day by accepting Saw Maung's application to change the name of the country as well as sending the UNDP's consultant, Dr. Tun Thin, to Burma and continuing to finance certain development projects. Many private firms around the world have entered into trade deals with the Saw Maung regime, thus supporting his point and explaining why democracy has failed so far in Myanmar today.

On July 5, the stalemate over power transfer and the continued military dictatorship were evident when Saw Maung spoke at the SLORC meeting: "I have repeatedly stated that until responsibility is transferred to a government that emerges according to the Constitution, we are to continue to attend our tasks—which will also contribute to our three tasks."[47]

This statement exactly duplicated the main point of the resignation speech given by Ne Win back in July 1988. These three tasks he spoke of were those mentioned in the Announcement No. 1/88 after the September coup, which included the restoration of law and order; provision of secure and safe transportation; and easing people's needs for food, clothes, shelter, and other items by providing assistance to co-operatives and the private sector.[48]

Since that speech, there has been a deliberate delay in the transfer of power with the postponement of the formation of the People's Assembly, the requirement for the drafting of a new and perfect constitution approved by the SLORC and holding of a national convention or referendum for the approval of the new constitution to be drafted not by the winning NLD but by all the winners. Most important of all, government spokesmen did not recognize the NLD as the majority winner of the election. Instead, they wiped the slate of the election result clean by asking all twenty-seven parties and six independents elected to meet with them and draw up the mythical new constitution.

On July 13, Khin Nyunt denied the initial promise made by Senior General Saw Maung of immediate power transfer to the NLD and bluntly stated that Daw Aung San Suu Kyi would not be released since she had repeatedly defied authority and infringed on the "Criminal Law as well as special laws."[49] He further charged the leader of the NLD in the absence of Daw Aung San Suu

Kyi, former colonel Kyi Maung, with slandering him and threatened a possible lawsuit against him. The paranoid attack on Kyi Maung was made in connection with the question of a potential Nuremberg trial of the military leaders raised in an interview by a foreign reporter named Dominic Faulder. Kyi Maung's answer to that question was that people would not take such an action, if there was a peaceful power transfer. After these rhetorical statements and accusations made by Saw Maung and Khin Nyunt, the final announcement that power would not be transferred to the NLD came out two days prior to the scheduled meeting of the NLD leaders at Ghandi Hall on July 29 to decide what to do and propose to the SLORC. The essence of the July 27 announcement by the SLORC was: "The SLORC, the Defense Services is not bound by any constitution. The SLORC is ruling the country by martial law. It is known to all that the SLORC is a military government and that it is recognized by countries of the world and the United Nations. . . . Accordingly, it is using the following three powers in governing Myanmar [Legislative Power, Administrative Power and Judicial Power]."[50]

It further warned that "the drafting of an interim constitution to obtain state power and to form a government" will not be tolerated and "effective action will be taken according to the law" against any party doing so.[51] Indeed, they kept their word by arresting the leader of the NLD, Kyi Maung, and Chit Khaing of Rangoon and six others on September 6, 1990. The arrest was made following the NLD Ghandi Hall Meeting's denouncement of the SLORC's shameful delay in power transfer and demand for the formation of a Constituent Assembly and the release of Suu Kyi.

As the year 1990 ended, the NLD in central Burma was virtually decimated with all of its Central Executive Members except four (U Aye Swe, U Lwin, U Shwe, and Daw Mynint Myint Khin) under house arrest or in jail. The SLORC intensified its crackdown on the opposition by arresting many more NLD members and dissident Buddhist monks. On December 7, the government source (Khin Nyunt) disclosed that some 49 more NLD members (35 elected candidates and 14 activists) and 77 monks were arrested for planning to set up an illegal government and plotting to assassinate government officials. According to the NLD source, the total number of its members arrested since the elections was 500. The exact number of the arrested NLD candidates who won the elections is not known.

Under the relentless crackdown on opposition politicians, a cousin of Suu Kyi, Dr. Sein Win of the Party for National Democracy (the son of U Ba Win, General Aung San's older brother who was also killed in the 1947 assassination of General Aung San and his Cabinet members), who won the May 27 election from the Pegu District, and seven NLD members defected to the Thai border. On December 18, they set up a provincial government named the National Coalition Government of the Union of Burma in alliance with the Democratic Alliance of Burma (DAB) at Manerplaw, the headquarters of DAB located some 130 miles southwest of the Thai city, Chiang Mai. The DAB is an armed coalition of twenty-one ethnic minority and political dissident groups formed in 1988. Dr. Sein Win was named the Prime Minister of the eight-member Cabinet of this newly formed provincial government, which was made up of candidates elected in the May 27 elections.

According to the DAB's Media Release dated December 17, 1990, the basic aims and objects of the provincial government are:

1. To remove the SLORC military dictatorship, restore internal peace, harmony, and democracy, and build a democratic society;

2. To convene the National Assembly for the election of a national government, and to entrust the National Assembly with the task of drafting a new constitution;

3. To hand over power to the National Assembly, and to dissolve the provincial government.

In the interim period, pending the removal of the SLORC military dictatorship, the provincial government will govern through an advisory body known as the Supreme Council made up of elected members of the NLD, the members of the Executive Committee of the DAB, and members of both organizations.

Following this move by the opposition, the military regime stripped the eight opposition politicians of their legislative seats. The Central Executive Committee of the NLD of central Burma also reportedly expelled the seven NLD members who had defected to save its own very existence. This action of the NLD may not succeed in stopping the SLORC from declaring it an illegal organization. The success of the newly formed coalition leadership in overthrowing the military dictatorship in the 1990s will depend ultimately upon its ability to generate both mass mobilization inside Burma and outside support.

NOTES

1. EIU, *Country Report* 1990, p. 47.

2. A low-ranking government officer earned a monthly maximum income K550, the new pay scale of a gazetted officer.

3. The most vivid and detailed descriptive account of the political upheavals of 1988 was written by Bertil Lintner, *Outraged*. Also, Moksha Yitri, "The Crisis in Burma: Back from the Heart of Darkness," *Asian Survey* (Berkeley: University of California, June, 1989).

4. See for detail, Bertil Lintner, "March Student Riots, Unrest Reviewed," *Bangkok Post*, April 17, 1988.

5. *Aung Gyi's Letter* (Rangoon, June 6, 1988), p. 1.

6. Ibid., p. 4.

7. Ibid., p. 6.

8. Ibid., p. 7.

9. Ibid.

10. U.S. Department of State, *Country Reports On Human Rights Practices for 1988* (Washington, D.C.: U.S. Government Printing Office, 1989), p. 741.

11. FEER, April 21, 1988, pp. 34–35.

12. See Foreign Broadcasting Information Service, *Burma* (Washington, D.C.: U.S. Government Publication, April 22, 1988), pp. 39–41. From now on it will be referred to as FBIS.

13. Ibid., p. 41.

14. See Lintner, pp. 112–114.

15. From the source of *Address by Party Chairman U Ne Win to the Opening Session Extraordinary Congress of the BSPP At the Saya San Hall in Kyaikkasan Grounds*, Rangoon, on 23 July (Recorded). p. 3.

16. FBIS, *Burma*, August 1, 1988, p. 29.

17. Lintner, p. 161.

18. See The U.S. Committee for Refugees, *The War is Growing Worse and Worse: The Refugees and Displaced Persons On the Thai-Burmese Border* (Washington, D.C.: American Council for Nationalities Service, May 1990), p. 2.

19. From the taped interviews (in Burmese) of U Nu and Daw Aung San Suu Kyi by U Oung Myint Tun of the British Broadcasting Corporation, August 30 and September 10, 1988.

20. *Working People's Daily*, Rangoon, August 30, 1988.

21. Lin Neumann, "Dark Days in Burma," *The Sunday Times*, London, December 4, 1988.

22. Ibid.

23. Loc.cit. Ibid.

24. Jonathan Sikes, "Strict Burmese Regime Vowing Change, Elections," *The Dallas Morning News*, May 18, 1989, p. 44A. Also, Amnesty International, *Unlawful Killing of Peaceful Demonstrators*, September 29 and October 7, 1988 (London: Amnesty International, 1988).

25. From the *Working People's Daily, Press Summary*, October, 1988, pp. 29–30.

26. The Burmese Embassy, Bangkok, December, 1988. The announcement was made to be in effect until December 30, 1988.

27. "U.S. Says Rangoon Killing Returnees," *Bangkok Post*, January 7, 1989.

28. See *Working People's Daily*, Rangoon, September 18 and October 10, 1988.

29. FBIS, June 27, 1989.

30. From the source of "Daw Aung San Suu Kyi's Interview" (in Burmese), *Burma Review*, New York, September, 1989, p. 10.

31. See "Interview with Aung Gyi: I Trust the Army," *Asiaweek* (Hongkong, July 21, 1989).

32. FBIS, August 9, 1989, pp. 43–45.

33. The SLORC Ministry of Information, *Burma Communist Party Attempts to Seize Political Power* (in Burmese) (Rangoon: Ministry of Information, August 5, 1989), pp. 3–7.

34. Ibid., pp. 60–62.

35. FEER, August 18, 1988, p. 39.

36. *Working People's Daily* (in Burmese), Rangoon, February 2, 1990.

37. Ibid.

38. International Human Rights Law Group, *Report on the Myanmar Election* (Washington, D.C.: International Human Rights Law Group, May 19, 1990), p. 5.

39. FBIS, December 29, 1989, p. 34.

40. *Working People's Daily*, (see note 36).

41. See Steve Erlanger, "Burmese Military Is Forcing Mass Migration from Cities," *New York Times*, New York, March 21, 1990.

42. Ibid.

43. FBIS, March 14, 1990, p. 41.

44. EIU, *Report No. 1, 1990*, p. 25.

45. See "the Announcement No. 895 of the General Election Commission," (30th June, 1990), *The Working People's Daily*, Rangoon, July 1, 1990.

46. FBIS, June 19, 1990, p. 28.

47. FBIS, July 5, 1990, p. 42.

48. Ibid.

49. See FBIS, July 17, 1990, pp. 40–43.

50. Ibid., p. 42.

51. Ibid.

11

The Burmese Way to Capitalism and the Future of Burma

The period from 1988 to 1990 may be viewed as a deployment of ostensible economic reforms similar to that of the late 1970s when Ne Win attempted to open the economy slightly to the outside world to obtain the necessary foreign aid to sustain his dictatorship. The common goal of these reform measures has been to fortify the military might of the Burmese Army to crush political opposition. The future of Burma with respect to the prospect of democratization of its polity will ultimately depend upon whether these economic strategies of the "Burmese Way to Capitalism" and "Open Economy" succeed or fail in amassing the necessary foreign exchange and funds to sustain the military campaigns against the political and ethnic rebels inside and along the borders of Burma. Thus far, the present military junta seems to be quite successful in obtaining external funds from a number of countries whose economic interest superseded their concern for atrocious violations of human rights by the military rulers.

THE BURMESE WAY TO CAPITALISM?—THE EXOGENOUS FACTORS

At the very outset, it will be stated that "the Burmese Way to Capitalism" is a charade and it is the same old state capitalism controlled and managed by nineteen military commanders of the SLORC with a giant network of state enterprises and controls. The economic base of political power, which has been the main determinant of military dictatorship, has not been reduced. Instead, it has been enlarged by the military "Robber Barons" in the name of privatization or decontrol of the economy. The policies of an "open economy" and "liberalization of trade" or the cliché "the Burmese Way to Capitalism" by which Colonel David Abel came to fame as the minister of two separate ministries, the Ministry of Trade and the Ministry of Finance and Planning, are thus far a political ploy to put Burma's untapped natural resources up for sale.

Beginning in 1989, the Saw Maung regime announced legalization of trade, particularly the border black market trade, and entered into a series of trade concession agreements with China and Thailand. This effort at the ostensible liberalization of the economy and the concession trade agreements entered into with China and Thailand were assessed by the *Nation* of Bangkok as follows:

> Burmese leader Saw Maung appears to have been trying to gain control of a big chunk of illegal trade, said as much as 50 percent of Burma's total trade turnover. Illegal trade practices are currently in the hands of Burmese ethnic groups rebelling against Rangoon. . . . The source seems to be saying that the concession-trade is only an illusion created by the Burmese government, which is hoping for political results without having to take responsibility for any failures. The source implies that the "true" trade is the black market.[1]

This legalization of the border trade was made for the economic purpose of capturing tax revenue from traders, on the one hand, and politically subduing the ethnic minority rebels by crippling their economic base for armed struggles, on the other.

EASTERN VERSUS WESTERN ECONOMIC POLICIES TOWARD BURMA

In terms of volume and value, the major countries that have entered into trade and investment deals with the present military regime are Asian countries—Thailand, China, Singapore, South Korea, and Japan on both government and private levels. As for the West, the governments of major powers have taken a strong stance against the Saw Maung regime by adopting economic sanctions or rather by not giving foreign aid. Hence, this seems to suggest that there is a different approach between the West and the East in dealing with Burma.[2] A Thai reporter presented these two opposing approaches as follows:

> While members of the western world see sanctions as a means to press for human rights and democracy in Burma, their eastern counter-

> parts—notably Thailand, Singapore, China, South Korea and Japan—regard the advancement of economic relations as a way to inspire political developments, Asian style.... At a time when the West applies sanctions to pressure Rangoon back to some sense, the East seems bent on trading with Burma on the calculation that a more prosperous economy would spur political liberalization.[3]

The validity of this dichotomy is not truly convincing. Although the U.S. government and the governments of the European Economic Community countries did not resume aid or strike economic deals with Myanmar on the ground of human rights abuses, a number of private firms from these nations have entered into various ventures with the illegitimate government of Saw Maung. As of January 5, 1990, the *Working People's Daily* reported that altogether 270 contracts were signed by the SLORC with foreign companies; some of these firms were Dai Ichi (Japan), Thip Than Pong Company and Mae Sot Forest Industry (Thailand), Daewood Corporation (South Korea), Exxon, Amoco, Coca-Cola, Pepsi-Cola, and Unocol (U.S.), Premier Petroleum Myanmar Ltd. (U.K.), Petro Canada, Fritz Werner of West Germany, Renault of France, Nestle of Switzerland, IAEG of Austria, BHP of Australia and Shell of Holland.[4]

THE THAI FACTOR

Since the military coup of 1988, Thailand has been Saw Maung's most important helper in achieving the goal of crushing the democracy movement. It has cooperated with the Burmese Army in subduing the student and minority rebels along the Thai-Burmese border and entered into over twenty different trade concessions in teak and fishing rights involving some eighteen different Thai companies owned and controlled by the relatives of General Chaovalit. Indeed, the so-called oriental view was naturally spearheaded by the Deputy Foreign Minister of Thailand, Praphat Limpaphan, at a recent Thai-Burmese relations seminar held at Chiang Mai University.[5] During and after the political upheavals of 1988, General Chaovalit had already successfully established immensely beneficial economic deals for his family-owned companies and Thailand with the Saw Maung regime.

The role the military political elite of Thailand has played so far must be considered as one of the most detrimental obstacles in the Burmese people's struggle against the military dictatorship. Despite the resignation of General Chaovalit as the Deputy Premier in early 1990, the present Thai government continues to deport hundreds of Burmese political refugees by declaring them to be illegal immigrants. All the border outpost towns which served as the conduit for giant black market trade, Mae Sot, Myawaddy, Ranong, and Three Pagoda Pass, for example, have become port authorities for both tax-collection by the Burmese Army and shipment of political refugees back to central Burma by the Thai border police and military units.

The relative importance of the Western economic sanctions, which are not yet fully enforced, versus the active Eastern trade and other economic deals may be a debatable issue in helping Burma emerge out of the darkness of political repression and economic poverty. The reality, however, is that when the economic interest of a nation is put to the test, the interest in human rights abuses or the promotion of democracy usually takes a second seat. Thailand's own deforestation and the need for Burmese teak are the stark reality responsible for its official collaboration with and support of one of the most ruthless regimes in the world. The sale of arms by China, Singapore, and Pakistan also testifies further to this reality. Unfortunately, the correct stance of economic sanctions taken by the United States and other major Western powers against Burma has been relatively less important than the Eastern stance of trade and aid. The latter has contributed greatly to the fortification of the military might of Saw Maung and the potential demise of freedom fighters in Burma today.

THE CHINESE FACTOR

The second most important provider of tax revenues from border trade has been the People's Republic of China which entered into a bilateral trade agreement with the Saw Maung regime on August 5, 1988. The agreement was signed between two state enterprises of the Yunan Province Import Export Corporation of China and the Myanma Export-Import Corporation of Burma. In addition, a clearance account agreement for bilateral trade was signed between the China Bank and the Myanma Foreign Trade Bank. Since then, Chinese goods have been flooding the markets at major urban centers. The Burmese authorities announced that the Sino-Burmese border trade was open to private entrepreneurs, although in reality it was a measure to incorporate the existing black market trade into the official enterprise system.

For the last twenty-eight years, China and Thailand have competed for the huge black market border trade of Burma. As the trading activities of one declined, the other usually picked up momentum to supply the scarce consumer and producer goods at major urban centers of Burma. These two countries have been the busiest with frequent diplomatic and trade missions for the purpose of entering into numerous trade agreements with the military regime to exploit the forests, mines, and fishery of Burma. Opium and jade dominate the Sino-Burmese border trade, while teak and fishery preoccupy the Thai-Burmese joint-ventures. The border trade with these two countries is partially controlled by the ethnic rebels along the various black market routes of the Shan, Kachin, and Karen states. The political developments and conditions affecting the border trade with these two nations are going to be the critical factor in the economic future of Burma.

The latest developments in Sino-Burmese relations were the first confirmed shipment of munitions by China to Rangoon in August 1990 and an arms deal of over $1 billion toward the end of 1990. It is not really surprising that the military regime of Burma has turned toward China in light of the two countries' common heritage of "nightmare states" and experiences of political upheavals and massacres of demonstrators in 1988 and 1989. Both of them are steadfast in their goal of crushing the democracy movement with no compunction in killing and violating the fundamental human rights of their people. Chinese military aid will certainly play a major role in the political future of Burma as the Western powers continue to exert pressure on the military regime for the restoration of democracy and "freedom."

THE JAPANESE FACTOR

There was an important development for the Myanmar Road to Democracy in 1989. The political pressure exerted by the United States and the West was felt by the major economic power of Asia, Japan. According to the *Financial Times* of London, Japan had halted its economic assistance to the SLORC government on the basis of its violations of human rights such as the arrest of Daw Aung San Suu Kyi, U Tin U, and other political dissenters.[6] Although on the governmental level Japan has not officially resumed aid, it is the only country which has officially recognized the illegitimate military regime of Burma today. With respect to Japan's continued role in relieving the foreign debt pressure or an indirect aid to the military regime in 1990, Harn Yawnghwe spoke correctly:

> If we [Burmese abroad] keep quiet, governments will take the most expedient route and continue dealing with the Saw Maung regime. For example, JAPAN has already given the regime a debt-relief grant of Yen 3.5 billion (US$ 23.5 million). This grant canceled a payment on Japanese loans which was repaid in March. Although Japanese officials say that the grant is not a resumption of aid to Burma and an endorsement of SLORC, the military saw it differently. The grant was received on July 23 and on July 27, SLORC declared that it would not hand over power to the NLD.[7]

Furthermore, many private Japanese firms have joined Thailand and other nations to invest in Burmese oil, mining, forestry, and fishing. It is more than likely that Japan will not sever its historical economic interest in Burma and abandon the immense role it has played as the largest creditor to finance the economic ventures of military rulers since 1962.

The total amount of external financing of Burma since 1988 is not exactly known, but from various private and public reports it may be estimated at over $2 billion in aid, trade concession agreements, and joint-ventures. Of these, the percentage distribution of the sources of funds are roughly 20 percent ($400 million) from private foreign investment in timber, 18 percent ($360 million) in department stores, hotels, and tourism, 12.5 percent ($250 million) in oil and gas, 7.5 percent ($100 million) in fishing and mining, and over 40 percent from the source of Japanese investments and the sale of the Tokyo Burmese Embassy in 1989/1990 at the understated official price of $236 million (the private estimated value of the sale was $600 million).[8]

The Japanese contribution to the external financing of the Saw Maung regime included $24 million in government aid and $10 million for a highway project. The long-term commitment of the Dai Ichi Company of Japan to invest in the development of Burma's infrastructure was $14 billion covering a period of ten to fifteen years. If the sale of the Burmese Embassy is included, the total financing by Japan would be more than 50 percent of the external funds raised by the present military regime of Saw Maung. It was also reported that outstanding aid of some $247 million is waiting to be approved by the Japanese government. It is safe to assume that the two most important countries funding the prolongation of the military dictatorship over Burma today are Japan and Thailand.

THE U.S. FACTOR

Thus far, the United States and the twelve European Economic Community governments have stood firm in halting aid, not officially recognizing the legitimacy of Saw Maung's regime, and calling for an end to political oppression, although diplomatic relations are maintained. Four basic actions were taken by the U.S. Government: the adoption of Senate Resolution No. 464 condemning the killings and demanding restoration of democracy; the cancellation of the General System of Preference (GSP) status of Burma; the pending Proposal of Trade Sanctions (Senate Bill 822) by Senator Patrick Moynihan passed by both houses which has yet to become an official sanction; and three other Senate and House Resolutions for humanitarian assistance, one of which was adopted by the Congress in November 1989 allocating $250,000 of humanitarian aid to the Burmese refugees.

It should be pointed out that these actions of the United States took more than a year and a half of delay to relieve the plight of thousands of refugees along the Thai border. Further delays of definitive actions against the SLORC are likely in view of the more urgent need to solve the Persian Gulf crisis. The actions taken by the United States and the West so far seem ineffective in either causing economic havoc or promoting democratization of Burma. Thus, the SLORC has been turning to China, which shared with Burma the suppression of "freedom," and other Asian countries. However, the hopeful sign of various actions taken by the United States is that Ne Win's past strategy of anticommunist campaigns, which has been vehemently deployed by the present regime to discredit the opposition and receive western support, is not working.

THE UN AGENCIES

It was also reported that the visiting team of the International Monetary Fund and the World Bank, which were approached by the present military regime for development loans, left Burma unimpressed by the charades of "an open economy" and "the Burmese Way to Capitalism." However, the United Nations Development Programme, the Food and Agricultural Organization, the World Health Organization, and UNICEF continue funding some of the development projects by virtue of Burma's entitlement of aid as a least developed country. Many civil servants of the present regime continue to travel abroad under the aforesaid United Nations agencies' programs indicating that there is a fundamental flaw in the stance and policy of this prestigious international organization. The Universal Declaration of Fundamental Human Rights and its violations by an illegal government seem not to count in the membership in this organization, on the one hand, and the entitlement of aid enables violators to receive funding for projects, which can lead to further violations of human rights, on the other.

Although the United Nations Commission on Human Rights looked into the human rights abuses inside Myanmar since March 1989 at its Geneva Meeting and later received the Burmese delegation in February 1990 to reply to the charges made by various human rights organizations, no specific official actions have been taken to either denounce or sanction the military regime. In fact, under the pretense of holding "free and fair multiparty democratic general elections" and that "the government is looking forward to the day when they would be able to hand over power to the duly elected government,"[9] the Burmese delegation indicted both the reputation of the UN Commission and other critics for making groundless accusations of human rights violations. Now that the military regime of Saw Maung has unequivocally reneged on its promise by not even officially recognizing the May 27 election results let alone handing over the power to the majority winning party of the NLD, it will be interesting to see how the UN and many nations react to this clear violation of the fundamental right of the Burmese to choose and install a government according to their will and wish.

THE ENDOGENOUS FACTORS FOR BURMA'S FUTURE

The economy of Myanmar under the SLORC management has remained essentially the same despite the official cliché and policy of "the Burmese Way to Capitalism." The basic structure and function of the double dual economy have not been altered in that the nominal official economy coexists with the giant black market economy, now ostensibly labeled "the free market," while the gap between the "center" and the "periphery" with respect to production function or modernization continues to widen. The new twist of the "open economy" of Saw Maung has been to legalize internal and external trade without giving up the control of major industries, and to enlarge military economic power by expanding the scope of state capitalism. Since the SLORC's illegal seizure of political power, it has maintained almost complete control of economic activities and industries of major foreign exchange earning power by entering into hundreds of joint-ventures with various private foreign firms in oil, forestry, gems, and fishery.

STATE CAPITALISM AND CONTROLS

The old governmental superstructure with various ministries, fifty-five State Economic Enterprises (SEEs), eleven State Corporations, and thousands of co-operatives has largely remained intact and controls the economy of Burma. The key industries of forestry, oil, mining, gems, and fishery with foreign-exchange earning capacity are still the state monopoly. This is evident in the fact that more than forty trade concessions of teak and a number of fishing rights were successfully made by Abel directly with a dozen or so countries. The most prominent countries among the foreign investors are Thailand (more than 90 percent of teak concessions), Japan, China, Korea, Singapore, and Australia.

These concessions and the legalization of border trade were made with the single purpose of obtaining scarce foreign exchange to finance the all-out military campaign against the minority insurgents, student rebels, and all other political foes. The recognition of the regime by Japan, which has resumed informal aid; the permission by the Thai government—which has teak-logging interests—for Burmese military incursions in its territory; the annual Burma gems emporium successfully held; the granting of onshore oil exploration rights to many countries; and the other foreign ventures in Myanmar—all of these seem to indicate economic interests superseding the issue of human rights violations in international economic relations. The sadness in all of this is that an illegitimate regime's military strength is fortified, and it continues to oppress the Burmese people with the arms financed by the free world.

The clearest evidence of the fake privatization and open door economic policy or *perestroika* of the SLORC is to be found in a number of stringent rules, regulations, and restrictions placed on private traders engaged in external trade. First, there are strict licensing requirements imposed upon private traders and their individual transactions. Nineteen categories of goods for import and export are specified by the Ministry of Trade which issued licenses at a fee plus an additional license for each consignment of export and import. Second, restrictions are imposed on border trade by banning the export of sixteen important products, including rice, teak, cotton, maize, rubber, etc. Third, all private exporters and importers cannot deal freely in foreign exchange except through the Myanma Foreign Trading Bank.

The purpose of the so-called legalization of border trade by the SLORC since 1988 has been simply to set up ten custom stations at the Thai, Chinese, Indian, and Bangladesh borders to collect custom duties. All fourteen different countertrade agreements signed were between the Myanmar Export Import Services (MEIS) and foreign countries or companies. Both the private sector and the State Economic Enterprises of the SLORC participated in these agreements. However, all of these agreements were made in kind rather than in cash or money to indicate that nothing really has changed in the border trade of Myanmar except for the fact that the border trade has now become an officially legalized source of revenues for the military regime.

Further evidence of the nominal nature of this supposed open door economic policy can be discerned in the control of foreign exchange by the present military regime. For example, the exchange rate has been fixed at about K6.5 per US dollar, and the Central Bank of Burma, the Myanma Foreign Trading Bank, and the Myanma Export Import Services monopolize all foreign exchange transactions and flows into Myanmar. It is interesting to note here also that the reason for maintaining a fixed exchange rate given by the Chairman of the SLORC, Saw Maung, is very intriguing. According to the *Working People's Daily*, the following is how Saw Maung intelligently explained the foreign debt burden and why the foreign exchange rate must remain fixed:

> He warned against reducing the foreign exchange rate of Myanmar because it was most likely that the rate would be reduced again and again. He also warned that if it was carried out hastily, future generations would suffer. Dealing with debts, General Saw Maung said that the country became one of the Least Developed Countries (LDC). Becoming an LDC, the country got debt relief. He assured, however, that debts would not increase because the government was undertaking joint ventures and the Investment Law was in existence. Chairman of the State Law and Order Restoration Council General Saw Maung said that the government was not going to stay on for long and it would not make future generations suffer by altering the exchange rate.[10]

This interesting rationale for not devaluing the Burmese kyat to avoid sufferings by future generations is not only intriguing but also places a tremendous burden of inability to sell to foreign buyers on the part of the present generation of private exporters. His naive interpretation and ignorance of the foreign exchange rate adjustment mechanism as well as his confidence in reducing foreign debt by simple joint-ventures confirm once more the lack of technical sophistication on the part of the military rulers in general. It also reflects the same technical incompetence shown by his mentor Ne Win whose foreign exchange transactions and indictment of foreign advisers were described earlier.

The real impact of this irrational policy of fixed exchange rate has been on the private traders. Since the state imposed total foreign exchange control, the proceeds of foreign sales made by private traders are paid by the central monetary authorities in Burmese local currency which is overvalued several times above the black market rate. As a result, the real value of exports is not received and private merchants alone suffer phenomenal translation losses in their foreign sales. As for the state, foreign exchange proceeds from these private foreign transactions have been highly profitable and helpful in augmenting the foreign exchange reserves. Consequently, the majority of private external trade has been conducted more or less on a bilateral barter basis in the same black market centers along the Sino- and Thai-Burmese borders.

One other subject General Saw Maung spoke of deals with how the status of Myanmar as one of the least developed countries in the world can be changed. He said confidently that:

> Furthermore, it was said that the country has declined to a status of LDC because of mismanagement during the past 26 years. Have we really become poor by being a LDC? Are you aware of privileges that accrue to a LDC? It is easy to stop being a LDC. Every government that comes to power can apply to have the status canceled. Why have we become LDC? I have learnt that the prices of commodities are very high today. Then what measures have we taken before to bring down the prices? I would like to mention a matter regarding rice. According to accounts kept, rice was sold at losses of 324.1 million kyats in 1984–85, 353.1 million kyats in 1985–86 and 392.7 million kyats in 1986–87. The prices of fertilizers and petroleum, of railway fares and airfares were also at a loss. That was why our country became a LDC.[11]

He went on further to explain that his regime cured this problem of loss by introducing market mechanisms whereby prices rose and the government made a profit [presto no longer a LDC?]. This ludicrous theory of inflation and miraculous panacea for underdevelopment by introducing market mechanisms and price hikes to avoid state losses do not seem to be working very well lately in Burma which is under siege by stagflation, an outstanding foreign debt of over $4.5 billion, and a debt service ratio of over 25 percent in 1990. Perhaps, the SLORC should keep Burma's status of a LDC a while longer for the privilege of debt relief recently given by Japan.

THE IMPACT OF STATE CAPITALISM AND "LEGALIZATION OF TRADE": POSITIVE OR NEGATIVE

To recapitulate the basic theme of this study, the assessment of the Burmese social character, modernization, and economic performance has always been made in a dichotomous vein by many writers. The present state of affairs in Burma has been assessed in the same way, although there seem to be very few positive appraisals of the military regime's human rights violations and of putting up Burma's resources for sale. Yet, some authors and interested trading partners of Burma praised and welcomed the opportunity to invest and exploit the untapped natural resources that have remained latent for nearly thirty years in the isolated Burmese economy.

The classic positive view and appraisal of the benevolent impact of the military economic policy for Burma are represented by the views of a well-known sycophantic British political scientist and historian of the military rule over Burma, Robert Taylor. He is about the only Western academician defending the military actions as benevolent and has been allowed to travel freely in Burma with red carpet treatment by his military host. His works and views were discussed earlier in this study. His recent articles and works have been extensively used by the Saw Maung regime as an authoritative account of the Burmese Way to Capitalism and its beneficial effect on Burma and its people. Without using empirical data and evidence of privatization and a truly open economy, he wrote:

> The government's policies since the 1988 coup have begun the process of opening up Burma's economic system to one more similar to its ASEAN neighbours. With the help of the United Nations Development Programme and other agencies, privatization and other liberalization programmes are being implemented. Foreign investment is again possible and real economic growth could be rapid. The army and the successful parties [which ones?] at least seem to agree on this.[12]

These observations and projections of the future economic growth of Burma are contrary to the real nature of state capitalism held tightly by the military "Robber Barons," on the one hand, and to the historical reality of economic difficulties being confronted by a host of former totalitarian regimes, the Soviet Union, Poland, and Czechoslovakia, for example, in their efforts to restructure their economies by a surgical privatization, on the other. It is more likely for Burma to face economic crises, and, conversely, less likely for Burma to experience a rapid economic growth in view of its relative retrogression for the last thirty years with respect to modernization and the depressed state of technology. It is almost certain that the economic retrogression of Burma will continue rather than being replaced by the rapid economic growth envisaged by Taylor.

His evaluation and recommendations are totally contrary to the historical evidence of the gross military mismanagement of the Burmese economy, which succeeded in making the Golden Land, generally recognized as immensely rich in natural resources, one of the least developed countries in the world. Nothing is going to change overnight to augment the low technological base of the economy by inviting foreign investments and putting Burma up for sale to the relatively more developed economies of the ASEAN nations and the world. Neither the terms of trade nor world market conditions seem to favor Myanmar's potential for rapid economic growth. This view is consistent with that of many observers who see through the charades of Saw Maung's regime and recognize that the nominal liberalization programs are a political ploy for fortification of military might to sustain its illegitimate government. As J. R. Saul wrote:

> U Ne Win, Myanmar's ruler, and his generals have reduced the richest country in Southeast Asia to such an impoverished state that, with a few hundred million dollars of hard currency per year, the system can be run and enough will be left over to fill the generals' pockets. Until the repression of 1988, these funds were a combination of foreign investments [foreign aid] and drug money. Some people in Washington [also Thailand and other ASEAN countries] believe that opening up Myanmar to foreign investment represents an opportunity for political liberalization. They are wrong. Foreign investment is the single most important element keeping the generals in power with their repressive policies and support of the drug lords.[13]

Indeed, economic liberalization and political repression are incompatible for the flowering of democracy as well as economic growth. Although private enterprises are nominally allowed, their operations have been confined to minor economic areas of small businesses. The truth of the above evaluation can be supported by the fact that neither internal nor external private firms are really allowed or able to enter and compete against the more than fifty different giant state enterprises of the military regime which has a monopoly on every key industry of major foreign exchange earning power.

One other evidence of the claim on economic power and privilege by the generals of the SLORC can be found in the nonpublicized one-step promotion of all the nineteen military commanders whose new artificial ranks and titles remind one of the omnipotent titles and ownership of everything by the Burmese kings. General Saw Maung is now addressed as the "Senior General," formerly a nonexistent rank in the armed services, while Brigadier Khin Nyunt, Colonel Abel, and others all became "Generals" with higher salaries and greater privileges. This is similar to the People's Deputies' Emoluments Law passed in 1975 which phenomenally increased the top military administrators' salaries and other privileges. There are also luxurious new homes and real estate built and expanded for the generals in the exclusive sections of Rangoon among which the old Bogyoke Ywah No. 1 and the new Bogyoke Ywah No. 2 (General's Village or Villa No. 1 and No. 2) are the most conspicuous.

The single most important evidence of this military control of the riches and enterprises of Burma was the creation of a giant enterprise called the Union of Myanmar Economic Holdings Limited totally owned and operated by Defense Services personnel, veterans, and military regimental organizations. It is reminiscent of the Defense Service Institute and the Burma Economic Development Corporation associated with the names of Brigadiers Tin Pe and Aung

Gyi in the 1950s and early 1960s. The military owned and operated companies numbered more than fifty prior to the military coup of 1962. This giant military capitalist venture was established by law on February 19, 1990 with an initial capital of K10 billion (roughly $1.5 billion) for the welfare of the generals, their military associates, and families.[14]

Apart from this giant military corporation under the direct control of the Ministry of Defense, which is ostensibly called the State/Private Joint Venture (JVC) No. 9, there are eight other similar JVCs dealing with agriculture, fishery, trade, construction, hotel, and medicines under the direct control of the SLORC. The Ministry of Trade and Foreign Investment Commission dictate and control all other joint ventures formed, which is propagandized as "the SLORC's economic endeavors paving the way with flowers—56 Joint-Ventures [formed]" in the *Working People's Daily*. Hundreds of JVCs between the State and domestic and foreign business firms have been formed to perpetuate state capitalism.

According to the Index of Foreign Firms: January to December 1990 (*Burma Alert No. 1, Volume 2,* January 1991) compiled by Harn Yawnghwe, the total number of foreign firms from around the world that entered into trade, investment, and joint-venture agreements with the SLORC is over two hundred. The number of foreign firms in order of ranking were 76 Thai firms, more than 90 percent of which were in teak, 33 Japanese firms, 28 Singaporean firms, 14 Hongkong firms, 13 Korean firms, 10 American firms, and 7 Australian firms. Most of these firms were required to pay a signature bonus in foreign exchange or a bribe up front, which was as high as $5 million for a $15 million oil project, as in the case of Petro-Canada, to the Foreign Investment Commission chaired by Major General Abel, the Minister of Trade as well as Finance and Planning. The estimated initial signature bonuses in 1989/1990 alone were between $50 and $55 million.

According to the Foreign Investment Law, which was promulgated in December 1988 and began operating in May 1989, foreign investment is allowed only outside the twelve areas that are primarily reserved for the state under the State Economic Enterprise Law. The twelve areas represent a total state monopoly of major industries. All of these state restrictions and capitalist ventures of the SLORC represent a scrupulous enlargement of the economic base of the military rulers to control the political power. In short, the so-called open market–oriented economy of Myanmar of the present military "Robber Barons" is a revamped military command economy of the past socialist state of Burma.

THE ECONOMIC PERFORMANCE OF BURMA (1988–1990)

The production of rice and other agricultural produce was supposedly privatized, but the state quota system of delivery and price control were indirectly kept intact. The state distribution shops and co-operatives have not been dismantled and the same phenomenal price differentials between the official and

Figure 13
Scarcity Index October 1989 Black Market Prices

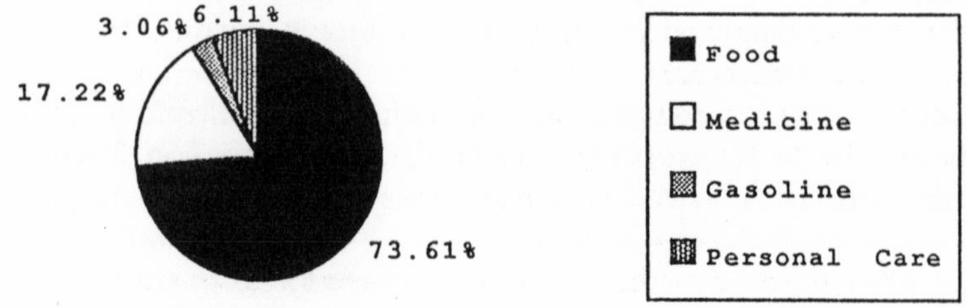

Source: U.S. Embassy, *Shadow Survey*, Rangoon, October, 1989.

the "free market" prices persist to plague the economic life of the people. Inflation and the cost of living index in the so-called liberalized economy of Burma have not only not subsided but rather have increased rapidly to nullify Taylor's glorious vision of a rapid real economic growth (see Figure 13).

This scarcity index was calculated on the basis of the so-called free market prices of various items in each category. It indicates the phenomenal cost of food for an urban family in its monthly budget despite the upward adjustment of the pay scale of government workers and civil servants by about 110 percent.[15] For example, between July 1988 and July 1989, the prices of three types of good quality rice, Ngakywe, Meedon, and Emata rose by 127, 188, and 188 percents respectively in Rangoon, while the price of low quality rice, Ngasein, rose by 260 percent. The price of sesame oil rose by 71 percent, while the price of onions rose by 367 percent. These three items, rice, cooking oil, and onions, are the main components in the Burmese diet. With the exception of goat meat, other basic meat prices rose on average by about 50 percent. The overall composite average rise in the prices of seven basic necessities was given as 76 percent showing the consequences of the ostensible liberalization measures taken by the military regime.[16]

These rises in the prices of basic necessities were attributed by the military regime to traders who were charged with "obstructing flow of commodities region-wise" and "lack of co-operation; there are indications of manipulation of commodity prices and that legal action to be taken against those who adversely effect public welfare."[17] It has a familiar ring of holding the "black marketeers" and "black money-holders" responsible for causing inflation and opposing the construction of the socialist economy, as Ne Win claimed when his demonetization measures were undertaken in the late 1980s. The military junta set up various divisional Committees for Reducing Commodity Prices (CRCP) demanding that the "free private traders" bring down prices by command of the military commanders. The Chairman of the Rangoon CRCP dictated that: "The rice traders are required to strive for bringing down the prices of rice by distributing it through brokerage centers and wholesale shops at prices to be fixed by the Rangoon Division Rice Traders Association. It is necessary for rice traders to sell rice at reasonable price for the welfare of the public."[18]

In fact, it was reported that the private traders were forced to sell rice and other commodities at below cost to the state collection centers or at par with the official distribution prices of the same old co-operatives and newly created welfare shops. These restrictions and requirements imposed on the private traders and their activities indicate that there have not been any major changes in the functioning of the military command economy which restricts economic freedom by arbitrary laws.

The clearest example of the gross mismanagement of the economy by the unskilled and uneducated military managers seems to be in the same area of distribution and price control of basic necessities. In an effort to combat poverty and appease the impoverished urban population, the SLORC instituted welfare shops or military discount shops to sell rice and other products to the poor at discount prices. The result was the same as before, shortages at these shops caused by black marketeering. It also hiked the pay scale by more than 300 percent for civil servants financed by new money, thereby inadvertently increasing the money supply. The net effect was a wage-price spiral in the "free market" fueled by the declining productivity and hoarding of goods by private traders. The price of rice and other products has skyrocketed three to ten times above the official prices set at these shops.

The price per *pyi* (4.69 pounds) of good quality rice, Ngakywe, for example, climbed above K30 (roughly 5 U.S. dollars) in 1989 compared with K20–25 in the middle of the political crisis of 1988. The price per *pyi* of low quality rice, Ngasein, which was rarely consumed by the average Burmese wage earner prior to 1962, soared above K20 in the black market compared with K6 at state welfare shops in July and reset at K8 and K9 in August. The pay scale hike of the lowest K100-2-110 monthly income of a poor urban government servant to K450-25-600 to alleviate the economic hardship was not sufficient to counter the relatively greater rise in the prices of basic consumer goods. For example, a person earning this new K450 monthly pay must spend K320 per month on low quality rice alone, assuming the monthly consumption of 16 *pyis* at a cost of K20 per *pyi*. If he is married, then the cost of rice consumption would be K640 which is beyond his monthly income. Thus, for an urban family of more than three even those who earned K1,000 would face a below subsistence level of existence.

In rice distribution, the former government agency, the Agricultural and Farm Produce Trade Corporation (AFPTC), was simply renamed the Myanma Agricultural Produce Trading (MAPT), and did not purchase paddy during the period of political upheavals in 1987–88. It was manned by the same personnel from former People's Councils of the B.S.P.P. with the new name of Law and Order Restoration Councils all over Burma. In 1988–89, the MAPT began procuring paddy by reinstituting the former state buying depots of the AFPTC with the new name of Central Collection Centers, once more forcing farmers to sell at low prices relative to the free market prices. Despite Saw Maung's claim of the state buying agencies' profitable operations by hiking the procurement price, the free market price of rice was higher than the state offered price. The result has been a massive hoarding of basic necessities generating empty shelves at state welfare shops and co-operatives reminiscent of the state-controlled cooperative shops in the Socialist Republic of the Union of Burma.

Agricultural and export performance of Burma during the fiscal year 1988–89 further testify to the continuing journey of Burma toward poverty. For example, rice and broken rice topped the list with a decrease of some 84 percent from the year before. Earnings from these declined by 79 percent valued at \$3.8 million. A total of only 23,684 metric tons of regular rice (\$4.52 million worth) and 24,108 tons of broken rice (\$3.8 million worth) were exported. The export and income from rice dropped by 88 percent and 85 percent respectively. Compared with the annual average export of roughly 100,000 metric tons in the years immediately prior to the political turmoils of 1988, these figures definitely indicate the limping economy of Burma.[19]

In 1989/90 the price per gallon of gasoline, governmentally controlled and rationed at 4 to 5 gallons a week per family, climbed above K150 in the black market relative to the government distribution price of K16. The U.S. dollar had been trading over-the-counter at K60 or more, even though the official exchange rate averaged K6.5 in recent months. As before, the SLORC blamed private merchants and traders for causing these price differentials with their greedy speculation and hoarding for profit. Despite the huge stockpile of rice at state warehouses as a result of the 1988 political unrest, the prices of basic necessities continued to rise in 1989–1990. The rise in general price levels since 1988 was caused both by hoarding of goods by private traders and by monetary policies of price and wage hikes, introduction of K200 new notes and an increase in government deficit and money supply. The key macroindicators of the economy of Burma shown in Table 9 may be used to confirm the continuing trend of the Burma Road to Poverty.

Since these macro-economic indicators are derived primarily from the sources of the Ministry of National Planning and Finance and the Central Bank of Myanmar, the reliability of some of these data is suspect, especially the growth rate of GDP for the year 1989/90 and the rate of inflation implicated in the consumer price indices. The real growth rate of 7.4 percent for 1989/90 may be deemed as inflated due to the underestimation of the inflation rate for

Table 9

The Macro-Economic Indicators of the Burmese Economy (1987-1990)*

Domestic Economy	1987/1988	1988/1989	1989/1990
Population (in millions)	38.6	39.29	40.03
GDP at 1985-86 prices (in millions of kyats)	K53,178	K47,096	K50,562
Growth Rate of GDP	-4.2%	-11.4%	7.4%
Consumer Price Index(1986=100)	126.53	155.0	191.73
% Change of Currency in Circulation	-29.1	49.85	55.62
Labor force (in millions)	15.813	16.036	N/A
Government Deficit (% of GDP)	6.0	10.0	14.4
Trade and Balance of Payments (in millions)			
Trade Balance	-$370.497	-$190.259	-$274.888
External Public Debt	$4,257	$4,500	$5,679
Debt Service Ratio	50.78%	25.45%	25.25%
Foreign Exchange Reserves	$63.7	$110.8	$146.1
Exchange Rate per US$1			
Official	K6.44	K6.57	K6.69
Black Market	K50	K60	K70

*The data for 1988/89 are provisional actual and for 1989/90 are provisional estimates. Sources: Ministry of National Planning and Finance (Social and Economic Indicators, 1990), Central Statistical Organization and Central Bank of Myanmar, IMF, World Bank and US Embassy.

that year by the government at about 30 percent relative to a more realistic rate of perhaps 60 percent. Thus, the true rate of growth may be between 3 and 4 percent.

The indirect evidence of this realistic lower rate adjusted for higher rate of inflation is supported by the sustained growth rates of currency in circulation, government deficit, trade deficit and black market exchange rate for the US dollar given in Table 9. From private sources, the rate of inflation in Rangoon and other cities in 1989/1990 and in the early months of 1991 has been in double or triple digits depending upon products. The gap between the official prices and open market prices has remained as large as before indicating that the Burmese economy remains under seige by its built-in political foes of accelerated inflation and impoverishment of the masses.

THE LEGACIES OF THE BURMESE KINGS REVIVED

All of the above economic actions undertaken by the SLORC have two backward political linkages to Ne Win's dictatorship and the despotic practices of the Burmese kings. They reaffirmed the ownership and control of everything by the numinous state with the modern cliché of the Burmese Way to Capitalism. Vital industries and enterprises remain in the hands of the military rulers whose control of their production, export, and joint-ventures with foreign firms is complete. The programs of building roads, bridges, and face lifting Rangoon and a very few other cities were launched in the tradition of a Burmese king. In a way, it is similar to the custom of a bad Burmese monarch constructing pagodas, monasteries, and lakes for the atonement of the sins committed during his reign.

With respect to this customary practice of a ruler, Ne Win spoke of the nature and character of the Burmese back in 1959 when he reigned over Burma as an interim Premier. He carried the kingly title of Thado Thiri Thudama Wungyigyoke Ne Win when he addressed the Security Council Conference of the Burmese Army held at the Defense Services Headquarters in Rangoon on December 24, 1959. His assessment of the weakness of the Burmese character was as follows:

> People of our country are very shallow and low in standard with respect to their belief and thinking. The people of Burma have many weak national habits among which is the habit of forgetting things quickly. What it means is that if a person commits a misdeed, everybody will indict and label him as an extremely bad individual at the time he commits it. But later if the same person does something nice or cunningly pretends to behave nicely, the rest of the folks forget the wound and consider him to be the nicest person. Therefore, a human being is not always good or not always bad but a changing being.[20]

He went on further to explain how a woman whose husband was killed by someone who went berserk, shouting, crying, and telling how he was killed at the time of the killing. One month or so later, at the court, she told the authorities that there was no point or personal profit in charging the accused sitting next to her with the crime and to let bygones be bygones. The moral of this story was that, whether as an individual or a nation as a whole, the "Burmese are weak in remembering the misdeeds committed by power-holders."[21] This national characterization of the Burmese is essentially the same as the one made by Major Allen Yule a century before upon his visit to the Kingdom of Ava: "They are cheerful and singularly alive to the ridiculous; buoyant, elastic, soon recovering from personal or domestic disaster . . . indifferent to the shedding of blood on the part of their rulers, yet not individually cruel, temperate, abstemious, and hardy, but idle, with neither fixedness of purpose nor perseverance."[22]

By psychologically projecting his own cynical unconcern for the Burmese people's human rights, Ne Win continually took advantage of this weakness in the Burmese social character. He also emphasized many times that the Burmese people deserved the kind of government he created since they chose to accept and tolerate it. He has persistently employed the Machiavellian tyrannical tactic of all-out assault or punishment followed by a deliberate delay in time to cool down the frenzy of the moment of his crimes. He would also later dole out rewards to those who were totally subjugated to heal the wounds he had inflicted.

All the post-1988 political strategies deployed by the present military regime of Saw Maung mirrored Ne Win's beliefs and practices showing that he and he alone has been responsible for various actions and policies designed to destroy the democracy movement in Myanmar. Building bridges and gardens, and at the same time fortifying various defense service offices and barricades, requiring the people of Rangoon by force to clear the dirty ditches and painting the houses and buildings white, and delaying the transfer of power to the winning party of the May 27, 1990, election, all of them point to the Big Father pulling the string from behind the speeches and actions of Saw Maung and Khin Nyunt. The pattern of the SLORC actions has been to wait and reduce the psychological frenzy of the masses to a state of inertia. Whether or not this will work again in the future to prolong the military dictatorship in Myanmar is a question yet to be answered. Thus far, the Burmese do not seem to be forgetful as evidenced by many memorial services and sporadic demonstrations held regularly under the guns of the military rulers inside Burma.

BURMA'S ECONOMIC CHALLENGE AND TRANSITION IN THE 1990S

At this juncture, it is pertinent to note that a number of Burmese and Western scholars have recently written on the economic future of Burma with recommendations and panaceas based upon the historical performances and economic policies of the past in a book entitled *Myanmar Dilemmas and Options: The Challenge of Economic Transition in the 1990s.* Mostly using the unreliable statistical data of the Burmese government, both the editors and others dealt with past macroeconomic performances by demarcating two basic periods, one of economic stagnation (1962–1974) and one of "recovery or reversing the trend" (1974–1987). They did not mention the enormous external resuscitation in the form of foreign aid received by the General Ne Win regime in the late 1970s and 1980s. For example, an average per capita growth rate of 2.5 percent was given for the past twenty-eight years, which certainly contradicts the facts presented in this study and Burma's attainment of the least developed country status in 1987.[23] The majority of the analyses and evaluations of the Burmese economy were descriptive and barely scratched the surface of the fundamental issues and dilemmas of Burma. For example, U Tun Wai wrote: "One has to understand the past and the present in order to meaningfully plan the economic future. In this task, one should not be wedded to "isms", be it capitalist or socialistic. What counts most is a pragmatic assessment of the past failures and successes, reasons for the results and lessons to be learned so that the same mistakes are not made again."[24]

This statement sounds highly benevolent and rational, but hardly pragmatic. His whole analysis did not touch upon the gross military mismanagement of the economy and giant black market to give a true understanding of the past. Neither did he analyze the real nature and intentions of the legalization of trade by the present military regime's pretentious "Burmese Way to Capitalism." This study has shown that the obsession of the consecutive political leadership of Burma with monolithic "socialism" of the Sino-Soviet type and the "statism" of the past Burmese kings has been the major obstacle to what modern men would term rational actions and policies. The Burma Road to Poverty or what went wrong with a country of immense richness in natural resources causing it to attain the least developed country status is largely a story of "failed isms" in the pursuit of a negative utopia. Ideologies or "isms" are not out of fashion in both the developed and the less developed countries around the world. The "statism" of Burma will remain the main stumbling block for its economic future. U Tun Wai's recommendation of "stock-taking and restructuring"[25] ignores further the depressed state of technology, particularly the managerial and innovative capacity of the military "Robber Barons" in Burma, as a consequence of the brain drain and discrimination against private entrepreneurs and the educated.

None of the studies analyzed and appraised the role played by "the military managers" and the basic structure of the double dual economy of socialist Burma, particularly the giant black market and its significance, over the last twenty-eight years. The economic base of the military dictatorship forms the key dilemma for the future of Burma and to suggest, as Badgley did, that Burma be remodeled by "political innovation" [?], restructuring the Army and changing the nonexistent constitution[26] following the models and examples of the Western democracies and other countries is a dream rather than what is happening inside Burma today. The historical continuum of the military control of wealth, resources, and political power will persist and the so-called "Burma and Asia-Pacific Dynamism" of volkes misses the enormous technical and absolute advantage enjoyed by the Pacific nations over Burma in striking joint-ventures, trade concessions, and investments, on the one hand, and the goal of fortifying the military might of the ruling junta, on the other.[27]

The technological trap of primitive and traditional modes of production in both the large agricultural and small modern sectors of the Burmese economy created by the inept policies of the military managers is not likely to be sprung by the ostensible legalization of internal and border trade. The monetary and fiscal policies of the present military regime have been to impose arbitrary taxes and collect revenues from both private Burmese citizens and traders more than to institute the reforms suggested by U Tun Wai and U Myat Thein in their recommendation of "stock-taking" and "supply-leading" development policies.[28] U Tun Wai and U Myat Thein are recommending state initiation and intervention to stimulate the transformation of "the economic culture" of the people which seems to have degenerated during the past twenty-eight years. However, rampant corruption, theft, and violations of the economic rights of the people of Burma have been the main features of the past and present functioning of the Burmese economy. It is this retrogression that will be the largest obstacle to the economic development and modernization of Burma in the future.

FUTURE ECONOMIC PROSPECTS

Based upon these historical facts on the functioning of the economy and polity of Burma, a number of conclusions may be drawn with respect to its future economic prospects. First and foremost, the economic development of Burma cannot and will not occur without the central prerequisite of establishing "a government whose authority to govern is derived from the consent of the people." This is supported by the historical economic performances of the negative utopian states of totalitarian governments around the world. In the words of Daw Aung San Suu Kyi, "Burma is struggling for her second independence" from the military dictatorship which must be achieved first before anything else for the future economic growth of Burma. Even if this prerequisite is achieved, Burma will confront monumental problems in repairing the enormous damages inflicted upon the human resources by almost three decades of military dictatorship.

Second, since this prerequisite is lacking in Burma today, the depressed state of technology and the technical incompetence of the military managers will remain the major obstacles to Burma's future economic development. The richness of Burma in natural resources, as a parameter of potential economic development, is not constant since the population of Burma has been increasing at an annual rate of over two percent over the last three decades. This increased ratio of population to land and the rapid depletion of natural resources that are being put up for sale to foreign investors are going to be additional factors for the perpetuation of the Burma Road to Poverty.

Third, in the short run the state monopoly of key industries and the present flow of external private capital into Burma from more than a dozen nations are likely to produce a temporary and illusory resuscitation of the dying economy. This is reminiscent of the past external pump priming of the limping economy of Burma by a host of Western governments and international agencies in prolonging the life of the military command economy. Thus far, more than two hundred foreign private firms and some specialized agencies of the United Nations have provided the necessary funds resulting in the military fortification of the present regime. The two most important Asian countries that have helped most for the survival of the present military regime are China and Thailand.

China, which like Burma had closed its books on the democracy movement, has become the largest supplier of arms and military technology since 1988 as evident in the arms deal of over $1 billion in 1990, while Thailand has been the main exploiter of Burma's teak, fishery, gems, and opium and the major exporter of manufactured goods to Burma since 1962. As of today, some sixty-seven different Thai firms have struck trading and investment deals with the SLORC which is by far the largest number of firms from a single country. The majority of these firms are in teak-logging and fishing industries. As for the industrial nations, the two major historical donors of Japan and West Germany continue to play a vital economic role in helping the military regime. Their respective firms of Fritz Werner and Dai Ichi continue to invest heavily in financing the arms factories, heavy industries, and infrastructure projects of the Defense Services.

The historical interest and role of Japan as the major investor and donor of aid to the military regimes of Burma are not likely to wane in view of the huge arrears of Japanese debt accumulated by Burma and Japan's own economic interest in the untapped natural resources of Burma. This is evident in the fact that Japan has been the only country which officially announced its recognition of the military regime of Saw Maung as a legitimate government of Burma soon after the 1988 fake military coup. In transportation, public utilities, television, and other manufacturing industries, Japanese firms have always dominated all other foreign firms in Ne Win's Burma. This tradition continues in Burma today. For example, the Dai Ichi firm alone committed $14 billion in 1989 to finance a long-term investment project in infrastructure for a period of ten to fifteen years.

Fourth, the governments of the West have not been doing the rescuing. Major powers have stopped their aid to the military regime since 1988. Instead, private sectors in both the West and Asian countries have taken up that function. However, the most dominant investors are Japan and the neighboring Asian countries such as China, Thailand, Singapore, South Korea, and Hong Kong. They are going to be the major determinant of Burma's future in the 1990s. Putting up the untapped natural resources of Burma for sale to the technologically superior foreign firms of these Asian countries, which have depleted their own natural resources in their modernization, may well produce an Asian takeover and economic bankruptcy of Burma in the long run. Indirect evidence of this can be found in Burma's deteriorating terms of trade.

Last, in spite of this success in attracting private foreign capital and investments, the same old problem of hyperinflation plagues the Burmese economy today. It is being brought about by a host of inept monetary measures such as phenomenal pay hikes, increased procurement prices for paddy, massive real estate loans to various civil servants sympathetic to the military government, and deficit financing of the military build up. They were financed primarily by pumping new money into circulation without concomitant rise in productivity. The result has been double and triple digit inflation rates for the majority of basic necessities.

Except for rice which is down from K25 per *pyi* in 1989 to K14 per *pyi* in January 1991 in the open market relative to the official distribution price of K8.50 per *pyi* at the military welfare shops, the prices of all other basic necessities in the urban communities have been rising at a rapid rate. Between 1990 and 1991, the open market prices of basic necessities have soared upward by double digit inflation rates, e.g., from K50 to K75 ($12.50) per viss of cooking oil, from K2 to K3.50 ($.60) per egg, and from K50 to K70 ($11) per viss of fish. The price per gallon of gasoline, rationed at four gallons a week and sold at K16 per gallon by the government, now soared above K200 per gallon in the black market compared with K100 a year ago. As for foreign products, a pack of Marlboros is sold for K54 or $9 and a bar of Lux soap for K24 or $6 at the official exchange rate of K6 = $1. The US dollar has been trading in the black market at a price as high as K72 relative to K50 in the middle of the 1988 political upheaval and K60 a year ago.

The clearest indicators of Burma's actual and potential economic decline are to be found in a continual annual trade deficit of over $250 million since 1988 and the mounting foreign debt of over $5.6 billion, and the increasing ratio of debt payments to export proceeds of over 25 percent. According to the source of the *Economic and Social Indicators* (published unofficially by the Ministry of Planning and Finance of the Government of the Union of Myanmar, March 1990), the balances of the trade deficits for the years 1988/1989 and 1989/1990 (provisional) and 1990/91 (planned) were K1,250 million, K1,839 million, and K2,788 million. The terms of trade deteriorated between 1988/89 and 1989/90 which were given as 74.3 percent and 80.8 percent. The projected or planned terms of trade for 1990/91 was 81.2 percent.

As of March 31, 1989, the same report gave the total external debt (disbursed and undisbursed) of Myanmar owed to multinational and bilateral donors as US $5.679 billion with bilateral aid, commercial loans and credit accounting for $4.243 billion or roughly 75 percent of total external debt. The outstanding Japanese aid and loans alone amounted to $2.951 billion or roughly 52 percent of the total external debt. However, the foreign exchange reserves derived mainly from all the trade concessions and joint-ventures entered into with foreign firms showed an increasing trend of $63.7 million, $110.8 million, and $146.1 million for 1987/88, 1988/89, and September 1989. The annual external debt servicing ratio (foreign exchange proceeds from trade and services to debt payments) for the same period was over 25 percent. As of September 1989, the ratio of foreign exchange reserves to total external debt was only 2.57 percent, indicating the persistent problem of external debt burden.

All these negative indicators of the economic performance of Myanmar since 1988, along with the accelerated double and triple digit inflation rate (depending upon the products) represent a formidable built-in political foe to the present military rulers. The historical cyclical pattern of relaxing and tightening the controls of the economy, as well as opening and closing the country, is likely to occur again. The continued economic decline and impoverishment of the masses may also precipitate another political upheaval and the ensuing killing fields in the future.

BURMA'S POLITICAL CHALLENGE AND TRANSITION IN THE 1990s?

This study was based upon the premise and hypothesis that the main cause of the Burma Road to Poverty has been the attempt of the consecutive political leadership of independent Burma to travel back in time to the glorious society of peace and prosperity of the past ancient Burmese kingdoms. The Burmese political leaders' view of the past is "not really historical, in the proper sense of the term, at all" and "they search for the past not so much for the causes of the present as for the standard by which to judge it; that is, for the unchanging pattern upon which the present ought to be modeled, but which through accident, ignorance, indiscipline, or neglect it so often fails to follow."[29] The socio-political developments during the last thirty years of military rule may best be depicted as the dialectical process of two opposing forces: the centripetal "exemplary center" or "negara" imposing authority and the arbitrary rule of force from the top down and the center outward, and "the dispersive periphery" or "desa" with its intrinsic tendency of fragmentation and the power element from the bottom up and inward.

This duality of power elements persists in the contemporary polity of Burma creating a historical spectacle of reviving the traditional myths of state. As a consequence, the more the military leadership aspired to claim its scope of power and control, "the more fragile the political structure supporting it, for the more it was forced to rest on alliance, intrigue, cajolery, and bluff"[30] as well as brute force. The collapse of the socialist republic and the present state of affairs in Burma may be thought of as the political drama of military warlords who rely upon the cultural ideal of the "consummately expressive or desacralized state" and strive to subdue opposition at all cost and extend their ability to mobilize men and materials so as to legitimize its authority and power. In so doing, they seem to be working against "the grain of a form of political organization whose natural tendency, especially under intensified pressures for unification, was toward progressive fragmentation."[31] In short, they had created a nightmare state of Pyidawchah—a country of repression, socio-political and economic decay, and retrogression back to the dark ages of the Burmese kings.

The evidence of the continuum of traditional despotic and totalitarian practices of Ne Win has been compiled and documented by the U.S. State Department, Amnesty International, Asia Watch, and other human rights groups. Some of this evidence includes the prohibition of freedom of expression and peaceful assembly, arbitrary arrest without fair trials and torture of thousands of political dissidents and prisoners, execution of hundreds of student and political rebels, the forceful use of human porters to wage war against the political rebels, forced or compulsory labor, extrajudicial execution and torture of ethnic minorities, and an endless list of violations of the human rights of the people of Burma. The number of imprisoned people has been reported to be as high as 30,000 since 1988, while hundreds have been executed and thousands abused and tortured.[32] In the words of Amnesty International, "many of Myanmar's political prisoners, including NLD leaders Aung San Suu Kyi and Tin U, are prisoners of conscience"[33] arbitrarily detained and arrested by the military rulers with neither conscience nor respect for the sanctity of human life mandated by the sacred religion of Buddhism.

CONCLUSION

In light of the social, political, and economic analyses of the Burma Road to Poverty presented in this study, a few conclusions may be drawn with respect to the future of Myanmar and its Road to Democracy. The main obstacle on this road has been the army, dominated by hard liners controlling the "center," reviving ancient despotic practices and deploying the modern arsenal of military intelligence and weapons. The entrenchment of power in the hands of nineteen military commanders of the SLORC under the direct command and tutelage of Ne Win is not likely to wane overnight and make room for civilian politicians to install democratic institutions. The estimated military strength of the Burmese armed forces and paramilitary groups totaled close to 300,000 with the armed forces accounting for 215,000; in comparison the NDF has a combined force of 35,000 and the communists 10,000.[34] These numbers are likely to be different today in favor of the Burmese armed forces, since there are reports that the government has been mobilizing more recruits and adding new divisions.

The second obstacle relates to the traditional handicap of factionalism among opposition groups, particularly the disparaged factions of formerly purged political leaders. This is the traditional legacy of past polities—the ancient, the colonial, the civilian, and the Ne Win totalitarian polities. With the exception of Daw Aung San Suu Kyi, the rest of the opposition leaders are formerly subdued leaders with no power and unity among themselves to oppose the "center." There are also multiple political groups led by children of civilian politicians of the U Nu era vying for leadership inside and outside Burma. For example, the US-based Committee for Restoration of Democracy (CRDB) is led by Tin Maung Win, the son of U Win, a former minister of U Nu, while

Thanmani Bo Khin Maung led a separate Thailand-based organization with Ko Aung, son of U Nu, and Zali Maw, son of Dr. Ba Maw. There is also a separate Bangkok-based organization led by Dr. Tin Myint U and Daw Aye Aye Thant, son-in-law and daughter of the late U Thant.

Factionalism cuts across various organizations both inside and outside Burma. The feuds and splits within the major overseas opposition group of the CRDB in the United States, the United Kingdom, West Germany, and other countries testify to this problem. Apart from the CRDB, there is a myriad of groups and separate individuals with mutual mistrust opposing the present military regime in various foreign countries. This is not truly unique or unusual since most tradition-bound political refugees and defectors suffer from the same lack of unity and organizational efficiency as the Burmese inside Burma. However, the sad result of all these factions has been the prolongation of military rule. The military intelligence service has been taking full advantage of this weakness and using tactics to intensify the fragmentation inside and outside Burma.

The third and perhaps the most serious obstacle relates to the psychological trauma and moral decay suffered by the people of Burma, which the military dictatorship has deliberately and systematically caused to bring out the worst social character and habits, born out of the rupture of moral fibres, values, and integrity under a system of unjust rule. The traditional authoritarian ways of life that have been reinforced by the military dictatorship of Ne Win are not likely to change quickly and, in fact, will persist to put the Burmese society in a state of social inertia for development. Fear, mistrust, and survival of the fittest usually outweigh the notions of social justice, common good, and fellowship in a nightmare state. They were generated by the "double negatives" and the reign of terror deployed by what Orwell called the Ministry of Truth of Ne Win and the military intelligence officers. It will be immensely difficult to overcome this injury inflicted on the psyche and character of the people of Burma by almost thirty years of dictatorship.

One of the positive results of the 1988 political upheavals and the present violations of human rights by the SLORC has been the loss of respect for the army on the part of a large segment of the Burmese populace, which has been held in conditions of grinding misery, fear, and peonage for almost thirty years. The single most important lesson the Burmese have learned is that their own government can be manifoldly more cruel and atrocious in violating their fundamental rights than all the previous foreign rulers of Burma. Indeed, as Daw Aung San Suu Kyi shrewdly and correctly perceived, the people of Myanmar are struggling for "second independence" and "freedom from fear" under the siege of their own army. This struggle will continue in spite of the phenomenal odds against its immediate success.

Although it is not quite certain, the naked aggression, killing, and indiscriminate violations of the rights of the people of Burma seem to have caused a temporary subsiding of the traditional mistrust and hatred between the majority

Bamahs (Burmese) and the minority ethnic groups whose need of mutual help to fight the common foe seems to supersede their ancient ethnophobia. The army, however, is constantly provoking this ancient social disease of various ethnic groups and emphasizing again and again the issue of ethnic minorities' wish to secede from the Union of Burma. Thus far, it has failed to put a large enough wedge between the majority Myanmahs or Bamahs and the minorities to destroy their steadfast demand for democracy and a legitimate civilian government. As to the future, whether or not this temporary union of ethnic groups will endure is uncertain. Yet, it is one of the inadvertent consequences of the ruthless military rule over Burma. One can only hope that it has an everlasting effect of cooperation and mutual trust leading to the construction of a viable socio-political and economic system so that all people of Burma can call their country Shwe Pyidawthah or Golden Land of Peace and Prosperity once again.

Meanwhile, the double dual economy of Ne Win's socialist republic continues to function and the military managers have been strangled by a giant black market infested with corruption, theft, and shortages of goods for the poor. The same technical incompetence and gross mismanagement of the economy by unskilled military managers will take Burma further down the Road to Poverty. It is more than likely that the same old economic malaise of a command economy of state capitalism will once again put Burma on edge for future political turmoil. In the end, if the historical experiences of a mismanaged military command economy are correctly assessed, the economic policy of putting up the untapped natural resources of Burma for sale will produce the same kind of economic disaster and poverty for Burma with a glaring and greater inequality of wealth and income distribution between the military power-holders and the simple folks.

There are also some speculations about and reports of dissent among the ranks within the army to suggest a potential coup or power struggles in the inner circles which may result in political turnover. Thus far, they remain speculations and hopes at best, although in terms of historical experience, there is a potential for the downfall of rising stars like Saw Maung, Khin Nyunt, and Abel. The ousting of the two Tin Oos, after their rapid rise to fame and power in 1976 and 1983, and the purging of Brigadiers Aung Gyi, Tin Pe, and others are precedents, showing the moves made by Ne Win to guard his political throne. The same fate may well be in store for Saw Maung, Khin Nyunt, and Abel. The key determinant of this lies in the person of the aging Ne Win and his power to command loyalty from these personalities and others. So far his power and personality cult have not waned and the process of permanent purge seems to be continuing.

As to the future of Daw Aung San Suu Kyi and her political leadership, as well as the political future of Burma, there are a number of possible outcomes. After the visit of a prominent Japanese political figure, Mr. Watanabe, the benefactor of Burma, Saw Maung promised to release Daw Aung San Suu Kyi upon the condition that she leave her native land and cease to be a politician. The likelihood of her departure gives rise to the possibility of waging a war from outside and mobilizing supporters to overthrow the present regime, similar to the cases of Premier Bhutto of Pakistan or President Aquino of the Philippines or President Chamorro of Nicaragua, with the help of the United States and other Western democracies. Such a course cannot be initiated by her voluntarily for she will lose credibility; hence the people and rebels must urge her to form a formidable opposition force of military strength. This, however, is a remote possibility.

On the other hand, the most likely case is that she will continue to stay in Burma under house arrest to symbolically taunt the scared military commanders and wait for potential mass demonstrations or breaks in the ranks of the Army or both. Without breaks in the ranks of the Burmese Army, the possibility of downing the superior armed forces is unlikely. Yet, if such an incident of people's revolt and power similar to the case in the Philippines should occur and succeed in installing her as the legitimate political leader, there is still a future possibility of power struggles and political fragmentation resulting in her being dethroned by the military commanders as in the case of Premier Bhutto. In any event, the governing of Burma and restoring democracy face monumental problems mentioned previously.

Despite these complexities as to the future outcome of Burma's struggle for freedom, one thing remains certain. The Burmese Army has lost its political legitimacy, credibility, and the respect of the majority of the people of Burma as evidenced in the May 27 election results. Those who committed the atrocious crimes in the political upheavals of 1988 and subsequent violations of human rights up to the present are cornered psychologically and politically with fear and insecurity for their future, hence the reason for the continued deployment of the rule of force. The tradition-bound masses are in a similar situation of fear and insecurity confronting the ruthless and overpowering military rulers, hence the reason for the psychological warfare with traditional signs and symbols. The most recent event in which images of Buddha wept or oozed blood and changed shapes or showed swelling of the breast, stirring people across the country, reflects symbolically the collective psyche and wish of the Burmese to be free from the yoke of military rule. Particularly, it reflects their hope and wish to free Suu Kyi who in their minds has become the only real contender for the political throne, *min lawn*, in the legendary image of her father, General Aung San.

Recently, the Burmese Buddhists have evoked the traditional method of reading signs of changes in the shapes of Buddha images as omens for future political change and the demise of the military. In particular, they interpreted the phenomenon of Buddha images' swollen breasts as the signal that the next ruler of Burma is to be a woman in the person of Daw Aung San Suu Kyi who has been under house arrest since July 1989. As in the nationalist movement against the British, the movement against the military rule today receives a new and, perhaps the most powerful impetus, from the awesome traditional political force of the Buddhist clerical order. It was initiated and radiated from the central and sacred city of Mandalay where the leading Buddhist cardinals and the rebellious monks reside.

In October 1990, the leaders of the Buddhist clerical order undertook cultural sanctions against the military and their families by refusing to accept the feeding of monks (a deed of merit for a Buddhist) and to perform funeral services (a necessary act for the proper departure of the spirit from the body). It was also reported that in the streets the monks pay homage to the soldiers and military commanders as Buddha. This action is considered sacrilegious and harmful to Buddhists who extol the clergy as equal in rank and reverence to Buddha himself in Burmese Buddhism.

This cultural taunting of bad rulers by the leading clergy of Upper Burma spread to other Buddhist monks across Burma and apparently caused some psychological trauma to the military rank and files. Indeed, being Burmese and Buddhist is synonymous and these cultural sanctions may well be the most potent weapon against the Burmese army.

Consequently, the military rulers have countered these sanctions as the Burmese kings and General Ne Win did in the past by invading over a hundred monasteries and arresting several monks as well as banning many Buddhist monk organizations. The senior abbots were forced to stop their boycott for fear of arrest and subjugation. However, many thousands of young monks continue to employ sanctions against the military rulers. Thus far, the military power-holders do not seem to be daunted by either the traditional religious sanctions or the modern standards of international law and human rights. They stand impervious to and indignant at the Western pressure for releasing opposition leaders and indictments of human rights violations by various human rights organizations. Indeed, the Army recently surrounded various foreign embassies to detain and question Burmese national employees, causing a minor uproar of protest by foreign diplomats for this violation of the international rules of conduct.

The myth of the mother goddess of earth combined with the hero myth has been revived in the person of young and charismatic Suu Kyi for the people of Burma who have seen many contenders for Ne Win's throne fall over the course of the last thirty years. It is not accidental that in the traditional societies of three major religions, Catholicism (Philippines and Nicaragua), Islam (Pakistan), and Buddhism (Burma), four women political saviors have emerged to taunt and overthrow the dictatorial regimes. To the tradition-bound people, all of them symbolize a benevolent heroine in the images of their respective male relative political heroes, father or husband, exalted above the discredited and subdued politicians. Perhaps this is the major reason why Suu Kyi, who spent all her adult life abroad away from the troubled Golden Land, with no previous practical political experience, as in the cases of President Aquino, President Chamorro, and Premier Bhutto, became the torchbearer and leader to slaughter Ne Win, the evil captor holding the Burmese in military bondage.

All four leaders are truly "accidental politicians" whose lives are not contaminated with the politics of power struggles and corruption of the past like the formerly subdued politicians. The ancient political myths of the godly ruler and hero are revived and epitomized in their personalities to free the people from the evil dictatorial and totalitarian rulers. Suu Kyi and the contemporary politics of Burma share the same pattern of political development as seen in the Philippines, Pakistan, and Nicaragua, and the same or similar scenarios may occur in the future political drama of Burma. Be that as it may, traditional myths, symbols, and thrones in the theater states of traditional societies of the Third World are not out of fashion and their significance cannot and must not be underestimated.

The recent development, when the United Nations Human Rights Commission sent an independent human rights expert, Madam Sadako Ogata, to probe into the human rights abuses beginning on November 4, 1990, may perhaps lead to a positive step toward democratization. As before, the head of the Burmese delegation to the United Nations General Assembly Meeting in October, General Ohn Kyaw, accepted and welcomed this mission of inquiry in his speech on October 19. It remains to be seen what kind of cooperation the SLORC will give her. However, it seems very unlikely that her positive findings and subsequent denunciations by the United Nations will make the kingly Burmese Generals voluntarily give up the political reign to restore democracy and human rights.

So far, all indicators point to a continuum of relentless repression of any political opposition activity inside Burma. The religious sanctions initiated by the senior abbots of Mandalay have been forcefully dealt with. In Rangoon, soldiers forcefully crushed NLD members on hunger strikes in Insein Jail, killing and injuring some. The latest action taken by the military regime is that the few remaining NLD spokesmen are forced to sign documents under duress for drafting the Catch 22 "perfect constitution" and promising to refrain from any sedition against the regal orders of the SLORC or face handcuffs. Amnesty International has led a worldwide campaign for the restoration of human rights and democracy in Burma beginning on November 7, 1990. This should exert further international pressure for the release of Daw Aung San Suu Kyi and thousands of political "prisoners of conscience" from the jails of Myanmar.

Although the political future of Burma looks gloomy, Daw Aung San Suu Kyi remains the brightest star for the Burmese as well as the world. Recognizing her role in Burma's movement for democracy, Norway awarded her the **1990 Rafto Prize of Human Rights** in Norway on November 4, 1990. She is the fourth recipient of the Award which was instituted in 1987. Previous winners were leaders from the Eastern European countries who spearheaded democracy movements. The Award appropriately states its reasons:

> Aung San Suu Kyi personified Burma's movement for democracy. Through her courageous and devoted work for Human Rights and

Democracy, Aung San Suu Kyi has become the focal point of the Burmese opposition demanding an end to the iron-fisted military rule in the country, restoration of fundamental human rights and democracy. In this dark period of the history of Burma, Aung San Suu Kyi has earned enormous respect both from her fellow-citizens and from international human rights community.

On January 22nd, 1990, she was awarded the **1991 Sakharov Prize** by the European Parliament. The **Sakharov Prize** was first instituted in 1988 by the Liberal Group of the European Parliament upon the consent of Andrew Sakharov, the world renowned Russian human rights dissident and Nobel laureate, to use his name. The previous winners of the award were Nelson Mandela of South Africa, sharing it with the widow of Antonin Marchenko (the Russian dissident who died in prison), in 1988 and Alexander Dubcek of Czechoslovakia in 1989.

The enlarged Bureau of the European Parliament selected Suu Kyi as the recipient of the 1990 Sakharov Award from a short list of three candidates submitted by the Political Committee. Two other famed candidates in the list were Fang Lizhi of China and Lászlo Tökes, the Romanian Bishop of Hungarian origin. This second consecutive award of an even greater prestige and honor bestowed upon her by the international community permanently placed her name among the top leading human rights leaders of the world.

In February 1991, the Czechoslovakian President, Vaclav Havel, led a group of other prominent human rights leaders in nominating her for **the 1991 Nobel Prize**. It is further confirmation of the world respect she has earned for the inspiring role she continues to play in the restoration of fundamental human rights and democracy in Burma from behind the walls of the house which has been her prison since July 1989.

The following lines from W. E. Henley's poem, which was her father's favorite, befit her enormous strength, courage, and dedication to human rights:

Out of the night that covers me,
Black as the Pit from pole to pole
I thank whatever gods may be
For my unconquerable soul.
Beyond this place of wrath and tears
Looms but the Horror of the shade,
And yet the menace of the years
Finds, and shall find, me unafraid.

Richard Lovelace's "stone walls do not a prison make nor iron bars a cage" exemplifies the unconquerable spirit of Daw Aung San Suu Kyi of Burma. From behind the wall of house arrest, she rises and shines as the symbol of hope for freedom and human rights to the people of Burma and the world. She will remain the enduring beacon of light, dispelling the darkness which has fallen upon the Golden Land, and inspiring "freedom from fear" in the nightmare state of Burma.

The political saga of Burma since the fake military coup of September 1988 is nothing really new in the annals of military dictatorship around the world. The massacre in Tiananmen Square on June 4, 1989, in China (far less in number of deaths and violence than the Burmese massacres of 1988), the slaughtering of unarmed demonstrators by Pinochet on the occasion of the Pope's visit to Chile, the violence and killings by Noriega in the Panamanian elections, the Chinese mass slaughter of the Tibetan Buddhist monks, and the case of Myanmar all share thousands of deaths followed *in tandem* by massive crackdowns on dissidents by armed oppressors. One can only hope that the United Nations, the United States, and major Western democracies will help the subjugated Burmese people by pressuring their citizens and allies to halt economic dealings with and denounce the illegitimate SLORC government in a combined multinational effort.

NOTES

1. FBIS, February 13, 1989.
2. Suphaphon Kanwirayothin, "The Carrot, Not Stick, Will Liberalize Burma," *Bangkok Post*, May 17, 1990, cited in FBIS, May 17, 1990, p. 21.
3. Ibid.
4. See for details, *The Working People's Daily*, Rangoon, January 6, 1990 and Harn Yanghwe's *Burma Alert Nos. 1–9* (Quebec: Privately Published Papers, 1989–1990).
5. Kanwirayothin, (see note 2).
6. See Roger Mathews, "Burma Abandons Efforts at Reform," *Financial Times*, London, November 9, 1989.
7. Harn Yanghwe, *Burma Alert No. 9*, September 1990, p. 2.
8. These estimates were arrived at by the diligent efforts of Harn Yanghwe who has been tracking all foreign aid and investments from various sources in journals and government newspapers.
9. From the private source of *The Myanmar Delegation's Reply*, February 27, 1990.
10. *The Working People's Daily*, Rangoon, November 25, 1989, p. 6.
11. Embassy of the Union of Myanmar, *Myanmar (Burma), No. 21, 90*, Washington, D.C., September 4, 1990, pp. 7–8.
12. Permanent Mission of the Union of Myanmar to the U.N., *Myanmar, Press Release No. 19/90*, New York, June 22, 1990, p. 2.
13. J. R. Saul, "Drugs, Torture—And Western Cash," *New York Times*, April 18, 1990.
14. See The Government of the Union of Myanmar, Ministry of Trade, *Formation of the Union of Myanmar Economic Holdings Limited, Notification No. 7/90*, Yangon, February 19, 1990.

15. See *The Working People's Daily*, Rangoon, March 4, 1989, p. 2.

16. From the source of a privately conducted Random Survey, *Free Market Retail Prices of Some Essential Food Items in Rangoon between 1987 and 1989*.

17. *The Working People's Daily*, Rangoon, March 7, 1989, p. 1.

18. *The Working People's Daily*, Rangoon, March 8, 1989, p. 1.

19. From the source of U.S. Embassy.

20. Excerpt from *Ne Win's Speech* (in Burmese) at the Conference of the Defense Services Security Councils, Rangoon, December 21–24, 1959.

21. Ibid.

22. C.J.F.S. Forbes, p. 44.

23. Mya Than and J.L.H. Tan, eds., p. 3. and p. 53.

24. U Tun Wai, "The Myanmar Economy at the Cross Road: Options and Constraints," Mya Than and Tan, eds., p. 50.

25. Ibid., p. 41.

26. John Badgley, "Remodelling Myanmar," Mya Than and Tan, eds., pp. 267–268 and pp. 285–286.

27. See R. W. Volkes, "Burma and Asia-Pacific Dynamism: Problems and Prospects of Export-Oriented Growth in the 1990s," Mya Than and Tan ed., pp. 233–241.

28. U Myat Thein, "Monetary and Fiscal Policies for Development," Mya Than and Tan, eds., p. 85.

29. Geertz, *Xlegara*, p. 19.

30. Ibid.

31. Ibid.

32. See *News From Asia Watch*, Washington, D.C., September 15, 1989 and August 14, 1990. Also see, Amnesty International, *Burma: Extrajudicial Execution and Torture of Members of Ethnic Minorities* (London: Amnesty International, May 1988).

33. Amnesty International, *Burma (Myanmar): Prisoners of Conscience in Myanmar, A Chronicle of Developments Since September 1988* (New York: Amnesty International, November, 1989), p. 72.

34. See Karin Eberhardt, *Burma in Brief* (Washington, D.C.: International Center for Development Policy, April, 1989).

Bibliography

BOOKS AND ARTICLES

Adas, M., *The Burma Delta: Economic Development and Social Change on an Asian Rice Frontier, 1852–1941* (Madison: University of Wisconsin Press, 1974).

Adloff, R. and V. Thompson, *The Left Wing in Southeast Asia* (New York: William Sloane Associates, 1950).

Altizer, J. J., *Mircea Eliade and the Dialectic of the Sacred* (Westport: Greenwood Press, 1975).

Andrus, J. R., *Burmese Economic Life* (Stanford: Stanford University Press, 1947).

Aung, Maung Htin, *The Stricken Peacock: Anglo-Burmese Relations* (Hague: Martinus Nijhoff, 1965).

Badgley, John and Jon A. Wiant, "The Ne Win-BSPP Style of Bama Lo," Joseph Silverstein ed., *The Future of Burma in Perspective: A Symposium* (Athens: Ohio University Center of International Studies, 1974).

Bigandet, P., *The Life or Legend of Gautama: The Buddha of the Burmese* (London: Trubner & Co., 1880), Vols. I and II.

Binns, B. O., *Agricultural Economy of Burma* (Rangoon: Government Printing and Stationery, 1948).

Bruma, Ian, "The Road to Mandalay," *New York Book Review* (New York: New York Times, October 23, 1986).

Cady, J. F., *A History of Modern Burma* (Ithaca: Cornell University Press, 1958).

Campbell, J., *The Inner Reaches of the Outer Space: Metaphor as Myth and as Religion* (New York: Harper & Row, 1986).

Cassirer, E., *The Myth of State* (Garden City: A Doubleday Anchor Co., 1955).

Christian, J. L., *Burma* (London: Collins, 1945).

Collis, M., *Trials in Burma* (London: Faber & Faber, 1938).

Correspondent at Rangoon, "King Thebaw," *The Times Weekly Edition*, London, December 25, 1885.

Eberhardt, Karin, *Burma in Brief* (Washington, D.C.: International Center for Development Policy, April, 1989).

Embree, J. F., "Thailand—A Loosely Structured Social System," Hans-Deiter ed., *Loosely Structured Social Systems: Thailand in Comparative Perspective* (New Haven: Yale University Southeast Asia Studies, 1969).

Erlanger, Steve, "Burmese Military Is Forcing Mass Migration from Cities," *New York Times*, New York, March 21, 1990.

Forbes, C.J.F.S., *British Burma and Its People: Native Manners, Customs, and Religion* (London: Spottswood & Co., 1878).

Frazer, Sir James George, *The Golden Bough* (New York: The Macmillan Company, 1963).

Furnivall, J. S., *Colonial Policy and Practice* (New York: New York University Press, 1956);

———, *The Economy of Burma* (Rangoon: Privately Published Paper, January 28, 1952);

———, *The Governance of Modern Burma* (New York: Institute of Pacific Relations, 1958);

———, *Progress and Welfare in Southeast Asia* (Shanghai: The Willow Pattern Press, 1941).

Geertz, C., *Local Knowledge: Further Essays in Interpretive Anthropology* (New York: Basic Books Inc., 1983);

———, *Negara: The Theatre State in Nineteenth-Century Bali* (Princeton: Princeton University Press, 1980).

Glass, L., *The Changing of Kings: Memories of Burma 1934–1949* (London: Peter Owen, 1985).

Green, Timothy, "Jade is Special, As Are the Risks in Bringing It from Mine to Market," *Smithsonian Magazine* (Washington, D.C.: Smithsonian Institute, July 1986).

Gyi, Aung, *40-Page Letter* (In Burmese) dated May 9, 1988 and *Letter* dated June 6, 1988.

Gyi, Maung Maung, *Burmese Political Values: The Socio-Political Roots of Authoritarianism* (New York: Praeger Publishers, 1983).

Hagen, E. E., *The Economic Development of Burma* (Washington, D.C.: National Planning Association, July 1956);

———, *The Theory of Social Change: How Economic Growth Begins* (Homewood: The Dorsey Press, 1962).

Hallet, Mr. Holt, "Burmah: Present and Future," *Times Weekly*, London, December 25, 1885.

Howe, Irving ed., *1984 Revisited: Totalitarianism in Our Century* (New York: Harper & Row Publishers, 1983).

Htoo, Maung (R.A.S.U.), "The Last Journey to Democracy," *Burma Review* (New York: Privately Published Journal, February, 1990).

Jesse, F. T., *The Lacquer Lady* (New York: The Dial Press, 1979).

Jung, Carl G., *Man and His Symbols* (Garden City: Doubleday & Company, 1964).

Kamm, Henry, "Socialist Burma: Pervasive Poverty, Indifferent Military Rule," *The New York Times*, New York, June 25, 1975.

Kanwirayothin, Suphaphon, "The Carrot, Not Stick, Will Liberalize Burma," *Bangkok Post*, May 17, 1990.

Kin, U Pe, "The Seeds of Pinlon Accord" (In Burmese), *Collected Articles of the Working People's Daily, Vol. 4* (Rangoon: Ministry of Information, March 1989).

Kyar, U Hpo, *A Brief Modern History of Burma* (In Burmese) (Rangoon: Myanma Gonyai Press, 1937).

Lintner, B., *Outrage: Burma's Struggle for Democracy* (Hongkong: Far Eastern Review Publishing Company, June 1989).

Lowenthal, Richard, "Beyond Totalitarianism," Irving Howe ed., *1984 Revisited: Totalitarianism in Our Century* (New York: Harper & Row Publishers, 1983).

Lu, Maung Shwe, *Burma: Nationalism and Ideology* (Dhaka: The University Press, 1989).

Mathews, Roger, "Burma Abandons Efforts at Reform," *Financial Times*, London, November 9, 1989.

Maung, Maung, *Burma and General Ne Win* (New York: Asia Publishing House, 1969);

———, *A Trial in Burma: The Assassination of Aung San* (Hague: Martinus Nijhoff, 1962).

Maung, Mya, *Burma and Pakistan: A Comparative Study of Development* (New York: Praeger Publishers, Inc., 1971);

———, *A Genesis of Economic Development in Burma* (Ann Arbor: Ph.D. Dissertation, 1961);

——— "Socialism and Economic Development of Burma," *Asian Survey* (Berkeley: University of California, December 1964); "The Burmese Way to Socialism Beyond the Welfare State," *Asian Survey* (Berkeley: University of California, June 1970); "Violence in Golden Land," *Fletcher Forum of World Affairs* (Medford: The Fletcher School of Law and Diplomacy, Summer 1989); "The Burma Road from the Union of Burma to Myanmar," *Asian Survey* (Berkeley: University of California, June 1990).

F. T. Morehead, *The Forests of Burma: Burma Pamphlet No. 5* (Bombay: Orient Longmans, 1956).

Muller, Christian, "Burma's Splendid Isolation," *Swiss Review of World Affairs* (Zurich: Swiss Review of World Affairs, May 1975).

Myint, U. Hla, "Economic Theory and Underdeveloped Countries," *The Journal of Political Economy* Vol. LXXIII, No. 4 (1965).

Myint, Myo, *The Politics of Survival in Burma: Diplomacy and Statecraft in the Reign of King Mindon* (Ithaca: Ph.D. Dissertation submitted to Cornell University, May, 1987).

Myint, U Tun, *Ten Great Stories* (In Burmese) (Rangoon: Baho Press, 1989).

Neumann, L., "Dark Days in Burma," *The Sunday Times*, London, December 4, 1988.

Nu, U, *Forward with the People* (Rangoon: Ministry of Information, 1955);

———, *From Peace to Stability* (Rangoon: Ministry of Information, 1951);

———, *U Nu, Saturday's Son* (New Haven: Yale University Press, 1975).

Nyunt, Khin Maung, *Market Research of Principal Exports and Imports of Burma with Special Reference to Thailand (1970/71 to 1985/86)* (Bangkok: Chulalongkorn University, March, 1988).

Orwell, G., *Burmese Days* (New York: Time Incorporated, 1962).

Overholt, William H., "Dateline Drug Wars: Burma: The Wrong Enemy," *Foreign Policy* (Washington, D.C.: Foreign Policy, Winter 1989).

Perakumbar, Ashok, "Burma's Signboard Socialism," *Orientations*, February 1975.

Pern, B. R., *A History of Rangoon* (Rangoon: American Baptist Mission Press, 1939).

Phayre, A., *History of Burma* (London: Trubner & Co., 1883).

Ping, Ho Kwon, "The Cautious Search for Success," *Fareastern Economic Review*, Hongkong, January 18, 1980.

Praphanphon, Pon, "Mae Sot: The Day That City Fell Silent," Joint Publication Research Service (JPRS), *Burma* (Washington, D.C.: JPRS, January 6, 1988).

Pye, L., *Politics, Personality, and Nation-Building: Burma's Search for Identity* (New Haven: Yale University Press, 1962);

———, "Armies in the Process of Modernization," and "The Army in Burmese Politics," John J. Johnson ed., *The Role of the Military in Underdeveloped Countries*, (Princeton: Princeton University Press, 1962).

Pye, Maung Maung, *Burma in the Crucible* (Madras: The Diocesan Press, 1951).

A Retired Burmese Army Officer, *Thuelo Lu* or *That Type of Man* (In Burmese) (Koln: Committee for Restoration of Democracy in Burma, West Germany, 1988).

San, Aung, *Burma's Challenge 1946* (Rangoon: The New Light of Burma Press, 1946).

Sarkisyanz, E., *Buddhist Backgrounds of the Burmese Revolution* (Hague: Martinus Nijhoff, 1965).

Saul, J. R., "Drugs, Torture—And Western Cash," *New York Times*, New York, April 18, 1990.

Saunders, K. J., *Gotama Buddha: A Biography* (New Delhi: Light and Life Publishers, 1978).

Scott, J. G. (Shwe Yoe), *Burma From the Earliest Times to the Present Day* (London: T. Fisher Unwin, Ltd., 1924);

———, *The Burman: His Life and Notions* (New York: W. W. Norton & Co., 1963);

———, *Gazetteer of Upper Burma and the Shan State* (Rangoon: Government Printing Office, 1900), Part I, Vol. II.

Scully, L. and Frank N. Trager, "Burma 1979: Reversing the Trend," *Asian Survey* (Berkeley: University of California, February, 1980).

Seagrave, S., "Burma on Edge," *Geo: A New View of Our World* (New York: Grunner & Jahr USA Inc., 1979).

———, "Burma's Golden Triangle: Warlords, Spooks, Narcs, Mercenaries & Missionaries," *Soldier of Fortune* (Denver: Soldier of Fortune, May, 1984).

Shaing, U Tin ed., *The Glass Palace Chronicle* (In Burmese) (Rangoon: Pyigyi Munnaing Pitaka Press, 1963).

Shin, Daw Mya Saw (translator), *The Constitutions (Fundamental Law) of the Socialist Republic of the Union of Burma* (Washington, D.C.: The Library of Congress, June 1975).

Silverstein, J., *Burma: Military Rule and the Politics of Stagnation* (Ithaca: Cornell University Press, 1977);

——— ed., *The Future of Burma in Perspective: A Symposium* (Athens: Ohio University Center of International Studies, 1974);

——— ed., *Independent Burma at Forty Years: Six Assessments* (Ithaca: Cornell Southeast Asia Program, 1989);

———, *Insurgency and Rebellion in Burma* (Hawaii: Privately Published Paper by Defense Intelligence College, United States Pacific Command, March, 1989).

Sleth, Andrew, *Death of a Hero: The U Thant Disturbances in Burma, December 1974* (Nathan: Griffith University, April, 1989).

Smith, D. E., *Religion and Politics in Burma* (Princeton: Princeton University Press, 1965).

Steinberg, David I., *Burma: A Socialist Nation of Southeast Asia* (Boulder: Westview Press, 1982).

Symes, Michael, *An Account of an Embassy to the Kingdom of Ava Sent by the Governor-General of India in the Year 1795* (Edinburgh: Constable and Company, 1827).

Takamuri, S. and S. Mouri, *Border Trade: Southeast Asian Black Market* (In Japanese) (Tokyo: Kobundo Publishers, 1984).

Taylor, R., *The State of Burma* (Honolulu: University of Hawaii Press, 1987).

Than, Mya, "Little Change in Rural Burma: A Case Study of a Burmese Village (1960–1980)," *SOURJOURN* Vol. 2, No. 1;

——— and J. L. H. Tan, eds., *Myamar Dilemmas and Options: The Challenge of Economic Transition in the 1990s* (Singapore: Institute of Southeast Asian Studies, 1990).

Than, Tin Maung Maung, "Burma in 1987: Twenty-Five Years after the Revolution." *Southeast Asian Affairs* (Singapore: Institute of Southeast Asian Studies, Spring 1988).

Thaung, U, "Burma: A Case Study in Press Repression," *Freedom At Issue, No. 16* (New York: Freedom Foundation, May–June, 1981).

Thompson, Virginia, *Notes on Labor Problems in Burma and Thailand* (New York: Institute of Pacific Relations, 1954).

Thwin, Michael Aung, *Pagan: The Origins of Modern Burma* (Honolulu: University of Hawaii Press, 1985).

———, "1948 and Burma's Myth of Independence," Joseph Silverstein ed., *Independent Burma at Forty Years: Six Assessments* (Ithaca: Cornell Southeast Asia Program, 1989);

———, "The Role of *Sasana* Reform in Burmese History: Economic Dimensions of a Religious Purification," *Journal of Asian Studies*, August 1979.

Tin, Pe Maung and G. H. Luce, *The Glass Palace Chronicle of the Kings of Burma* (Rangoon: Rangoon University Press, 1960).

Tinker, H., *Burma Struggle for Independence 1944–48* (London: Her Majesty's Stationery Office, 1984;

———, *The Union of Burma* (London: Oxford University Press, 1961).

Trager, F. N., "Democratic and Authoritarian Rule in a Not So Newly Independent Country," Joseph Silverstein ed., *The Future of Burma in Perspective: A Symposium* (Athens: Ohio University Center of International Studies, 1974).

Trager, H., *Burma Through Alien Eyes: Missionary Views of the Burmese in the Nineteenth Century* (New York: F.A. Praeger, Publishers, 1966).

Tucker, Robert C., "Does Big Brother Really Exist?", Irving Howe ed., *1984 Revisited: Totalitarianism in Our Century* (New York: Harper & Row Publishers, 1983).

Tun, U Aung Than, *Four Eras of Burmese Laws* (In Burmese) (Rangoon: Kalaung Pyan Press, 1968).

Tun, U Saw, "Tales of a Burmese Soothsayer," Hiram Haydn and John Cournos, eds., *A World of Great Stories* (U.S.A.: Crown Publishers, 1961).

Tun, U Than, *Ancient Burmese History: Studies in Burmese History No. 1* (In Burmese) (Rangoon: Mahah Dagon Press, 1964).

Wai, Tun, *Burma's Currency and Credit* (Bombay: Orient Longmans, Ltd., 1953);

———, *Economic Development of Burma from 1800 to 1940* (Rangoon: University of Rangoon, 1961).

Walinsky, L. J., *Economic Development in Burma 1951–60* (New York: The Twentieth Century Fund, 1962).

Walzer, Michael, "On 'Failed Totalitarianism,'" Irving Howe ed., *1984 Revisited: Totalitarianism in Our Century* (New York: Harper & Row Publishers, 1983).

Yawnghwe, C. T. (Eugene Thaike), *The Shan of Burma: Memoirs of a Shan Exile* (Singapore: Institute of Southeast Asian Studies, 1987).

———, "The Burman Military: Holding the Country Together?" Joseph Silverstein ed., *Independent Burma at Forty Years: Six Assessments* (Ithaca: Cornell Southeast Asia Program, 1989).

Yawnghwe, Harn, *Burma Alert Nos. 1–9* and *Burma Alert No. 1, Vol. 2, 1991* (Quebec: Privately Published Papers, 1989–1991).

Yoon, Won Z., *Japan's Scheme for the Liberation of Burma: The Role of the Minami Kikan and the "Thirty Comrades"* (Athens: Ohio University Center for International Studies, 1973).

DOCUMENTS AND NEWSPAPERS

Amnesty International, *Burma: Extrajudicial Execution and Torture of Members of Ethnic Minorities* (London: Amnesty International, May 1988);

———, *Unlawful Killing of Peaceful Demonstrators, September 29 and October 7, 1988* (London: Amnesty International, 1988).

———, *Burma (Myanmar): Prisoners of Conscience in Myanmar, A Chronicle of Developments Since September 1988* (New York: Amnesty International, November 1989).

Asia Watch, *News From Asia Watch*, Washington, D.C., September 15, 1989 and August 14, 1990.

Asian Development Bank, *Loan, Technical Assistance and Private Sector Operations Approval, No. 89/09* (Manila: Asian Development Bank, September 1989).

Asia Week (Hongkong).

Bangkok Post (Bangkok).

Burma Facts and Figures: Burma Pamphlet No. 9 (London: Longmans, Green & Co., 1946).

Burma in Brief (Washington, D.C.: International Center for Development Policy, April, 1989).

Burma Rice: Burma Pamphlet No. 4 (Bombay: Orient Longmans, 1956).

The Burma Socialist Programme Party, *The System of Correlation of Man to His Environment* (Rangoon: Ministry of Information, January 17, 1963).

———, Central Organization Committee, *Party Seminar 1965* (Rangoon: Sahpai Beikhman Press, February 1966).

———, *Lanzin Thating* (In Burmese), Rangoon, November 6, 1985.

The Burmese Embassy, *Myanmar News*, Washington, D.C., 1989–1990.

Census of India 1931: Vol. XI, Burma, Part I (Rangoon: Government Printing & Stationery, 1933).

European Intelligence Unit, *EIU Country Profile 1989–1990, Burma* (London: EIU, 1990).

Fareastern Economic Review, *Asia Year Books* (Hongkong: Fareastern Economic Review, 1960–1990).

Fareastern Economic Review (Hongkong).

Financial Times (London).

Government of the Socialist Republic of the Union of Burma, *Pyithu Hluttaw Reports*, 1974–1988.

Government of the Union of Burma, *Constitution of the Union of Burma* (Rangoon: Government Printing & Stationery, 1948).

———, *The 1958 Union of Burma Penal Code, Vol. VIII* (Rangoon: Ministry of Justice, 1958).

The Government of the Union of Myanmar, Ministry of Trade, *Formation of the Union of Myanmar Economic Holdings Limited, Notification No. 7/90*, Yangon, February 19, 1990.

International Human Rights Law Group, *Report on the Myanmar Election* (Washington, D.C.: International Human Rights Law Group, May 19, 1990).

International Monetary Fund, *International Financial Statistics, World Bank Reports* and United Nations, *Financial Year Books*.

Nation (Bangkok).

New York Times (New York).

Permanent Mission of the Union of Myanmar to the U.N., *Myanmar, Press Release No. 19/90*, New York, June 22, 1990.

Report of the Burma Provincial Banking Enquiry Committee (Rangoon: Government Printing & Stationery, 1931).

The Revolutionary Council, *The Burmese Way to Socialism: The Proclamation of the Revolutionary Council Philosophy* (In Burmese) (Rangoon: Ministry of Information: April 30, 1982);

———, *A Short History of the Actions of the Revolutionary Council* (In Burmese) (Rangoon: Union of Burma Buddhist Affairs Association, March 2, 1974).

Season and Crop Report (Rangoon: Government Printing & Stationery, 1941).

The Socialist Republic of the Union of Burma, *Report to the Pyithu Hluttaw on the Financial, Economic and Social Conditions* (Rangoon: Ministry of Planning and Finance, 1987–1990).

The U.S. Committee for Refugees, *The War is Growing Worse and Worse: The Refugees and Displaced Persons On the Thai-Burmese Border* (Washington, D.C.: American Council for Nationalities Service, May 1990).

U.S. Department of State, *Country Reports On Human Rights Practices for 1988* (Washington, D.C.: U.S. Government Printing Office, 1989).

———, "U.S. and Burma Reaffirm Bonds of Friendship and Cooperation," *Department of State Bulletin No. 55* (Washington, D.C.: Department of State, October 3, 1966).

U.S. Embassy, *1984 CERP 004: The Foreign Economic Trends Report for Burma* (Rangoon, June 18, 1984).

———, *Shadow Surveys*, Rangoon, 1987, 1988, and 1989.

———, *Foreign Economic Trends Report: Myanmar (Burma)*, Rangoon, November, 1989.

U.S. Government, Foreign Broadcasting Information Service (FBIS), *Reports on Burma*, Washington, D.C., 1987–1990.

West German Government, *Landerkurbericht: Birma* (Bundesministerium Fur Wirtschafliche Zusammennarbeit, January 7, 1988).

Working People's Daily, Rangoon, 1970–1990.

Index

About the Author

MYA MAUNG is Professor of Finance in the Boston College School of Management. He is the author of *Burma and Pakistan: A Comparative Study in Development* as well as articles and monographs on development in Burma and other Asian countries.